Public Sector Performance, Corruption and State Capture in a Globalized World

This collection examines the difficult task of reforming governments worldwide to meet citizens' needs and aspirations. It advances constructive efforts to enhance public accountability while recognizing the complex ways in which corruption, greed, and state capture undermine the legitimacy and performance of government. The contributors are political scientists, lawyers, and economists who bring a cross-disciplinary approach to their chosen subjects. The first group of chapters deals with public sector performance, development, and public participation. Complementary pieces by a practitioner and a scholar confront the challenges of achieving reform in countries with difficult political environments and extensive poverty and inequality. The second group emphasizes the way corruption and state capture limit the accountability and effectiveness of governments in both developing and wealthy countries. The contributions consider the institutional roots of dysfunctional government and their links to the private sector. Taken together, the volume surveys a wide range of topics with theoretical arguments and empirical findings that provide insights into real-world problems and policymaking dilemmas. Inspired by Susan Rose-Ackerman's fifty-year exploration of public policymaking, public law, and corruption, the collection will be an invaluable resource for researchers, academics, and policy makers working in the areas of Public Law, Anticorruption, and Political Economy.

Susan Rose-Ackerman is Henry R. Luce Professor Emeritus of Law and Political Science, Yale University. She has published widely on comparative administrative law and public policy and on the political economy of corruption. Her book, *Corruption and Government* (CUP, 1999, 2d edition with Bonnie Palifka, 2016), is a standard political-economic reference on the topic.

Routledge Research in Public Law

Available titles in this series include:

Rule of Law in Crisis
Constitutionalism in a State of Flux
Edited by Martin Belov

Lawfare and Judicial Legitimacy
The Judicialisation of Politics in the case of South Africa
Kate Dent

Public Administration and Expertise in Democratic Governments
Comparative Public Law in the Twenty-First Century
Edited by Susan Rose-Ackerman

Comparative Administrative Law
Perspectives from Central and Eastern Europe
Edited by Ieva Deviatnikovaitė

For more information about this series, please visit:
https://www.routledge.com/Routledge-Research-in-Public-Law/book-series/RRIPL

Public Sector Performance, Corruption and State Capture in a Globalized World

Edited by Susan Rose-Ackerman

Routledge
Taylor & Francis Group
LONDON AND NEW YORK

First published 2024
by Routledge
4 Park Square, Milton Park, Abingdon, Oxon OX14 4RN

and by Routledge
605 Third Avenue, New York, NY 10158

Routledge is an imprint of the Taylor & Francis Group, an informa business

British Library Cataloguing-in-Publication Data
A catalogue record for this book is available from the British Library

ISBN: 978-1-032-52429-0 (hbk)
ISBN: 978-1-032-54301-7 (pbk)
ISBN: 978-1-003-41623-4 (ebk)

DOI: 10.4324/9781003416234

Typeset in Times New Roman
by Deanta Global Publishing Services, Chennai, India

Contents

Figures

Tables

Contributors

Manuel Balán is Associate Dean at the Faculty of Arts at McGill University in Montreal, Canada, and Associate Professor in Political Science and International Development Studies. His research focuses on governance, rule of law, corruption, and anti-corruption policies.

Ximena Benavides is Postdoctoral Associate and Lecturer in Ethics, Politics, and Economics at Yale University; Postdoctoral Resident Fellow at Yale Law School's Information Society Project, and Affiliated Faculty at the Yale Institute for Global Health. She holds a Masters (LL.M.) and a Doctorate (J.S.D.) in Law from Yale Law School.

Marc L. Busch is the Karl F. Landegger Professor of International Business Diplomacy at Georgetown's School of Foreign Service. He writes on international trade policy and law, and he served two terms as a "cleared advisor" on technical trade barriers to the Department of Commerce and the US Trade Representative.

Weitseng Chen is Associate Professor, National University of Singapore (NUS) Faculty of Law. He specializes in comparative Chinese law in Greater China, with an emphasis on law and development. His published books include *Regime Type and Beyond: The Transformation of Police in Asia* (2023) and *Authoritarian Legality in Asia: Formation, Development and Transition* (2019).

Kevin E. Davis is the Beller Family Professor of Business Law at New York University School of Law. His research and teaching concern the relationship between law and economic development, with particular emphasis on anti-corruption law, commercial law, and measurement of the performance of legal systems.

Nancy Hite-Rubin is Affiliated Faculty at Tisch College, Tufts University. She holds an LL.M. in Law and Economics from the University of Hamburg and a Ph.D. in Political Science from Yale. Her research focuses on comparative political economy and international relations, especially corruption, informality, and clientelism. She has published in both policy-focused outlets and academic journals.

Stephen B. Kaplan is Associate Professor of Political Science and International Affairs at George Washington University. He specializes in the political economy of global finance and development, China's overseas foreign investment, and Latin American economic policy. His recent book, *Globalizing Patient Capital: The Political Economy of Chinese Finance in the Americas* (2021) examines China's financial investments in the developing world.

Daniel Kaufmann is a Senior Fellow at Results for Development, and at the Brookings Institution (non-resident). He is president emeritus of the Natural Resources Governance Institute and a visiting professor in the Economics Department of the University of the Philippines. He was a director at the World Bank, leading work on governance and anti-corruption.

Stephen Kosack is a political scientist whose work focuses on political and economic development, particularly how governments can become responsive and effective for people without unusual wealth, privilege, or other advantages. He is an associate professor at the Evans School of Public Policy and Governance at the University of Washington, Seattle.

Jana Kunicová is Practice Manager at the World Bank, currently covering digital development in West and Central Africa. Since joining the Bank in 2006, her work has taken her to over 60 countries across Africa, Asia, and Europe, including field postings in Senegal, Kenya, and Malaysia. She holds a Ph.D. in political economy from Yale University.

Kalle Moene is Professor Emeritus of Economics at the University of Oslo. His research and teaching focus on inequality, institutions, and governance in rich and poor countries.

Bonnie J. Palifka is Associate Research Professor in the Economics Department at Tecnologico de Monterrey (Mexico), Lecturer at Yale University, the founder of the Academia against Corruption in the Americas conference, and co-author (with Susan Rose-Ackerman) of the second edition of *Corruption and Government: Causes, Consequences, and Reform.*

Mariana Mota Prado is Professor and William C. Graham Chair in International Law and Development at the Faculty of Law, University of Toronto, Canada. Her research focuses on law and development and on comparative administrative law. Her published books include *Institutional Bypasses: A Strategy to Promote Reforms for Development* (with Michael Trebilcock, 2019), and *Advanced Introduction to Law and Development* (with Michael Trebilcock, 2nd ed. 2021).

Tina Søreide is Professor of Law and Economics at the Norwegian School of Economics (NHH) in Bergen, Norway. Her research and teaching focus on the interaction between governance and corporate misconduct. Since 2022, she has taken a leave from NHH to serve as Director General at the Norwegian Competition Authority.

Jennifer L. Tobin is Associate Professor of Public Policy at the McCourt School of Public Policy, Georgetown University. She earned her Ph.D. at Yale University and has worked at the Brookings Institution, the World Bank, Oxford University, and microfinance institutions in Uganda, Haiti, and Mexico. Her main research interests are in the political economy of development.

Natalia A. Volosin holds LL.M. and J.S.D. degrees from Yale Law School, where she learned from Susan Rose-Ackerman, whose theories she follows as a prominent anti-corruption campaigner in Argentina. She led the Criminal Investigations Body at the General Attorney's Office (on leave) and is now senior columnist for national media.

1 Foreword and overview

Susan Rose-Ackerman

In late August 2022, two dozen scholars from around the world came to Yale Law School to contribute original essays inspired by my 50-year exploration of public policymaking, public law, and corruption in the modern world. This volume is one of two resulting from that conference, proposed by my Yale Law School colleague Jerry Mashaw and by two graduate students Ximena Benavides and Eugenio Garcia-Huidobro. The companion volume, *Public Administration and Expertise in Democratic Governments*, concentrates on contemporary issues in public law from a comparative perspective.

The essays in the present volume examine constructive efforts to promote reform and good government worldwide, on the one hand, and the complex ways in which corruption, greed, and state capture undermine the legitimacy and performance of government, on the other. Building on my book, *Corruption and Government*, as well as my other relevant scholarship, the essays make fascinating connections and draw on various fields of study and parts of the world. Connected with my work on corruption, Tina Søreide and Paul Lagunes invited the conference participants to help finance an especially appropriate gift. With the funds raised, they purchased hard copies of my books on corruption and donated them to the library of the University of Kiev. The gift was planned in 2020 before Russia's invasion of Ukraine, but it has now become especially meaningful.

I am grateful to the contributors to both volumes for their interesting and insightful essays. At the conference, colleagues and students from different times and places in my career met and shared common scholarly interests. The resulting discussions in the sessions and over breaks and meals were lively and fascinating. I am very proud and happy to have helped support the careers of such a wonderful collection of creative and committed scholars and policy advisors.

The event was funded by a generous grant from the Law School's Oscar M. Ruebhausen Fund. It was originally planned for the summer of 2020 and was delayed twice by the corona-virus pandemic. Jerry and I discussed holding a virtual conference online in 2021, but rejected that option as inconsistent with the goal of bringing people together whose main connection was a shared link to myself and my scholarship. Renee DeMatteo, Senior Manager for Conferences and Events, stayed with the project from the beginning, and she was absolutely essential in keeping the project on track through the pandemic delays. My long-time administrative assistant, Cathy Orcutt, provided her usual very high level of patient support for

DOI: 10.4324/9781003416234-1

the organization of the event and management of the flows of draft papers. As I moved toward manuscript submission, Quiana Atkinson took Cathy's place and has helped me to bring the book projects to fruition with grace and skill.

In this essay, I introduce this volume's contents and illustrate how the contributions relate to each other and to my own work. Of the eleven chapters, five are by political scientists, four by lawyers, and three by economists, but all the authors bring a cross-disciplinary approach to their chosen subjects. Most of the authors are scholars with academic appointments, and three have had distinguished careers as policy advisors and advocates. Everyone has contributed to contemporary policy debates in their home countries and internationally.

The chapters fall into two broad, but overlapping, groups: *Public Sector Performance, Development, and Public Participation*; and *Corruption, State Capture, and Policymaking*. Taken together, they survey a wide range of topics, and their theoretical arguments and empirical findings provide insights into real-world problems and policymaking dilemmas.

The volume begins with the complementary essays by *Jana Kunicová*, a World Bank manager, and *Stephen Kosack*, a professor at the University of Washington. Each has faced the challenge of achieving reform in countries with difficult political environments and extensive poverty and inequality. Both authors confront, not the lack of research per se, but rather, the difficulty of making it relevant to real-world conditions on the ground.

Kunicová examines the disconnect between academic research and findings that can be put to work to achieve concrete results in polities that lack crucial resources and skills. Outsiders bearing results and reform proposals may be dismissed as interlopers who do not understand local conditions, and this attitude may reflect the truth. Kunicová has spoken with many of the most thoughtful and experienced contemporary policy analysts and practitioners, many of whom she has worked with during her World Bank career. She shows that those who seek to improve conditions on the ground in developing countries must go beyond amassing macro- and micro-data. They also need a deep understanding of the interplay between public and private motives and incentives that may not fit neatly into conventional economic models. Uncomfortable truths must be faced so that aid and lending programs have a realistic chance of benefiting the intended populations even when no massive redistribution of power and wealth is possible given existing resources and political will.

Stephen Kosack comes at a related issue from the perspective of a researcher who helped to organize a major randomized controlled trial (RCT), currently a state-of-the-art research technique. The research project took place in villages in Indonesia and Tanzania, and it sought to discover if facilitated, grass-roots participation by women could help improve the delivery of local services for maternal and child health. No participants were paid and no extra funds were provided for service provision. The results showed no statistically significant difference in health outcomes between control and test villages. Did this mean that encouraging local participation in service delivery should be abandoned with the focus shifting to more funding and trained personnel and supplies? Kosack argues, instead, that if one looks at specific, village-by-village results, one sees that local women's agency led to a wide range of specific local initiatives that improved the delivery of services in myriad ways that were not captured in aggregate statistics. These results complement Kunicová's overview and suggest the value people place in having a say in key aspects of their life and participating in improving their community. As a consequence, he argues for combining programs that fund goods and services and provide expert personnel with opportunities for intended beneficiaries to participate.

The other three chapters in this section focus on specific programs that raise important issues related to economic development. In their chapter, *Weitseng Chen and Mariana Mota Prado*, law professors in Singapore and Toronto, study pawnshops, a worldwide source of credit for low-income households without access to conventional bank loans. The authors document the complex interactions of state, market, and the law in Brazil, Mexico, and Taiwan, providing a typology that captures the roles performed by the state vis-à-vis the private sector. In Brazil, the state monopolizes the pawnshop sector (replacement model). Mexico allows a free market in pawnshops (absence model), and in Taiwan public and private pawnshops competed until the 1990s (competition model), followed by a smaller role for public pawnshops, who serve those who are unable to access the private one (complementary model). These differences have led to systematic differences in benefits and costs. A set of "best practices" is difficult to find because of the importance of cross-country differences. However, some institutional arrangements can be corrupt, inefficient, or excessively costly, and, even with public provision, interest rates are very high.

The next chapter is by *Jennifer L. Tobin*, a political scientist, and *Marc L. Busch*, a specialist in international trade policy. It examines a U.S. program that imposes zero tariffs on exports from those less-developed countries that implement a set of labor standards itemized in the statute. Their careful empirical work shows that the program has had no impact on national labor policies, and they conclude that the program has the wrong focus. It should have targeted industries, not overall national policies to influence the treatment of labor. Thus, this chapter, like the chapter by Stephen Kosack, argues that there is much to learn from null results that allow one to examine the fine structure of policy impacts.

The final chapter in this section by *Stephen B. Kaplan* critiques central bank policymaking worldwide in the face of a vexing trilemma. Kaplan, a political scientist with experience as a banker, has written insightfully about Chinese investment in Latin America. Here, he takes a broader focus to illuminate a puzzle facing all central banks. Macroeconomic policy, rather than simply facing the tensions between price stability and unemployment, now includes the operation of the financial markets on a global scale. This trilemma is not easy to resolve with conventional monetary and fiscal policy at the country level. It requires not just new tools in individual countries but also cross-national efforts that are bound to conflict with the policy goals and political realities of many individual nation states. Thus, this section ends by highlighting the global nature of the development challenges facing nation states and international aid and lending organizations. With that in mind, the second section of the volume turns to specific governance pathologies, especially corruption and state capture by economic elites.

The chapters grouped under the heading: *Corruption, State Capture, and Policymaking*, build on my own long-standing interest in the institutional roots of dysfunctional government and their links to the incentives and opportunities arising in the private sector. Insights from law, economics and political science illuminate the various chapters, which confront a range of diverse but related topics.

The first essay, by *Natalia A. Volosin,* a prominent anti-corruption voice in Argentina, critiques anti-corruption policy initiatives in that country that have echoes worldwide. Drawing on my institutional perspective on corruption, she argues that Argentina moved from state capture to bilateral monopoly and, more recently, to kleptocracy. She articulates structural weaknesses that have resisted efforts at reform, and she argues that so-called anti-corruption reforms instead turned the law and judicial proceedings into weapons to overthrow pro-poor governments. The structural problems that she discusses are not unique to Argentina; thus, her deep knowledge of that country can illuminate reform efforts elsewhere. Reform needs to go beyond efforts to improve law enforcement and ought to confront institutional weaknesses in the state and in the private sector that create incentives for payoffs.

Bonnie J. Palifka, an economics professor at Tecnologico de Monterrey, was my co-author on the second edition of my book: *Corruption and Government: Causes, Consequences and Reform*, published in 2016. I would not have thought of issuing a second edition without Bonnie's encouragement, commitment, and hard work. Her PowerPoint presentation summarizing the book's messages was above my own skill level and has been used by each of us to introduce our work to audiences worldwide. The volume remains a basic source for anyone interested in understanding the institutional roots of corruption. Her chapter for this volume, co-authored with *Manual Balán*, takes up an important issue in the anti-corruption discussion. A free media environment and active civil-society watchdogs are essential for shedding light on corrupt dealings that might otherwise remain secret. Yet, revealing malfeasance can cause the public to think that corruption is entrenched. Palifka and Balán, instead, argue that scandals reported in the media indicate that the corrupt do not operate with impunity. Rather, the vigorous reporting of scandals, not subject to repression by the state, is a positive sign that can lead to better public anti-corruption policies and law enforcement against public officials and private actors who benefit from corruption. Their empirical data covers countries in Latin America and the Caribbean before and during the COVID-19 emergency, a situation that created new incentives for corruption. Increased reporting on corruption in 2020 is associated with more transparent government institutions. Assuming that the actual level of corruption increased everywhere as the pandemic spread, this result suggests that more transparent polities will have a better chance of eventually limiting corruption than more closed systems with few investigative journalists able to publicize scandals.

Kevin E. Davis, a distinguished analyst of corruption in international business as it affects government–business relations worldwide, distinguishes between business lobbying of political actors and outright bribery to gain an advantage. He points to the ways in which overseas corruption accusations can be used to further domestic political agendas in investors' home countries as well as to influence the careers of political leaders in other countries. He points to the problematic nature of corruption allegations in international affairs that may, in practice, undermine the role of domestic firms and politicians as well as discredit overseas politicians. He makes an effort to sort out legitimate from illegitimate efforts to mix political and legal goals.

Staying with the theme of corruption by business firms, the economists *Kalle Moene and Tina Søreide* consider how laws against corporate bribery vary across national borders, a topic of interest to multi-national firms considering where to invest. What characterizes the most 'actionable definitions' of corruption? For efficient law enforcement, should reform-friendly countries select a precise definition of liability or a definition with a broader scope? Considering foreign bribery in the light of the increasing use of non-trial resolutions, they explain why, for a given scope of liability, lower precision in the definition of liability impedes anti-corruption law enforcement. They draw on OECD data on the scope and precision of corporate liability in 36 jurisdictions. Their study shows that countries that perform well in terms of the OECD's definition of corporate bribery, also perform well on a range of other governance indicators, and that they are better able to enforce corporate liability. A broad scope of liability can make criminalization of foreign bribery appear more functional than it is in reality because it is correlated with other features of good governance. Correlation is not causation.

Next, *Nancy Hite-Rubin*, a scholar of the political-economy of development, examines a troubling empirical regularity. Across countries, increases in both defense spending and foreign procurement of military equipment by the most relatively corrupt countries are associated with rising foreign direct investment (FDI). Teasing out the causal pathways is a difficult task, but Hite-Rubin's empirical work suggests some answers. Military suppliers may try to obtain favorable contract terms through corrupt arrangements with powerful public officials, and these efforts, in some cases, show up in cross-country FDI data. These activities introduce two types of distortions. First, the global defense industry practice of contract bundling and "buy back" stipulations are arguably anti-competitive and inefficient, and, second, the FDI itself may hide payoffs and special favors granted to powerful local actors so that the dollar value of FDI is a poor measure of its social value to the country. Hite-Rubin's essay builds a political-economy framework and formalizes two hypotheses for why FDI, counterintuitively, chases military spending into the world's most corrupt markets.

The contributions by Davis, Moene & Søreide, and Hite-Rubin all raise troubling issues that ought to be confronted by those interested in limiting "grand corruption" that can undermine political and economic development goals.

The last two chapters broaden the frame to consider "state capture", that is, a polity where elites have been able to unduly influence government so that state institutions and their actions unduly benefit powerful private business and wealthy elites at the expense of ordinary citizens, especially those at the low end of the income scale. *Daniel Kaufmann*, an economist with a long career at the World Bank, was an early proponent of including anti-corruption and governance in the Bank's policy work. First at the World Bank, and then engaging in leadership work on governance with think tanks and civil-society organizations, collaborating with others, he moved beyond the study of bribery in particular deals to consider state capture, a worrisome trend across the globe, including in many wealthy countries. Influence flows through campaign contributions that make politicians beholden to their financial backers. The impact of private power on public officials also occurs via lobbying, the revolving-door hiring of ex-officials, and the provision of in-kind benefits, such as luxury trips. Furthermore, state capture can, he argues, also occur inside the state if autocratic leaders gain control and use public institutions to benefit themselves and their narrow inner circle, which also often includes oligarchs. His chapter is noteworthy in providing and analyzing a first dataset with preliminary cross-country measures of the extent of state capture both across the globe and over time. Frequently, countries with low levels of conventional corruption in the form of illegal bribery and malfeasance, such as many in industrialized countries, score less well on measures of overall state capture. Further, some prominent wealthy and middle-income countries have experienced a significant increase in the extent of state capture since the late nineties.

As an illustration of state capture at work, *Ximena Benavides*, draws on her extensive work on pharmaceutical companies' response to the US opioid crisis and the COVID-19 pandemic. She shows that firms' pursuit of profits had devastating health effects, including the deaths of thousands of people. Two fundamental problems arise in the social provision of healthcare and health. First, healthcare is a "credence" good that consumers are unable to evaluate on their own. They must rely on expert medical-care providers. If healthcare is covered by public or private insurance, it is subject both to moral hazard and, if coverage is not mandatory, to adverse selection. Second, the lower levels of health experienced by those of low income or who are otherwise disadvantaged cannot be remedied unless the state provides both healthcare and environmental and product regulations, funded by governments. Thus, Benavides' essay presents a sobering picture for readers from the U.S. and other wealthy countries. The destructive effects of lightly regulated oligarchic markets can occur in high-income countries as well as in the developing world. The consequences will affect all citizens but will be especially acute for those with limited income and wealth.

This volume emphasizes public-policy issues that have long engaged my scholarly interest in government performance—both constructive efforts to combine competence with democratic accountability and an awareness of the many ways that individual self-interest and outright malfeasance can undermine state action and circumvent democratic accountability. Of course, the topics are necessarily selective, reflecting the authors' own particular interests and talents. However, even the most focused essays on labor standards, pawnshops, and the opiod crisis raise broader issues of governments' ability and willingness to respond appropriately to policy challenges. The essays on broader topics pose challenges both to researchers seeking to understand the complex interactions between factors that influence political and economic conditions and to policymakers and citizens aiming for governments that are both technically competent and democratically responsible. Reformers need both a deep commitment to a set of ethical principles of good government and an appreciation of the incentives facing real-world actors in an imperfect world.

Public sector performance, development, and public participation

2 Improving public sector performance in developing countries

Practice meets scholarship

Jana Kunicová [1]

Public sector performance failures are seemingly ubiquitous around the globe. Hardly a day goes by without headlines in the press suggesting that public money is mismanaged or outright misused; petty bribery is rampant; civil servants are unmotivated, prone to nepotism or poorly trained; or government agencies fail to coordinate with each other. As a result, the quality of public services suffers, or citizens must navigate a bureaucratic maze to access them. These issues can be observed in both developed and developing countries but are generally exacerbated by lower levels of economic development.

Improving public sector performance requires an understanding of how governments work and how public-policy decisions are made. Social scientists and practitioners alike recognize this issue but adopt somewhat different approaches. This chapter focuses on the gap between how academicians and practitioners study public sector performance in developing countries. It defines and classifies these differences, asks why they arise, whether there is value in bridging them, and if so, how to go about it.

The chapter begins by highlighting key differences in the questions that practitioners and academicians ask, the methods they employ, and their relevant timelines. It then explores the reasons for this gap by outlining three key tensions between the worlds of scholarship and practice: scientific precision versus different ways of knowing; parsimony versus complexity; and specialization versus a broader skillset. To illustrate these tensions, it highlights the example of two social sciences, economics and political science, and their relationship to the work of the World Bank. In describing these tensions, the chapter makes it clear that much can be gained by alleviating them. This provides a way to think more systematically about building bridges between practice and scholarship. What academic frameworks are most useful for practitioners? What can practitioners offer academicians? Finally, what practical steps can be taken in the academic world and by development institutions, such as the World Bank, to enable more systematic cross-fertilization between practice and scholarship?

To begin with definitions, "public sector reform" refers to improvements in the way governments work; "public sector performance" is a related term that emphasizes the results of such reform – e.g., better public services delivered. Public sector reform is undertaken around the world, in advanced as well as developing economies, but this chapter focuses largely on the latter. By referring to "scholars" or

DOI: 10.4324/9781003416234-3

"academicians," I mean social scientists, most often political scientists and economists, who research these issues and are generally based at academic institutions. In contrast, "practitioners" are policy and development professionals working with governments on public sector reform, including staff in the operational arms of international financial institutions. These are, of course, "ideal types." Many people straddle both worlds and do not fit neatly in either box; this spectrum is discussed in detail below. Relatedly, aside from drawing on both academic and policy literature, this chapter unavoidably contains a set of personal retrospectives and reflections, given that I started my career in academia and transitioned to the World Bank almost two decades ago.

Finally, because the focus is on public sector reform, it is difficult to avoid the politics of development writ large. Development work, including macroeconomic reforms, infrastructure expansion, or service delivery in health and education, entails interfacing with political actors making political decisions. After all, these reforms are delivered by governments who face political incentives and constraints. They also take place in a particular institutional context and create winners and losers. Although practitioners may need to remain apolitical due to their institutions' mandate, understanding the politics behind a reform is critical for its design and implementation. Put simply, development institutions need to be informed about politics, but not driven by it.

Improving how governments work: The gap between academicians and practitioners

Improving how policy decisions are made and how governments work is – or should be – one of the major concerns of both policy circles and academia. However, scholars and practitioners differ in the specifics of *what* questions they ask, *how* they answer these questions, and the *timelines* they are willing to accept to arrive at what they consider to be satisfactory answers. To paraphrase Lant Pritchett (2020), an academic discipline is a group of people who decide what counts as a question and what counts as an answer. The study of public sector performance in developing countries is a vivid example of a field where the questions and answers posed by academicians are not always the same as those posed by practitioners.

Different questions

As part of my work at the World Bank over the past 17 years, I have had the privilege of seeing the veritable "policy kitchen" up close and personal in over 60 developing countries on four continents. In practice, this means working closely with ministers of finance and their deputies, heads of agencies, but sometimes also with prime ministers and heads of state on designing and implementing public sector reforms. The World Bank often supports these reforms with financing, be it general budget support or specific financing for reform projects and programs. Aside from financing, the Bank also provides client governments with "advisory services and analytics," which offer just-in-time advice or more long-term analytical support to public sector reforms. As an institution, it has a stake in the design and implementation of these reforms and uses its own administrative budget to fund the underpinning analysis.

The types of questions that senior policymakers in developing countries ponder on a daily basis are usually technical and inherently political. Below are a few that recently arose in connection with my own engagement with World Bank projects:

In a middle-income African country, I led a team of World Bank staff that worked with policymakers on a reform program to reduce the footprint of the state in the economy and spur private-sector-led growth. Our task included helping to design a privatization bill that would speed up the process of offering state-owned enterprises for sale while providing the necessary transparency and accountability guardrails for the privatization process. The government, however, faced the additional task of managing the opposition's challenge to the bill and maintaining broad-based popular support for the government's reforms.

In a middle-income country in East Asia, a high-level reform champion asked the World Bank how to reduce entrenched nepotism in the civil service, despite decades-long structural opposition and sabotage of reform attempts by those who benefited from the status quo. Is the automation of civil-service examinations the answer? Or are there other transparency features that would be more effective in achieving the desired outcome?

In a low-income country in Africa that is emerging from decades of fragility and is in the process of state-building, I advised on a reform program that grappled with fundamental questions pertaining to the design of a supreme audit institution. What is the right set of checks and balances that would guarantee the independence of the auditor general when the parliament risks politicizing the selection process? What is the right balance of power between the president and the parliament in hiring and firing the auditor general, given the government's fragility, the constitutional structure, and the nature of political competition? What will work best in safeguarding the integrity of public accounts without the whole reform being instrumentalized as a political tool?

As a political economist by training, these questions are at the heart of why I chose my discipline a quarter century ago: they are at the intersection of fundamental issues in development economics and political science, where economic growth, political institutions, power, and incentives are tightly intertwined. Carefully disentangling these issues is challenging, but critical for getting the reforms right and pushing development forward.

However, although touching on similar themes, these questions are quite different from those that engage today's academicians as they formulate their research questions. As an illustration, consider the papers published in a recent issue of the *American Political Science Review*. Jessica Rich (2023) studies the tradeoff between accountability and bureaucratic capacity in developing countries, using the case of Brazil to ask whether increasing accountability by outsourcing social-sector programs ended up decreasing state capacity in the long run. Nicholas Kuipers (2023) also focuses on easily overlooked tradeoffs when he examines the effect of civil-service examinations in Indonesia on the attitudes toward the state, social cohesion, and state legitimacy. Are there unintended consequences of merit-based recruitment if those who fail form negative attitudes toward state? Mallory Sorelle (2023) studies the politics of financial sector reform, specifically the causal mechanisms through which regulatory policymaking affects consumers' political action. Is grassroots political action more or less likely, given how particular policies are designed?

Clearly, the issues that these scholars chose to study are related to the concerns of policymakers, but they are necessarily *narrower* and *less context specific* than policy-focused analysis. A policymaker will certainly want to know whether promoting accountability will affect state capacity, whether more transparent civil-service recruitment through national examinations will affect social cohesion and state legitimacy, or how a particular reform design may spur or hinder the political mobilization of winners and losers from the reform. However, there is no straight line from causality to practical action. The policymaker will weigh all these issues in the context of the particular political environment, reform priorities, and timelines. Therefore, the questions that policymakers ask concern how these factors play out in their own polity, including the level of development of the country, existing formal institutions, informal power structures, timing, and the like. As a result, the analysis underpinning such policy advice is necessarily broader than these academic papers, focuses on specific context, and often synthesizes various methods and perspectives under a much shorter timeframe. In sum, the practitioner's task is to help the policymaker craft entry points for change, which requires a range of practical skills and compromises. Because most academics do not engage with this complexity, this undercuts the possibility for constructive dialogue.

The loss of context specificity is the flipside of the academic quest for generalizability of findings. A case in point are the issues captured in Dean Karlan and Jacob Appel (2012). Using empirical analysis and the modern thinking in behavioral economics, including randomized control trials (RCTs), the authors distill the most generalizable "seven ideas that work in the fight against poverty:" microsavings, reminders to save, prepaid fertilizer sales, deworming, remedial education in small groups, chlorine dispensers of clean water, and commitment devices. This is what we *know*, rigorously and scientifically, based on decades of empirical research. However, this is a very parochial menu to offer most development agencies and all governments, even if they are very evidence-minded. Even though data tell us that these interventions work for development, it is hard to imagine a politician or a policymaker who would run for office on a platform solely based on these ideas. Although the list presents very reasonable options, policy is built on much more encompassing, bigger issues. Agendas for action are not simply shaped by suggesting that governments implement excellent empirically supported ideas. Country counterparts have ideas of their own, as do donors. The task for the evidence-oriented practitioner is to figure out whether and how to incorporate very specific interventions supported by empirical academic research into a much more multifaceted policy agenda. In other words, although improving development outcomes may involve implementing some of the initiatives documented to work by Karlan and Appel, programs for public sector reform will necessarily be much wider ranging.[2] Political feasibility and bundling of reforms will most certainly be at the forefront.

In sum, the politics of public sector reform is challenging to both study and navigate, but at the same time, it is at the heart of reform choice, design, and implementation. Reformers themselves must also take politics into account. Designing and supporting reforms requires asking questions that are at the same time more context specific and broader than the questions asked in academic research.

Different timelines

Another key difference is the timeframe. In the policy world, timeframes are driven by policy and electoral cycles. When a new government is elected in democracies (even imperfect ones), there is usually a honeymoon period of up to a year when difficult reforms can be pushed through. This is when the key context-specific questions require answers. Decision-makers don't have the luxury of spending time on extensive data collection, survey design, or randomized control trials; instead, descriptive statistics, rapid surveys or qualitative analysis are often utilized in these cases to guide policy design or advice on implementation.[3]

Similarly, when the World Bank prepares a country partnership framework (CPF) which guides its engagement in a country for the period of four or five years, it has roughly a year to prepare the report. The Bank collects and analyzes data on what worked or did not work in the previous CPF period. Usually this includes a meta-analysis of other policy-driven analytical work that the Bank has conducted during the CPF period. Examples include Systematic Country Diagnostics that attempt to disentangle medium-term constraints on poverty alleviation and reduce inequality in the country; Country Economic Memoranda that analyze the medium-term drivers of growth; and Public Expenditure Reviews that look at the amounts and composition of public spending. These are the so-called "core diagnostics" that the Bank conducts for each country during each CPF cycle. The timeframes are driven by the Bank's budget allocation protocols, which are constrained by fiscal years, and rarely span more than a year.

In contrast, timeframes are generally longer in academia. Research design, data collection, field experiments, and drafting can often stretch over multiple years. The peer review process and publication in academic journals further extends the timeframe. For example, the *American Political Science Review* advises its authors on its website that "it still takes over a year from submission to acceptance for articles to be published," which is similar to other top journals in political science, economics, and other social sciences (Huisman & Smits, 2017). Publication and tenure incentives are usually multi-year, and, more generally, there is rarely an immediate pressing need to answer a research question by a particular deadline. Because, in academia, the questions are less context specific and the findings strive for generalizability, the answers have a certain timelessness. The academic purpose is less to answer a question in real time and more to create a solid, unassailable, unquestionable building block in the timeless body of knowledge. Hence, scholars accept long time horizons to find answers.

Different methods

There is another reason for the longer timeframes for finding acceptable academic answers compared with practice. Methods have evolved to be ever more sophisticated, often requiring larger and more granular datasets that take more time to assemble, clean, analyze, and to run robustness checks. Both structural models and RCTs, which have gained much popularity in developmental economics and in political science in recent decades as a veritable 'gold standard' for the evidence on cause and effect (see, for example, Wantchekon & Guardado, 2011),[4] take much effort and time to design. Scholars worry about scientific precision, external validity, and generalizability of findings, contributing to the body of knowledge and pushing the boundaries of what is knowable in social science.

The policy arena asks broader, context-specific questions, and operates under tighter timelines that influence the methods used to arrive at answers (or at what count as answers to other practitioners, but perhaps not to academicians). One could say that epistemological purity is generally less important in the policy world. The underlying data and resulting analyses tend to be less sophisticated, and the methods less "cutting edge." Instead, the analysis is often based on multi-disciplinary approaches, including constructing and interpreting descriptive statistics and correlations, combined with case studies, and using other qualitative methods, including typologies and analytic narratives.

Astutely, Michael Woolcock (2007) observed that policy analysts and practitioners make use of three core competencies throughout their careers: "the skills of *'detectives'* (data collection, analysis, and interpretation), *'translators'* (reframing given ideas for diverse groups), and *'diplomats'* (negotiation, conflict mediation, and deal making)." Extrapolating, one could say that academicians spend their careers honing their skills as detectives, while practitioners must acquire broader skills and be comfortable wearing different hats while tackling pressing questions of how to improve the way governments work.

Perhaps most importantly, practitioners' answers must respond to context-specific questions and come at just the right time when policymakers can use them to make decisions. To summarize, what count as questions for development practitioners are the questions that *need* to be answered given real-world imperatives, rather than the questions that *can* be answered by a specific method or with a certain "rigor."

Why this gap? A taxonomy of tensions

The comparison of questions, timelines, and methods used in academia and policy circles suggests a set of tensions between these two worlds. These tensions include scientific precision versus different approaches to *knowing,* parsimony versus complexity, and a preference for specialization versus a broader skillset.

Scientific precision versus different ways of knowing

As discussed above, modern social sciences have become significantly more "scientific" in recent decades. The methods have become considerably more sophisticated and mathematical, requiring large-n datasets or experiments to test hypotheses.[5] Collecting such data or designing and running experiments takes time. In contrast, in the policy world, advice is required in specific contexts and in real time. Even if it were possible to collect granular data, design the empirical tests, or run experiments in these specific contexts, the timelines are compressed; hence, the analytical work in the policy world places less emphasis on the latest methodology and more on triangulating various types of knowledge.

This is linked to broader epistemological questions. What is knowable? Are we offering policy advice on well-founded, justified beliefs, or are these glorified opinions? Are we telling stories or presenting evidence (and is this a correct dichotomy in the first place)? I am reminded of an anecdote involving a Nobel-prize winning macroeconomist, who was asked at a function celebrating his contributions to knowledge what he thought of a pressing policy issue of the day. He demurred, responding that much more research needed to be done to answer the question. However, in reality policymakers needed to make decisions and act in real time to tackle such issues, taking into account *what we know at a given moment* about not just the economic rationale but also the political, institutional, and social context. What is telling, however, is that scholars are much less inclined to offer recommendations unless they are certain about the scientific validity of their answers.

As a practitioner, I accept that my answers to pressing policy questions are less precise in a scientific sense, simply because they do not undergo the same rigor of large-n analysis, robustness checks, or external validity tests as they do in academic social-science research. However, I must make sure that my answers are correct with a *good-enough* probability. This requires rooting them in the body of relevant knowledge, but also triangulating different types of information and approaches.[6]

Reflecting on the body of knowledge in political science and anthropology, James Scott (2012) wrote about different ways of knowing, coining the terms of *official* and *vernacular* orders of knowledge. *Official order* refers to the government's knowledge of local realities, based on the particular points of view of government officials, often shaped by exercising power and need for control. In contrast, *vernacular order* is based on knowledge of local realities through the lived experience of those who receive government services. Each of these 'orders', Scott argues, represents a valid way of knowing, but the official order often uses scientifically grounded information to exercise power. The lack of scientific arguments (or even their presence to the contrary) does not make the vernacular order any less legitimate.

Building on Scott's distinction, David Lewis, Dennis Rogers, and Michael Woolcock (2014) add a concept of an *academic knowledge order*, which they define as "a mode of reasoning familiar to people who hold advanced degrees, are organized into different disciplines, and are trained in how to speak with each other, their immediate colleagues, and collaborators."

In a similar vein, one could define a *policy-knowledge order* as a mode of reasoning used by people working in the development field, who reference a broader set of qualitative and quantitative research across social sciences and use the considerable practical experience of many person-years working with governments and observing how policymakers make decisions. Paraphrasing Daniel Kahneman (2011), the policy-knowledge order is based not only on "slow thinking" that requires explicit data collection and analysis, but also on "fast thinking" based on implicit data contained in observed and lived experience. Formulated this way, one could imagine a bridge between the two orders, in which the policy-knowledge order generates potential research questions for the academic-research order, which then proceeds to test them according to its own standards of scientific rigor.

Parsimony versus complexity

Complexity is the world where practitioners function. They are looking for a specific solution to a specific problem in real time. Social scientists, in contrast, are interested in findings that are generalizable based on their research. Their incentives are to produce work that is elegant and parsimonious, based on issues that can be modeled and where granular, high-quality data can be collected for empirical validation. Ideally, social-science models would help practitioners cut through complexity and provide sound frameworks to answer specific questions. Academic empirical findings would also ideally help establish building blocks of hard scientific knowledge which can be the basis for sound policy advice.

However, few academic social scientists have spent time running programs in the public sector, and they often lack deep knowledge of how processes of change unfold in practice or how policies are implemented. Practitioners do know these processes first-hand but often struggle to find the time or incentives to think about them systematically and rigorously.

As a result, the rift between the two worlds is widening. As academic questions become ever-narrower and research methods more and more sophisticated, many academically trained practitioners become less interested in following findings reported in academic journals. This is not because of the lack of intellectual curiosity but because the assumptions behind theoretical models tend to be too far removed from reality and because rigorously tested empirical findings are too narrow to be relevant for policy advice. At the same time, social scientists have little incentive to invest considerable amounts of time in understanding how things work in practice, given that what is generally valued by academic journals is not the depth or richness of real-world understanding, but rather parsimony and generalizability.

Yet striving for parsimony is only useful if it helps to cut through real-world complexity. If the scholarly community has little first-hand understanding of that complexity, the models become self-referential and of little value in explaining and guiding change in the real world. Examples of work that successfully navigates this divide and is rooted firmly in the complex realities are produced by scholars who either have significant policy experience or cared to invest in gaining a deep understanding of the real world. It is worth contemplating a few recent examples spanning the methodological spectrum in social sciences that do bridge this gap.

As an example of a rich context-specific work in a top academic journal, consider a *Quarterly Journal of Economics* article co-authored by academicians and World Bank practitioners that focuses on corruption in customs (Chalendard, Fernandes,

Raballand, & Rijkers, 2023). The paper offers a new methodology to detect corruption in customs and tests it on granular data from Madagascar's main port. The methods are sophisticated, formal, and quantitative; the context is very specific and yet generalizable to similar settings. The development of this new methodology was rooted in the authors' multi-year, first-hand experience in customs reform in Madagascar and other low-income countries. At the same time, the authors were not deterred by the seeming imperfection of the data available and continued to refine their analysis (using academic rather than practitioners' timeframes). As a result, the paper combines the best of both academic and practitioners' worlds: rigorous and generalizable analysis deeply anchored in the complex realities of real-world, public-sector reform.

Yet, much policy-rooted research that cuts through the complexity of public sector reform in developing countries is qualitative. For example, Brian Levy, formerly a World Bank staffer who is currently on the faculty of Johns Hopkins University, believes that the academic work that is most useful for practitioners involves thinking *typologically*. Reform entry points vary by place and time, but practitioners are not systematic about articulating types; hence this is where academicians can add value. His 2014 book *Working with the Grain: Integrating Governance and Growth in Development Strategies* asks what it would take to initiate and sustain reforms in low-income countries. The book is built around a typology for distinguishing among contexts in four broad groups of countries, according to whether polities are dominant or competitive, and whether institutions are personalized or impersonal. Context specificity then leads to identifying alternative options for governance and policy reform. In some contexts, these could involve strengthening formal institutions, while in others it requires supporting the "islands of effectiveness" that emerge. As Levy writes, his goal was to provide an orienting framework for practitioners, "capable of filling the gap between 'best practices' hubris, on the one hand, and, on the other, the despair disguised as humility [that follows from] the notion that every country is unique and that there is little to be learned in one setting that can be helpful in another" (Levy, 2014). This sheds helpful light on a long-standing debate at the World Bank between the *best practice* and the *best fit*: best practice would suggest that "one size fits all," but the notion of best fit risks the implication that each context is unique. Typologies bridge this gap.

Another classical approach in policy-anchored research is the use of *case studies*. Despite having taken a backseat to quantitative methods in modern social science, a recent edited volume co-authored by academicians and practitioners makes a convincing case for their use (Widner, Woolcock, & Nieto, 2022). Case studies can have a valuable role both in development practice and in furthering social science, including discussions of how to ensure internal and external validity. An excellent example of case studies that chronicle public sector reform in developing countries is a program of the Princeton School of Public & International Affairs, called *Innovations for Successful Societies* (ISS). Run by Jennifer Widener, an academician keenly interested in real-world complexity, ISS is committed to focusing on questions or problems that arise when governments engage in building an institution or delivering a service. As the ISS website states, "often the most creative and successful ideas are generated internally, framed by people who have deep knowledge of local conditions. ISS enables practitioners to tell their unique stories and join a knowledge network of reform-minded public servants from around the globe. ISS case studies distill these conversations into a tool for learning, for cross-cutting analysis, and for scholarship."[7] This distinctive program is based at a university but provides a platform for real-world public sector reformers to tell their stories. The way that these case studies are framed and developed is different from typical case studies in academia. Instead of being highly stylized, they are rooted in context, operational detail, and pay specific attention to reform leaders and their perspective. ISS's intent is for these case studies to lead to hypotheses that social scientists can further test but that first draw out a real problem from the operational detail and context.

Specialization vs broader skillset

Academicians tend to specialize in research. Individual researchers acquire and maintain considerable and highly specialized skills in modern social-science methods, so some argue that they should continue specializing in theoretical modeling or empirical methods. After all, these are different skills from those needed for policy dialogue, advocacy, and management of development programs. The value-added of researchers is in developing models and frameworks, as well as building a body of empirical knowledge backed by rigorous data analysis. This knowledge can then be used by practitioners for policy advice. In other words, academically trained practitioners can apply their training by basing policy advice on the latest cutting-edge academic research, while using other skills for policy dialogue, project management, and other tasks. Thus, the argument goes, scholars should specialize in what they do best, which will, in turn, inform the work of practitioners.

However, related to the discussion in the previous section, this argument holds only insofar as academicians produce policy-relevant research. It weakens if researchers know too little about how things work in practice to make reasonable assumptions in their models. Similarly, if academic journals place a premium on high-tech empirical analysis, it will incentivize researchers to ask ever-narrower questions that can be answered with large-n data using sophisticated methods. Such analysis is of little interest or importance to practitioners. Clearly, building bridges between scholarship and practice would be of mutual benefit.

An interesting example of different approaches to building such bridges is the difference between the research departments at the World Bank and the International Monetary Fund (IMF). The World Bank research department (Development Research Group, or DECRG) resembles a social science department at an academic institution, staffed mostly with economists and a few other social scientists. Being housed at the World Bank, the topics that these researchers study focus on international development, but there is limited cross-fertilization with the everyday operational work of the Bank. DECRG staff tend to build their entire careers within that department, without any requirement to move in and out, although they are required to provide 13 weeks of their time each year in cross-support to other parts of the Bank.[8] In contrast, IMF staff who join the Fund's research department are required to rotate to operations after two years to gain first-hand experience in how reform processes work through policy dialogue and technical assistance.

As someone who started her career as an academician and made a transition to a policy practitioner, I can offer a personal reflection. I was trained in a quantitative vein of political science and in economics. As a scholar, I gravitated toward rigorous scientific approaches. Like most of my colleagues, I specialized in research, even though I was keenly interested in the workings of policy and international development. In retrospect, however, had I invested five or even ten years working in the development policy world before embarking on a Ph.D., my academic approach would have been even more interdisciplinary. Eighteen years into my World Bank tenure, having grappled with many of the thorny issues of development, I am much humbler about what is knowable and, indeed, actionable using quantitative methods of social science. To come closer to finding answers to some of the key questions in development, I believe we need not just specialized knowledge of economics and political science, but also history, sociology, anthropology, and humanities, more broadly. Moreover, we need not only individuals who specialize in each of these disciplines but also those who can synthesize and weave them into convincing narratives, distilling complexity into clear frameworks and compelling stories. I have learned that the most useful and powerful types of knowledge in development lie at the intersection of disciplines.

An example: Economics and political science at the World Bank

So far, I have referred to social sciences as if they were a single academic discipline. However, there are important differences in how economics and political science relate to the world of practitioners in international development. For specificity, I will use the example of World Bank operational work as a proxy for the development practitioners' realm, as this is the environment with which I am most familiar.

Although macroeconomics concerns itself with economic growth and development, political science studies how governments and institutions work. In theory, it should be as relevant as economics for understanding how developing countries can improve their public sector performance. But, in practice, the profile of political science is much lower among practitioners and in international development in general. The World Bank has a position of a Chief Economist, but no similar position for a political scientist who would advise Bank management and client governments on the issues of public sector reform and institutional development.[9]

Economics and political science face different types of challenges in building bridges with the policy world. Economics is in many ways better positioned than political science. The research department at the World Bank, or DECRG, is in theory designed as a vehicle to bridge the gap between academic approaches in economics and development policy. As discussed above, DECRG is not always successful at doing so because its functioning is not fully integrated into the daily operational and policy advice work of the Bank. At the same time, the prestigious position of Chief Economist of the World Bank Group (who is also Senior Vice President for Development Economics and hence the head of DECRG) serves as a powerful bridge between cutting-edge ideas in economics and the practitioners' world. As a rule, Chief Economists are influential academicians who come to the Bank for two to four years and influence policy direction and advice that the World Bank dispenses to its client governments. The list of former chief economists is long and illustrious, including Anne Krueger (1982–1986), Stanley Fischer (1988–1990), Larry Summers (1991–1993), Joe Stiglitz (1997–2000), Nicholas Stern (2000–2003), Justin Lin (2008–2012), Paul Romer (2016–2018), and Carmen Reinhart (2020–2022).

Political science faces a particular predicament. For the first 50 years of its existence, the World Bank could not talk about politics due to the strict interpretation of its mandate as apolitical in the World Bank Articles of Agreement. The Bank's focus is on lifting millions of people around the world out of poverty, but it does this through providing grants, loans, and policy advice to governments. Because of this direct relationship with governments, there is a limit to the Bank's ability to engage in political discourse and analysis. Only since 1995, after the seminal legal opinion by Ibrahim Shihata, the World Bank's General Counsel, related to prohibition of political activities in the World Bank, has the strict interpretation of the Articles of Agreement been somewhat relaxed. At a minimum, the Bank acknowledged that it needed to understand member states' underlying political dynamics to be effective. During the 1996 Annual Meetings, the World Bank President James Wolfensohn delivered his famous "Cancer of Corruption" speech (Wolfensohn, 1997). For the first time in the Bank's history, its leader discussed the issues of transparency, accountability, and institutional capacity of governments. In the same speech, Wolfensohn committed to fight against corruption, which, in his words, redistributed from the poor to the rich and distorted public expenditures. This was the first time that the Bank had inched toward talking about politics and to taking a stance that could be interpreted as political.

The 1997 World Development Report (WDR), *The State in a Changing World*, explored the role of the state and the capability it needed to deliver: in particular, "choosing how to do things – how to deliver basic services, provide infrastructure, regulate the economy – and not just whether to do them at all. The choice of approach might appropriately vary with a country's institutional capability." Following the 1997 WDR, the World Bank greatly expanded its operational engagement with governance and public sector reform around the globe.

In the past 25 years, much progress has been made in thinking politically at the Bank. At present, the Bank directly analyzes and supports the reform processes of governing and public institutions, as well as governance and anti-corruption more broadly. Today, the Governance Global Practice is one of the largest practice areas in the World Bank, comprising almost 800 development professionals who work with governments around the world on reforming public sector institutions, public financial management, public procurement, anti-corruption, and justice sector reform – through financing development projects, policy advice, and analytical work.[10] Pushing the analytical frontier on governance at the Bank, the 2017 WDR,

Governance and the Law, broke another taboo by looking explicitly into how political power is distributed and its effect on development.

On the operational side, the Bank's expanded work in fragile, conflict-affected, and violent (FCV) situations requires it to be more attuned to political analysis. In FCV countries, the Bank conducts periodic Risk and Resilience Assessments, which require understanding the drivers of conflict and resilience. In addition, the institution now routinely commissions "political economy analysis" for its country strategies or major engagements, framing economic problems with features of individual or group interests.

And yet, major constraints persist in using the definitions, frameworks, and tools of political science in the Bank work (cf. Carothers & Gramond, 2013). Most key governance concepts that the Bank uses do not come from the discipline of political science; they are, in fact, "home-grown" in the institution. For example, the concept of *state capture* was coined in the World Bank Policy Research Working Paper by Joel Hellman, Geraint Jones, and Daniel Kaufmann (Hellman, Jones, & Kaufmann, 2000). The *accountability triangle* for service delivery comes from the 2004 WDR. Even the very concept of *governance*, as used by the Bank, came from a World Bank White Paper (World Bank, 1991).

Upon reflection, this is perhaps unsurprising. It would not be appropriate for the Bank to talk about political science concepts such as *regimes, selectorates* or *electorates, kleptocracies,* or even *democracies* as contrasted with *autocracies*. This is because these concepts describe power relationships among actors, which is squarely outside the Bank's mandate. At the same time, the Bank can and does use more neutral descriptors of governments and their public sectors: *high- vs low-capacity public sectors*; *fragility vs stability*; *low-, middle-, or high-income country*. These terms, although clearly connected with different technical considerations, often correlate with some of these power relationships. Still, Bank-coined terms related to governance, accountability, and corruption reflect the Bank's reality of trying to push the envelope of these reforms in practice, but on its own terms, in the tight space that it navigates.

Meanwhile, political science as a discipline has kept evolving. Especially as taught in the graduate programs at the top US academic institutions over the last few decades, political science has become more quantitative and formal, pushing qualitative methods into the background (Emmons & Moravcsik, 2019). Paradoxically, even though modern political science looks more like economics, it is in a sense more insulated from the policy world. Unlike economics through the institution of the World Bank Chief Economist, political science is not part of the policy back-and-forth with the Bank and other development institutions. This limits the necessary cross-fertilization between academic ideas in political science and real-world issues. In addition, applied economics is an established discipline in a variety of prestigious think tanks and public-policy schools; in contrast, "applied political science," as a concept applied to the politics of comparative international development, is not well established (cf. Andres & Beecher, 1989). All these factors lead to the greater insularity of the discipline and its distance from the pressing questions that practitioners of international development face. Hence the growing divergence in the questions, methods, and timelines between the academic political science and the real-world politics of development.

Policy-relevant research and research-informed policy analysis: What the two worlds can learn from each other

The discussion thus far clearly implies that both the scholarship and the practice of public sector reform in developing countries would be better off if more bridges were built between the two worlds, with more cross-fertilization and exchange of experiences, ideas, and approaches to follow. This is particularly true for the task of improving public sector performance around the world, which entails political actors making and implementing decisions.

There are many things that academicians can learn from practitioners. The academic questions asked about public sector reform in the developing world would be more policy-relevant if the scholars invested more into learning about how policymaking and implementation process really work; how key policymakers make decisions; how to identify champions of reform; how to leverage islands of excellence; and the importance of context beyond the narrow question or field of study. At the same time, practitioners can benefit from thinking about public sector reform more systematically in any given country context. In a sense, this requires cutting through two different types of fog: one is the complexity of real-world conditions, and the other is the plethora of existing scholarly frameworks (some more useful than others for the reasons discussed above) that could help make sense of real-world phenomena.

From the practitioners' point of view, what are some examples of useful academic frameworks that allow one to make sense of the real-world complexity of public-sector reform in developing countries? I present a very partial list, for the purposes of illustration only, which includes concepts and frameworks that I have relied on in my own work after transitioning from academia to policy and operational work.

Albert Hirschmann's seminal *exit, voice, and loyalty* framework is indispensable for thinking about how and under what conditions different groups in the society support reforms, with a clear link to power and institutions (Hirschmann, 1970). When thinking about the interaction between states and markets and the evolving role of the state, Karl Polanyi's classic work on the linkage between the development of the modern state and the market economy is a good starting point (Polanyi, 1957). Linking the themes of Hirschmann and Polanyi, Joel Migdal proposed a frame to think about the role of the state in the developing world as it is underpinned by society and its traditional structures (Migdal, 1988). Susan Rose-Ackerman founded the field of political economy of corruption, anchoring our thinking about incentives and constraints for politicians and bureaucrats to engage in graft (Rose-Ackerman, 1978, 1999; Rose-Ackerman & Palifka, 2016). Mancur Olson and the line of research that his work inspired provides a powerful way of thinking about how different modes of governing, authoritarian or democratic, may influence growth and development (Olson, 1993). Joel Hellman provided a framework for thinking about simultaneous transitions from autocratic to democratic forms of government and from plan to market, asking fundamental questions of how the interaction between winners and losers from these reforms results in partial reform equilibria (Hellman, 1998). More recently, Douglas North, John Wallis, and Barry Weingast explored the nature of political settlements and their impact on when political violence breaks out, helping to underpin the analysis of the nexus between violence, political fragility, and development (North et al., 2009, 2013). Brian Levy assesses ways to approach public sector reform in different types of political and institutional contexts (Levy, 2014).

Perhaps unsurprisingly, classical political economy frameworks dominate this illustrative list, especially those focusing on institutional reform and power dynamics underpinning the support for and resistance to reform. In addition, the frameworks for the study of the relationship between the state and markets, as well as those focusing on the formation of states and cessation of violence, are also crucial for policy-oriented work. As noted above, the World Bank and other development institutions cannot discuss the interaction between power and institutions in the countries they serve, but their work must recognize the complexity surrounding these issues. Paradoxically, due to the nature of the Bank's work and its proximity to policymakers, Bank staff also have much first-hand, nitty-gritty detailed knowledge and data, both quantitative and qualitative, pertaining to these issues. At the same time, academicians can and should study these questions, further developing useful frameworks that would help practitioners cut through the fog of practical real-world complexity. However, the access and exposure of academicians to the relevant practical information remains limited for the reasons discussed earlier.

Academicians and practitioners are, of course, stylized types. There are institutions, programs, work-streams, and individuals that successfully straddle the two worlds. However, underpinning the argument in this chapter is the fact that such "hybrids" are few and far between, and *ad hoc* rather than mainstream. Among public-policy schools and research centers, the Blavatnik School of Government at Oxford stands out as producing academically informed research about public sector performance that is deeply grounded in operational realities. The same is true of the *Innovations for Successful Societies* program at Princeton discussed above. The University of Manchester supported the *Effective States and Inclusive Development* (ESID) research program, a 26-country partnership funded by UK government. ESID furthered the study of political settlements and their implications for reform entry points, resulting in a useful volume (Kelsall et al., 2022). Among think tanks, the Center for Global Development produces excellent policy-informed research on public sector reform.

There is also research-informed World Bank analytical work on public sector-performance, but it does not always reach academic economics or political science departments. Academicians tend to be most familiar with the World Bank research department (DECRG) working papers on the subject, including its sections, such as Bureaucracy Lab or Development Impact Evaluation (DIME). However, as discussed earlier, these are closer to academic research than to everyday policy work done by the Bank, with minimal cross-fertilization with the Bank's operational departments. The *World Development Reports* (WDRs), flagship annual publications of the Bank led by DECRG with the participation of staff from operational teams, are reasonably well-disseminated in academia. Over the years, three of them dealt explicitly with public sector reform-related issues: the role of the state (WDR, 1997), service delivery and accountability (WDR, 2004), and governance and the law (WDR, 2017). Their role is precisely to inform the work of the Bank by offering relevant up-to-date analytical frameworks, rather than to analyze data obtained through the institution's own operational engagement.

In contrast, scholars might be less familiar with much of the analytical work produced by operational departments of the Bank that deal with public sector reform in a much more granular, operational way. As mentioned earlier, these include the so-called *core diagnostics*: standard reports that the Bank conducts every four or five years in each country where it engages. These include: *Systematic Country Diagnostics* (analysis of constraints on achieving the twin goals, poverty alleviation and shared prosperity, regularly underpinned by institutional analysis); *Country Economic Memoranda* (analysis of the sources of growth for each country, followed by the institutional and policy reforms required in the medium term to achieve it); *Public Expenditure Reviews* (detailed disaggregated analyses of public spending, often with an institutional dimension); and *Climate Change and Development Reports* (identifying mitigation and adaptation strategies for green growth, including institutional assessments). Aside from these regular reports, there are hundreds of demand-driven analytical and advisory pieces produced every year that deal with specific issues of public-sector reform based on requests from client countries; this advice can be country specific, regional, or global in nature.

The Bank's operational analytical work is a good place to start for those academicians who are interested in delving into real-world complexity and understanding the current issues arising in developing countries that strive to improve their public sector performance. Yet, although each set of core diagnostics has a public sector and institutional dimension, these regular reports deal with broader issues of development. To focus on public sector performance, the Bank produced a global report in 2018 that drew on the hitherto tacit knowledge of about 800 staff in its Governance Global Practice. Its goal was to tease out broader lessons from the Bank's own operational experience with improving public sector performance (World Bank, 2018). The next section highlights its approach and findings.

An example: World Bank global report on public sector performance: what works on the ground in the developing world, and why[11]

The World Bank's global report, entitled *Improving Public Sector Performance through Innovation and Inter-Agency Coordination* (World Bank, 2018), argues that positive change is possible in many low- and middle-income countries that attempt to reform their public sector. Reforms can improve how public money is managed, how civil servants are motivated or trained, how agencies coordinate among themselves, and how all of this translates into better service delivery.

The report presents 15 country cases of such reforms and shows that such change does not necessarily require large financial investments or complex information technology (IT) systems. What these cases have in common, instead, are three or more of the following five interconnected drivers of success:

- **High-level political leadership** is needed because few, if any, of the innovations are a purely technocratic exercise. Leaders need to find ways to collaborate with a wide range of internal and external stakeholders to overcome inherent opposition. In addition, visible political leadership is helpful, but a key high-level technician at the helm of the lead agency is instrumental for success.
- **Institutional capacity building** within existing institutions is a common element across many of the successful cases. Successful lead agencies, even if newly established, often build on existing traditional systems and structures. For reforms to endure, one ultimately needs to create sustainable institutions.
- **Incentives** matter, both at the institutional level (e.g., through government-wide systems and structures that shape institutional objectives, and program-monitoring systems) as well as at the level of civil servants (e.g., through performance targets and reward systems).
- **Increased transparency** can help deliver change in public sector performance by breaking down government silos and ensuring inter-agency information-sharing and publishing or disseminating performance information. Transparency can also be a powerful driver for changing incentives.
- **Technology**, while not a panacea, is present in two-thirds of the featured cases. The reformers applied relevant, even basic, IT tools and know-how to their specific functional requirements and did not over-design their efforts. Furthermore, technology is rarely a stand-alone solution; rather, it needs to be accompanied by policies and procedures to change behavior. IT also helps to change incentives and often increases transparency.

The case studies in the report provide ample illustrations of how change occurred in practice, including the following vignettes:

Rwanda's leadership gave incentives to local governments to improve their performance by fusing the traditional leaders' public pledge (known as *imihigo*) with a modern idea of performance contracts for high-level civil servants. The President's Office began by using these powerful non-monetary incentives to get mayors across the country to set development targets for their districts and deliver on them, resulting in measurably better development outcomes at the district level.

In Pakistan, a simple mobile text messaging system and robocalls created a powerful feedback mechanism, through which citizens provide information to their leaders about the quality and availability of public services in real time. After piloting this intervention in the province of Punjab, the national passport office has since taken the approach on board and attributes citizen feedback to helping them slash the processing time for passports from three weeks to ten days.

In Indonesia a simple automation of the entrance exam for civil servants cut corruption and nepotism in civil-service recruitment. Now the database of questions is tightly controlled, and results are posted in real time outside the testing center, dramatically reducing opportunities for preferential hiring.

How were these and the remaining 12 cases in the report selected? Nominations of successful cases were solicited in 2017 from all Governance Global Practice staff at the World Bank, based in both the headquarters in Washington and in over 140 offices around the world. The goal was to capitalize on the collective knowledge of those working with governments on public sector reform. Out of 54 nominations received, 15 cases were selected by a panel of ten senior public-sector specialists (core team) at the Bank, following an agreed selection framework. The cases had to meet several criteria: they had to document new (innovative) attempts to solve old (pernicious) problems; they had to contain "innovations" rather than "inventions;" and demonstrate their impact (though not necessarily through an existing impact evaluation). Methodologically, the departure point for the case structure were the cases from *Innovations for Successful Societies*, which were adapted to the specificity of the World Bank projects, while rigorously following the tenets of qualitative inference (cf. Widener et al., 2022).

What can we say, based on these case studies, about how public sector reforms materialize? One size, of course, does not fit all; different solutions may be appropriate for different contexts. Trial and error is expected, and flexibility is key on the path to finding the best fit for a particular challenge and context. Progress is possible if governments keep trying to improve, even while stumbling. They need to learn from pitfalls and adapt their approaches to achieve the desired change. These ideas are encapsulated in the well-known Chinese saying, "crossing the river by feeling the stones." This means that each experiment that worked for some governments can be a stepping stone for others, but each one needs to be tried out, and possibly adjusted to the specific context at hand. Documenting such experiences thus becomes important as an inspiration or catalyst for further trying and adapting, rather than as a prescription for an approach that can be directly emulated.

For practitioners, this is actionable advice. For scholars, the report may generate further questions, including testable hypotheses, or the need to propose or refine the theoretical framework. If the report has these effects, that would be a positive step toward building bridges between the practice and scholarship.

Concluding thoughts: Additional ideas for building bridges

Throughout this chapter, I have given ample reasons for scholars who study public sector reform in developing countries to be more involved with the world of practitioners. In particular, academicians might want to invest in understanding what the World Bank does operationally. There is a treasure trove of information and data, along with the tacit knowledge of the Bank staff, that may lend itself to academic study. Bank staff have unprecedented access to high-level policymakers, as well as to other stakeholders, including donor governments, private sector representatives, civil society, and the media. Academicians could think about how to leverage the practitioners' understanding of the policy and implementation process. Further, World Bank projects support reforms that sometimes run into implementation challenges, but other times work well. The Bank has systematically documented both successes and challenges and these can be analyzed. There are also millions of transactions recorded in the financial management and procurement data for World Bank projects; there are hundreds of potential research questions that can be explored.

At the same time, practitioners can also do more to nurture systematic links with academia. The Bank has made much of its data public but could do even better. The Governance Global Practice (GGP) at the Bank could create platforms that would systematically give incentives to scholars to interact with its staff on the issue of public sector reform. The creation of a new central unit in the GGP in 2023, focused on public institutions, data, and analytics, provides an excellent entry point when there is momentum developing for managing global knowledge about public sector institutional reform. Finally, if the Bank considered re-introducing the office of the Chief Institutional Economist, it could help tremendously in connecting with both institutional economics as well as political science as a discipline, creating avenues for more systematic cross-pollination and tighter links.

On balance, the analysis in this chapter points to the value of both academic and practical approaches to thinking about public sector reform. They are different and quite complementary. It is useful to have scholars working to develop a rigorous body of knowledge that practitioners can draw on to provide just-in-time advice to governments and nudge the reform process forward. At the same time, the chapter also argued strongly that the world would be a better place if academicians and practitioners were more attuned to each other's approaches and knowledge. Their differences notwithstanding, the two worlds are in need of more bridges. Building them begins with nurturing curiosity, understanding, and respect for each other's knowledge on both sides, which can then lead to more institutional platforms for exchange between the academic and policy worlds.

Notes

1 The views expressed here are solely the author's and do not necessarily reflect those of the World Bank, its Executive Directors, or the countries they represent. The author would like to thank, without implicating, the following colleagues and collaborators for helpful conversations and comments on earlier drafts: Edouard Al-Dahdah, Robert Beschel, Zubair Bhatti, Paulo Correa, Keith Hansen, Joel Hellman, Arturo Herrera, Ivailo Izvorski, Dani Kaufmann, Phil Keefer, Brian Levy, Norman Loayza, Lant Pritchett, Gael Raballand, Martin Raiser, Susan Rose-Ackerman, Jennifer Widener, Michael Woolcock, and Albert Zeufack.

2 There are other powerful critiques of Karlan & Appel's (2012) book as a summary of what is known about fighting poverty. For example, Pritchett (2020, 2022) shows that nearly all variation in a country's headcount poverty rate (across countries and over time) is accounted for by the median income of the country. Because, by definition, a country's median income is not affected by programs targeted to those with less than median income, that country's level and growth rate of median income has little to do with deworming or other initiatives described by Karlan & Appel (2012).

3 Sometimes, policy advice is required in real time, in which case it is more akin to "thinking fast" in the Kahneman (2011) sense, when many person-year experiences are distilled into a judgment call. The World Bank has a number of formal processes

where such judgement calls are made, including decision meetings (DMs). DMs are formal corporate reviews of all lending and analytical work that include peer reviews and written comments from key corporate departments, generally with a director-level chair responsible for guidance and decisions, including judgment calls. Operations or analysis with higher stakes require higher authority for judgment calls; then, decision meetings become regional operational committee (ROC) meetings, chaired by a vice-president, or operational committee (OC) meetings, chaired by the Managing Director for Operations

4 The status of RCTs as "gold standard" in social science is increasingly being challenged on the grounds of external validity; see Bedecarrat et al. (2020).

5 In political science, Cassandra Emmons & Andrew Moravcsik (2019) find that all top tier political science departments offer courses in quantitative research methods, but only over a half offer qualitative method training, in a marked decline in the past two decades.

6 See Lewis, Rodgers, & Woolcock (2014) for a provocative argument in favor of using different lenses to push forward the knowledge of development solutions. According to the authors, these approaches are found not only in development economics, political science, sociology, and anthropology, but also in history, literature, and film.

7 See https://successfulsocieties.princeton.edu/about/how-we-work, accessed on July 10, 2023.

8 It is important to note that the Bank produces the vast majority of its analytical work not through DECRG, but through its operational departments. I discuss this in the following section. However, the work of DECRG staff is most directly comparable to that of academicians, as they are required to publish their work in academic peer-reviewed journals. In addition, although DECRG would be a large academic department – with about 100 researchers – it is a minuscule percentage of World Bank professional staff, which has more than 10,000 employees in 140 offices around the globe.

9 The closest in spirit was a short-lived position of Chief Institutional Economist, occupied by Joel Hellman, in 2010s. Admittedly, Chief Institutional Economist is different from Chief Political Scientist, but the mandate was closest to understanding political and economic incentives. After Joel Hellman's departure from the Bank, the office was disbanded.

10 Out of 800 Governance staff, roughly half carry out the Bank's fiduciary compliance – financial management and procurement in projects. Formerly a "back-office function," the lines between back-office and client-facing roles have now been blurred, as financial management and procurement staff often contribute to client dialogue focused on public financial management reform and public procurement reform, including transparency, accountability, and anti-corruption.

11 This section expands on my blogpost published on the World Bank's *Governance for Development* blog: https://blogs.worldbank.org/governance/five-drivers-improving-public-sector-performance-lessons-new-world-bank-global-report

References

Andres, G., & Beecher, J. (1989). Applied Political Science: Bridging the Gap or a Bridge Too Far? *PS: Political Science & Politics*, *22*(3), 636–639. https://doi.org/10.2307/419633

Bédécarrats, F., Guérin, I., & Roubaud, F., eds. (2020). *Randomized Control Trials in the Field of Development: A Critical Perspective*. Oxford Academic. https://doi.org/10.1093/oso/9780198865360.003.0004

Carothers, T., & Gramont, D. (2013). *Development Aid Confronts Politics: The Almost Revolution*. Carnegie Endowment for International Peace. https://doi.org/10.2307/j.ctt6wpk93

Chalendard, C., Fernandes, A., Raballand, G., & Rijkers, B. (2023). Corruption in Customs. *The Quarterly Journal of Economics*, *138*(1), 575–636. https://doi.org/10.1093/qje/qjac032

Emmons, C. V., & Moravcsik, A. M. (2019). Graduate Qualitative Methods Training in Political Science: A Disciplinary Crisis. *PS: Political Science & Politics*, *53*(2), 258–264. https://doi.org/10.1017/s1049096519001719

Hellman, J. S. (1998). Winners Take All: The Politics of Partial Reform in Postcommunist Transitions. *World Politics*, *50*(2), 203–234. https://doi.org/10.1017/s0043887100008091

Hellman, J., Jones, G., & Kaufmann, D. (2000). Seize the state, seize the day: State capture, corruption, and influence in transition economies. World Bank Policy Research Working Paper No. 2444 (Washington).

Hirschman, A. O. (1970). *Exit, Voice, and Loyalty*. Harvard University Press.

Huisman, J., & Smits, J. (2017). Duration and Quality of the Peer Review Process: The Author's Perspective. *Scientometrics*, *113*(1), 633–650. https://doi.org/10.1007/s11192-017-2310-5

Kahneman, D. (2011). *Thinking, Fast and Slow*. Penguin UK.

Karlan, D., & Appel, J. (2012). *More Than Good Intentions*. National Geographic Books.

Kelsall, T., Schulz, N., Ferguson, W. D., Hau, M. V., Hickey, S., & Levy, B. (2022). *Political Settlements and Development*. Oxford University Press.

Kuipers, N. (2023). Failing the Test: The Countervailing Attitudinal Effects of Civil Service Examinations. *American Political Science Review*, *117*(3), 891–908. https://doi.org/10.1017/S0003055422001149

Levy, B. (2014). *Working with the Grain*. Oxford University Press.

Lewis, D., Rodgers, D., & Woolcock, M. (2014). *Popular Representations of Development*. Routledge.

Migdal, J. S. (1988). *Strong Societies and Weak States*. Princeton University Press.

North, D. C., Wallis, J. J., & Weingast, B. R. (2009). *Violence and Social Orders*. Cambridge University Press.

North, D. C., Wallis, J. J., Webb, S. B., & Weingast, B. R. (2013). *In the Shadow of Violence*. Cambridge University Press.

Olson, M. (1993). Dictatorship, Democracy, and Development. *American Political Science Review*, *87*(3), 567–576. https://doi.org/10.2307/2938736

Polanyi, K. (1957). *The Great Transformation*. Beacon Press.

Pritchett, L. (2020). Randomizing Development: Method or Madness? In Bédécarrats, F., Guérin, I., & Roubaud, F. (eds.), *Randomized Control Trials in the Field of Development: A Critical Perspective*. Oxford Academic. https://doi.org/10.1093/oso/9780198865360.003.0004

Pritchett, L. (2022). National Development Delivers: And How! And How? *Economic Modelling*, *107*. https://doi.org/10.1016/j.econmod.2021.105717

Rich, J. (2023). Outsourcing Bureaucracy to Evade Accountability: How Public Servants Build Shadow State Capacity. *American Political Science Review*, *117*(3), 835–850. https://doi.org/10.1017/S0003055422000892

Rose-Ackerman, S. (1978). *Corruption*. Academic Press.

Rose-Ackerman, S. (1999). *Corruption and Government*. Cambridge University Press.

Rose-Ackerman, S., & Palifka, B. J. (2016). *Corruption and Government* (2nd Edition.). Cambridge University Press.

Scott, J. C. (2012). *Two Cheers for Anarchism*. Princeton University Press.

Sorelle, M. (2023). Privatizing Financial Protection: Regulatory Feedback and the Politics of Financial Reform. *American Political Science Review*, *117*(3), 985–1003. https://doi.org/10.1017/S0003055422001071

Wantchekon, L., & Guardado R. J. (2011). Methodology Update: Randomised Controlled Trials, Structural Models and the Study of Politics. *Journal of African Economies*, *20*(4), 653–672. https://doi.org/10.1093/jae/ejr029

Widner, J., Woolcock, M., & Nieto, D. O. (2022). *The Case for Case Studies*. Cambridge University Press.

Wolfensohn, J. D. (1997). 1996 Annual Meetings Speech. *Trends in Organized Crime*, *2*(4), 39–39. https://doi.org/10.1007/s12117-997-1072-5

Woolcock, M. (2007). Higher Education, Policy Schools, and Development Studies: What Should Masters Degree Students be Taught? *Journal of International Development*, *19*(1), 55–73. https://doi.org/10.1002/jid.1300

World Bank. (1991). *Proceedings of the World Bank Annual Conference on Development Economics*. Washington, DC. https://documents1.worldbank.org/curated/fr/595181468739238386/pdf/multi-page.pdf

World Bank. (2018). *Improving Public Sector Performance: Through Innovation and Inter-Agency Coordination*. Washington, DC. https://documents1.worldbank.org/curated/en/833041539871513644/pdf/131020-WP-P163620-WorldBankGlobalReport-PUBLIC.pdf

World Development Report 1997. (1997). World Bank Publications.

World Development Report 2004. (2004). World Bank Publications.

World Development Report 2017. (2017). World Bank Publications.

3 The strength of weak effects

Stephen Kosack

One result of the international commitment to participatory development (e.g. OECD 2008) is that hundreds of organizations around the world have developed a range of participatory programs that seek to improve the transparency and social accountability of public services. A growing number of randomized controlled trials (RCTs) find that although these programs can sometimes cause transformative improvements (Christensen et al. 2021; Banerjee et al. 2018; Björkman and Svensson 2009), they often have null or weak effects on health care, education, infrastructure, and other public-service outcomes (Raffler, Posner, and Parkerson 2019; Lieberman, Posner, and Tsai 2014; Ananthpur, Malik, and Rao 2014; Banerjee et al. 2010; 3ie 2018).

One program with null effects on public-service delivery was a community scorecard offered to 200 communities in a 2014–15 RCT in Indonesia and Tanzania. I was part of a team of researchers and practitioners who designed the RCT and evaluated its effects. The program sought to make maternal and newborn health care services more transparent and facilitate discussions to encourage community members to deliberate on barriers to pregnant women accessing quality health care services and create a plan of activities through which they could improve the responsiveness, accountability, and effectiveness of those services. Two years after it, maternal and newborn health care outcomes were not significantly different on average from those in 200 similarly stratified communities where the program was not offered.

To many who heard the null results of the RCT in Indonesia and Tanzania (including this author) the implication was that the program had no effect on maternal and newborn health care.[1] Given the nature of this program, the lack of impact reinforced concerns about the effectiveness of programs that seek to improve public services by providing information and encouraging participation.

But a null only indicates that the confidence interval around the average estimated impact of a common cause includes 0, and thus that the null hypothesis of no impact cannot be rejected. And in fact, the program's effects were not zero. A mixed-method evaluation, involving both the typical cross-sectional comparison of hypothesized outcomes after the program as well as interviews, observations, focus groups, and ethnographic studies before, during, and after it, shows that concealed in the program's average null effects was participation that was often empowering and that led to tangible improvements to local health care provision in a significant

DOI: 10.4324/9781003416234-4

proportion of communities. Taking account of the varied effects suggests a different interpretation of the program's null effects on average outcomes, with different implications for understanding how and in what circumstances programs like this can empower communities to improve public services.

Null effects and empowered participation

The 200 communities where this program was offered were randomly selected to be representative of health care outcomes across two provinces of Indonesia, Banten and South Sulawesi, and two regions of Tanzania, Dodoma and Tanga. In each community, a facilitator from a nongovernmental organization[2] spent several weeks conducting a survey and gathering stories of experiences among community members with their maternal and newborn heath and health care. The facilitator then invited a group of approximately 15 people broadly representative of the community and interested in trying to improve their maternal and newborn health care, particularly non-elites, to attend six community meetings over a period of approximately three-to-four months. The facilitators offered information, time, and space to discuss and deliberate, and encouragement and help with making and adjusting plans.

Numerous case studies and several randomized controlled trials have found that this kind of approach can repair or improve trust in providers and the responsiveness of public services, reduce corruption and waste, improve infrastructure, and increase knowledge and understanding about public services among communities they serve. In some cases, it has been found to increase awareness and alleviate principal-agent failures in the systems that deliver public services sufficiently to cause transformative improvements in public service outcomes. In 2004, in Uganda, an RCT of a similar program found that it was sufficient to improve immunization rates, treatment practices, waiting times, and practitioner absenteeism, and increase clinic visits by 20%. As a result, a year later there were one-third fewer deaths among children under five years old than in communities in a control group (Björkman and Svensson 2009). A follow-up study found sustained improvements four years later (Björkman Nyqvist, de Walque, and Svensson 2017). A 2011 RCT in Sierra Leone of a similar program in Uganda found similarly significant effects (Christensen et al. 2021).

Evidence collected two years after the scorecard program in Indonesia and Tanzania does not indicate that it had this kind of transformative effect. Instead, all the evidence points to one conclusion: that the program had null average effects on health care outcomes. In interviews two years after the program, recently pregnant women did not describe significantly different experiences with maternal and newborn health care in communities where the program was offered compared to communities in the control group. They were not significantly more likely on average to deliver in the facility or seek pre- and post-natal care. Interviews with staff and observations of clinics also indicate that the clinics in communities where the program was offered were not significantly more accessible, better or more fully equipped or equipped, or otherwise delivered better care than clinics without these meetings. Average indicators of these outcomes improved substantially in the two years after the program started in both Indonesia and Tanzania, but on average these improvements were insignificantly different from improvements in communities in the control group where the program was not offered (Arkedis et al. 2021).

What do these null effects mean? Randomized controlled trials are unrivaled in the precision of their estimates of the significance of the average impact of a common cause like a development program. This same precision of interpretation is not possible with a null result. Yet null results are often read to indicate that there was no impact. A study of a randomized replication of the Uganda scorecard program in 2014–15 concluded that it had no effect on utilization or child health outcomes and only small, barely significant effects on other health care outcomes, showing the weakness of this kind of bottom-up approach (Raffler, Posner, and Parkerson 2019). A randomized evaluation of an experimental citizen training and participation program in Karnataka, India found that it had no effect on schools, health, sanitation, irrigation, roads, access to government programs, or tax compliance. Although all improved, the improvements were insignificantly different on average from improvements in communities in the control group not offered the program. An ethnographic study of the program is called "The Anatomy of Failure" (Ananthpur, Malik, and Rao 2014).

But a null only indicates that the confidence interval around the average estimated impact of a common cause includes 0. In estimates of effects in the RCT in Indonesia and Tanzania, the 95% confidence intervals around 0 are small: generally less than one standard deviation in outcomes across the province or region. But they also include effects on birth with a skilled provider, birth at a facility, ante- and post-natal care, and other health care outcomes that ranged from slightly harmful, on average, to slightly positive.

The RCT of this program was a mixed-method evaluation, involving both the typical cross-sectional comparison of hypothesized outcomes after the program, as well as interviews, observations, focus groups, and ethnographic studies before, during, and after the program, to identify hypothesized effects and process-trace the mechanisms underlying them and methods for identifying unexpected outcomes and unanticipated processes (Figure 3.1).

Data from these interviews, observations, and focus groups consistently indicate that the program's effects were not the transformative improvements measured by evaluations of similar programs in other contexts. In the average community, participants were not able to traverse the complex causal paths from planning actions to realizing tangible improvements. Yet evidence from focus groups two years after the program and process-tracing interviews, observations, and ethnographic studies during the program also consistently shows substantial and sustained participation in almost all communities in Indonesia and Tanzania. Not all of participants' activities were successful, and in some communities, participation in the program was disappointing and seen as a waste of time. But in significantly more, participating in the program reinforced participants' perceptions of their capacities to improve their communities as members of those communities and citizens of Indonesia and Tanzania. In most—83 of 100 communities in Indonesia; 95 of 100

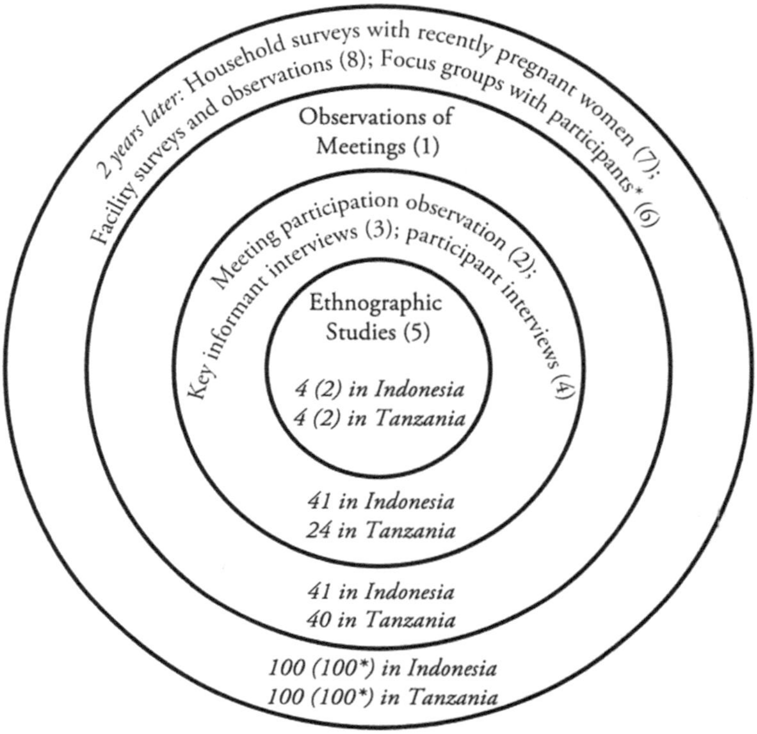

Figure 3.1 Data on participation and efficacy.

Source: Author

in Tanzania—participants saw their efforts making a difference to maternal and newborn health care in their communities. And in 41 communities in Indonesia and 30 in Tanzania—a much larger proportion than typical thresholds for statistical significance—the evidence consistently indicates that participants' activities led to tangible changes in their access to quality maternal and newborn health care that were noticeable and memorable to them and others in their community.

Most participants' activities led to relatively limited changes in existing practices and policies, such as expanded clinic hours or changes in outreach to pregnant women. Even the tangible changes were relatively modest and specific, such as a more private delivery room or a new delivery bed, a new information board or suggestion box, or a new nurse or midwife. These changes varied widely between communities. The activities that led to these improvements were also not unusual: most were similar to activities for improving maternal and newborn health that were already happening in communities in the control group ($p < .1$ for 12 of 15 types of activities in both countries). The normalcy of participants' activities and the subtlety and variability of the resulting changes weakened their aggregate impacts on health care outcomes measured across all the communities where the program was offered compared with communities where it was not.

Yet the normalcy of participants' activities and the subtlety and variability of their effects were also strengths. Participants' activities were locally appropriate efforts to work with providers, officials, and others in their communities to fix problems community members perceived in their access to quality health care. And these activities led to innovations in prior practices and policies, improvements in materials and programs, new feedback mechanisms, and small but locally important changes and additions to existing infrastructure, and many other changes that were noticeable and memorable to participants and others in their communities.

Significance and insignificance in an RCT

In one of the hundred communities in Indonesia where the community scorecard program was offered, participants knew of family, friends, and neighbors who had had difficult pregnancies and deliveries but who were reluctant to go to the health facility. These women thought using the facility was expensive and that the help of a midwife was all that they needed. As a result, participants worked with the health facility to develop a coordinated information campaign to get the word out about its services, what women needed around the time of birth, and the importance of delivering in a facility. Some went door-to-door with this message. In later interviews, they expressed pride in the results of their activities. The facility reported that pregnant women were visiting the facility more regularly. The village head subsequently attempted to make these outreach efforts an official activity, with help from the village budget.

In a community in Tanzania, many, though not all, community members already knew that they were less likely to have problems with birth if they delivered in a facility. But they found the nurses there were frequently rude and unhelpful, leading many to avoid them. So participants decided to create a suggestion and comment box, whose responses they would then use to highlight the best provider of the month, and pooled resources to offer the winner a small amount of money to show their appreciation.

In another Tanzanian community, community members knew of the importance of delivering in a facility, but there was no facility nearby. So they decided to create one. They pooled their resources to clear land, contribute timber, sand, and other supplies, and began building.

These are not outliers or isolated examples. In almost all communities in both countries where the program was offered, participants in focus groups two years after the program recalled specific activities they had tried to improve their health care. In a significant proportion of communities—39 of the 100 communities in Indonesia and 41 of the 100 in Tanzania—participants also recalled lacking the resources, knowledge, or willingness to see their efforts through, remembered those with whom they tried to engage ignoring them, being unwilling to help, or otherwise being unsuccessful in alleviating problems with their health care that they had decided in the meetings to try to fix. But in almost all communities in both countries, participants recalled that at least one of the activities they had planned had been successful. When asked to reflect on their efforts overall, participants in 83 of the 100 communities in Indonesia and 95 of the 100 communities in Tanzania thought their efforts had improved health care in their community.

When asked in these focus groups why they thought their efforts had improved health care, the improvements they described were often general and unspecific, such as greater community awareness or staff who were more accessible, not tangible changes that they recalled as resulting specifically from their efforts. But in 41 communities in Indonesia and 30 in Tanzania, participants recalled changes in their health care or access to it among their communities resulting from their efforts that were specific and tangible, and that may have made a difference to their access to quality maternal and newborn health care. These included new or improved buildings, staff, and ambulances; information boards and birth preparedness materials that may have made facility services easier to understand and therefore access; waste bins, toilets, and sources of clean water; staff living at or near the facility; and many more. These changes are also reflected in observations and interviews after the program ended and in process-tracing interviews during the program. In 65 of the 200 communities where interviewers spoke shortly after the program with those who attended meetings and with others in the community, they heard about similar changes in 26 (40%). In 17 of these communities (26% of the 65 in this subgroup), similar changes were observed in facilities or described in interviews with recently pregnant women two years after the program.

Table 3.1 lists both the specific and unspecific changes participants recalled as resulting from their efforts.

These changes did not add up to significant improvements in measures of community maternal and newborn health care outcomes two years later, such as whether recently pregnant women gave birth at the facility or the content of the care they received, on average, across all the communities where the program was offered. A new facility, such as the one participants in the story at the start of this section were trying to build, might lead to transformative effects on maternal and newborn health care. But major infrastructure improvements like this were rare. Most of the tangible changes in Table 3.1 were more limited and specific additions or changes to existing programs, policies, or infrastructure that on their own were less likely to cause significant improvements in health care outcomes. The activities that led to them were also not unusual. Among recently pregnant women interviewed two years after the program, awareness of most of the kinds of activities participants planned was not significantly higher in communities where the program was offered than in communities in the control group ($p < .1$ for 12 of 15 types of activities in both countries; see Arkedis et al. 2021).

Yet the data also show that the program's null average effects did not mean that there were no effects. Instead, they show how participants in a significant proportion of the randomly selected communities where this program was offered used it to make noticeable, memorable changes to their community's maternal and newborn health care that they and others in their communities thought were improvements. Given the nature of this program, these effects challenge the conclusion

Table 3.1 Changes recalled by participants

*General, unspecific changes**	*Specific, tangible changes*
Staff are more accessible (excludes staff staying in facility or village)	An ambulance
Services now available 24 hours	A new oxygen tank
Better equipment or drugs (unspecified)	A new building
General community awareness	New staff
Health worker attitude or performance	A new generator
Decreased cost or improved affordability	New or improved road
Activities in local birth clinics (*posyandu* in Indonesia)	New or improved rooms at the facility (such as delivery room or inpatient room)
Improved sanitation or clean water at facility (without specifics)	New information board or specific information that is now included on an existing board (such as cost or the midwife's phone number)
More women giving birth in the facility	No expired medicine at the facility
Household toilets	A new toilet
Cooperation with facility	A service or arrangement for cleaning the facility
Collected data	Access to clean water
Vague improvement in "access"*	A new pharmacy
Vague renovations or improved building	A new or improved maternity waiting home
New outreach services	Electricity
	A new local birth clinic (*posyandu* in Indonesia)
	Distribution of birth preparedness stickers
	New beds
	A new registration counter
	New waste bins
	A new suggestion box
	Staff who now stay in or near the facility

Source: Kosack et al (2019)

* General or unspecific changes include, for example, participants describing the road as generally "improved" or the ambulance as "available," rather than remembering specific improvements, such as a new ambulance, a new arrangement for cleaning the facility, new staff, or specific improvements to the road to the facility.

often drawn from the mixed RCT results that programs that only offer information and encourage participation are often irrelevant to empowering communities to improve their public services.

Information and facilitated meetings

The community scorecard program was minimalist. It was designed only to make the workings of each community's maternal and newborn health care services more transparent and to provide discussion spaces to encourage community members to deliberate on and then try a plan of activities that they thought would improve the quality of, and access to, maternal and newborn health care services. They might implement the activities themselves or engage with others in their communities or with providers, officials, journalists, NGOs, or anyone else they thought needed to be involved. Otherwise, the program provided no incentives or additional resources, authority, expert advice, or other support to those who attended the meetings. Instead, the program was designed to ensure that whatever participants did outside the meetings would be voluntary and unprescribed, community-led efforts that used existing capacities, based on knowledge from lived experience as users of health care services, members of these communities, and citizens of Indonesia or Tanzania.

The information provided in the program consisted mostly of stories and statistics about basic features of the local system for delivering maternal and newborn health care and barriers to that system being responsive, accountable, and effective in serving the community. Facilitators first spent time in each community surveying health care facilities and women who had recently given birth about their experiences with maternal and newborn health care. Facilitators then invited a group of approximately 15 interested community members to attend six community meetings over 3–4 months. At the first meeting, facilitators discussed statistics and stories from the survey they had conducted, as well as evidence of the importance of delivering and seeking pre- and post-natal care at a modern health facility for reducing common risks to mothers and children in pregnancy and birth. A scorecard of statistics from the survey about potential barriers to pregnant women in the community having access to quality maternal and newborn care was displayed on a wall: for example, the proportion of people the facilitator had talked to who were unable to get to the facility, who had to pay a bribe or high fees, who thought the facility was dirty, ill-equipped, or not sufficiently private, or who were mistrustful of nurses or doctors. The facilitator also provided one other kind of information: stories of how other communities, mostly in the immediate vicinity of the community, had fixed local problems with health services, schools, water systems, and other public services, such as problem-solving with teachers or health facility staff or asking local officials for help.

At the second meeting, held shortly after the first, facilitators then encouraged participants to develop plans of activities through which they themselves, or with health providers, community leaders, public officials, or others in their communities, could alleviate the barriers they perceived in their community's access to quality maternal and newborn health care. At subsequent meetings, facilitators encouraged participants to discuss these plans with the broader community, give the plans a try, reflect on their progress and make adjustments, and plan for how to maintain their efforts once the facilitator was no longer holding meetings.

Within the growing empirical literature on participatory development, programs that offer only information and space for discussion and deliberation to improve public services with available resources and existing authority are often found to have null average effects in RCTs. In addition to the studies mentioned in the introduction, Banerjee et al. (2010) find that a program in India that provided information to Village Education Committees on their role and activities, and to community members on administering a basic reading test, failed to increase the involvement of community members in education or the efforts of teachers, and had no effect on learning outcomes. Lieberman, Posner, and Tsai (2014) find similar results from a similar program in Kenya. Olken (2007) finds that a program that encouraged communities in Indonesia to monitor and hold officials accountable for resource leakage in road construction were unable to match local officials' ability to hide their malfeasance; only audits by higher level officials made a difference. More generally, a review of the experimental evidence in 21 countries from 25 evaluations of community-driven development (CDD) programs finds that these programs rarely improve public services and often fail to encourage much participation.[3] A broader review of nearly 500 programs (Mansuri and Rao 2013) finds that although collective action that originates locally ("organic" participation) can improve accountability and outcomes, participation that is encouraged ("induced") by outside actors like the facilitators in a community scorecard program is likely to be marginal, captured by elites, and irrelevant to the deeper inequities, conflicts, and institutional failures preventing more responsive, accountable, and effective use of available resources and capacities for delivering public services.[4]

Yet despite these challenges to this kind of program empowering communities to improve public services, numerous case studies show that the approach can be effective,[5] and the RCT literature is not conclusive. The community scorecard approach that was found to cause significant improvements in maternal and child health in Uganda (Björkman and Svensson 2009; Björkman Nyqvist, de Walque, and Svensson 2017) is particularly celebrated.[6] An RCT of a 2011 program in Sierra Leone similar to the 2004 community scorecard in Uganda found similarly significant improvements, including a 38% reduction in child mortality (Christensen et al. 2021). Banerjee et al. (2018) find that informing Indonesian citizens of their entitlement to rice subsidies led to a 26% increase in the subsidy they received. Andrabi, Das, and Khwaja (2017) find that informing communities in Pakistan of test scores from available public and private schools improved education outcomes. Reinikka and Svensson (2005, 2011) find that providing communities with information comparing funding they were receiving for schools with funding entitlements increased funds schools received as well as test scores. These RCTs show that programs that offer information and encourage participation to increase the transparency and social accountability of public services can sometimes significantly improve public service outcomes.

Learning more from an RCT

In RCTs, effectiveness is often defined as significant effects, or no effects; transformative, or irrelevant. In the growing literature on social accountability and transparency and accountability, most debates are about how and in what circumstances these programs improve the responsiveness, accountability, and effectiveness of public services. Yet the conclusions drawn from RCTs of these programs, which are increasingly the most influential empirical evidence in these debates, remain largely binary. Significant effects indicate that programs are effective and should be replicated. Insignificant effects indicate failures.

But participatory development programs are complex, and the evaluation in RCTs need not be so blunt. Transparency and accountability programs seek improved responsiveness, accountability, and effectiveness of complex bureaucratic hierarchies that deliver health care, education, water, sanitation, infrastructure, and other public services. Many scholars have argued that rather than seeking only estimates of average impact across a large number of treatments, RCTs should also seek to identify and explain as fully as possible the variation around that impact and the processes that led to it in different contexts.[7]

In the RCT of the community scorecard program in Indonesia and Tanzania, the evaluation of the program's effects relied on comparisons of averages of preregistered health care outcomes in communities where the program was offered with average outcomes in communities where it was not. In addition, the typical experimental approach was augmented with a number of other empirical methods designed to understand, reliably and from multiple perspectives, how the program was offered and received, the environments in which it was offered, and the causal pathways underlying any effects.

The basic methodology was the method of agreement and difference (Mill 1843), which takes advantage of observed regularities in otherwise dissimilar situations. Into that basic comparative logic, the approach incorporated a variety of alternative perspectives on rigorous and reliable methods for social inquiry.[8] Observed regularities were determined through structured interviews, focus groups, and observations of variation in participation and outcomes across subgroups of communities (Figure 3.1). These subgroups were selected randomly from the same national and regional stratifications as the broader RCT. Like the interviews and observations two years after the program, data collection methods for these additional observational, interview, and focus group data were designed to be unbiased, systematic, and replicable across diverse settings. Findings from them were integrated, so that each could help to compensate for the disadvantages of the others in verifying and exploring key observable implications of the program empowering community members to find ways to improve the responsiveness, accountability, and effectiveness of their community's maternal and newborn health care.

Altogether data from these additional methods allow an understanding of this program from distinct yet overlapping perspectives that each partly compensates for biases in the others. Meeting observations focused on general meeting dynamics: participants' interest and engagement in the conversations, the role of the facilitator, participants' deliberations at the start of the program around planning their activities, and participants' reflections on activities they had tried, challenges they had faced, and plans for the sustainability of their activities. In early meetings and the last program meeting, observers were also asked for their perceptions of how skeptical or optimistic participants appeared to be that their efforts would make a difference. These observations complement participants' perceptions of the efficacy of their activities as described in interviews and focus groups: the former entail observer bias but are also less susceptible to other biases inherent in asking participants themselves about their experiences and their perceptions of their capabilities. Meeting observers were also complemented by interviews with participants and observations of individuals' participation in meeting discussions, particularly for understanding differences in participation among education, gender, and age groups associated with empowerment and marginalization: differences that were less of a focus of meeting observations of general dynamics of each meeting. Participants' recollections and reflections in focus groups two years after the program provide a fifth complementary perspective involving recall and other biases, but less susceptible to biases or incentives toward socially desirable responses than interviews and observations during the program.

Most of these methods of comparative causal process-tracing of hypothesized methods and outcomes are familiar in evaluations of development programs, including RCTs. But in addition, the evaluation was also designed to explore hypotheses inductively generated during the program, by participants as well as researchers, that were unanticipated in earlier theory and unmeasured in the interviews, observations, and focus groups in Figure 3.1. To do so, the RCT also included evidence from a methodological approach that is still unusual in RCTs of development programs: ethnography. Four scholars lived for between six months and one year in or near eight of the 200 communities (two each in the two regions in Tanzania and provinces in Indonesia where the program was offered) as well as near four communities (one in each region or province) in the control group. During this time, these scholars undertook deep ethnographic studies to understand the perspectives of participants as they responded to and experienced it.

Ethnographic methods like these are rare in RCTs. There have been hundreds of randomized controlled trials to evaluate the impacts of development programs, including dozens of participatory development programs. But at the time of the program in Indonesia and Tanzania, only one other RCT of a similar program included ethnographic methods for understanding participants' experiences (Ananthpur, Malik, and Rao 2014).[9] Instead, researchers in RCTs typically seek to avoid bias by limiting analyses to measures of hypothesized mechanisms and outcomes pre-registered in pre-analysis plans. Many RCTs also employ mixed methods like those in Figure 3.1, but these interviews, observations, and focus groups are usually focused on hypothesized processes and outcomes. In understanding the impact of programs with complex, contextually contingent effects, such as this community scorecard, a deductive focus on hypothesized causal processes and outcomes measured cross-sectionally at specific times may be insufficient. Such methods may obscure, devalue, or exclude impacts and implications, and broader economic, social, political, and other contextual dynamics underlying them, that differ from hypothesized processes and outcomes or were unanticipated in metrics for evaluating them, but that were important and relevant to those who participated in the program.

In short, through this mixed-method approach, the RCT sought deeper understanding of the RCT's effects by placing the observable implications of the program's hypothesized mechanisms and effects under maximal deductive scrutiny from multiple perspectives, while also inductively exploring unanticipated processes and effects.

Interpreting a null

Given theory and the mixed findings in the existing RCT literature about the effects of these programs, it would not be surprising if the program encouraged little participation and had no effect. Participation in the program was encouraged and facilitated by someone from outside these communities. Although some facilitators were from neighboring communities, they were not typically from the community, and participants were generally aware that the program itself was partly supported by external organizations. Participation was also not externally empowered with resources, authority, or expertise beyond participants' existing capacities as members of their communities and citizens of Indonesia or Tanzania. Participants were provided with snacks at early meetings, and in Tanzania, small allowances were given to those who attended the first two of the six program meetings. But otherwise, the program provided only information and discussion space, not technical, relational, material, or financial resources to support any particular approach or to help participants with whatever they had planned. Whether for these reasons or others, the null results show a kind of weakness in the program and the bottom-up approach to participation, accountability, responsiveness, and effectiveness that it encourages.

Yet data from the mix of methods described above also consistently show that hidden in the insignificance of the program's average effects was substantial and sustained participation that participants and other community members saw making a difference to maternal and newborn health care in a significant proportion of communities. Interviews, meeting observations, and later reflections in focus groups suggest that participants in Indonesia and Tanzania began with varied expectations but were generally optimistic by the time they had created their plans. By the end of the program, participants in 5 of the 41 communities in Indonesia and 21 of the 40 communities in Tanzania where observers sat in on the final program meeting seemed to observers to be skeptical of the efficacy of their efforts. Two years later, participants in 39 of the 100 communities in Indonesia and 41 in Tanzania recalled lacking the resources, knowledge, or willingness to see their efforts through; remembered that those with whom they tried to engage ignored them or were unwilling to help; or described being unsuccessful in their efforts to fix problems with health care. But reflecting on their efforts overall, participants in 83 of the 100 communities in Indonesia and 95 in Tanzania described reasons that at least some of their activities had improved their community's maternal and newborn health care: feedback mechanisms, resolutions of disputes and bottlenecks in supplying facilities, new staff, raised awareness, improved materials, and existing programs that had become more interactive and helpful. And participants in a substantial proportion of communities—48 in Indonesia and 33 in Tanzania—perceived their efforts as successful enough to keep them engaged long after the program ended and the facilitator was no longer holding meetings. Some of their efforts were individual, but in about a quarter of communities in both countries—23 in Indonesia and 26 in Tanzania—participants also said that they were still meeting as a group.

In a large majority of communities, participants also described participating as personally beneficial. Some recalled participating as a waste of time; others said that they should have been paid for their efforts; others described being treated suspiciously by traditional birth attendants or by neighbors who thought that they were being paid. But in 65 of the 100 communities in Indonesia and 74 communities in Tanzania, not a single participant in the focus group described any cost or negative consequence from participating. And in 94 communities in Indonesia and all communities in Tanzania, more than three-quarters of participants in these focus groups described their participation as personally beneficial. When asked why, many described gaining knowledge or experience speaking publicly about community issues, or other personal skills or experiences. But many also described pride in improvements they had made to their community's health care: in new ambulances, nurses, new or improved facilities; in community members being treated better at the facility; in helping those who had been reluctant to get services to go to the facility; in men accompanying wives more often to get care; or simply from having worked together to try to improve their communities. Most participants also described themselves as more or as confident in their personal efficacy than before the program began, particularly in Indonesia, where participants were less confident at the beginning of the program. Not all found it empowering: 7% of participants in Indonesia and 20% of participants in Tanzania described themselves in interviews after the program as less confident in their capacity to improve their communities than they had in interviews before the first meeting.[10] But in Tanzania, most of participants who had started out less than fully confident (13% of the 20%) told interviewers that they were more confident in their efficacy after participating in the program. And in Indonesia, where most participants had begun the program perceiving themselves somewhat (49%) or completely unable to improve their communities (12%), at the end of the program nearly half (46%) of participants told interviewers that they were more confident in their capacities to improve their communities.

Many of these findings are also reflected in the ethnographic studies in eight of these communities. Like data from the more deductive comparative process-tracing methods, they showed complex effects that were not universally positive, and left some participants disappointed and discouraged, but that also empowered many. The ethnographic studies also complement findings from the other methods by showing the more complicated reality of participating in this program. Participants sometimes felt social pressure to participate, and they were sometimes treated warily by others in their communities. Many participants were disappointed that the program did not provide more resources or support for their efforts. In one of the eight communities, the disappointment was so widespread that most participants abandoned their involvement at the very beginning of the program. Yet the ethnographic studies also show that in a significant proportion of these eight communities, participants' efforts led to tangible, identifiable changes that might have made a difference to health care or might at least offer a foundation for future improvements: a new midwife; more interactive exchanges with nurses about preparing for birth; new or renewed community outreach to pregnant women; more comprehensive birth preparedness planning materials. The activities that led to these changes were not unusual: these studies also show how history and memory influenced understanding of the program and responses to it by those who remained involved, particularly past experiences with community engagement, access to external resources from aid and philanthropy, efforts to improve maternal and newborn health care, and the capacity and involvement of the state in community development. Yet these studies also show that participants' efforts differed in important ways from what had come before, reflecting participants' efforts to correct lapses or gaps in staffing and facility capacities, mend disconnections and distrust, share information, or improve existing materials and events, with outcomes that varied widely from community to community.

Finally, like the other data sources, the ethnographic studies show that in all but one of these eight communities, community members who remained engaged in the program seemed to experience their participation as empowering. Partly empowerment came from outcomes. But there was also more to whether and how participants were empowered through their involvement in it than whether their efforts led to improvements in the health care. Empowerment also came through developing new skills, using statistics and other information to understand public problems, sharing knowledge with communities, voicing stories and experiences, engaging purposefully and often constructively with health providers and local officials, and, for a few participants, simply participating for the first time in the public sphere.

In short, evidence from multiple perspectives consistently shows that participants in most communities took substantial and sustained advantage of the opportunities the program offered to discuss their access to quality maternal and newborn health care and deliberate on how they could improve it, and that they almost always tried at least a part of the highly varied approaches they planned. Interviews, observations, and reflections years later all suggest that their participation was perceived as improving a valued public service in their communities. For a substantial number, participation was empowering. While trying the activities they had planned, participants in approximately half of communities in Tanzania and one-eighth of communities in Indonesia became skeptical that their efforts were improving their health care. Years later, participants in a quarter of communities in Tanzania and one-third of communities in Indonesia recalled the effort as costly or at least partly a waste of time. In most communities, however, participants appeared confident that they could sustain improvements in their health care and described themselves as more or as confident in their personal capacity to improve their communities than before the program began. Years later, participants in almost all communities recalled particular activities that they remembered as having improved their health care. And in a significant proportion of communities, participants saw and later recalled tangible changes from their activities that were noticeable and memorable to them and to others in their communities.

So what? Implications of a null

Why does it matter that the null average effects of the program did not mean no effects?

First, because interpreting the null average effects of this program as no effects ignores effects caused by the activities of participants that were apparent to them and to others in their communities. One of the first principles of the international commitment to participatory development is including the views of participants.[11] Years later, participants in most communities recalled how their activities had made a difference to their communities' access to quality maternal and newborn health care. Although most of their reasons were not specific and difficult to triangulate with other interviews and more specific observations, in 41 communities in Indonesia and 30 in Tanzania, participants' efforts led to changes that were specific and tangible, and that may have made a difference to their communities' access to quality maternal and newborn health care. Interviews and observations during the program in a subgroup of communities show similar changes in a similar proportion. The effects of these changes did not add up to significant average improvements in outcomes across all the communities where the program was offered compared with average outcomes in communities where it was not. But they were noticeable and memorable in the communities where they occurred.

Second, despite the weakness of their average impact on outcomes, these effects were innovations or solutions to particular problems faced by diverse communities. Their wide variability (Figure 3.1), and the similarity of these activities that led to them to the kinds of activities that were already common in the area, were both weaknesses in affecting health care outcomes consistently across the 200 communities where the program was offered. Yet their variability and normalcy also reflect adaptability and local appropriateness: specific changes in practices, policies, and infrastructure that complemented existing resources and capacities across communities with a range of political, economic, social, and geographic differences. The effects of the community scorecard program in Indonesia and Tanzania were informed and encouraged by facilitated meetings, but depended on capabilities, local knowledge, and lived experience that participants in the meetings already possessed as members of their communities and citizens of Indonesia or Tanzania. The results thus indicate that across a wide range of contexts, a program of information and encouraged participation led to community-led efforts that complemented existing resources and capacities for improving maternal and newborn health care services.

This study has important limits that are caveats on the generalizability of these findings. Within the broader group of programmatic approaches to social accountability or transparency and accountability, the community scorecard program in this RCT was relatively short-term, informal, locally focused, and community-led. Unlike many programs, it did not provide additional resources or authority. The co-design and piloting of the program with researchers and staff of nongovernmental partner organizations prior to the RCT led to differences between it and other community scorecard programs. Finally, the countries in which the program was offered shared maternal and newborn health care systems that, although under-resourced, with uneven access and quality, had long been the focus of resources and reforms, and had been improving steadily for decades. The findings may or may not generalize to programs and contexts without these characteristics.

But the results of this RCT also show the importance of looking more deeply before concluding that insignificant average effects mean no effects. They support a different interpretation of this community scorecard program's null average effects, with different implications for understanding how and in what contexts programs like this—one that simply offered information and facilitated meetings—can empower people to improve public services. The findings described in this chapter about the program's effects are also still consistent with it having null effects on community-level health care outcomes on average, across all 200 communities where it was offered. In some places and times, these programs have caused transformative improvements, sufficient to lead to very significant improvements in outcomes like infant mortality. This one did not. In that sense, its effects were weak. In the average community, participants were not able to traverse the complex causal paths from planning actions to realizing tangible improvements in their access to quality maternal and newborn health care. And in some communities, the program clearly was a failure. Some participants were treated with suspicion and resented that they were not paid for their participation or offered resources to support their plans. In a significant proportion, participants who remained involved later recalled that some of what they tried had failed. Some participants who had begun the program fully confident in their capacities to improve their communities described being less than fully confident after the program.

But for significantly more of those involved, participating seemed to be empowering. In most communities, participants later recalled how their activities had improved their community's access to quality maternal and newborn health care. And in a substantial group of communities—a much larger proportion than the typical threshold for statistical significance—participants saw improvements that were noticeable and memorable to them and others in their communities.

Overall, evidence from a range of perspectives consistently shows that hidden in the insignificance of the program's average effects was substantial and sustained participation that participants and others saw making a difference to maternal and newborn health care. The subtlety, normalcy, and variability of participants' efforts and the changes they led to weakened their average impacts on aggregate health care outcomes. But this same subtlety, normalcy, and variability were also strengths. Participants' activities helped to resolve disputes and bottlenecks in supplying facilities, facilitate hiring staff, raise awareness, set up feedback mechanisms, improve materials, and make existing programs more interactive. Altogether these effects were insufficient on average to significantly improve outcomes, at least without additional resources, expertise, authority, or other support. But they also suggest that in a significant proportion of communities, much of what was needed to fix some problems with access to quality health care was already available, and what was missing was the local perspective and engagement of interested community members. In some contexts, these programs are sufficient to cause transformative improvements. The results from this RCT suggest that even where these programs are insufficient on their own, they can be an empowering, locally appropriate complement to available resources and capacities for improving the responsiveness, accountability, and effectiveness of a valued public service.

Appendix

Mixed-method sources of data on participation and efficacy in this RCT include:

1. In 81 communities of the 200 where the program was offered—41 in Indonesia and 40 in Tanzania—trained observers attended three of the meetings and answered a series of questions about engagement, discussion, and decision-making in those meetings.
2. In 65 of these communities (41 in Indonesia and 24 in Tanzania), interviewers asked follow-up questions of several participants as well as of those with whom they engaged as part of their activities: providers, officials, their neighbors, and others.
3. In 35 of these communities (16 in Indonesia and 19 in Tanzania) a second observer noted the frequency with which meeting participants made distinct contributions during the discussions or discussed activities they would attempt or had engaged in outside the meetings.
4. In these 35 communities, interviewers asked all participants before the first meeting and after the last about their perceptions of their personal capacity to improve their communities (Bandura 1977, 1982). To allow more valid interpersonal comparisons, interviewers also asked participants to compare their perceptions of their own efficacy to three anchoring vignettes in which a person in a community like theirs tries to improve their school (Masset 2015; King et al. 2004).
5. In eight communities, four scholars lived for between 6–12 months in a small subgroup of eight of these 200 communities. They attempted inductively, self-reflexively, and comparatively to understand the perspectives of participants as they responded to and experienced the program, its impacts and implications for them, and the influences of broader historical dynamics in the political economy of development in and around these communities.
6. Two years after the program, an interviewer invited participants in all 200 communities to a focus group in which they were asked to reflect on the program and any activities they remembered, including challenges they had faced and any changes they had seen as a result.
7. Two years after the program, in all 200 communities where the program was offered as well as the 200 communities in the control group, an interviewer surveyed a random sample of women who had lived in the community for at least six months and had given birth in the last year (6,001 recent mothers in Indonesia and 6,008 in Tanzania). Prior to data collection, survey teams conducted an extensive listing exercise with village and hamlet leaders, formal and informal health care providers, as well as other informants, to prepare a list of all women who had lived for at least six months in the village and had given birth in the prior 12 month.
8. Two years after the program, interviewers also observed sample health facilities and surveyed health care providers about staffing, equipment, and the content and use of maternal and newborn health care services.

All subgroups of communities where researchers conducted additional interviews, observations, and ethnographic studies were selected randomly from the same national and regional stratifications as the broader RCT.

Acknowledgments

This is a book for Susan, of research that those fortunate to be her students hope exemplifies the kinds of legal and social-scientific scholars she taught us to be. For me, that has meant the kind of study this chapter focuses on, about questions of real-world significance to the delivery of crucial public services, using whatever methodologies and disciplinary insights would contribute to understanding them, and open to whatever answers the evidence supports. I will always be grateful for Susan's wisdom and guidance in helping me learn the means and ends of this kind of scholarship. I was privileged to be part of an incredible team involved in this study: co-PIs Jean Arkedis, Jessica Creighton, Dan Levy, Archon Fung, and Courtney Tomie, and a large group of scholars and practitioners including Sarah Alphs, Novi Anggraeni, Iqra Anugrah, Rexford Asiama, Megan Cogburn, Fatu Conteh, Sad Dian Utomo, Akshay Dixit, Eric Englin, the late Linda Gassama, the late Chris Grorud, Riska Hasan, Hannah Hilligoss, Takondwa Iman, Jenna Juwono, June Kambalametore, Kondwani Kaunda, Hilda Kigola, Samson Kiware, Mitchris Chapman Kodam, Agnes Lahai, Isaac Lyatuu, Esther Mtumbuka, Rohit Naimpally, Happy Ndomba, Didik Purwandanu, Mohamed Yunus Rafiq, James Rasaiah, Lindsey Roots, Rachmat Reksa Samudra, Emmanuel Sandy, Emmanuel Sapalado, Diego Shirima, Manpreet Singh, Musa Ansumana Soko, Wayan Suriastini, Astri Arini Waluyo, J. Preston Whitt, James Quophy Wumenu, Kankan Xie, and many others at the Indonesian Center for Regional Information and Studies (PATTIRO), SurveyMeter in Indonesia, the Tanzania branch of the Clinton Health Access Initiative, Ideas in Action in Tanzania, the Results for Development Institute, the Ash Center for Democratic Governance and Innovation at the Harvard Kennedy School, and the Evans School of Public Policy and Governance at the University of Washington. I am grateful to the Bill and Melinda Gates Foundation, the William and Flora Hewlett Foundation, and the U.K. Department for International Development, for their generous support of this study, and the Transparency and Accountability Initiative for coordinating it. Most importantly, I gratefully acknowledge the thousands of Indonesians and Tanzanians who were willing to give this program a try. I hope their experiences are reflected in this chapter. All errors are my own.

Notes

1 Susan, when she heard the results, thought they were troubling: that "people felt good, but nothing happened."

2 In Indonesia, a national network of research and policy advocacy organizations focused on regional and local governance; in Tanzania, the national branch of an international NGO focused on improving health service delivery and access.

3 3ie (2018). The review suggests that those who come to the meetings rarely participate in discussions or decision-making, and that women and traditionally disempowered groups are particularly unlikely to participate.

4 Cornwall (2002, 2004), Fox (2007, 2015) McGee and Gaventa (2011), Joshi and Houtzager (2012).
5 Numerous case studies also show that the approach can be effective. In a review of 180 programs in the UK Department of International Development's Empowerment and Accountability portfolio that used a range of approaches to social accountability participatory programs across 28 countries, Holland and Schatz (2016) found that those that invited citizen engagement almost always improved service delivery.
6 CARE has been using this approach around the world since 2002 (Gullo, Galavotti, and Altman 2016).
7 See Woolcock (2009, 2013), Ananthpur, Malik, and Rao (2014), van der Meulen Rodgers et al. (2020), de Haan, Dowie, and Mariara (2020), Zaveri (2020), Kvangraven (2020), Muller (2020), and Rao (2020).
8 In addition to Mill (1843), the approach draws from the conclusions and recommendations of comparative methodological scholarship including King, Keohane, and Verba (1994), Lieberman (2005), Seawright (2016), among others, as well as in international development (Stern et al. 2012; Woolcock 2013; Ananthpur, Malik, and Rao 2014).
9 Many scholars argue for integrating ethnographic methods in political science and development studies: see, among others, Cartwright (2011), Cartwright and Hardie (2012, 123–34), Thachil (2018), Drèze (2020), Das (2020), and Garchitorena et al. (2021).
10 An analogous concept is "self-efficacy"—an individual's belief in their capabilities (Bandura 1977, 1982).
11 See the 2005 Paris Declaration on Aid Effectiveness and the Accra Agenda for Action (OECD 2008)

References

3ie. 2018. "Does Community-Driven Development Build Social Cohesion or Infrastructure?" Working paper brief (Governance). London: International Initiative for Impact Evaluation.

Ananthpur, Kripa, Kabir Malik, and Vijayendra Rao. 2014. *The Anatomy of Failure: An Ethnography of a Randomized Trial to Deepen Democracy in Rural India*. Policy Research Working Papers. The World Bank.

Andrabi, Tahir, Jishnu Das, and Asim Khwaja. 2017. "Report Cards: The Impact of Providing School and Child Test-Scores on Educational Markets." *American Economic Review* 107 (6): 1535–63.

Arkedis, Jean, Jessica Creighton, Akshay Dixit, Archon Fung, Stephen Kosack, Dan Levy, and Courtney Tolmie. 2021. "Can Transparency and Accountability Programs Improve Health? Experimental Evidence from Indonesia and Tanzania." *World Development* (142): 105369.

Bandura, Albert. 1977. "Self-Efficacy: Toward a Unifying Theory of Behavioral Change." *Psychological Review* 84: 191–215.

———. 1982. "Self-Efficacy Mechanism in Human Agency." *American Psychologist* 37 (2): 122–47.

Banerjee, Abhijit V., Rukmini Banerji, Esther Duflo, Rachel Glennerster, and Stuti Khemani. 2010. "Pitfalls of Participatory Programs: Evidence from a Randomized Evaluation in Education in India." *American Economic Journal: Economic Policy* 2 (1): 1–30. https://doi.org/10.1257/pol.2.1.1.

Banerjee, Abhijit V., Rema Hanna, Jordan Kyle, Benjamin A. Olken, and Sudarno Sumarto. 2018. "Tangible Information and Citizen Empowerment: Identification Cards and Food Subsidy Programs in Indonesia." *Journal of Political Economy* 126 (2): 451–91. https://doi.org/10.1086/696226.

Björkman, Martina, and Jakob Svensson. 2009. "Power to the People: Evidence from a Randomized Field Experiment on Community-Based Monitoring in Uganda." *The Quarterly Journal of Economics* 124 (2): 735–69.

Björkman Nyqvist, Martina, Damien de Walque, and Jakob Svensson. 2017. "Experimental Evidence on the Long-Run Impact of Community-Based Monitoring." *American Economic Journal: Applied Economics* 9 (1): 33–69.

Cartwright, Nancy. 2011. "A Philosopher's View of the Long Road from RCTs to Effectiveness." *The Lancet* 377 (9775): P1400–01.

Cartwright, Nancy, and Jeremy Hardie. 2012. *Evidence-Based Policy*. New York: Oxford University Press.

Christensen, Darin, Oeindrila Dube, Johannes Haushofer, Bilal Siddiqi, and Maarten Voors. 2021. "Building Resilient Health Systems: Experimental Evidence from Sierra Leone and the 2014 Ebola Outbreak." *Quarterly Journal of Economics* 136 (2): 1145–98.

Cornwall, Andrea. 2002. "Making Spaces, Changing Places: Situating Participation in Development." IDS Working Paper 170. Sussex: Institute of Development Studies.

———. 2004. "New Democratic Spaces? The Politics and Dynamics of Institutionalised Participation." *IDS Bulletin* 35 (2): 1–10.

Das, Sabyasachi. 2020. "(Don't) Leave Politics out of It: Reflections on Public Policies, Experiments, and Interventions." *World Development* 127: 104792.

Drèze, Jean. 2020. "Policy beyond Evidence." *World Development* 127: 104797.

Fox, Jonathan. 2007. "The Uncertain Relationship between Transparency and Accountability." *Development in Practice* 17 (4–5): 663–71.

———. 2015. "Social Accountability: What Does the Evidence Really Say?" *World Development* 72 (August): 346–61.

Garchitorena, Andres, Megan B. Murray, Bethany Hedt-Gauthier, Paul Farmer, and Matthew H. Bonds. 2021. "Reducing the Knowledge Gap in Global Health Delivery: Contributions and Limitations of Randomized Controlled Trials." In *Randomized Control Trials. A Critical Perspective*, edited by Florent Bédécarrats, Isabelle Guérin, and François Roubaud, 152–56. Oxford: Oxford University Press.

Gullo, Sara, Christine Galavotti, and Lara Altman. 2016. "A Review of CARE's Community Score Card Experience and Evidence." *Health Policy and Planning* 31 (10): 1467–78.

Haan, Arjan de, Gillian Dowie, and Jane Mariara. 2020. "To RCT or Not, Is Not the Question: Methods for Policy-Relevant Research on Gender Equality." *World Development* 127: 104794.

Holland, Jeremy, and Florian Schatz. 2016. *Macro Evaluation of DFID's Policy Frame for Empowerment and Accountability*. London: ITAD. https://itad.com/wp-content/uploads/2017/06/EA-Macro-Evaluation-Technical-report-Dec16-FINAL.pdf.

Joshi, Anuradha, and Peter P. Houtzager. 2012. "Widgets or Watchdogs? Conceptual Explorations in Social Accountability." *Public Management Review* 14 (2): 145–62. https://doi.org/10.1080/14719037.2012.657837.

King, Gary, Robert O. Keohane, and Sidney Verba. 1994. *Designing Social Inquiry: Scientific Inference in Qualitative Research*. Princeton, NJ: Princeton University Press.

King, Gary, Christopher J.L. Murray, Joshua A. Salomon, and Ajay Tandon. 2004. "Enhancing the Validity and Cross-Cultural Comparability of Measurement in Survey Research." *American Political Science Review* 98 (1): 191–207.

Kosack, Stephen, Grant Bridgman, Jessica Creighton, Courtney Tolmie, Preston Whitt, and Archon Fung. 2019. "Encouraging Participation, working paper." Harvard Kennedy School: Ash Center for Democratic Governance and Innovation.

Kvangraven, Ingrid Harvold. 2020. "Impoverished Economics? A Critical Assessment of the New Gold Standard." *World Development* 127: 104813.

Lieberman, Evan S. 2005. "Nested Analysis as a Mixed-Method Strategy for Comparative Research." *American Political Science Review* 99 (3): 435–52.

Lieberman, Evan S., Daniel N. Posner, and Lily L. Tsai. 2014. "Does Information Lead to More Active Citizenship? Evidence from an Education Intervention in Rural Kenya." *World Development* 60: 69–83. https://doi.org/10.1016/j.worlddev.2014.03.014.

Mansuri, Ghazala, and Vijayendra Rao. 2013. *Localizing Development: Does Participation Work?* Washington, DC: World Bank.
Masset, Edoardo. 2015. "Measuring Empowerment in Rural India Using Vignettes." *Journal of Development Effectiveness* 7 (3): 346–56.
McGee, Rosie, and John Gaventa. 2011. "Shifting Power? Assessing the Impact of Transparency and Accountability Initiatives." *IDS Working Papers* 2011 (383): 1–39.
Meulen Rodgers, Yana van der, Anthony Bebbington, Catherine Boone, Jampel Dell'Angelo, and Arun Agrawal. 2020. "Experimental Approaches in Development and Poverty Alleviation." *World Development* 127: 104807.
Mill, John Stuart. 1843. *A System of Logic*. London.
Muller, Seán M. 2020. "The Implications of a Fundamental Contradiction in Advocating Randomized Trials for Policy." *World Development* 127: 104831.
OECD. 2008. *Paris Declaration on Aid Effectiveness (2005); Accra Agenda for Action (2008)*. Paris: OECD. http://www.oecd.org/dac/effectiveness/34428351.pdf.
Olken, Benjamin A. 2007. "Monitoring Corruption: Evidence from a Field Experiment in Indonesia." *Journal of Political Economy* 115 (2): 200–49. https://doi.org/10.1086/517935.
Raffler, Pia, Daniel N. Posner, and Doug Parkerson. 2019. "The Weakness of Bottom-Up Accountability: Experimental Evidence from the Ugandan Health Sector." Working Paper.
Rao, Vijayendra. 2020. "Evidence-Based Development Needs a Diversity of Tools, with a Bottom-up Process of 'Embedded' Dialogue." *World Development* 127: 104823.
Reinikka, Ritva, and Jakob Svensson. 2005. "Fighting Corruption to Improve Schooling: Evidence from a Newspaper Campaign in Uganda." *Journal of the European Economic Association* 3 (2/3): 259–67.
———. 2011. "The Power of Information in Public Services: Evidence from Education in Uganda." *Journal of Public Economics* 95 (7–8): 956–66. https://doi.org/10.1016/j.jpubeco.2011.02.006.
Seawright, Jason. 2016. *Multi-Method Social Science: Combining Qualitative and Quantitative Tools*. Cambridge: Cambridge University Press.
Stern, Elliot, Nicoletta Stame, John Mayne, Kim Forss, Rick Davies, and Barbara Befani. 2012. "Broadening the Range of Designs and Methods for Impact Evaluations." Working Paper 38. London: DFID.
Thachil, Tariq. 2018. "Improving Surveys Through Ethnography: Insights from India's Urban Periphery." *Studies in Comparative International Development* 53 (3): 281–99.
Woolcock, Michael. 2009. "Toward a Plurality of Methods in Project Evaluation: A Contextualised Approach to Understanding Impact Trajectories and Efficacy." *Journal of Development Effectiveness* 1 (1): 1–14. https://doi.org/10.1080/19439340902727719.
———. 2013. "Using Case Studies to Explore the External Validity of 'complex' Development Interventions." *Evaluation* 19 (3): 229–48.
Zaveri, Sonal. 2020. "Making Evaluation Matter: Capturing Multiple Realities and Voices for Sustainable Development." *World Development* 127: 104827.

4 Finance, state-owned enterprises, and development

A comparative study of pawnshops in Brazil, Mexico and Taiwan

Weitseng Chen and Mariana Mota Prado[1]

Despite being one of the oldest forms of credit, development scholars and policymakers have not devoted much attention to pawnshops. The basic arrangement is simple: goods are provided as guarantee for a small loan (often in cash) and kept in possession of the creditor, who is authorized to sell the goods if the debtor defaults. Such a form of credit is accessible because borrowers do not require bank accounts, credit history and/or employment. While their existence precedes banks, pawnshops have been described as fringe banking, as their operations occupy the periphery of financial markets.[2] Yet, they play an important role, especially in developing countries: the value of the loans is often small, being beneficial to low-income, marginalized groups, similarly to microcredit.[3] Indeed, in Latin America, pawn shops are apparently an access to credit mechanism for the unbanked.[4] Considering how much attention the law and development literature has paid to access to credit,[5] the dearth of interest in pawnshops in development circles seems puzzling.[6]

Pawnshops also offer insight into the possible roles of government banks and state-owned financial institutions. Some state-owned pawnshops are long established and persist to this day, as in Brazil. Others have been privatized in waves of neoliberal reforms, as in Taiwan. Some countries have always relied on private markets to offer such services, as in Mexico. While the specialized literature on state-owned enterprises (SOEs) has extensively mapped the complex ways in which state and market interactions may promote economic growth,[7] especially in the finance sector,[8] less attention has been paid to the role of state-owned or state-linked financial institutions in promoting financial inclusion and increasing access to credit. Pawnshops offer us an opportunity to explore that.

The pawnshops in Brazil, Mexico and Taiwan show four different institutional arrangements. To explore these arrangements, we propose a typology of the complex relationships between state and markets:

1. *The replacement model:* in Brazil, the state established a monopoly over pawnshops in the 1930s and has maintained it since.
2. *The absence (free market) model:* in Mexico, the state never had a direct presence in the pawnshop business, but global economic integration seems to have changed how private businesses have managed their risks (and consequently the type of services they offer).

DOI: 10.4324/9781003416234-5

3. *The complementary model:* after a period of intense liberalization in the 1990s, pawnshops are primarily private in Taiwan today, but they are heavily regulated by the state. Only two public pawnshops remain, catering to the most vulnerable.
4. *The competition model:* in the early days, Taiwan had public pawnshops, to provide more protection to debtors from possible exploitation by private pawnshops.

Despite their differences, our four case studies are characterized by a puzzling convergence: all three countries currently have special terms set by the state for pawn brokerage services for the most vulnerable groups, regardless of the level of state intervention in the industry. Often these exist through direct state intervention or state-linked institutions. Moreover, the state may reduce its direct presence in markets, replacing it with effective regulations. On the other hand, the state may maintain its presence in the industry without performing a strong social assistance role (e.g. Brazil in the 1990s). In light of the different roles of the state in the pawnshop industry, we conclude the chapter with a brief speculation of the normative implications of our analysis.

This chapter is inspired by and celebrates Susan Rose-Ackerman's influential scholarship. In our case studies; we embrace the type of comparative sensitivity that has been the hallmark of Susan's career. By examining the experience of multiple countries, Susan's research in comparative law allowed readers to see the richness of diverse legal arrangements on their own terms, rather than forcing countries to conform to a pre-determined blueprint.[9]

Case studies: overview

Pawnshops offer a unique opportunity to examine the complex relationship between state and markets in the financial sector. Focusing on financial institutions allows one to narrow the debate about the specific functions and the role that the state may perform in this sector. Yet, there are significant variations in how financial institutions are structured depending on the services they offer (e.g. savings banks, development banks, commercial banks, investment banks, and non-bank financial institutions).[10] As such, the focus on pawnshops offers a useful strategy to narrow the scope of analysis to avoid comparing apples to oranges.

Pawnshops serve a very specific function, offering one-off credit transactions whenever individuals are confronted with emergencies. They offer access to credit to individuals who are neither the most destitute (since they have possessions to offer as collateral), nor privileged enough to dispense with this type of service. As such, they perform a social welfare function as a financial safety net during times of crises to those who may not be at the bottom of the pyramid but are (or could easily become) vulnerable populations.

Pawnshops offer a perfect case study because there is great variation around the world and over time in terms of their ownership, structure, and function.[11] By analyzing three countries, Brazil, Mexico and Taiwan, we capture existing variations, while also focusing on developing countries.

First, we will look at a state monopoly, classified as the *replacement model* in our typology. In Brazil, pawn brokerage became a monopoly of a state-owned bank (Caixa Econômica Federal) in 1934 and remains so to this day. Therefore, there is one public pawnbroker in the country and no (legal) private pawnshops. Pawnshops are used by the unbanked and people with bad credit records, with the middle-class resorting to these services only to meet unexpected financial shortfalls.[12]

Second, we will analyze Mexico, where there is no direct state provision of pawnshops. This creates the second category in our typology: the *absence model*. State presence is also not heavily felt in the regulation of private pawnshop operations and the poorest of the poor resort to private philanthropic institutions, that offer not-for-profit pawn brokerage. More recently, however, private pawnshops associated with commercial banks have started to rely on international capital markets to distribute risks. Here, international capital markets serve as a functional substitute to domestic legal regulations to control risks.

Third, we will look at Taiwan, which has both private and state-owned pawnshops, with the *competition* and *complementary models* existing during different time periods. Before the 1990s, state-owned pawnshops dominated Taiwan's markets, operating in direct competition with private pawnshops. After the 1990s, following a wave of neoliberal reforms, the state retreated from the pawnshop market and closed down most state-owned pawnshops. Today, only two continue to operate, located in two major cities. While private pawnshops have thrived since the neoliberal reforms, the remaining two public pawnshops continued to operate, but in a more cost-conscious and non-profit fashion than their private counterparts. The state has transformed them into part of the social safety net.

Replacement model: Brazil

Brazil's pawnshop industry has evolved over time. Until 1861, the Brazilian model was entirely private and unregulated. In 1861, the Brazilian government created public pawnshops, which coexisted with private pawnshops but offered more favorable conditions for the loans.[13] Thus in the nineteenth century, Brazil transitioned from a private model to a complementary model (similar to Taiwan today);[14] it was only in 1934 that pawnshops become a state monopoly and remain so to this day. Currently, Caixa Econômica Federal, a state-owned bank, is the only financial institution authorized to offer these services.

In 1934, President Getúlio Vargas adopted a series of reforms designed to modernize and strengthen the Brazilian state to finance productive economic activity and promote industrialization. One of these reforms was to turn philanthropic state-owned institutions called Caixas Econômicas into robust financial institutions that could help promote savings and thus finance government spending and promote economic growth.[15]

To achieve that, Vargas granted all Caixas a monopoly over pawnshops and lotteries, along with a series of transformations that made Caixas financial institutions like commercial ones (e.g. offering mortgages for urban real estate).[16] These transformations generated significant results: from 1934 to 1940, loans from Caixas grew from 6% of the credit offered by commercial banks to 10.5%.[17] In 1969, during the military dictatorship, there was another restructuring, which remains to this day: a single, state-owned bank controlled by the Federal Government called Caixa Econômica Federal. The decree that merged the multiple Caixas into one institution and created the modern Caixa also guaranteed the continuation of its monopoly over pawn brokerage.[18] During the 1990s, Brazil adopted a series of neoliberal reforms, and promoted the privatization of numerous SOEs, including numerous state-owned banks. Caixa was reorganized according to American management models, and in compliance with the rules of the Basel Accord.[19] Yet, neither Caixa nor pawn brokerage services were part of the transition to private, foreign and market-based banking.[20]

Before 1934, Caixa was known as the "bank for the poor," offering accessible credit to vulnerable groups. The monopoly over pawnshops reinforced the public image that the bank has a social mission, which persists to this day.[21] Today, Caixa Econômica Federal is the only bank that is present in every one of the 5,562 municipalities in Brazil[22] and is used for payment of numerous governmental benefits, such as pensions and other welfare programs, as well as governmental subsidies and bailouts. Moreover, the bank offers numerous services, including being the primary financier for urban housing in the country.[23]

While Caixa has a presence in every municipality in Brazil, not all municipalities have branches, and not all branches of Caixa offer pawn brokerage. As of 2007, only 433 branches offered such services.[24] In 2014, the number had increased to 463.[25] While limited in their geographical reach, Brazilian state-owned pawnshops have become more accessible over time regarding the goods accepted as collateral: earlier only precious metals and stones (gold, silver, and diamonds) were accepted as guarantees for loans, but this changed in 1937, when they started accepting other valuables. In 1991, the system changed again to accept only jewelry.[26] Today, in addition to jewelry, Caixa accepts valuable pens, watches, and silverware.[27] The goods offered as collateral are evaluated by highly specialized staff at Caixa, who are trained to work in the pawnshop department. Staff are only allowed to provide loans worth up to 80% of the value of the good (going up to 100% in only exceptional cases), but Caixa only evaluates the goods based on the raw material, disregarding value-adding craftsmanship.[28] This is designed to reduce the risk of not recouping the loan when selling the asset. If the debtor defaults, Caixa is authorized to sell the goods through an online auction. The item is displayed on Caixa's website and interested parties can make bids using the bank's ATMs.[29] Caixa only keeps the amount of the outstanding loan; if there is a surplus, it goes to the debtor.

Caixa's pawn loans offer one of the lowest interest rates in the Brazilian market. While the average interest rate charged by banks in Brazil is 60% a year, Caixa's average interest rates for pawn loans are around 20% a year.[30] Given the high interest rates set up by the Brazilian Central Bank, banks loans can be offered for up to 100% a year, while credit cards charge more than 240% year.[31] Therefore, in terms of cost for consumers, pawn brokerage is one of the cheapest forms of credit available in the Brazilian market. While they may benefit consumers, it is unclear how profitable Caixa's pawn brokerage services are. One non-official source claims that despite offering one of the lowest interest rates in the market, and even more generous conditions to low-income clients, pawn brokerage services are one of the most profitable operations of Caixa, representing more than 20% of their revenue in 2009.[32]

In the early 2000s Caixa made its pawn brokerage services more accessible to vulnerable consumers. The micro-pawn loan (*micro penhor*) had reduced interest rates and was available to debtors who were unbanked or had an average balance in their bank account of less than 1,000 reais (US$370 in 2005). It only covered goods valued between 50 and 600 reais.[33] Within two months of its launch, Caixa had 214,000 micro-pawn loans, lending a total of 51 million reais.[34] In 2009, the conditions to access the micro-pawn brokerage became more generous: the lower interest rates also became available for those with a bank account with an average balance in a checking account (or investments) of 3,000 reais (US$600 in 2022). In these cases, the credit was limited to a maximum of 1,000 reais (US$200 in 2022) and the interest rate was 1.7%/month.[35] As a result, micro-pawn loans increased 47% from 2009 to 2010.[36] This service continues to be offered to this day.

These changes were part of a larger government effort to promote financial inclusion, through access to credit for the lower classes.[37] As a result, between 2004 and 2014, consumer credit in Brazil had increased 658%, totaling US$297 billion. Pawnshops were part of this process, having increased both in total volume and in number of clients.[38] Between 2010 and 2014, the pawn-loan portfolio of Caixa doubled, reaching US$670 million.[39] Between 2015 and 2017, Caixa's pawn-loan portfolio increased on average 11% a year.[40] By 2019, the pawn-loan portfolio had increased to US$1billion (R$5 billion).[41]

Caixa makes access to the service very simple. The debtor needs to come in-person to one of the branches equipped to evaluate the collateral, and once the good has been evaluated, they can obtain cash on the spot. The debtor only needs to provide a piece of identity, proof of address, and social insurance number.[42] This makes the service accessible to those with bad credit history, no bank account, or without employment or regular income. While the loan is up to 85% of the value of the good for most clients, for those who have a job and receive their salaries through Caixa, the loan can be up to 100% of the value of the collateral.[43]

The free market (state absence) model: Mexico

After Mexico gained independence in 1821, there were no longer restrictions on lending money at high rates of interest, creating opportunities for pawnshops to open and make high profits.[44] Freestanding pawnshops emerged in Mexico by the 1830s, offering higher-interest collateral loans[45] These pawnshops were called *casas de empeños* in legislation and *montepíos* colloquially.[46] During the Porfiriato (1876–80; 1884–1911) pawning establishments expanded and the private pawning industry was characterized by larger capitalizations and high interest rates.[47] The private pawnshop industry in Mexico is lightly "regulated".[48] While the Federal Consumer Protection Bureau (PROFECO) requires registration and provision of information by pawnshops, interests rates and conditions for the loans are largely unregulated.[49] The pawnshop industry is also subject to various administrative and general business regulations in the areas of tax compliance, customs, consumer protections, money laundering, and public safety, among others.[50] Yet, even these light regulatory demands are not always strictly enforced.[51]

Of the approximately 6,000 to 8,000 pawnshops in Mexico, most only offer loans for jewelry or small consumer electronics.[52] Full-service pawnshops are estimated at fewer than 1,500.[53] Common goods accepted as collateral in full-service pawnshops include jewelry, watches, consumer electronics, cars, power tools, household appliances, sporting goods, and musical instruments.[54] In a 2012 study, PROFECO found that most private pawnshops charge a monthly interest rate of 11.5%, while most banks charge 6%.[55] According to the World Bank, private pawnshops in Mexico charge an annual percentage up to five times higher than traditional banks.[56]

The majority of pawnshop clients in Mexico are people earning low incomes and unbanked individuals.[57] For individuals without a fixed or steady income, it is difficult to obtain formal credit or loans from banks.[58] According to the World Bank, only 37% of individuals above 15 years old have a bank account[59] and less than 15% have a credit card in Mexico.[60] Since about 90% of consumer transactions in Mexico are cash-based,[61] pawnshops are an accessible way to quickly obtain cash since borrowers do not need a job, credit history, or a co-signer.[62] A 2014 survey showed that 45% of individuals surveyed in several urban areas in Mexico use informal financial services such as pawnshops, non-bank savings institutions, and entrusting savings to a family member.[63] Pawnshops are used for everyday life, business, and emergencies, with the busiest seasons for pawn loans taking place during the Christmas holidays, back-to-school week in the fall, and Easter holidays.[64] Individuals, including those with steady incomes, might take out pawn loans to pay off extra bills and cover living expenses while waiting for their next payroll.[65]

Pawn brokerage underwent significant transformations in the 1990s, thanks to the transformation of their related business sector—microcredit lending. Microcredit lending in Mexico was traditionally structured as a not-for-profit, charitable service. However, many microcredit lenders in Mexico began to transform themselves into formal financial institutions to expand their market reach by using customers' savings for lending,[66] becoming profitable operations. In this process, microfinancing institutions sought capital injections from international investors through the issuance of bonds and equity globally. The tendency observed in the microcredit financing extended to pawnshops, revealing a stunning trait of Mexican pawnshops that differentiate them from their counterparts in Brazil and Taiwan.

Nowadays, pawn brokerage services in Mexico are highly profitable and thus attract foreign investors. For-profit pawn lenders nation-wide grew from an estimated 600 branches in the early 2000s, to more than 5,000 in 2017.[67] For instance, FirstCash, Inc., a pawnshop operator listed in NASDAQ, has been swiftly acquiring pawnshops in Mexico, where more than half the nation's municipalities lack traditional bank branches.[68] The lack of banking services implies a lucrative business for pawnshop owners, who can charge monthly interest rates of about 18% .[69] Despite this exploitative rate, the revenues of pawn-loan interests accounted for only 27% of FirstCash's revenue in Mexico in 2020. Most of its revenue came from selling goods, such as scrap jewelry and retail merchandise obtained through defaults in loans.[70]

Pawn brokerage services are also offered by financial institutions, such as banks. Bank Azteca, for example, is one of the major microcredit providers in Mexico, established in the early 2000s. As the first bank for the poor, it does not require clients to have a job in the formal sector but requires collateral for loans. Bank Azteca sends its agents to customers' homes to assess the value of their assets before offering secured loans. Bank Azteca takes possession of the collaterals upon default and sells them at their own stores across the country. Due to the high risks associated with these loans, Bank Azteca charges interest rates higher than those of formal banks, but lower than the rates charged by for-profit pawnshops. In 2005, for example, annual percentage rates (APRs) of pawnshops, Bank Azteca, and traditional banks were 220%, 130%, and 40% respectively. Bank Azteca's main competitors are pawnshops, since most of their customers have no access to formal banks either.[71] Studies show that the use of pawn shops declined in the municipalities where the Bank opened branches.[72]

The competition between pawnshops and Bank Azteca blurs the conventional distinction between pawnshop and microfinancing; in fact, it makes Bank Azteca, as well as other commercial microcredit providers in the country, operate much more like pawnshops. Like many pawnshops, the sale of seized collaterals accounts for a much larger share of their revenue than the revenue from interest payments.[73] That being said, there still exist conventional, non-for-profit microcredit providers in Mexico, such as Financiera Independencia, that do not take any collateral and instead grant microloans only to individuals who meet various criteria, such as microbusiness operators, mothers with at least one child under the age of 18, or people earning minimum wages in the formal sector.[74]

Microcredit providers who resort to pawn brokerage services in Mexico, such as Bank Azteca, are able to offer lower interest rates than traditional pawnshops, not because of the distinctive nature of their business, but because of their institutional capacity. Large financial institutions' (e.g. banks) personnel capacity and nationwide branches greatly improve their collection and repossession mechanisms. When necessary, they can subsidize microfinancing with the revenues from other business segments. But most importantly, in contrast with conventional pawnshops, microfinancing institutions offering pawn loans rely upon international capital markets, distributing their risks globally and at the same time obtaining capital injections. This strategy is possible due to the immense potential for profitability in this market. The country's top six microcredit providers, all listed companies, are large financial groups, with bonds or equity issued and listed in major stock markets worldwide, including stock exchanges in Singapore, the US, Dublin, and Luxembourg.[75]

While Mexico's free market model remained largely unchanged over time, with neither state-owned pawnshops nor restrictive governmental regulations, the growth of pawn brokerage services in the 1990s was remarkable. Our inference is that Mexican financial institutions are not able to reduce operational risks domestically, but distributed such risks globally by issuing notes and equity to global investors. In this way, the expansion of the domestic market shares was due to injected capital from the proceeds of such global capital offerings.

One important consequence of this strategy is that Mexican for-profit operations have limited capacity to perform a social function by offering a safety net to the most vulnerable groups. The state has decided not to offer an alternative directly, but has used a private philanthropic organization, Monte de Piedad ("Monte"), for such purpose.

Monte de Piedad, once a public institution, has been a Private Assistance Institution (IAP) since 1927, but is still heavily regulated by the Private Assistance Board for the Federal District.[76] Formed to provide social and humanitarian assistance,[77] IAPs carry out their activities with private assets but cannot seek profit.[78] The Private Assistance Board closely supervises IAPs and approves all of their operating activities.[79] These regulatory bodies are generally composed of a combination of government officials and representatives of the regulated institutions.[80] This suggests that while Mexico has an absence (free market) model, the government still plays an important role in this charitable private organization to keep pawn brokerage accessible to vulnerable groups.

Monte continues to provide among the lowest interest rates in Mexico, offering around 3 to 5% per month depending on the good being used for collateral.[81] At Monte, the value of the loan compared to the collateral good is an average of 89% for jewelry,[82] 49% for cars, and 50% for miscellaneous items.[83] Monte provides pawn loans ranging from 30 pesos up to thousands of pesos for most items except livestock, food, and weapons.[84] Monte has 230 branches in large cities and in the countryside, and over three million families take out pawn loans from their network each year.[85]

Hybrid model in Taiwan: competition and complement

Public pawnshops in Taiwan have a colonial origin. Japan colonized Taiwan from 1898 to 1945, and created the first public pawnshop in Taiwan in 1918. When the Nationalist government, led by the Kuomintang Party (KMT), took over Taiwan after WWII, it allowed these public pawnshops to continue operating, with the same personnel in their management offices. Both the Japanese and its successor Nationalist governments attempted to limit the operation of private pawnshops, due to concerns that they might exploit the poor. In contrast with their private counterparts, public pawnshops were regulated and monitored by the state and played a major role in providing access to credit for individuals and small-sized firms.[86]

Under the Nationalist government's authoritarian rule between 1945 and the 1980s, public pawnshops were also used to offset the harsh consequences of developmental policies. Throughout Taiwan's remarkable economic take-off between the 1950s and the 1980s, the government implemented a policy of financial repression, which favored state-owned banks, big firms, and strategic industries over ordinary people, small and medium-sized firms. These policies drove large groups of people to the informal sector. Hence, in the early 1950s, the Nationalist government started to use public pawnshops to address concerns about exploitative practices and disputes associated with shadow banking. Public pawnshops had interest rates as low as 3–5% per month, compared to the 13–15% per month charged by private pawnshops.[87] Public pawnshops were made part of the social safety net, as not-for-profit microcredit providers. At this time, like its colonial predecessor, the Nationalist government formally introduced a model of competition between public and private pawnshops. [88]

To exclude commercial lending from the operation of its public pawnshops, the government skillfully adjusted the list of acceptable collateral for public pawnshops. For example, only light-weight jewelry made of gold and weighing no more than 37.5g was acceptable as collateral at public pawnshops. To small and medium-sized firms, this limitation rendered public pawnshops an impractical source of commercial financing, as larger amounts of finance were needed, using common corporate assets as collateral.[89] Rather, entrepreneurs and owners of small- and medium-sized firms turned to private pawnshops for assistance, becoming a main driver of the development of private pawnshops.[90] This alternative social safety net was mainly accessible to political supporters of the Nationalist authoritarian regime: middle-class public servants working for the army, public schools, all levels of government, or else retired military personnel. Furthermore, retired military personnel were given priority to apply for the licenses to operate private pawnshops.[91]

Under this competition model, private pawnshops were resilient and competitive compared to public pawnshops backed by the state. Their competitiveness is attributable to the inflexibility and restrictions imposed by the state. For example, while gold was a common form of assets held by households and individuals at the time, public pawnshops could not accept many forms of gold, such as gold bars. This was because the state wanted to reduce the incentive for people to hold gold, which was a concern for the country's foreign reserves. Also, public pawnshops were not permitted to accept diamonds as collateral, as they did not have the necessary skills to assess its value. In comparison, as private pawnshops were not subject to some of these restrictions, or simply ignored and circumvented such restrictions,[92] they remained competitive, despite charging higher interest rates.

In the 1990s after Taiwan's democratization, the government decided to transform the role of public pawnshops into one that was only complementary. This was influenced by the rise of privatizations across the world. As a result, various economic restrictions were lifted, and the political considerations behind maintaining public pawnshops became less appealing. The new liberal government assumed that, in a competitive market, banks would have latitude in finding optimal interest rates to attract new clients that once relied on pawnshops and shadow banks under financial repression.[93] As such, the government decided to close all public pawnshops except for two, in Taipei and Kaohsiung, the two largest cities in the country. These two public pawnshops have some branch offices in their respective city districts. For example, Taipei's public pawnshop has six branches, with four to six employees in each a branch office.

Although public pawnshops significantly shrank in numbers, the remaining two public pawnshops have expanded their social services to cast a wider social safety net under the democratic government. The employees, who need to pass a rigid, nation-wide public servant exam, are all public servants with solid professional training and educational backgrounds. In addition to evaluating the collateral, they have developed online auction platforms to sell collateral upon default by debtors, similar to Caixa in Brazil and private pawnshops in Mexico. They also began to collaborate with other governmental agencies to provide a wider range of social services, such as job searching and employment training for their clients.

While public pawnshops nearly ceased to operate amid the privatization process, private pawnshops were not squeezed out of the market by large private banks. Rather, private pawnshops have thrived in free markets ever since. By 2015, the numbers of private pawnshops had increased to 2,023 across the country, while only two public pawnshops remained.[94] This means that the competition model has now been replaced by a complementary model, in which private pawnshops dominate the market. The question is why private pawnshops in Taiwan have not only survived but thrived in a competitive, free, and modern financial market in which other private banks and financial institutions also operate.

In this new complementary model, the dominant position of private pawnshops is attributable to their ability to utilize the mature legal system that was overhauled after democratization. Taiwan's fast-growing economy gave rise to demands for greater liquidity, but this expanding market came with greater risks and costs regarding contract enforcement, evaluation and sale of collaterals, and other disputes. As a result, private pawnshops lobbied for more regulation. Unlike traditional informal banking that relies on reputational networks and collective responsibility to reduce transaction risks,[95] private pawnshops in Taiwan chose a very different approach to managing their risks: they resorted to the formal legal system to reduce their reliance on reputational networks.

Private pawnshop owners realized that the law can be an efficient tool to reduce transaction costs and formalize their operations. In 2007, Taiwan's Civil Code was amended to recognize a new type of right crucial for private pawnshops—pledge for commercial purposes. This new type of right not only legalizes the pawnshop business but also facilitates their operations by, for example, simplifying the process of selling collateral in case of default. Also, the Association of Private Pawnshops successfully lobbied for the Act on Pawnshop Business in 2010.[96] The Pawnshop Act reduces transaction costs for pawnshop business. For example, the procedure for selling collaterals upon debtor's default has been streamlined and simplified by the new legal regime. Property registration offices now recognize pledge contracts provided by pawnshops as legitimate proof for the purpose of registering property transfers. The Pawnshop Act also helps reduce business risks inherent in private pawnshops' business model. For example, debtors are now required by the Act to provide fingerprints;[97] in this way, the pawnshops, as creditors, can easily identify their clients and check their criminal record. Also, the Pawnshop Act substantially reduces the restrictions on collateral by stipulating a short list of assets not allowed for use as collateral.[98] In this way, pawnshops are allowed to significantly expand the types of acceptable collateral. The Pawnshop Act also provides that pawnshop owners are entitled to request police assistance when needed.[99] This helps pawnshops owners deal with tough clients or illegal collaterals being offered. Disputes could be resolved on site preemptively rather than leading to a future default. In other words, the government is willing to share the burdens and transaction costs of private pawnshops by offering institutional support.

Private pawnshops' successful legal approach to reducing business risks and preventing disputes gave rise to increased profitability, thereby enabling further investment in high-tech equipment to better evaluate the collateral offered by debtors, such as diamonds and other precious jewels. Some also began to provide professional training for their staff to improve evaluation skills, and to invest in other facilities such as surveillance systems and safe storage.

While legal protections have allowed the market to expand, fierce market competition has ensued, changing the nature of the private pawnshop business. Aiming to grab a share of increasing profits, large firms began to offer pawn brokerage services and to compete with traditional pawnshop operators. For example, several well-established car rental companies, with nation-wide business networks, began to offer loans to be secured by borrowers' cars. With the newly recognized commercial pledge right, these lenders could obtain sufficient legal security without keeping the borrowers' car. Technology such as GPS tracing devices also helped to reduce lenders' risks, as they can easily locate the cars or any movable collaterals under pledge, while still allowing their use by borrowers. With such convenience, car owners began to switch to these financial service providers as needs for cash arose. If a default happens, these firms minimize costs by simply moving the cars at issue into their car rental or used car trading business. As a result, within a few years, their borrower-friendly services and full-scale business capacity have snatched from pawnshops almost all the customers that would use cars as collateral.[100]

To survive fierce competition, private pawnshops have transformed themselves into financial service providers too by providing swift services and hence being able to charge high service fees. Although the Pawnshop Act allows private pawnshops to charge only a 2.5% monthly interest rate, pawnshops charge additional service fees, usually about 5% per month. With an effective monthly rate of 7.5% (or 90% a year), they aim to serve middle-class and upper middle-class customers rather than the poor. Public pawnshops are not the competitors of private pawnshops anymore; rather, public and private pawnshops serve very different customers and are complementary to each other in Taiwan's non-bank financial service sector.

By contrast, public pawnshops remain risk averse and much less flexible. Not driven by profitability, public servants of public pawnshops are inclined to undervalue collateral so as to reduce the risk of default by decreasing the value of loans offered.[101] For example, they do not take certain types of collaterals that might depreciate too fast or are subject to volatile market conditions.[102] In theory, public servants' risk averse attitudes could lead to the limited accessibility of public pawnshops. In practice, however, due to the changing nature of private pawnshops, state-backed reputation, and low interest rates, public pawnshops are still able to attract many customers and, therefore, remain self-sufficient and sometimes even profitable.[103]

Although they are much more profitable than their public counterparts, private pawnshops do not seem to be able to replace the remaining two public pawnshops.[104]

Those solidly trained employees of public pawnshops have been performing well in producing other social services, including employment consultation. For senior and disabled citizens who need to borrow, public pawnshops also offer mobile services. As a result, the total lending amounts of the remaining two public pawnshops increased steadily over the past three decades.[105]

As such, private and public pawnshops are now complementary to each other in terms of beneficiaries and the services provided. While public pawnshops remain as institutions serving the underprivileged, profit-driven private pawnshops target customers with better assets who need fast cash. They effectively operate in different markets. Although public pawnshops have never been a monopoly, the state has had a wide latitude in defining itself as a regulator, a competitive market participant, or a provider of a safety net for the poor. Taiwan's complementary model suggests that, to benefit truly vulnerable groups, some form of state intervention is required, especially in a market dominated by profit-driven private pawnshops.

Pawnshops, states and markets

The cases from Brazil, Mexico, and Taiwan provide some interesting lessons about the relationship between states and markets, including state-owned or state-linked companies, in serving the most vulnerable groups in the population. Our case studies illustrate that some market arrangements may increase access to finance, especially for vulnerable populations, but there are still limitations for the poorest of the poor.

Both Mexico and Taiwan show that private provision and market competition can increase poor people's access to credit. In both countries, however, private pawn brokerage services have become a profitable investment for large financial institutions and international investors, resulting in service to the middle-class rather than the poor. As such, the role of the state in the pawnshop markets remains significant. In Taiwan, it is the remaining two public pawnshops that still bear the original obligation of offering cheap and accessible credit for the underprivileged. The Mexican case shows that the internationalization of pawn brokerage services offers slightly better conditions to the poor than the ones offered by traditional pawnshops. However, profitability expectations of international investors leave the poor susceptible to exploitation. The most vulnerable groups still rely on the generous conditions offered by Monte, the government-controlled philanthropic organization. In contrast, Brazil shows that the public provision of pawn brokerage may not provide a safety net for the poor either, as the state-owned pawnshops only recently created accessible conditions to the most vulnerable.

Mexico and Taiwan also offer contrasting examples of how private markets can make services more accessible to vulnerable groups. Taiwan shows that regulation neither hurts profitability of private pawnshops nor diminishes their interests. Instead of relying on markets to distribute risk, as microlending institutions do in Mexico, the state shares risks with creditors by offering them better legal protection, such as policing power, new types of legal rights, or easier procedures to liquidate collaterals. The law helped expand rather than limit the private pawnshop markets in Taiwan. However, both state provision of pawn brokerage services and effective regulation to reduce risks of creditors ultimately come at the expense of taxpayers. This explains why Taiwan shifted from the competition model (with a larger role for the state in providing the service) to the complementary model (with a smaller role for the state in providing the service, but a much larger role in regulating it). Yet, resorting to state regulations depends on strong institutions and legal systems, which are not present in all developing countries.

The contrasting cases of Mexico and Taiwan suggest that some policy options imply a redistribution of risks and benefits among stakeholders, including creditors, debtors, investors, and taxpayers. Such a redistribution requires not only institutional capacity of the state, but also political will and supporting political economic conditions. Taiwan, in this regard, seems to provide the textbook example, relying on state intervention initially to discipline market forces, and then replacing the state intervention with state regulation to perform the same function. Taiwan also offers an example of how state regulations may effectively protect and benefit both debtors and creditors and could reduce the risks of criminal activity as well as the financial exposure of pawnshops. Its transition to a liberal model is thus marked by a heavy reliance on the effectiveness of laws and the legal system.

The expansion of Mexican pawnshops and microcredit institutions resonates with their counterparts in Taiwan, with private operators prevailing and dominating the market. The difference is that, while Taiwanese pawnshops resorted to legal systems to reduce business risk, Mexican pawnshops and microcredit providers rely primarily on international capital markets. In this regard, international capital markets serve as a functional substitute for the domestic legal system and market institutions to reduce risk in order to expand the scale of market and increase the profitability of Mexico's microfinancing market.

Mexico seems to provide a case study where limited state capacity and lack of an effective legal system simply did not allow for either direct state provision of the service or a healthy expansion of the private market for pawnshops, at least until recently. Nonetheless, as the Mexican model shows, even in countries without effective institutions, creditors may find other forms of reducing risk, especially if they can access international markets.

Brazil, in contrast, adopted a state monopoly over pawnshops in the 1930s.Two congressional bills are trying to end the monopoly[106] to increase access to credit by offering the service in localities not covered by the state. Those opposing the end of the monopoly argue that the state would not be capable of monitoring and/or effectively regulating the private provision of such services, leading to abusive conditions under a profit-driven private pawnshop structure.[107] There are also concerns that private pawnshops will facilitate criminal activity, such as money laundering and sale of stolen goods.[108] Some claim that existing concerns can be addressed either by regulation (PL 230/19), or by restricting pawn loans to established financial institutions, such as banks (PLC 78/21). In other words, if these bills were approved, Brazil would either be adopting the Taiwanese model or an adapted version of the Mexican model (restricting the service to large financial institutions which have fewer incentives to resort to abusive conditions, or engage with criminal activity).

Finally, our case studies show a convergence toward some form of state-linked model to address the need of the poor that runs in parallel to traditional services. All three countries analyzed, despite very different roles of the state, have converged toward a dual-track arrangement for access to pawn brokerage services, with favorable terms for vulnerable groups. In other words, with or without direct state interventions, pawnshops of three countries have developed state-linked arrangements that preserve the social function of pawnshops. Taiwan had ensured a safety net for its most vulnerable population even before its successful transition to a market-oriented model and continues to deliver public services through its public pawnshops. In Brazil, public pawnshops were originally created to provide accessible services to vulnerable people. After neoliberal reforms, the state continues to rely on pawnshops as profitable operations, but since the 2000s they also offer special services for the poor. Mexico maintains a form of social safety through the philanthropic private institution Monte de Piedad, through direct regulation and close oversight. Interestingly, the convergence toward a dual-track pawn brokerage services in all three countries demonstrates pluralist trajectories and does not seem to be associated with particular models of state intervention in the economy.

Conclusion

Considering how central the topic of access to credit has been in the law and development literature, is there a way of structuring pawnshops that ensures accessibility and sustainability of credit? It is undeniable that the internationalization observed in Mexico helps with the sustainability of microfinancing and pawnshops, and may also increase accessibility. But the poorest of the poor do not seem to be contemplated by private for-profit providers during the process of internationalization. Taiwan's complementary model seems to offer a textbook example of good synergy between state, market, and the law, despite the limitations in the state-owned system designed to benefit the most vulnerable. Yet, not all developing countries can replicate this model due to variations in state, institutional, and legal capacity. As Brazil embarks on a Congressional discussion about ending state monopoly of pawnshops, further lessons may be learned. Until then, our case studies point to various advantages and risks of different levels of state intervention or reliance on markets, along with a list of factors that constrain the choices available in different contexts. Although far from comprehensive, we believe this typology of state roles in pawnshops may help those interested in exploring how to increase access to credit around the world, but especially in developing countries.

***

Notes

1 Authors' names are in alphabetical order of last name, as both authors contributed equally to the piece. We are grateful to Ben Maclean-Max and Foti Vito for excellent research assistance and editorial suggestions. All remaining errors are ours.
2 John P. Caskey, Fringe Banking: Check-Cashing Outlets, Pawnshops, and the Poor (1994).
3 See, e.g., Jerzy Eisenberg-Guyot et al., From Payday Loans to Pawnshops: Fringe Banking, the Unbanked, and Health, *Health Affairs* 37(3) 429 (2018); Tatsuki Inoue, The Role of Pawnshops in Risk Coping in Early Twentieth-Century Japan, 28 *Fin. Hist. Rev.* 319 (2021); and Abdul Ghafar Ismail & Nor Zakiah Ahmad, Pawnshops as an Instrument of Microenterprise Credit in Malaysia, 24(11) *Int. J. of Soc. Econ.* 1343 (1997).
4 Arturo G. Santillán et al., Pawnshops: Are they Really a Solution for the Vulnerable Population?, 6 *Ecoforum* 1(10) 2 (2017).
5 For an overview of the literature, see Mariana Mota Prado & Michael J. Trebilcock, *Advanced Introduction to Law and Development* (2021), Chapter 10. For more recent pieces, see, for instance, Orkun Akseli, Financial Inclusion, Access to Credit, and Sustainable Finance: What Role for the UNCITRAL Model Law on Secured Transactions?, 84 *Law & Contemp. Probs.* 181 (2021); Carlos Madeira, The Impact of Interest Rate Ceilings on Households' Access to Credit: Evidence from a 2013 Chilean Legislation, 106 *J. of Banking & Finance* 166 (2019).
6 There are, of course, exceptions. See, e.g., F.J.A. Bouman & R. Houtman, Pawnbroking as an Instrument of Rural Banking in the Third World, 37(1) *Econ. Dev. and Cult. Change* 69 (1988); Siti Malikhatun Badriyah et al., Private Pawnshop Registration as an Effort to Develop Small and Medium Enterprises in Indonesia, 12(7) *Int. J. of Innovation, Creativity, and Change* 174 (2020).
7 For an overview, see Michael Trebilcock, State-Owned Enterprises, in *Encyclopedia of Law and Economics* (Alain Marciano & Giovanni Battista Ramello, eds., 2022).
8 For an overview of the literature, see Robert Hockett, Public Actors in Private Markets: Towards a Developmental Finance State, 93 *Wa. U. L. Rev.* (2015).
9 Susan Rose-Ackerman, American Administrative Law Under Siege: Is Germany a Model?, 107(6) *Harv. L. Rev.* 1279 (1994); Susan Rose-Ackerman, *Democracy and Executive Power: Policymaking Accountability in the US, the UK, Germany and France* (2021).
10 Kurt E. von Mettenheim, Federal Banking in Brazil: Policies and Competitive Advantage, 5–28 (2010).
11 See, for instance, Inoue, *supra* note 3; Ismail & Ahmad, *supra* note 3; Bouman & Houtman, *supra* note 6; Heiko Schrader, *The Role of Pawnshops in the Life Strategies of Lower Income Groups: A Preliminary Study in St. Petersburg/Russia*, Working Paper No 316, Universität Bielefeld (1999); Susan Payne Carter & Paige Marta Skiba, Pawnshops, Behavioural Economics, and Self-Regulation, 32 *Rev. of Banking & Fin. Law* 193 (2012) (focusing on the USA).
12 Dan Horch, Brazil's Middle Class Finds a Lifeline at the Pawnshop, *NY Times*, Dec. 2003.
13 Decreto No. 2.723, de 12 de Janeiro de 1861, *Col. Leis Imp. Brasil*, 1 (11) (Brazil). ww2.camara.leg.br/legin/fed/decret/1824-1899/decreto-2723-12-janeiro-1861-556013-publicacaooriginal-75580-pe.html. Kurt E. von Mettenheim, *Monetary State Craft in Brazil: 1808-2014*, 46 (2020). Alexis Cavicchini Teixeira de Siqueira, *A História dos Bancos no Brasil* 49 (2007).
14 Until the 1930s state-owned pawnshops were called *Montes de Socorro*, while private ones were known as "Casas de Prego" or "Casas Belchior". *Ibid.* at 49.
15 *Ibid.* at 53. Von Mettenheim, *supra* note 10, 101–144. Flavio Silveira et al., A Presença Do Estado No Setor Financeiro Brasileiro: O Caso Da Caixa Econômica Federal, 11(1) *Rev. E. de Gestão Organizacional* 132, 147 (2013).

16 Decreto No. 24.427, de 19 de Junho de 1934, Diário Oficial da União [D.O.U.] de 3.7.1934 (Brazil). www2.camara.leg.br/legin/fed/decret/1930-1939/decreto-24427-19-junho-1934-498355-publicacaooriginal-1-pe.html.
17 Siqueira, *supra* note 13 at 50.
18 Decreto-Lei No. 759, de 12 de Agosto de 1969, Diário Oficial da União [D.O.U.] de 26.8.1969 (Brazil), artigo 2. www2.camara.leg.br/legin/fed/declei/1960-1969/decreto-lei-759-12-agosto-1969-374148-publicacaooriginal-1-pe.html.
19 Flavio Silveira et al., *supra* note 15 at 151; Marcelo Milano Falcão Vieira & Diana Costa de Castro, A Presença Do Estado No Setor Financeiro Brasileiro: O Caso Da Caixa Econômica Federal, 11(1) *Rev. E. de Gestão Organizacional* 132, 151 (2013); see also von Mettenheim, *supra* note 10 at 130.
20 von Mettenheim, *supra* note 13 at 159.
21 Flavio Silveira et al., *supra* note 15.
22 Siqueira, *supra* note 13 at 313.
23 von Mettenheim, *supra* note 10 & *supra* note 13.
24 Siqueira, *supra* note 13 at 313.
25 Horch, *supra* note 12.
26 Siqueira, *supra* note 13 at 49.
27 *Penhor Caixa*, Caixa Econômica Federal, www.caixa.gov.br/voce/credito-financiamento/penhor/Paginas/default.aspx.
28 Horch, *supra* note 12.
29 *Vitrine de Joias*, Caixa Econômica Federal, https://vitrinedejoias.caixa.gov.br/Paginas/default.aspx.
30 Ramon Wiest and Giácomo Balbinotto Neto, Assimetria de Informação e Garantias no Mercado de Crédito: O Caso das Operações de Penhor, 1(2) *RJLB* 1853, 1858 (2015).
31 Horch, *supra* note 12.
32 Fenae, Caixa Anuncia Novidades na Modalidade de Empréstimo do Tipo Penhor (2009).
33 Lúcia Helena Alves Müller & Décio Soares Vicente, Vão-se os Anéis: Uma Abordagem Antropológica do Penhor como Instrumento de Crédito, 4(2) *Rev. Espaço de Diálogo e Disconexão* 4 (2012).
34 InfoMoney, Micropenhor da CEF supera expectativas e atinge R$ 51 milhões em empréstimos, *InfoMoney*, www.infomoney.com.br/minhas-financas/micropenhor-da-cef-supera-expectativas-e-atinge-r-51-milhoes-em-emprestimos/.
35 FENAE, *supra* note 31.
36 Müller & Vicente, *supra* note 33 at 5.
37 Lúcia Müller, Negotiating Gifts and Debts: Financialization policies and the Economic Experiences of Low-Income Social Groups in Brazil, 11(1) *Vibrant* 191 (2014).
38 Müller & Vicente, *supra* note 33 at 5.
39 Horch, *supra* note 12.
40 Wellton Máximo, Movimentação do Penhor da Caixa cresce 11.4% em 2016, Agência Brasil (2016); Fábio Massalli, Penhor da Caixa movimenta R$ 7.2 milhões no primeiro semestre deste ano, Agência Brasil (2017).
41 Projeto de Lei Complementar n.º 230/2019 (Brazil).
42 Caixa Econômica Federal, *supra* note 27.
43 Massalli, *supra* note 40.
44 Marie E. Francois, A Culture of Everyday Credit: Housekeeping, Pawnbroking, and Governance in Mexico City, 1750–1920, 264 (2006).
45 Ibid. at 4.
46 Ibid.
47 Marie E. Francois, When Pawnshops Talk: Popular Credit and Material Culture in Mexico City, 1775–1916, 255 (Ph.D. dissertation, University of Arizona) (1998).
48 First Cash Financial Services, Inc., Annual Report (Form 10-K) (Feb. 17, 2016).

49 Ezcorp, Inc., Annual Report (Form 10-K) (Dec. 05, 2019) ("PROFECO regulates the form and terms of pawn loan contracts (but not interest or service charge rates) and defines certain operating standards and procedures for pawnshops, including retail operations, and establishes registration, disclosure, bonding and reporting requirements. There are significant fines and sanctions, including operating suspensions, for failure to comply with PROFECO's rules and regulations."). *See also,* Susanne Soederberg, *Debtfare States and the Poverty Industry: Money, Discipline and the Surplus Population,* 201 (2014).
50 Ibid.
51 Santillán et al., *supra* note 4.
52 First Cash Financial Services, Inc., *supra* note 48.
53 Ibid.
54 Ibid.
55 Santillán et al., *supra* note 4.
56 *Mexico Financial Inclusion Development Policy Financing*, The World Bank, https://documents1.worldbank.org/curated/en/661091561168880162/pdf/Mexico-Financial-Inclusion-Development-Policy-Financing-Project.pdf. *See also,* Santillán et al., *supra* note 4.
57 Santillán et al., *supra* note 4.
58 Ibid.
59 Account ownership at a financial institution or with a mobile-money-service provider (percentage of population ages 15+)— Mexico, The World Bank, https://data.worldbank.org/indicator/FX.OWN.TOTL.ZS?locations=MX.
60 Credit card ownership (percentage age 15+)—Mexico, The World Bank, https://tcdata360.worldbank.org/indicators/h15dc8779?country=MEX&indicator=3360&viz=line_chart&years=2011, 2017.
61 Benjamin D. Mazzotta and Bhaskar Chakravorti, The Cost of Cash in Mexico 1 (2014), https://sites.tufts.edu/digitalplanet/files/2020/03/CCMEX-final-web.pdf.
62 Los Angeles Times, Pawnshops part of life in Mexico, *The Denver Post* (Dec. 18, 2005), www.denverpost.com/2005/12/18/pawnshops-part-of-life-in-mexico/.
63 Mazzotta & Chakravorti, *supra* note 61 at 16.
64 Los Angeles Times, *supra* note 62; William Booth, Mexicans pawn their valuables with 'Aunt Pity', The Seattle Times (Feb. 27, 2010), www.seattletimes.com/nation-world/mexicans-pawn-their-valuables-with-aunt-pity.
65 Los Angeles Times, *supra* note 62.
66 Financiera Independencia, Offering Memorandum of 8.000% Senior Notes due 2024, (July 12, 2017) 88.
67 Ibid.
68 Brendan Case, US Pawnshops Find Success in Mexico, *Seattle Times* (Sept. 20, 2011).
69 Ibid.
70 Ibid.
71 Bank Azteca did not aim to compete with traditional relational banking either, since the costs of borrowing from friends and relatives are significantly lower. In 2005, while the APR of Bank Azteca is 130%, the APR of borrowing from friends and relatives could be as low as 0%. In fact, Bank Azteca did not open branches in areas where relational banking dominates. See Claudia Ruiz, *From Pawn Shops to Banks: The Impact of Formal Credit on Informal Households*, The World Bank Policy Research Paper No. 6634 (2003).
72 Ibid.
73 Each pawnshop has a main source of revenues according to their business model and expertise. Some rely on interest payments by borrowers while others would depend on the sale of seized collaterals.
74 These microcredit providers design various loan products for various types of customers. Each product has a different interest rate based on the risk portfolio of different

types of borrowers. *See*, e.g., Financiera Independencia, Offering Memorandum of 8.000% Senior Notes due 2024, pp. 94–95 (July 12, 2017).

75 They are Financiera Independencia, Banco Compartamos, Banco Famsa, Credito Real, Banco Coppel, and Grupo Elektra (which owns Bank Azteca).

76 María E.R. Ibarra, El Monte de Piedad de México: su Origen y Desarrollo, 41 *Revista Internacional de Ciencias Sociales* 12, n. 90 (2021). *But see* the official website, indicating 1922 as the date: *Órgano de Gobierno*, Nacional Monte de Piedad, www.montepiedad.com.mx/conocenos/organo-de-gobierno.

77 Nonprofit Law in Mexico, Council on Foundations, https://cof.org/content/nonprofit-law-mexico.

78 Ibid.

79 Mexico Legal Analysis, International Center for Not-For-Profit Law, www.icnl.org/resources/civic-freedom-monitor/mexico.

80 Westlaw, *Charitable organisations in Mexico: overview | Practical Law,* https://content.next.westlaw.com/practical-law/document/Ibf82551a895... e=Default&contextData=(sc.Default)&viewType=FullText&firstPage=true at 6.

81 Guía de Servicios, Nacional Monte de Piedad, www.montepiedad.com.mx/storage/tasas-y-costos.pdf.

82 Ibid.

83 Ibid.

84 Los Angeles Times, *supra* note 61..

85 Quiénes Somos, Nacional Monte de Piedad, https://www.montepiedad.com.mx/conocenos/quienes-somos.

86 Wan-Yu Chen (陳宛妤), Legal Transplant and Traditional Finance Activities, 89, Master's thesis, National Taiwan University College of Law (2004).

87 Shih-Feng Hung (洪士峰), State and Pawn: The Genealogy of the Public Pawnshops in Postwar Taiwan, 57 *Thoughts and Words Journal* 1, 14 (2019).

88 By 1953, there were 12 public and 195 private pawnshops.

89 United Daily, *Ministry of Finance Explains the Restriction on Pledge against Gold* (放寬銀錢業抵押, 外傳並不確; 財部日內有解釋 飾金抵押有限制), December 30, 1956, at 3; Hung, *supra* note 86.

90 Hung, *supra* note 87, at 18.

91 Ibid. at 37.

92 Shih-Feng Hung, Licitness, Legitimatizing Illicitness and Illicitness: Pawn Transactions in Taiwan, 194–2010*,* 52 *Taiwanese Journal of Sociology* 79, 115 (2013).

93 Hung, *supra* note 87, at 21.

94 Ibid., at 1.

95 Relational banking is common for those unbanked people in a tight-knit community, in which creditors are able to rely on reputational networks and collective responsibility as a functional substitute to a formal legal system.

96 Hung, *supra* note 87, at 40.

97 Act on Pawnshop Business, Art. 15 (Taiwan).

98 Ibid., Art. 16.

99 Ibid., Arts 23–25.

100 Ibid.

101 Hung, s*upra* note 87 at 38.

102 Apple *Daily, Public Pawnshops Accept Only Rolex* (Dec. 7, 2012), https://tw.appledaily.com/headline/20121207/O2EW55OQYM22S7NCHGIHVJQFIE/.

103 Interviews conducted by Weitseng Chen (13 July 2022).

104 Ibid. The interest rates charged by Taipei City's Public Pawnshop is 5.4% per year for low-income citizens, persons with disabilities, and indigenous people, 7.44% per year for local residents of Taipei, and 8.16% per year for any other people. While public pawnshops provide much more affordable financial services than their private counterparts, at times they need budgetary support by city governments.

105 Hung, *supra* note 86 at 28.
106 FENAE, Papel social em risco: Câmara aprova fim da exclusividade do penhor da Caixa (Jun. 2, 2022), www.fenae.org.br/portal/fenae-portal/papel-social-em-risco-camara-aprova-fim-da-exclusividade-do-penhor-da-caixa.htm. FENAE, *Fim da exclusividade do Penhor na Caixa é desmonte de patrimônio público* (Jun. 3, 2022), www.fenae.org.br/portal/fenae-portal/fim-da-exclusividade-do-penhor-na-caixa-e-desmonte-de-patrimonio-publico.htm.
107 Léia Coelho, *Fim do Monopólio de Penhor pela Caixa Economica Pode Aumentar Empréstimos Predatórios*, Jornal Da USP (Aug. 2021), https://jornal.usp.br/atualidades/fim-do-monopolio-de-penhor-pela-caixa-economica-pode-aumentar-emprestimos-predatorios/.
108 Projeto de Lei, *supra* note 40.

Selected References

John P. Caskey, *Fringe Banking: Check-Cashing Outlets, Pawnshops, and the Poor* (Russell Sage Foundation;1st edition, New York, NY 1994).

Wan-Yu Chen (陳宛妤), Legal Transplant and Traditional Finance Activities, Master Thesis, National Taiwan University College of Law (2004).

Marie E. Francois, *A Culture of Everyday Credit: Housekeeping, Pawnbroking, and Governance in Mexico City, 1750–1920* (University of Nebraska Press, Lincoln & London, 2006).

Shih-Feng Hung (洪士峰), State and Pawn: The Genealogy of the Public Pawnshops in Postwar Taiwan, 57 *Thoughts and Words Journal* 1 (2019).

Shih-Feng Hung (洪士峰), Licitness, Legitimatizing Illicitness and Illicitness: Pawn Transactions in Taiwan, 1945–2010, 52 *Taiwanese Journal of Sociology* 79 (2013).

Kurt E. von Mettenheim, *Federal Banking in Brazil: Policies and Competitive Advantage* (Routledge, New York, NY 2010).

Claudia Ruiz, *From Pawn Shops to Banks: The Impact of Formal Credit on Informal Households*, The World Bank Policy Research Paper No. 6634 (2003).

5 Developing countries' utilization of GSP

Labor standards, the margin of preference, and the demand for zero tariffs

Jennifer L. Tobin and Marc L. Busch

Although the great majority of Susan Rose-Ackerman's work has been in the fields of corruption and administrative law, her influence on positive political economy extends to fields ranging from regulation and federalism, to investment and trade. As a professor working with students (including one of the co-authors of this article) her mentorship often went beyond corruption and administrative law to emphasize the importance of understanding both the comprehensive nature of policies and the importance of interdisciplinary approaches. In this chapter, we bring a political and economic framework into play to understand the conditions underpinning the generalized system of preferences (GSP), an important trade policy that is meant to bring greater development to low-income countries. As with Susan's work on corruption, we draw attention to the incentives and behavior created by different institutional designs in the creation and working of GSP. But perhaps more importantly, her conceptual framework on the interplay between good governance and economic and social development speaks directly to our work on how a policy intended to have a positive social outcome—better labor standards—might not be achieving this goal, due to a lack of understanding of the institutional framework.

In Bangladesh in April of 2013, Rana Plaza—which housed five garment factories—collapsed, killing over a thousand workers and injuring more than 2,500 others.[1] The collapse was directly attributable to sub-standard conditions for workers in those garment factories, with investigations determining that the building that housed the factories was constructed with sub-standard materials and had never been properly inspected[2] International reaction to the incident was swift. In the United States, President Obama suspended Bangladesh from its tariff-free market access to the United States under the Generalized System of Preferences (GSP) for "not taking steps to afford internationally recognized worker rights to workers in that country." The decision was actually in response to a petition filed more than five years earlier by the AFL-CIO calling for the Bangladeshi government to end labor abuses in the garment industry.

GSP is a one-way tariff program offered by nearly all high-income countries that allows duty-free entry into their markets for thousands of products made in developing countries. GSP is the centerpiece of most developed countries' "trade as aid" programs—that are meant to be a substitute for—or perhaps a complement to—foreign aid. But, as with all aid, GSP comes with conditions—such as respect for intellectual property rights, investor rights, and, perhaps most important, labor

DOI: 10.4324/9781003416234-6

standards. The conditional nature of GSP means that if countries violate these conditions, their exports can be suspended from GSP—and most suspensions are due to labor right violations.

The hope—at least from the importer-country—is that these suspensions, or even fear of the suspensions, should have an effect on workers' rights in the recipient country. This is particularly important in light of the fact that the US GSP program is currently suspended—and discussions of reauthorization are particularly focused on worker rights.

The conventional wisdom on GSP is that it serves to improve labor standards. Government reports and academic studies have long found that GSP conditionality motivates recipients to raise their labor standards. But nearly all of these studies take a supply-side approach, examining how US "suspensions" purportedly result in reforms.

If the conventional wisdom is right, that the conditionality in GSP has a positive impact on labor standards in recipient countries, then the evidence should also demonstrate a demand-side account—that exporters take the risk of their country being suspended from GSP into account when deciding whether or not to use GSP.[3]

Exporters weigh the costs and benefits of using GSP. The costs include substantial audit requirements, ensuring their export volumes remain below set quantitative limits, and abiding by "rules of origin" on domestic sourcing. The benefits include the *margin of preference* or the reduction in the tariff that an exporter would otherwise pay, namely the US's Most-Favored Nation (MFN) or non-MFN rate, depending on whether the recipient belongs to the World Trade Organization (WTO) or not. This margin is the literature's single best predictor of GSP utilization.[4]

Exporters have to calculate the risk that GSP can be suspended if their home country falls afoul of labor standards. In this sense, GSP conditionality should affect exporter decisions like the prospect of being subjected to other protectionist measures, such as an antidumping or countervailing duty. Specifically, exporters should "price in" this risk of being suspended when deciding whether GSP's margin is worth the investment in using the program. If labor standards matter, they should figure prominently in this regard.

Simply put, an exporter in a country with lower labor standards is at greater risk of suspension. To use GSP, this exporter will require a higher margin of preference. Conversely, an exporter in a country with higher labor standards is at less risk of suspension. It is thus likely to use GSP at a lower margin. We test our argument on a novel data set that allows us to examine GSP *utilization* at the four-digit tariff level on a country-product-year basis.

We use a two-limit Tobit model, and a specification curve, showing how our results hold up across other models, including a fractional logit, generalized method of moments, and standard gravity model. The specification curve results reveal a strong, positive effect of the margin, but show no effect of the interaction of this margin with the recipient's labor standards, or of labor standards alone. This lack of evidence casts serious doubt on whether GSP improves labor standards in developing countries.

Why does this matter? Dating back to 1976, the US has used GSP to pursue a variety of political goals, from encouraging compliance with intellectual property rights to adhering to investor rights.[5] Yet, worker rights stand out in the politics of GSP. Indeed, petitions to suspend a recipient, which are often filed by US interest groups, frequently mention labor standards. Moreover, the US House of Representatives is currently weighing legislation that would put *more* emphasis on enforcing "internationally recognized worker rights," making this a precondition for renewing the program.[6] Will a legislative rewrite make GSP more effective at promoting labor standards? Our paper suggests not, and we can pinpoint why: exporters can do little about labor standards at the country level, and would likely be far more responsive if these standards were assessed at the industry level.

Our paper proceeds as follows. First, we explain the costs and benefits of US GSP, and how a recipient's labor standards *should* inform an exporter's decision to use the program. Second, we detail our research design, describing the data and the models estimated. Third, we present our findings and robustness checks. Fourth, we conclude with some implications for GSP and, in general, for the use of trade preferences to leverage political influence more generally.

Generalized system of preference and labor standards

US GSP debuted in Title IV of the Trade Act of 1974, although the program did not launch until 1976. Like other countries' GSP programs, the US program takes the form of "trade as aid." It gives *non-reciprocal* tariff preferences to developing countries on a list of eligible goods. In other words, developing countries have access to US markets tariff-free without having to give this same access to US exporters. GSP is allowed under the WTO's *Enabling Clause*, which permits—*but does not require*—this preference to be given, despite the fact that it would otherwise violate MFN.[7] US GSP covers 5,000 tariff lines on imports from 119 developing countries. But the tariff preference comes with conditionality, meaning a recipient can be suspended if it does not comply with US-legislated political criteria. Labor standards stand out in this regard.[8]

In particular, the US legislation says that a recipient can be suspended if it does not "afford internationally recognized worker rights."[9] These include the right of association; collective bargaining; a prohibition on forced labor; a minimum age for child employment, a ban on the "worst forms of child labor;" minimum wages, hours of work, and occupational safety and health. Interest groups, especially unions, often petition to have the US conduct reviews of a recipient's compliance with labor standards, looking to have them suspended. The list of suspended countries includes Nicaragua (1987), Paraguay (1987), Chile (1988), Sudan (1991), Belarus (2000), Bangladesh (2013), and Thailand (2019 and 2020), for example.[10]

The US House of Representatives wants to do more. The proposed *Generalized System of Preferences and Miscellaneous Tariff Bill Modernization Act of 2021*,[11] would require a deeper "review of the laws of each beneficiary developing country relating to internationally recognized worker rights."[12] Its text would insert the "elimination of discrimination with respect to employment and occupation" and outlawing "violence or threats of violence against workers, including violence related to gender-based violence or harassment in the workplace and violence related to workers exercising or attempting to exercise any of the rights."[13] In other words, GSP would draw more on the covenants of the International Labor Organization (ILO). But does the *threat* of suspension change labor standards in recipient countries?

Government studies typically conclude that it does. For example, Europe's GSP, which also conditions tariff preferences on worker rights, is argued to have pushed Bangladesh to make a variety of key labor reforms.[14] Likewise, a "partial" suspension of Cambodia, mostly due to worker rights, is argued to have led the government to overhaul many of its laws.[15] The European Commission's biannual report also credits GSP with getting Bolivia to raise its minimum working age to 14 years old, Paraguay to vow to end child labor by 2024, and Sri Lanka to create "Child Labour Free Zones," which it credits with reducing child labor from 16% to 1% of total employment.[16]

The US also claims a long list of success stories involving GSP and labor standards. Thailand, for example, endured six years of GSP reviews, and took "steps to provide internationally recognized worker rights in a number of important areas" because of this scrutiny.[17] In addition, Bangladesh is argued to have increased its commitment to worker rights under threat of suspension, culminating in an agreement that involves input and monitoring by Canada and the International Labor Organization (ILO).[18] Indonesia also responded to threats of being suspended from GSP, changing labor laws the US had found problematic since the early 1990s.[19]

As more evidence of a link between GSP and labor standards, consider the fact that developing countries complain about it. They insist that the conditionality creates too much uncertainty about their market access. In advance of the 1999 WTO Ministerial, for example, Cuba, the Dominican Republic, and Honduras proposed that "[p]reference-giving countries *shall not subject preferential market access to conditionalities*, whether trade-related or not," or "initiate any form of unilateral action against preference-receiving countries."[20] India has been just as vocal in its opposition, demanding that the link "*is in violation of the 'enabling clause' of GATT relating to GSP which clearly sets out that GSP must be non-discriminatory*, non-reciprocal and generalized."[21] Yet, when asked to rule on conditionality, the WTO has upheld it. In a dispute filed by India against the European Communities (EC), called *EC—Tariff Preferences*, the WTO's Appellate Body said that countries should "ensure that identical treatment *is available to all similarly-situated GSP beneficiaries*,"[22] but did *not* rule against conditionality per se.

The problem with much of the literature on GSP is that it is cast at the level of the *recipient* country. As Hafner-Burton, Mosley and Galantucci (2019) explain, labor standards need to be examined at the product level. This is because suspensions of recipients are a "rare event," but suspensions of specific products are not. This suggests the decision of exporters to use GSP should be more informative with respect to any link between tariff concessions and labor standards.

To better understand when exporters would take labor standards into account when deciding whether or not to use GSP, we must first understand the costs, benefits, and risks of using GSP.

The costs of using GSP

An exporter incurs three main costs in using GSP. First, there is the paperwork. On a per-shipment basis, exporters must submit a wealth of audited information, and meet five-year record-keeping requirements. A tariff bill under GSP places the letter "A" in front of the good's eight-digit tariff code, but it falls on the exporter to verify that all ("A") or some ("A*") suppliers are eligible for GSP, or that the good is one of the 1,500 additional items that would be eligible from a least-developed country ("A*").

Second, there are trade volume concerns, known as "competitive needs limitations" (CNLs), that must be monitored on a yearly basis. These are quantitative caps on the import of a good from a given recipient by year. Specifically, CNLs restrict goods from a country that accounts for 50 percent of the total value of US imports, or exceeds a dollar value, set at $155 million in 2012. Waivers from CNLs can be had, but these require that the exporter make its case using eight-digit tariff data, which is difficult. For example, in 2018, Kazakhstan received a one-year waiver on "ferrosilicon chromium," a product that had been under a CNL the previous year, but the effort was costly. There is another waiver for goods that have not been produced in the US over the previous three years, but through 2019, only one has been issued, reflecting a high bar on submissions. In short, CNLs, and waivers from them, add exporter costs to using GSP.

Third, and most importantly, there are rules of origin. Exporters must track and be able to audit their use of inputs from upstream suppliers to ensure compliance with thresholds for the content by value of eligible products. This means that, to get a tariff preference, an exporter may have to rework its supply chain to meet these rules. US legislation requires that, to be eligible for GSP, the good "must be the growth, product or manufacture" of a recipient, with domestic materials, and direct costs of processing, equal to *at least* 35 percent of the appraised value. The cost of audits can be onerous, particularly where the rules of origin are subject to change.

To put this cost in perspective, take the example of the North American Free Trade Agreement (NAFTA). Most of NAFTA's rules of origin were so costly to comply with that some 80 percent of Mexican trade with the US was conducted under WTO rules, rather than going through the lower tariffs of NAFTA.[23] The US Chamber of Commerce worries about this happening under a renewed GSP, warning that "[t]hese revisions could lead foreign governments to conclude that *GSP's compliance burdens outweigh its economic benefits*."[24] As in preferential trade agreements, the value of a GSP tariff preference has to be weighed against the cost of adhering to a rule of origin that may require a substantial overhaul of the exporter's supply chain.

The benefits and risks of using GSP

GSP is a zero-tariff on eligible goods. The value of this preference is measured against the US MFN or non-MFN tariff (depending on whether the recipient is a member of the WTO), in other words the difference between the tariff that would apply and duty-free market access. This margin of preference is the literature's best predictor of the use of GSP.[25] Keck and Lendle, for example, find that it is the key to explaining GSP utilization across Australia, Canada, Europe, and the United States.[26] Likewise, Hoekman, Martin and Primo Braga introduce a volume of empirical studies by stressing the centrality of the margin, warning that its "erosion" relative to MFN poses challenges for developing countries.[27] Alexandraki and Lankes take this erosion concern a step further, explaining that exporters risk losing markets under GSP, given the proliferation of preferential trade agreements, for example.[28] In our data across all four-digit tariffs, GSP's margin ranges from zero to a high of 38 percent.

What the literature has never done, and what we do here, is *scale* this margin by the risk of being suspended over labor standards. Exporters price in the risk of being subjected to various protectionist measures, such as antidumping or countervailing duties, for example. Sourcing from upstream suppliers in China, which is the world's number one target of antidumping duties, is riskier in this regard than sourcing from upstream suppliers in Canada. Likewise, exporters in countries that have lower labor standards are likely more at risk of being suspended than exporters in countries that have higher labor standards.

This begs the question: do exporters *know* how their country scores on labor standards? Yes. First, and most obviously, they are being informed by the importers in the United States to whom they sell. Second, trade associations in the US and recipient countries keep exporters up to date, not only on labor standards reviews, but GSP revisions and renewals. Third, an exporter's home government, oftentimes in conjunction with the US government, invests resources to inform exporters about, and conduct training on, labor standards. Ethiopia's government, for example, routinely posts information on its website concerning GSP programs in the US and Europe. Recipient governments invest in tracking and sharing this information not just because of GSP, but because, under Section 307, the US can also seize imports produced by forced labor.

Taken together, we argue that if access to GSP has a positive impact on exporting country workers' rights, then we should expect exporters to price the risk of suspension into their decision over whether or not to utilize GSP. Our hypothesis is thus as follows:

> *A recipient with lower (higher) labor standards is at more (less) risk of being suspended, such that its exporters will require a higher (lower) margin to use GSP.*

Research design

Our unit of analysis is imports from GSP-eligible countries to the US at the country-product-year level, 1997–2011. Data are from the U.S. International Trade Commission.[29]

The dependent variable, GSP UTILIZATION, is defined as the fraction of GSP-eligible imports at the Harmonized Tariff System (HTS) eight-digit level that utilize either GSP or GSP+[30] when imported into the US. Formally, we calculate GSP UTILIZATION as:

$$y_{cjt} = \frac{X_{cjt}^{claim}}{X_{cjt}^{eligible}}$$

Where x^{claim} represents the total value of imports under GSP or GSP+, $x^{eligible}$ represents the total value of imports that were eligible for GSP, and *c,j,t* are the country, product and year, respectively.

If a good entered the US under an alternative trade scheme, we do not include it in the analysis. We only compare GSP UTILIZATION with the decision to export under the US's MFN or non-MFN rates. We obviously exclude cases where a country is *ineligible* for GSP treatment on a particular product or where some other exclusion was in effect. For example, US GSP includes CNLs eliminating or restricting utilization of these trade benefits when a good from a country (1) accounts for more than 50 percent of the total value of US imports of that good; or (2) exceeds a certain dollar value (i.e., $155 million in 2012). If, however, a country received a CNL waiver, or even a *de minimis* waiver, we include it in the analysis.

We have three variables of interest: (1) PREFERENCE MARGIN; (2) LABOR RIGHTS; and (3) their interaction. First, GSP PREFERENCE MARGIN is the difference between the US program's duty-free rate, and either its MFN or non-MFN rates. We use the World Bank's World Integrated Tariff Solution database to determine the average duty rates, available at HTS-8 level, for all products entering the United States under MFN or non-MFN rates, and subtract the GSP rate. Consistent with prior research, we expect GSP utilization to increase with the margin of preference.

Second, to measure LABOR RIGHTS, we use the Worker's Rights variable from the CIRI Human Rights Data Project. This measures the extent to which workers enjoy internationally recognized rights at work, such as freedom of association, prohibitions on forced labor, and acceptable health and safety conditions in the workplace. The variable is measured on a scale of 0–2, with 0 indicating that rights are severely restricted, and 2 indicating that rights were fully protected in a given year.[31] We expect that countries with lower scores will be less likely to use GSP, given concerns for suspension.

Third, we interact the PREFERENCE MARGIN with LABOR RIGHTS, the expectation being that countries with lower scores on the latter might be enticed to use this trade preference the larger the difference between GSP and either the MFN or non-MFN rate. Specifically, we expect the interaction of PREFERENCE MARGIN and LABOR RIGHTS to be negatively signed.

Appendix A displays summary statistics and data visualization of our variables of interest to help one to understand the variation across our variables of interest. Specifically, we illustrate the variation in GSP utilization and workers' rights across countries over time and in 2011, the most recent year in our dataset. Further, we illustrate the variation in our variables of interest within and across chapters and sectors of the HTS, and for a few countries. Of note is the wide variation in both the utilization and the preference margin, but the stickiness in labor rights. With such a large number of countries and industries, it is difficult to see patterns in summary statistics, so after describing our independent variables, we will rely on regression analysis to better understand the relationships between our variables of interest.

The remaining variables in our specification look at country-product characteristics that are likely to shape the costs of using GSP. We draw these from Hakobyan (2015), the most recent published work on the preference margin. First, firms need to comply with the rules of origin laid out in GSP. US GSP has relatively simple local content requirements (LCRs), Specifically, the value of local materials, plus the costs of processing, must equal "at least 35 percent of the appraised value of the article at the time of entry into the United States."[32] The cost of complying with local content requirements varies across countries, industries, and firms, but the less local content added to the product in the recipient country, the more burdensome it is for firms to satisfy LCRs and the less likely the firm is to utilize GSP. We deal with much of this variation by using fixed effects. Still, unprocessed primary products easily satisfy these LCRs, and thus we include a variable called PRIMARY EXPORTS, which is a dummy variable that takes the value of 1 if the product is classified as such. At the same time, LCRs are somewhat relaxed if the value of the good has been produced regionally. To account for this easing of LCRs, we include REGIONAL CUMULATION, a dummy that equals 1 if the beneficiary country qualifies for regional cumulation within any of the six regional associations in that year.

Next, we include IMPORT VALUE, the sum of preferential imports and MFN imports of a given product that are imported to the US. Here, we account for the potential of exporters to reduce utilization if their product is close to being terminated or limited for GSP benefits due to its strong competition with US domestic production. As we note above, the US terminates or limits GSP benefits for a given product line when that product (1) accounts for more than 50 percent of the total value of US imports for that good or (2) exceeds a certain dollar value (i.e., $155 million in 2012). If an exporter is approaching those limits, they may not fully utilize GSP.

Beneficiaries who are close to "graduating" from GSP—meaning they will soon be too wealthy to qualify—may utilize the program *less* in anticipation. We account for this with the variable GRAD ELIGIBILITY, an indicator that takes the value of 1 if the country *c* is in its last year of GSP eligibility and will graduate from GSP in the next year.

Finally, and importantly, exporters that are eligible for other preferential programs with less onerous requirements may utilize these programs instead of GSP. Indeed, it is possible that these other programs, even if not as generous as GSP in terms of a preference margin, would be preferred because the overhead cost of using them is less. We thus include OTHER PROGRAM, a dummy variable equal to 1 if the product originating in the beneficiary country is eligible for an alternative trade preference program in that year.

Model specification

The utilization rate is bounded between 0 and 1 with a number of observations at extreme values, so we use a two-limit Tobit model, which imposes that constraint, to estimate our main specification:

$$y^*_{cjt} = \beta_1 Preference\ Margin + \beta_2 Worker's\ Rights + \beta_3 Preference\ Margin$$
$$* Worker's\ Rights + \beta_4 Controls + \varphi_c + \omega_j + \tau_t + \varepsilon_{cjt}$$

Where y_{cjt} is the GSP Utilization rate of product *j* imported from country *c* at time *t*. *Controls* includes all of the control variables detailed above, φ is fixed country effects, ω are fixed product effects, τ are fixed time effects, and ε is an error term. We re-estimate this equation using more standard estimation techniques including OLS, fractional logit (which models the conditional mean as a logistic function ensuring that the predicted values fall between 0 and 1), and System GMM to deal with the potential for serial correlation and endogeneity in the OLS model. Although the size of the coefficient estimates and marginal effects varies across these estimation techniques, the signs and significance levels remain relatively consistent.

Findings

Table 5.1 reports the results of the above equation estimated by Tobit, OLS, Fractional Logit and System GMM. Focusing on our preferred specification, the Tobit in Model (1), we find that, as in other research on GSP utilization, there is a positive and statistically significant relationship between Preference Margin and GSP Utilization. Surprisingly, there is no statistically significant relationship between GSP utilization and either workers' rights alone, or the interaction of Labor Rights and Preference Margin. These relationships are consistent regardless of the econometric model used and their magnitude is incredibly small. Although an increase in the Preference Margin of 1 percent is associated with a 1 percentage point increase in the Utilization Rate, a one point increase in Labor Rights is associated with only a 0.1 percentage point increase in GSP Utilization—and again, this result does not approach statistical significance.

Because there is no standard model of GSP Utilization, a key concern is whether we have modeled the relationship appropriately. For example, different authors have used different estimation techniques and (or) included different controls. To gauge whether our null result is robust to different estimation techniques and controls, we run a specification curve analysis that allows us to examine how different choices in our econometric specification would have affected our findings.[33] We run 134 models that address any potential change to the specification. We exclude country, sector. and time fixed effects individually and combined; we exclude clustered standard errors, and alternatively cluster them at the HTS-2, 4 and 6 levels; we substitute our measure of Labor Rights with other political variables, including human rights, the existence of a military

Table 5.1 Regression models of GSP utilization

	(1) *OLS*	*(2)* *Tobit*	*(3)* *Fractional Logit*	*(4)* *System GMM*
Preference Margin	0.00730*** (8.14)	0.0157*** (7.11)	0.00861*** (7.48)	0.0864* (1.77)
Worker Rights	0.000458 (0.20)	0.00160 (0.30)	0.000825 (0.33)	0.217 (1.60)
Worker Rights* Preference Margin	-0.000362 (-0.62)	-0.0000798 (-0.06)	-0.000283 (-0.40)	-0.0501 (-1.57)
Primary Exports	0.0299*** (3.87)	0.123*** (5.71)	0.0373*** (3.61)	-0.631* (-1.78)
Import Value	0.0299*** (39.24)	0.0180*** (12.31)	0.0320*** (37.59)	0.00149 (0.09)
Regional Cumulation	0.0554*** (3.78)	0.135*** (3.78)	0.0574*** (4.06)	0.0397 (0.34)
Grad. Eligibility	0.0497** (2.80)	0.0950* (2.29)	0.0508** (2.89)	-0.00182 (-0.01)
Other Program	0.291*** (5.19)	0.481*** (4.50)	0.255*** (5.14)	
Constant	-0.00445 (-0.06)			0.443 (1.27)
Observations	206845	206845	206845	462542
Country Fixed Effects	X	X	X	X
Product Fixed Effects	X	X	X	X
Time Fixed Effects	X	X	X	X

Source: Prepared by authors
t statistics in parentheses;

** $p < 0.05$, ** $p < 0.01$, *** $p < 0.001$

alliance or trade agreement with the US, economic freedom, as well as the preference similarity with the US (based on ideological voting distance in the United Nations); and last, we include a series of variables often used in gravity models of trade, including distance, income, and population. Figures 5.1–5.3 display the specification curves focused on the coefficient estimates for the PREFERENCE MARGIN, LABOR RIGHTS, and their interaction, respectively, sorted by their magnitude. The shaded bars indicate the respective confidence intervals, and the light gray diamond indicates the main estimation model for the purpose of comparison.

These curves clearly demonstrate the robustness of our results. PREFERENCE MARGIN, the main predictor of GSP utilization in past studies, is significant at the

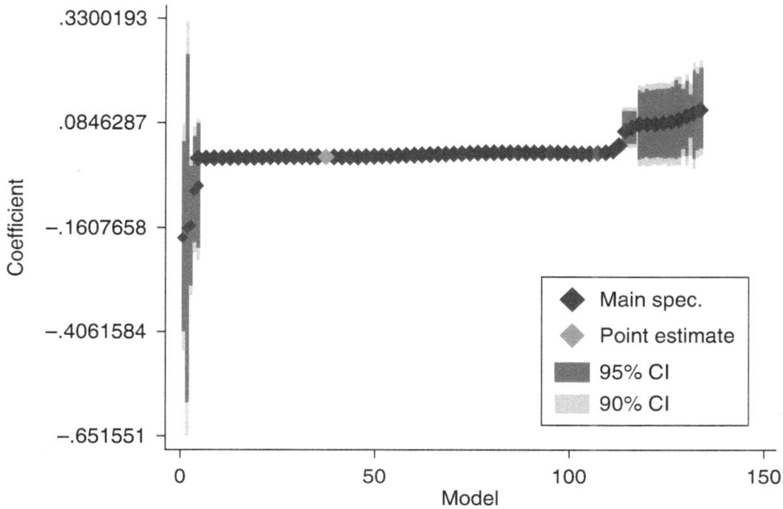

Figure 5.1: Specification curve of preference margin, dependent variable: GSP utilization.
Source: Prepared by authors

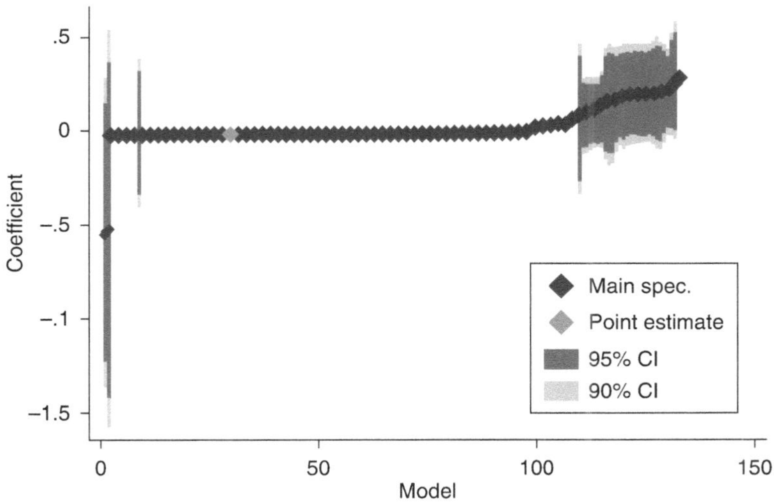

Figure 5.2: Specification curve of workers' rights, dependent variable: GSP utilization.
Source: Prepared by authors

90 percent level in 96 percent of our 134 models. This variable is only insignificant in four models, none of which include country-level fixed effects. This would be an odd choice in a model of trade flows, however, and thus we do not find it concerning. If anything, we take it as reassuring.

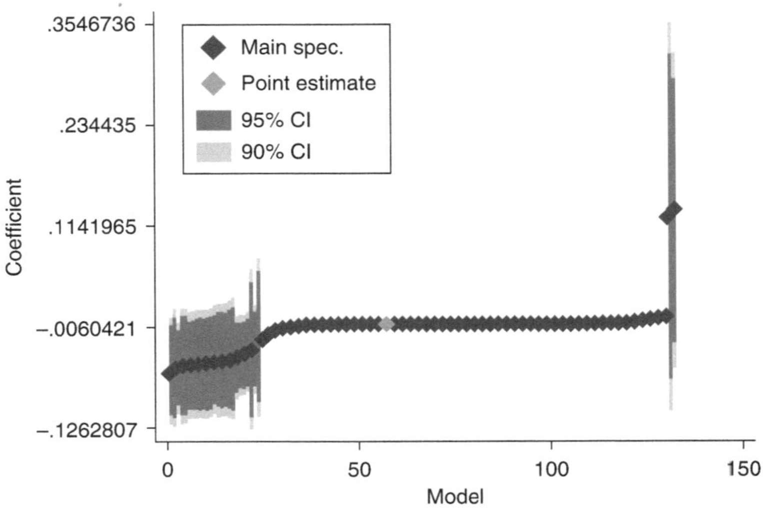

*Figure 5.3: Specification curve of Workers'Rts*PrefMargins, dependent variable: GSP utilization.*

Most critically, Labor Rights, as well as its interaction with Preference Margin, is similarly robust in terms of its *insignificance*. In fully 90 percent of our models, workers' rights are insignificant, and in 86 percent of our models, the interaction is insignificant. But as above, the models in which they are significant exclude either country or year fixed effects, which would be an unusual modeling choice in this case. We thus find these results reassuring as well.

Implications

Our null result defies the conventional wisdom that GSP has a positive influence on workers' rights in recipient countries. Labor standards, alone and interacted with the preference margin, and scrutinized from every possible angle, appear to shed no light on the demand for GSP.

Ours is not the only study to find this. In their supply-side account, Hafner-Burton, Mosley and Galantucci also find no evidence that labor standards explain GSP suspensions at the country-product level.[34] They explain that suspensions reflect yet another layer of US politics, making it more difficult to find confirming evidence. Our approach, which builds on the premise that exporters price in the risk of being suspended over labor standards, lets us hone in on exporters' responsiveness to different margins. And yet, like them, we end up with a null result.

What should we make of this null result? We submit that the link between GSP and labor standards is too *indirect*. There are many factors at the country-product-year level to model, and the literature has no doubt that the margin is the most important one. But labor standards are not measured at the country-product-year. At the country level, data on labor standards do not exhibit much year-on-year variation. This presents empirical challenges, and in our case leads us to run countless robustness checks. But it is also a problem for the exporters that are the subject of our study. The problem is that there is not much that these exporters can do about national labor standards writ large. To change labor standards, GSP needs to incentivize industry-level compliance, and needs to do this by offering audit methodologies that reward good behavior by an exporter's supply chain.

This type of industry-level audit is more consistent with the requirements of Section 307 of the US Tariff Act of 1930, which prohibits the importation of any good produced with forced labor, but there is still a long way to go. Petitions under Section 307, like those under GSP, point to data at the country level, rather than the industry- or firm-level. This is not helpful, as it means there is little that specific exporters and industries might do to demonstrate their compliance. To positively influence labor standards, a renewed GSP should focus attention on supply chains, not countries. The EU is moving in this direction with their recent proposal for a regulation prohibiting products made with forced labor from entering the Union market.[35] This regulation will make firms accountable for their supply chains—at least in terms of forced labor. Getting this right for the US will be even more important in the future, as GSP's margin continues to fall against the US MFN (and even non-MFN) tariffs. Our results point to an important conclusion for policy: the current design of GSP will not lead to improved workers' rights. It may simply be beyond the purview of a single exporter to influence their country's labor standards. And thus, without changing GSP to reward exporters for improving their individual rights, one of the main objectives of GSP—improved workers' rights—may be out of reach.

Notes

1 Butler, Saran and Thaslima Begum. "Abuses still rife: 10 years on from Bangladesh's Rana Plaza disaster." *The Guardian,* 24 April 2023.
2 Siddiqui and Uddin (2016) and Bossavie et al. (2019).
3 To use the GSP preference (as opposed to other preferences or the simple MFN tariff rate) importers must use the GSP's SPI code in their importation documentation in addition to having a host of documents prepared to support the claim. As we document below, this is not a simple process. For more information, see the USTR's GSP guidebook: https://ustr.gov/issue-areas/trade-development/preference-programs/generalized-system-preferences-gsp/gsp-program-i-0
4 See, for example Hoekman et al. (2008).
5 Tobin and Busch 2019.
6 H.R. 3975 "Generalized System of Preferences and Miscellaneous Tariff Bill Modernization Act of 2021," (117th Congress, 1st Session), p. 37.
7 Tobin and Busch 2019.
8 Mason (2004).
9 19 US Code § 2462(c)(7).
10 The years refer to the starting year of the suspension. Suspensions can last from a few months to an indefinite suspension.
11 As of the time of this writing, US GSP has still not been reauthorized.
12 HR 3975, "Generalized System of Preferences and Miscellaneous Tariff Bill Modernization Act of 2021," (117th Congress, 1st Session), p. 37.

13 HR 3975, "Generalized System of Preferences and Miscellaneous Tariff Bill Modernization Act of 2021," p. 42.
14 "Bangladesh to Reform Labour Laws to Retain Trade Benefits." Just-Style October 28, 2020.
15 "Cambodia: EU Partially Suspends Trade Preferences." Human Rights Watch February 13, 2020.
16 European Commission, "Joint Report to the European Parliament and the Council: Report on the Generalized Scheme of Preferences Covering the Period 2018-2019" (JOIN(2020) 3 final), p. 8.
17 "US Cuts to Thailand's Free-Trade Benefits Take Effect." Voice of America April 25, 2020.
18 Congressional Research Service, "Generalized System of Preferences (GS): Overview and Issues for Congress (2021)," p. 30.
19 Tsogas (2000).
20 WTO Document WT/GC/W/377. Emphasis added.
21 WTO Document WT/GC/W/123, 4. Emphasis added.
22 WTO Document WT/DS246/AB/R, paragraph 173. Emphasis added.
23 Congressional Research Service, "US-Mexico Economic Relations: Trends, Issues, and Implications" (Washington, DC: CRS, 2020).
24 Letter from Neil L. Bradley, Executive Vice President, Chief Policy Office and Head of Strategic Advocacy, US Chamber of Commerce, to Members of the House Committee on Ways and Means, December 1, 2021.
25 Congressional Research Service, "Generalized System of Preferences" (Washington, DC: CRS, 2002), p. 6; Congressional Research Service, "Generalized System of Preferences: Background and Renewal Debate" (Washington, DC: CRS, 2008), p. 24.
26 Keck and Lendle (2012).
27 Hoekman et al. (2008).
28 Alexandraki and Lankes (2004).
29 For 1997–2011, the USITC provides country and product eligibility for both GSP and GSP+. However, for 1989–1996, the USITC neither provides GSP+ eligibility nor disaggregates GSP imports into GSP and GSP+. This is a substantial limitation of the pre-1997 data; articles from numerous states may have been ineligible for GSP+ treatment during that period, but our analysis would treat their lack of GSP exports as a failure to use GSP. Thus, our primary results reflect the data available from 1997–2011.
30 GSP+ is a supplemental program that allows for duty-free import of additional products from least-developed countries. From here on we use GSP to refer to both GSP and GSP+.
31 Cingranelli, Richards, and Clay 2014.
32 USTR 2015.
33 Simonsohn et al. 2015, 2020.
34 Hafner-Burton et al. 2019.
35 Proposal for a REGULATION OF THE EUROPEAN PARLIAMENT AND OF THE COUNCIL on prohibiting products made with forced labour on the Union market - Publications Office of the EU (europa.eu)

REFERENCES

Alexandraki, Katerina, and Hans Peter Lankes. "The Impact of Preference Erosionon Middle-Income Developing Countries." *IMF Working Papers* 2004.169 (2004).

Bossavie, Laurent, Yoonyoung Cho, and Rachel Heath. "The Effects of International Scrutiny on Manufacturing Workers: Evidence from the Rana Plaza Collapse in Bangladesh." *World Bank Policy Research Working Paper* 9065 (2019).

Cingranelli, David L., David L. Richards, and K. Chad Clay. "The CIRI Human Rights Dataset." (2014). Available at: https://dataverse.harvard.edu/dataset.xhtml?persistentId=doi:10.7910/DVN/UKCPX

Hafner-Burton, Emilie M., Layna Mosley, and Robert Galantucci. "Protecting Workers Abroad and Industries at Home: Rights-Based Conditionality in Trade Preference Programs." *Journal of Conflict Resolution* 63.5 (2019): 1253–1282.

Hakobyan, Shushanik. "Accounting for Underutilization of Trade Preference Programs: The US Generalized System of Preferences." *Canadian Journal of Economics/Revue anadienne d'économique* 48.2 (2015): 408–436.

Hoekman, B., M. William, and P. Braga. "Quantifying the Value of Preferences and Potential Erosion Losses.–Ch. 1." *Trade Preferences Erosion Measurement and Policy Responses*. The World Bank (2008).

Keck, Alexander, and Andreas Lendle. "New Evidence on Preference Utilization." World Trade Organization Staff Working Paper No. ERSD-2012-12 (2012).

Mason, Amy M. "The Degeneralization of the Generalized System of Preferences (GSP): Questioning the Legitimacy of the US GSP." *Duke Law Journal* 54.2 (2004): 513–547.

Siddiqui, Javed, and Shahzad Uddin. "Human Rights Disasters, Corporate Accountability and the State: Lessons Learned from Rana Plaza." *Accounting, Auditing & Accountability Journal* 29.4 (2016): 679–704.

Simonsohn, Uri, Joseph P. Simmons, and Leif D. Nelson. "Better P-curves: Making P-Curve Analysis More Robust to Errors, Fraud, and Ambitious P-hacking, a Reply to Ulrich and Miller (2015)." *Journal of Experimental Psychology*: General 144.6 (2015): 1146–1152.

Simonsohn, U., J. P. Simmons, and L. D. Nelson. "Specification Curve Analysis." *Nature Human Behaviour* 4.11 (2020): 1208–1214.

Tobin, Jennifer L., and Marc L. Busch. "The Disadvantage of Membership: How Joining the GATT/WTO Undermines GSP." *World Trade Review* 18.1 (2019): 133–160.

Tsogas, George. "Labour Standards in the Generalized Systems of Preferences of the European Union and the United States." *European Journal of Industrial Relations* 6.3 (2000): 349–370.

USTR. U.S. Generalized System of Preferences Guidebook. Office of the United States Trade Representative Executive Office of the President, Washington, DC (2015).

6 The mandate trilemma

Central banking in an era of credit crises

Stephen B. Kaplan

During a late summer September day in 1920, a horse-drawn cart unexpectedly screeched to a halt on the corner of Wall and Broad streets in front of J.P. Morgan's four-story financial citadel. Within minutes, the wagon exploded, bombarding the block with metal projectiles and slaying more than 30 innocent bystanders. From Italian anarchists and communist sympathizers to attempted J.P Morgan Jr. assassins, there was no shortage of theories about the potential perpetrators of the catastrophic Wall Street bombing of 1920.[1] Notwithstanding two decades of FBI investigations, the case was eventually closed in 1940 and remains one of the bureau's biggest unsolved mysteries today.

Nearly a century later, a different eruption again shook Wall Street's architecture, and killed America's economy, but the crime was also left unresolved despite a lengthy list of culprits.[2] In the search for who was to blame for the 2008 global financial crisis, the lineup of institutional suspects ranged from mortgage brokers, investment banks and investors to credit rating agencies, regulators, and deregulating ideologues from across the political spectrum.[3] In terms of national regulators, one of the major post-crisis debates involved the U.S. Federal Reserve, and whether its prolonged period of low interest rates fed the financial frenzy. In the prelude to the 2008 crisis, the Federal Reserve had mainly kept interest rates low to offset lackluster U.S. demand following the Dotcom bubble-burst. However, low interest rates had also steadily become vital to the health of U.S. household finances. After the U.S. government, bankers, and regulators had all encouraged people to use cheap credit – and variable-rate mortgages – to help offset stagnating real incomes in the early 2000s, the health of America's household balance sheets had become dependent on low interest rates. In other words, it was becoming more difficult for economic officials to disentangle the soundness of the U.S. financial sector from the health of the U.S. economy.

Full employment – or attaining the maximum level of economic output – without price inflation was the key priority of the Federal Reserve's dual-mandate mission. However, domestic financial stability had implicitly crept into its institutional mandate, becoming a third informal target. Why? A shift away from the low interest rate environment of the early 2000s threatened to kill not only the financial bubble, but also the U.S. economy. Cheap credit was central to padding languishing household incomes. But the government had also channeled its low-cost funds unproductively. From investing in an inflated housing sector and regressively

DOI: 10.4324/9781003416234-7

cutting income taxes to funding oil-gouging wars in Afghanistan and Iraq, the American economy had become a paper tiger. Fearing the economic turmoil that could follow from piercing the financial bubble, central bankers balked at hiking interest rates. However, they had other regulatory tools, such as more prudent financial supervision (e.g. reducing maximum loan-to-value ratios or increasing capital-to-asset ratios) that could have dampened the bubble.[4] Counterfactually, it's unclear whether or not such financial regulation would have averted the crisis, but such actions were likely superior to employing the single tool of monetary policy to accomplish three different policy goals simultaneously: maximum employment, low inflation, and financial stability.

In this chapter, I develop a new theory about the Fed's mandate trilemma, suggesting the central bank's financial stability goals have complicated its ability to meet its dual mandate of full employment and price stability. By stretching its monetary policy operations to achieve three goals simultaneously, the Fed has created an impossible trilemma. To achieve financial stability and full employment, it tends to maintain easy credit conditions for longer than optimal, making eventual inflationary pressures more likely. The Fed is essentially sowing the seeds for greater volatility in the economy by amplifying swings from deflation to inflation.

To better understand these policy tensions and the Fed's monetary quandary, the chapter begins by developing two key concepts – the Phillips-curve trade-off and the history of the central bank dual mandate – before outlining the main theoretical framework. To examine these theoretical priors, I conduct a plausibility probe of the *mandate trilemma* by employing the case of the 2023 Silicon Valley Bank collapse. I find that the Fed's recent inflation-target overshoot reflected post-COVID credit concerns that translated into sustained quantitative easing measures, or excess monetary stimulus, that eventually sowed the seeds for financial and price volatility. Counterfactually, I argue if the Fed had instead relied more heavily on its banking supervision and financial regulatory power to provide financial stability, it could have more readily used monetary policy to hike interest rates after the pandemic and pre-empted price inflation.

Clarifying the concepts: the roots of the mandate trilemma

In the wake of the global financial crisis, Federal Reserve Board Governor Ben Bernanke announced the adoption of a 2 percent inflation target in January 2012. The choice seemingly reflected a pronounced shift toward inflation control within the long-standing debate about the primary aim of U.S. monetary policymaking: full employment versus price stability. Against this backdrop, however, the Obama administration emphasized the importance of the Fed's dual mandate, and, in particular, using monetary policy tools to ensure full employment.

The epic intellectual battle of 20th-century macroeconomics – Keynesianism and Monetarism – continued to dominate the field of macroeconomic policymaking in the 21st century. Historically, the debate between these two strains of intellectual thought had centered on a disagreement about the effectiveness of fiscal policy, specifically whether economic officials could successfully navigate a perceived unemployment-inflation trade-off, known as the Phillips-curve trade-off.[5]

Following 2010's post-crisis fiscal consolidation; however, policymakers had less scope politically to use fiscal policy to stimulate the economy. The crux of the intellectual debate spilled into the realm of central bank mandates, as monetary policy returned to being the primary macroeconomic tool in the U.S economy. To address the increased saliency of economic dislocations and job losses among voters, politicians increasingly turned to the central bank and its full-employment mandate. Before exploring the historic underpinnings of both the full employment and price stability elements of the dual mandate, let us first turn our attention to understanding the Phillips-curve trade-off.

The inflation-unemployment trade-off

In the halcyon days of the mid 20th century, these two governance approaches offered competing accounts of the effectiveness of government intervention. Keynesianism was more optimistic about policymakers' ability to exploit the Phillips-Curve trade-off, using economic policy to permanently create new jobs and growth. When facing an economic slump, Keynesianism held that the government could use expansionary monetary and fiscal policies to offset the adverse effects of an economic downturn. Creating new capacity and adding new jobs was expected to spur inflation, but only at very low levels of unemployment. Why? Wages and prices were deemed to be sticky. Workers might ask for higher pay, but these appeals were more likely when there was a booming economy and high demand for labor.[6]

By contrast, monetarism contended that inflation was a harmful by-product of expansionary economic policy. Championed by Milton Friedman, monetarism was first in vogue in the 1960s–1970s. It offered an explanation for the 1970s' puzzling rise of both inflation and unemployment. In response to economic stimulus, people adjusted their inflation expectations higher. Workers demanded better wages, and firms raised their prices. Inflation thus accelerated, undercutting any initial gains from the stimulus. In this regard, monetarists have claimed that there is a natural rate of unemployment, beyond which any attempts to spur economic activity only yield further inflation.[7] According to monetarism, the 1973 and 1979 oil shocks not only delivered a serious blow to economic growth, but also jolted inflation expectations considerably higher.[8] Lofty price expectations intensified the original shocks and dampened the benefits of expansionary policy. Hence, monetarists claimed the Phillips-Curve was vertical in the long run, rendering the effects of government stimulus ineffective beyond fueling further inflation.

Contemporary macroeconomics has sought to bridge the gap between these two schools of thought, with 'the neoclassical synthesis' advocating for economic governance to be principally conducted through an independent central bank that uses monetary policy to control inflation. At the turn of the 20th century, some scholars claimed that the *Great Moderation* – a period known for its sustained economic expansion, low inflation, and minimal economic volatility over two decades (mid 1980s to 2007) – reflected these improvements in monetary policy.[9] During this time, most mainstream economists had agreed on the importance of an autonomous central bank to insulate the economy from short-term partisan politics, finding that independent central banks are associated with greater price stability.[10]

The 2008–09 financial crisis provided a departure, albeit brief, from the neoclassical synthesis. The Bush and Obama administrations both subscribed to a traditional Keynesian view of the economy, hoping that a sizable fiscal stimulus would cushion the economic shock. Indeed, packaged in small government rhetoric, the turn-of-the-21st-century political economy was often characterized by budgetary cutbacks and diminished public goods.[11] When economic crises struck, however, public goods quickly became 'en vogue' once again. Ironically, during the *Great Moderation* decades, crises had often catalyzed heightened expectations of national government responsiveness.[12] For example, during the 2008 financial crisis, Federal Reserve Chairman Ben Bernanke promised to "do whatever was necessary," while newly-elected President Obama reiterated the central bank's message, saying "we have to do whatever it takes to get this economy moving again… [W]e shouldn't worry about the deficit next year or even the year after that… .[T]he most important thing is that we avoid a deepening recession."[13]

Following the initial countercyclical fiscal response to the 2008–09 crisis, however, the nation's *Imagine Dragon* brand of crisis politics quickly returned to its pre-crisis equilibrium. Departing from "Whatever It Takes" big government spending, the 'break me down, and build me up' cycle of fiscal policy once again dissipated. After tinkering with conventional Keynesian policy, politicians brought the central bank back to the center of managing the economy. The Keynesian consensus unraveled in the wake of the U.S. financial crisis as it spread to European nations, where there was greater technocratic support for fiscal consolidation.[14] With traditional Keynesianism fading from the policy picture, the contours of the economic ideological battle shifted back to the Federal Reserve, and its approach to central banking, specifically the utility of its dual institutional mandate. In the following pages, we'll define the Fed's dual mandate and delve into its politicization, before exploring how a mission-creeping third mandate of financial stability steadily eroded the Fed's technocratic capacity.

The Fed's dual-mandate history

Under the Federal Reserve Act of 1913 – signed by President Woodrow Wilson – the current Federal Reserve System was created with the aim of preventing future financial crises, following a series of financial panics and bank failures at the turn of the 19th century. Today, the Fed's most important task is governing monetary policy, which was formally codified under the Federal Reserve Reform Act of 1977, with the dual mandate of "promoting maximum employment" and "stable prices."[15] Formally, the Federal Reserve considers these two objectives of controlling inflation and unemployment as 'complementary,' taking a 'balanced approach' to its monetary policy governance.[16] Informally, however, the dual mandate has at times catalyzed public criticism over how the Fed should implement these two potentially competing objectives.

In the wake of the 2008 financial crisis, the Fed's performance in achieving its dual mandate was subject to considerable scrutiny, opening the door to such proposed governance reforms as a single mandate, or inflation-targeting. The incumbent Obama administration was in favor of maintaining the Fed's dual mandate, particularly in light of high unemployment, but it met growing political opposition. Notwithstanding the political saliency of high unemployment, the administration's renewed emphasis on the Fed's dual mandate ran counter to recent central banking practice.

Prior to the crisis, the Fed had operationally emphasized its credibility as an inflation fighter. For example, Fed officials rarely referenced the dual mandate, often communicating that "price stability was the surest way for monetary policy to keep unemployment down."[17] In the Fed's transcripts of its policy discussions, scholars find that the Federal Open Market Committee (FOMC)[18] increasingly emphasized inflation relative to unemployment between 1960 and 2010[19] – notwithstanding the Humphrey- Hawkins' Act of 1978's reiteration of the dual mandate.[20]

The lack of economic volatility during the *Great Moderation* had enabled an interpretation of the Fed's dual mandate that prioritized inflation control. In fact, the sustained economic expansion from the mid 1980s to 2007 had facilitated a temporary consensus about the Fed's operational mandate. Traditionally, the political economy scholarship had found that partisan incumbents differed in their economic policy goals. Republicans had tended to emphasize inflation control, while Democrats targeted low unemployment.[21] With unemployment averaging 5.5 percent in the two decades prior to the financial crisis, which was well below its 1982 peak of 11 percent, the Fed could prioritize price stability without much of a political cost. However, the unemployment shock (see Figure 6.1) stemming from the *Great Recession* (2007–09) heightened the saliency of unemployment

Figure 6.1 The great recession catalyzes unemployment saliency.

Source: U.S. Bureau of Labor Statistics, Unemployment Rate [UNRATE], retrieved from FRED, Federal Reserve Bank of St. Louis; https://fred.stlouisfed.org/series/UNRATE, September 28, 2023. In public domain

politically, reigniting debates about the Fed's dual mandate, and monetary policy more broadly.

As discussed above, on the heels of the 2008 financial crisis, policymakers maintained a partisan consensus in their Keynesian response to the crisis to help contain the economic shock. Initially, both the Bush and Obama administrations enacted fiscal stimulus measures to offset the economic downturn, which widened the U.S. fiscal deficit from 1.1 percent in 2007 to a whopping 9.8 percent by the end of 2009. The Fed reinforced this Keynesian response in the fiscal realm with extensive monetary stimulus, emphasizing its efforts to immediately counter rising unemployment in an environment of moderating inflation. Following its September 2008 meeting, the Fed also began to increasingly link the fate of labor and financial markets together, saying that "strains in financial markets have increased significantly and labor markets have weakened further… Over time, the substantial easing of monetary policy, combined with ongoing measures to foster market liquidity, should help promote moderate economic growth."[22]

Historically, Keynesians had been willing to use macroeconomic policy tools, including fiscal stimulus, to trade low unemployment for higher long-term inflation. However, beginning with the 1980s' neoclassical synthesis, Keynesians converged with Monetarists intellectually in supporting the legitimacy of central bankers as the main governors of the economy. During the *Great Moderation*, this meant targeting low inflation with monetary policy and containing budget deficits.

The unemployment shock created a political window in favor of Keynesianism, but it was short-lived as the policymaking consensus began to unravel in the period of fiscal consolidation that followed the *Great Recession*.[23] With real GDP growth averaging 2.2 percent between 2010 and 2015 – well below the U.S. long-term growth trend of about 3 percent – there was scope for greater fiscal stimulus economically, but not politically. Over the course of the next half-decade, the budget deficit steadily narrowed, reaching 2.4 percent by 2015 – in large part due to higher tax receipts from the economic recovery. That said, to some extent this pattern also reflected the emergence of the powerful fiscally conservative Tea Party within the Republican Party. After winning a sizable majority in the House of Representatives during the 2010 midterm elections, the Tea Party demanded sizable spending cuts from the Obama administration.

In an environment of post-crisis fiscal consolidation, traditional partisan debates about economic policy, such as growth versus inclusiveness, resurfaced in the monetary realm. The lack of fiscal space following the 2008–09 crisis meant partisan agendas increasingly focused on the Federal Reserve. Fiscal consolidation shrunk the budgetary power of politicians, who then shifted to other policy making forums to achieve their goals. With the central bank at the helm of the economy, the Fed's dual-mandate increasingly became a target of legislative and political battles.

Against this backdrop, the long-standing ideological debate between Keynesianism and Monetarism now centered on mandate politics. Keynesians supported using monetary policy to toggle between both the Fed's price stability and full-employment objectives, with the aim of stimulating near-term employment. By comparison, Monetarists were traditionally skeptical of fiscal stimulus, and hence, equally skeptical about the ability of monetary stimulus to control inflation and unemployment simultaneously. They instead believed that inflation control was the only viable pathway to ensuring sustainable growth and employment.

With unemployment at the center of the mandate debate, Congressional Republicans took their cue from Monetarists, and advocated for legislation to repeal the Fed's dual mandate in 2011.[24] Fretting about the Fed's extraordinary actions during the crisis, they thought that quantitative easing[25] – or the Fed's massive monetary stimulus to offset the economic shock – would undermine public faith in its inflation-fighting credentials. For example, the central bank more than quadrupled the size of its balance sheet over a half-decade – reaching US$4.5 trillion (25 percent of GDP) by the mid 2010's compared to US$850 billion (6 percent of GDP) prior to the crisis – catalyzing concerns about an overheating economy, and future price volatility (see Figure 6.2 below). Republican Congressman Kevin Brady, the Vice Chairman of the Joint Economic Commission, hoped to eliminate the Fed's dual mandate, claiming that "history proves the best way to maximize employment is to focus on achieving long-term price stability."[26] In other words, a single inflation-fighting mandate was optimal because otherwise "too many goals blur responsibility and accountability," as noted by John B. Taylor, a monetary economist and former U.S. Treasury official under the George H. Bush administration.[27]

By contrast, President Barak Obama nominated labor economist and former FOMC vice chair Janet Yellen as Federal Reserve Board Governor in 2014, with the charge of fulfilling both mandates.[28] In fact, Yellen viewed the unemployment rate (which was 7 percent at the end of 2013) as still too high at the time (see Figure 6.1), and advocated for "the mandate for the Federal Reserve to serve all the American people" saying "too many Americans still can't find a job and worry how they'll pay their bills and provide for their families."[29] Yellen took

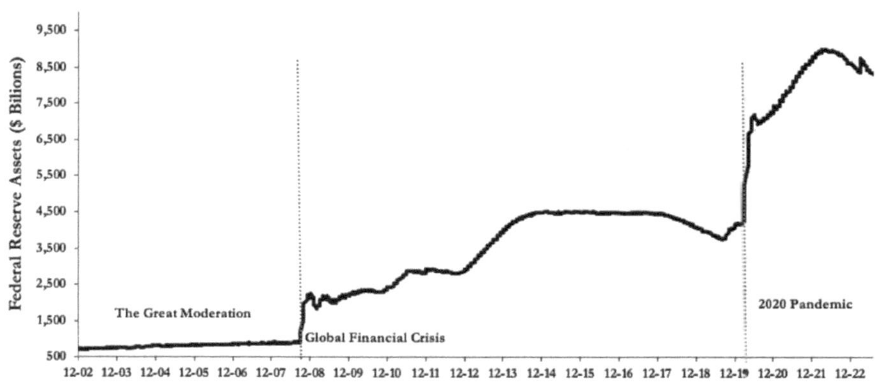

Figure 6.2 Quantitative easing expands the Fed's balance sheet.

Source: Board of Governors of the Federal Reserve System (US), Assets: Total Assets: Total Assets (Less Eliminations from Consolidation): Wednesday Level [WALCL], retrieved from FRED, Federal Reserve Bank of St. Louis; https://fred.stlouisfed.org/series/WALCL, September 28, 2023. In public domain.

a clear Keynesian approach to her interpretation of the mandate both as central bank governor, and later on in her career as U.S. Treasury Secretary. For example, she advocated for aggressive public spending in the wake of the COVID pandemic.

Against the backdrop of such shocks today, Congress has been reluctant to eliminate the Fed's statutory focus on full employment,[30] or its dual-mandate goal. However, despite the ongoing debate about the contours of the Fed's monetary policy, a third informal mandate has crept into its monetary operations over the course of the last two decades. As the global economy became more deeply securitized during the 1990s, the Fed began to increasingly use monetary policy to ensure the soundness of a growing financial economy. But, as Jan Tinbergen, the Nobel-Prize winning Dutch economist, stated: "The number of achievable policy goals cannot exceed the number of policy instruments."[31]

Theoretical framework: Financial stability blurs the dual-mandate mission

Following the 2008–09 financial crisis, the Federal Reserve has increasingly played a larger role in maintaining financial system stability. Compared to the limited government intervention that defined the last few decades of the *Great Moderation*, U.S. economic policymakers shifted to a Keynesian stance during the 2008 crisis largely because of their concerns about systemic risk. From March to September 2008, the collapse of Bear Stearns, AIG, and Lehman Brothers had triggered severe financial instability. Fearing a potential system-wide financial collapse, U.S. policymakers orchestrated rescue packages for Bear Stearns and AIG, and recapitalized major banking institutions, such as Bank of America, Citibank, and J.P. Morgan. Notwithstanding moral hazard concerns associated with bailing-out these institutions, economic officials thought the prevailing risk of financial collapse was too high. Banking institutions, such as AIG and Merrill Lynch, confirmed the worst of these moral hazard concerns by awarding bank managers billion-dollar bonuses, rather than realizing their losses or firing bank officials.

Against this fiscal backdrop, it was not only the national government that was exposed to moral hazard risk, but also the Federal Reserve. The central bank injected massive liquidity into the financial system by expanding its balance sheet to reduce the cost of capital and improve credit availability for households and businesses. These policy actions went beyond the central bank's typical money-market operations that were aimed at influencing short-term interest rates. They included quantitative easing, or the Fed's more than $4 trillion in purchases of long-term bonds aimed at reducing long-term interest rates by improving the flow of credit in the broader economy.[32] Quantitative easing was an effective policy tool at signaling the Fed's dedication to stimulating growth and jobs during the crisis, but also risked igniting inflation, fomenting asset bubbles, and ultimately undermining the central bank's accountability. These operations had ballooned the Fed's balance sheet, which had remarkably reached a post-pandemic pinnacle that was ten times the magnitude of its pre-crisis levels in 2007 (see Figure 6.2).

In a 2020 speech at the American Economic Association, former Fed Chairman Bernanke advocated for maintaining quantitative easing permanently in the Fed's toolkit as a recession-fighting instrument. Bernanke argued that low inflation inhibits the Fed from adequately targeting full unemployment because it contributes to low interest rates, which reduces the scope for conventional rate cuts.[33] By adding quantitative easing to the monetary policy arsenal, the new tool can ease financial conditions and stimulate the economy in such low-rate environments. According to Bernanke, "policymakers confronted with extraordinary circumstances must be prepared to think outside the box, defying orthodoxy if necessary."[34]

Chairman Bernanke's argument is sound technocratically, but underweights the importance of financial power. In other words, Bernanke suggests that quantitative easing works in part by "signaling policymakers' intentions to keep short rates low for an extended period."[35] Beyond the intended economic stimulus, however, I argue that 'defying the orthodoxy' sends another signal to financial institutions and market participants: *financial capital is, and will, remain cheap*! The Gordon Geckos and other Wall Street titans of the world who believe that 'greed is good' thus interpret such Fed actions as underwriting financial opportunities.

Given the important role that quantitative easing had in averting the credit crunch, its permanent existence in the monetary toolkit creates an implicit interest rate ceiling. Bankers and investors begin to expect that the Fed will "do whatever is necessary"[36] during a crisis to support systematically important banking institutions, sowing the seeds for a moral hazard problem. Why should banks constrain their financial margins or balance sheets today, if they know that the Fed stands ready to expand its balance sheet tomorrow in the name of financial stability? When such an implicit financial stability mandates creeps into monetary policymaking, it intensifies the tensions between the Fed's other formal mandates. In a Phillips-curve twist of Bernanke's original logic, financial stability concerns inhibit the Fed from adequately targeting inflation because they reduce the scope for traditional rate hikes. Low interest rates become necessary to contain the financial fallout from economic adjustment, and preserve the powerful financial status quo.

Financial stability and the law: Who's in charge?

The legal ambiguity underpinning financial stability governance further blurs the contours of the Fed dual mandate. According to U.S. law, financial stability does not fall under the purview of any single agency. That said, the Federal Reserve publicly acknowledges its role in promoting financial stability in concert with several other regulators.[37] For example, according to the Federal Reserve's website, among the Board of Governors' primary functions is to "promote the stability of the U.S. financial system" and "monitor financial system risks" to support "a healthy economy for U.S. households, communities, and businesses."[38]

Notwithstanding such informal precedence, financial stability is a challenging goal for monetary policy. It is difficult to define and measure compared to full employment or price stability. It does not have a single, quantifiable objective or metric of success. Perhaps, most importantly, financial stability decisions can involve questions about bankruptcy and bank management, which are inherently more political than monetary policy decisions.[39] For this reason, outside of the Federal Reserve and the Bank of England, most developed countries tend to have financial supervisory authorities that are independent from central banks.[40] Even when there is no autonomous supervisory authority, monetary policy has often been separated institutionally from banking supervisory functions.

Of course, a perfect separation between monetary and financial stability policies is not feasible because of their overlapping policymaking channels. Credit conditions may affect the transmission mechanism for monetary policy, and even disrupt the effectiveness of interest rates on the broader economy. For example, near-zero interest rates had little effect on banks' willingness to lend to clients when they fretted that their counterparties might default during the 2008 financial crisis. Within their monetary policy analysis, it is thus not unusual for central banks to identify long-term economic risks stemming from potential financial instability.

In many countries, central banks may even act as lenders of last resort,[41] but such financial roles are typically considered to be subordinate to monetary policy. For example, the Federal Reserve has a discount window – often used to lend to distressed financial institutions during crises. However, its role of providing funds to a few distressed banking institutions is secondary to open market operations. Most developed country central banks – with the exception of the European Central Bank (ECB), which is not a formal lender-of-last resort, have kept such financial stability lending 'subservient' to monetary policy.[42] Why? Monetary policy is centered on open market operations – or the buying and selling of U.S. Treasury securities to broadly influence market interest rates – which is distinct from financial stability policy that typically employs such instruments as supervision, regulation, and even lender-of-last resort policies.

The financial authorities were able to historically separate these two policy tools because the role of a lender-of-last resort had not changed much until recently. In 19th-century England, financial authorities first provided liquidity to the banking system when "no other lender [was] either capable of lending or willing to lend in sufficient volume to prevent or end a financial panic."[43] However, such historical cases of economic intervention had been limited to relatively rare financial crises. For example, as recently as 1968, a Federal Reserve report outlined that "it would be most unusual for the failure of a single institution or small group of institutions to have such significant repercussions as to justify Federal Reserve action."[44]

The mandate trilemma

In light of today's increased financial complexity and crisis frequency, however, individually distressed banks are more likely to pose a systemic risk to the entire financial sector than historically. The temptation for central bank authorities has been to increasingly use monetary policy (or open market operations) to affect broader credit conditions, given that the discount window was historically limited to containing the fallout from less systematically important entities. Increasingly, the Fed has even coordinated emergency lending to non-bank institutions that pose a systemic risk, including broker-dealers after the 1987 stock market crash, hedge funds during the Long-Term Capital Management (LTCM) crisis, and investment banks during the 2008 financial crisis.

Most recently, the Fed has used its balance sheet not only to provide greater monetary stimulus to catalyze jobs and growth during downturns, but also to extend liquidity to non-bank institutions using riskier instruments (e.g. mortgage-backed securities). The Fed's open market operations and lender-of-last-resort functions have thus increasingly blurred together over time to meet both its dual-mandate and financial stability goals. It even created a new policy tool, quantitative easing, to stimulate the economy when there are concurrent concerns about a liquidity trap, which happens when financial actors funnel their money in longer-term assets rather than broader lending.

To stimulate new lending, the Fed uses quantitative easing, or outright purchases of Treasury and mortgage-backed securities. Compared to the Fed's open market operations in short-term money markets which are meant to affect long-term interest rates through a transmission mechanism, quantitative easing is instead designed to ease long-term interest rates directly. In November 2008, the Federal Reserve announced the beginning of its quantitative easing policy, saying that its actions were intended "to reduce the cost and increase the availability of credit' and 'foster improved conditions in financial markets."[45] But, compared to the quantifiable targets of full employment and policy stability, how does the Fed measure such financial stability? What are the goals of its quantitative easing? Safeguarding system resiliency? Ensuring the steady flow of credit? Minimizing financial shocks?

Fed officials have often argued that quantitative easing is intended to ease credit conditions with the goal of stimulating the economy, and reaching 'maximum,' or full employment. To this end, scholars have found that quantitative easing tends to push long-term interest rates lower than otherwise projected without such unconventional measures (and under similar economic conditions).[46] Despite having such a measurable effect on interest rates, the key question is how market participants interpret such actions, given their role as financial intermediaries in the economy.

On the one hand, the Fed's extraordinary effort to ease credit conditions might prompt market participants to adjust their expectations for economic activity higher, as intended. However, they may also instead interpret quantitative easing as a sign the Fed will act unconventionally to curtail further financial turmoil, stoking market expectations of further financial rescues. Without such rescue expectations, the Fed's mandate ambiguity might not be as problematic. Given the Fed's recent history of unconventional actions during financial crises, however, it would be surprising if financial markets placed a non-zero probability on such rescues.

Against this backdrop, the legal ambiguity about the Fed's financial stability mission can thus create information asymmetries between central bank officials and economic actors, fomenting market misperceptions. One of the most salient episodes of the Fed promoting financial stability was during the aforementioned 1987 stock market crash. Known as the 'Greenspan put,' the Fed's willingness to supply accommodative monetary policy during the crisis meant investors were insured against downside risk. In other words, Fed stabilization policies had created market expectations of an asset price floor.[47]

Of course, the 'Greenspan put' is eerily similar to Bernanke's quantitative easing during the 2008 crisis. It was also aimed at supplying crisis liquidity, but arguably was interpreted by investors as buoying Treasury markets and ultimately providing an interest rate ceiling. Under such credit conditions, the Fed's financial stability focus creates a *mandate trilemma* where markets perceive that the Fed is less willing to tighten monetary policy to stave off inflationary pressures. An implicit financial stability mandate is thus at odds with an explicit price stability mandate, complicating the Fed's ability to reach full employment without overheating the economy.

In summary, U.S. monetary policymaking has often reflected a long-standing ideological debate about the existence of an unemployment-inflation trade-off. Keynesian thinkers are generally optimistic about fiscal policy's ability to stimulate the economy, without catalyzing near-term inflation. By contrast, Monetarists are deeply skeptical about such a trade-off. In the wake of the fiscal consolidation that followed the 2008 financial crisis, this policy debate moved into the monetary realm, and centered on the Fed's dual-mandate of "promoting maximum employment" and "stable prices."[48] Keynesians perceived a dual mandate as necessary in ensuring price stability effort did not undercut domestic employment, while Monetarists viewed a single inflation-target as the most efficient way to promote full employment.

The emergence of an implicit financial stability mandate has complicated these traditional debates by changing the Fed's ability to navigate potential unemployment-inflation trade-offs. Essentially, the Fed now faces a *mandate trilemma*, where it aims to simultaneously spur jobs and growth, stabilize the financial system, and control inflation. However, targeting both employment and financial stability with easier credit conditions potentially creates an inflationary bias in the system, making it harder to achieve the dual mandate. It also risks intensifying economic swings from deflation to inflation, as observed recently with the United States' pandemic recovery.

Empirical analysis: plausibility probe of the Silicon Valley Bank crisis

In the following pages, I conduct a plausibility probe of the chapter's theoretical priors, employing the case of the 2023 Silicon Valley Bank crisis. I claim that the Fed's focus on its implicit financial stability mandate as it emerged from the pandemic created a *mandate trilemma*, where it hoped to stimulate the economy and stabilize the financial system with a single monetary policy tool, complicating its ability to contain inflation. The Fed balked at hiking interest rates, believing inflation was transitory and fearing that tighter credit conditions risked disrupting the financial sector and derailing an economic recovery. In its attempt to meet all three of its objectives, however, inflation reared its ugly head by 2022, reaching its highest levels since the 1980s. The Fed's ongoing quantitative easing policy through early 2022 had signaled to markets that interest rates would remain low, creating expectations of an interest rate ceiling that was eventually pierced by higher-than-anticipated inflation.

Rather than using its regulatory and supervisory power to rein in financial sector excesses, the Fed's attempt to meet an implicit financial stability mandate with monetary policy left financial institutions exposed to interest rate volatility. When the central bank aggressively hiked rates to curb higher-than-anticipated inflation, a financialized economy that had relied on low interest rates was not prepared for the aftermath.

To better understand these dynamics, let us first turn to the Fed's monetary policymaking, the Federal Open Market Committee (FOMC), which regularly publishes policy statements following its meetings. We'll examine these statements one year into the pandemic, when the Fed decided to continue its quantitative easing program that it had restarted in March 2020 for the first time since the 2008–09 global financial crisis. Although the Fed had hoped to unwind these large-scale bond purchases, new COVID-19 variants had kept monetary authorities concerned about both the soundness of the banking system and the vitality of the economy.

In the wake of peaking COVID-19 variants in January 2021 and January 2022, the FOMC's summary statements emphasized the importance of using quantitative easing to ensure financial stability. For example, over the course of the 2021 calendar year, the FOMC had highlighted the same language about financial stability within the first page of its statement. "Asset purchases help foster smooth market functioning and accommodative financial conditions, thereby supporting the flow of credit to households and businesses."[49] To this end, the Federal Reserve stated in January 2022 that it would continue quantitative easing and further grow its balance sheet through March 2022 (see Figure 6.2). The Fed was once again "deploying its lending powers to an unprecedented extent"[50] to stabilize credit conditions, suggesting that beyond its typical dual mandate, financial stability had crept into the central bank's policy goals.

Notably, this unconventional policy designed to push long-term interest rates lower had lasted two-and-a-quarter years. By the spring of 2022, the Fed began to nominally pivot away from its monetary stimulus, inching its short-term monetary policy target higher, but it did not begin to unwind these long-term bond purchases until June 2022. By summer, the Fed was fully into a monetary tightening phase, hiking interest rates through its open market operations by more than two percentage points. The central bank also announced a new program to reverse its quantitative easing by reducing its bond holdings by $95 billion per month.

However, the Fed appeared to have missed the shift from a deflationary to inflationary environment by waiting to unwind these unconventional measures until summer 2022. Headed into summer, Federal Reserve Chairman Jerome Powell was firmly focused on controlling inflation. Compared to the ongoing emphasis on jobs and financial stability a few months earlier, Powell declared a war on inflation in the Fed's May 2022 press conference. According to Powell, "inflation is much too high and we understand the hardship it is causing…we're strongly committed to restoring price stability."[51] With the inflation rate breaching 8 percent, economic officials admitted that the Fed was too slow to hike rates. U.S. Treasury Secretary

Janet Yellen was quite candid in a 2022 interview, courageously referring to her 2021 remarks about 'transitory inflation,' saying "I think I was wrong then about the path that inflation would take."[52] To be fair, economic forecasting was not an easy exercise emerging from the pandemic. Not only were there persistent supply chain shortages, but there were also unexpected price shocks from higher energy and food prices.

That said, counterfactually, without the Fed's quantitative easing policies, long-term interest rates would have likely been higher.[53] Moreover, if this unconventional policy of massive balance sheet expansion were not made conventional, market participants would have been less likely to assume that there was an implicit interest rate ceiling. As with any economic crisis, there was a 'perfect storm' of potential causes of the 2023 Silicon Valley Bank crisis. That said, the Fed's choice to quell credit conditions with quantitative easing rather than greater regulations and supervision of the financial industry contributed to an environment of greed and easy credit that led to the regional banking crisis.

Though regional by name, neither Silicon Valley Bank (SVB) nor its financial problems were small, as its massive balance sheet expansion yielded the second largest bank failure in U.S. history. Given its Silicon Valley location, SVB specialized in financing and banking for venture-capital-backed start-up companies. The bank grew to be the sixteenth largest in America, with such well-known clients as Etsy, Fitbit, Pinterest, Roku, Roblox, Shopify, and Vox Media. Following the pandemic, its deposits spiked by 220 percent compared to an average increase of 26 percent at FDIC-insured banking institutions. Importantly, however, many of SVB's tech-savvy clients had deposited millions rather than thousands of dollars, meaning only $250,000 (the FDIC insurance cap) of their deposits had been insured. Leveraging this whopping deposit growth, SVB had invested in long-term bonds when rates were zero.

The blame for SVB's collapse reflects its own balance sheet mismanagement, but, importantly, quantitative easing also had a role by creating extremely accommodative credit conditions for almost two-and-a-half years. Counterfactually, if traditional financial stability tools (e.g., regulation and supervision) were employed to ensure stable credit conditions, financial authorities likely would have checked SVB deposit growth and balance sheet expansion. Instead, the Fed was left trying to provide financial stability through its monetary policy, once SVB's balance sheet had grown unchecked for several years. How did this happen?

After the Trump administration reversed the Dodd-Frank Act's regulatory reforms in 2018, regional banks were allowed to circumvent stress tests and financial regulations, with a new regulatory ceiling moving from $50 to $250 billion. Ironically, after such regional banks were deemed systematically *unimportant*, SVB's balance sheet had grown from a pre-pandemic $62 billion to a massive $212 billion by the end of 2022.

Against this backdrop, the Fed's own sizable balance sheet expansion had contributed to the eventual crisis by providing ultra-low interest rates for a sustained period of time. Financial actors were once again searching for yield, as they once did in the prelude to the 2008–09 financial crisis. Just as investment banks had once created asset-backed securities to provide their clients with a higher-return alternative to U.S. Treasuries, SVB bank offered its technology clients higher corporate deposit rates.

To match this deposit liability growth, SVB had also grown its financial assets. Quantitative easing had sent a signal to less-savvy financial investors like SVB that there was a near-term price floor on U.S. Treasury bonds, which accounted for a large share of its investment portfolio. SVB had invested more than $90 billion in long-term Treasury bonds, planning to hold them until maturity until inflation caught both the Fed and financial markets by surprise. Inflation that the Fed had once thought was transitory, continued to gather momentum, breaching a 10-percent annualized rate by March 2022, its highest level since 1982. By early March, Federal Reserve Chairman Jerome Powell had solidified tighter monetary policy expectations, saying before Congress that he was "inclined to propose and support a 25-basis-point rate hike."[54] As discussed earlier, however, the Fed did not officially begin unwinding its quantitative easing program until June 2022.

SVB had hoped to weather the storm over the next year, mostly because of its financial model. SVB lent venture capital to private technology companies, who would in turn funnel money back into banks deposits at SVB after their Initial Public Offering (IPO), or first stock issuance. During 2022, however, IPOs fell by about two-fifths amid higher-than-expected inflation and monetary policy tightening.[55] The plummeting IPO activity led to an erosion of their deposits from Bay area start-ups. The vast majority of these deposits exceeded the $250,000 ceiling that is insured by the Federal government. Without IPOs, tech companies withdrew their deposits to help cover their expenses, prompting SVB to sell its long-term bonds. The problem, however, was that SVB had bet that interest rates would remain low. When interest rates moved higher amid the Fed's 2022 tightening cycle, long-term bond prices fell which undercut these investments.

By March 2023, these bad investments had yielded $1.8 billion in after-tax losses, plunging its share price and catalyzing depositor withdrawals. The bank could not provide depositors with their funds, creating a credit crunch in the technology sector. SVB was caught in a vicious cycle of depositor withdrawals and falling bond prices, leaving it on the brink of insolvency. On March 12, the Federal Reserve, U.S. Treasury, and FDIC thus took the unusual step of guaranteeing all of SVB's deposits, saying it posed a major risk to the economy. They were careful to strike a balance, noting that the "bank's equity and bondholders [were] being wiped out. They took a risk as owners of those securities. They will take the losses." These unprecedented actions underscore the extent of financialization of the U.S. economy, which creates an implicit third mandate for the Federal Reserve to ensure the stability of the financial sector.

Concluding discussion

Banking supervision and regulation are much better instruments for containing financial sector excesses, but deregulation had left the Federal Reserve with the onus of ensuring financial stability. Ostensibly, based on the logic of the 2018 regulatory reversal of Dodd-Frank financial reforms, a regional bank should not have posed systemic risk. However, without greater financial supervision and stress tests, SVB's balance sheet grew too rapidly, eventually holding more than two-fifths of publicly traded venture-backed tech and healthcare companies as its bank clients. These financial linkages made SVB systematically important to the technology sector, and the sixteenth largest bank in the country. It also shows the political nature of financial stability, with the Biden administration intervening to protect Silicon Valley depositors, in part because of its concerns about the soundness the technology sector against the backdrop of geopolitical competition with China.

For this reason, financial stability should not be the purview of monetary policy. In the wake of the pandemic, the U.S. monetary authorities had hoped to avoid credit disruptions and facilitate an economic recovery with quantitative easing – a single blunt instrument of monetary policy. The central bank had developed quantitative easing to deal with the onset of deflationary crises following the 2008 global financial crises, intervening to ensure that low long-term interest rates would both stabilize credit conditions and stimulate the economy. However, given the balance sheet expansion associated with quantitative easing, it was not easy to reverse course in an inflationary environment.

An implicit financial stability mandate made this even more difficult, creating a lag in its responsiveness in controlling inflation in the wake of the pandemic. The Federal Reserve was placed in the unenviable position of employing one tool – interest rates – to simultaneously balance full employment, inflation control, and financial stability. Ironically, the Fed was caught in a catch-22, as its eventual shift to a more restrictive monetary policy fomented the type of financial disruptions it had hoped to avoid initially. Unfortunately, there is no clear escape from the mandate trilemma in a financialized world, other than the Fed exiting from this mandate ambiguity.

Notes

1 Federal Bureau of Investigation (FBI). *Wall Street Bombing of 1920.* www.fbi.gov/history/famous-cases/wall-street-bombing-1920.
2 Stiglitz (2009).
3 Ibid.
4 See note 1.
5 The Phillips curve is named after the British economist A. W. Phillips, who in 1958 observed a negative relationship between inflation and unemployment rates.
6 Samuelson and Nordhaus 1995.
7 Friedman 1968, 1970.
8 Revisiting the traditional Phillips curve trade-off, Milton Friedman and Edmund Phelps constructed a steeper Phillips Curve that accounted for the growth-diminishing effect of inflation expectations.
9 Bernanke 2004.
10 Alesina and Summers 1993.
11 McNamara 2002; Blyth 2002; Blyth and Matthijs 2017; Hopkin and Blyth 2019.
12 Roberts 2020.
13 Ibid.

14 Farrell and Quiggin 2017.
15 *Federal Reserve Reform Act*, Public Law 95-188, 91 Stat. 1387-91 (1977). Codified as amended in sections, 12 U.S.C.
16 *The Federal Reserve Board of Governors*. "What are the Federal Reserve's Objectives in Conducting Monetary Policy?" Sept. 26, 2013.
17 Taylor 2011.
18 The Federal Open Market Committee (FOMC) consists of twelve members – the seven members of the Board of Governors of the Federal Reserve System; the president of the Federal Reserve Bank of New York; and four of the remaining eleven Reserve Bank presidents. The FOMC holds eight meetings per year, where it reviews economic conditions, crafts monetary policy stances, and assesses the risks to its long-run goals of price stability and sustainable growth. For further details, see www.federalreserve.gov/monetarypolicy/fomc.htm.
19 Kaya, A., Golub, S., Kuperberg, M., and Lin, F. (2019).
20 The act requires the Federal Reserve Board to report to Congress twice a year on its monetary policy, and their relation to full employment and monetary policy (Goldberg 2013).
21 Hibbs 1977, 1987; Bartels 2008.
22 FOMC's policy statement on September 16, 2008.
23 Farrell and Quiggin 2017.
24 Goldberg 2013.
25 Quantitative easing was the Fed's trillion-dollar bond-buying campaign after the crisis to reduce long-term interest rates.
26 Lambert 2011.
27 See footnote 18.
28 Puzzanghera 2013.
29 Quote in Goldberg 2013.
30 The 1978 Humphrey-Hawkins Act mandates the promotion of both goals through the Fed's monetary policy.
31 Tinbergen (1952).
32 The Fed's long-term bond purchases included non-Treasury bonds, such as corporate bonds and mortgage-backed securities, with the aim of mitigating the credit crunch and encouraging long-term lending.
33 Bernanke 2020.
34 Bernanke 2015.
35 Ibid.
36 Bernanke as quoted in Roberts 2020.
37 Haltam and Weinberg 2017.
38 For further details, see www.federalreserve.gov/aboutthefed/the-fed-explained.htm
39 Crockett 2011.
40 Bank for International Settlements 2011.
41 Kaplan and Shim 2024.
42 See footnote 37.
43 Bagehot 1873.
44 Haltam and Weinberg 2017; Board of Governors of the Federal Reserve System (1968), 'Reappraisal of the Federal Reserve Discount Mechanism,' *Report of a System Committee*.
45 Federal Reserve Board Press Release, November 25, 2008. www.federalreserve.gov/newsevents/pressreleases/monetary20081125b.htm.
46 Toloui 2020.
47 Miller, Weller, and Zhang 2002.
48 See footnote 16.
49 FOMC Meeting Statements: January 27, 2021; January 26, 2022.

50 Transcript of Chairman Powell's Press Conference, April 29, 2020; www.federalreserve.gov/mediacenter/files/FOMCpresconf20200429.pdf.
51 "Fed raises rates by half a percentage point – the biggest hike in two decades – to fight inflation." *CNBC*, May 4, 2022.
52 "Yellen says administration was fighting inflation, admits she was wrong that it's transitory." *CNBC*, June 2, 2022.
53 See Toloui 2020.
54 *USA Today*. "Powell Says Fed Is Poised to Hike Interest Rates to Fight Inflation Despite Ukraine War, Market Sell-Off." March 2, 2022.
55 *World Economic Forum*. "The IPO Market Plummeted in 2022. Here's Why." Dec. 21, 2022.

References

Alesina, A., and Summers, L. (1993). 'Central Bank Independence and Macroeconomic Performance: Some Comparative Evidence.' *Journal of Money, Credit, and Banking* 25: 151–62.

Bagehot, W. (1873). *Lombard Street: A Description of the Money Market*. London: Henry S. King & Co.

Bank for International Settlements. (2011). 'Central Bank Governance and Financial Stability: A Report by a Study Group.' May.

Bartels, L. (2008). *Unequal Democracy: The Political Economy of the New Gilded Age*. Princeton, NJ: Princeton University Press.

Bernanke, B. S. (2004). 'The Great Moderation.' *Remarks at the Meetings of the Eastern Economic Association*, Washington, DC, February 20.

Bernanke, B. S. (2015). *The Courage to Act*. New York: W.W. Norton.

Bernanke, B. S. (2020). 'Presidential Address on the New Tools of Monetary Policy.' *Remarks at the 2020 American Economic Association (AEA)*, Washington DC, January 4.

Blyth, M. (2002). *Great Transformations: Economic Ideas and Institutional Change in the Twentieth Century*. Cambridge: Cambridge University Press.

Blyth, M., and Matthijs, M. (2017). 'Black Swans, Lame Ducks, and the Mystery of IPE's Missing Macroeconomy.' *Review of International Political Economy* 24(2): 203–31.

Board of Governors of the Federal Reserve System. (1968). 'Reappraisal of the Federal Reserve Discount Mechanism.' *Report of a System Committee*. Volume 1. Federal Reserve Bank of St. Louis.

Crockett, A. (2011). 'Central Bank Governance Under New Mandates.' BIS Papers No. 55.

Farrell, H., and Quiggin, J. (2017). 'Consensus, Dissensus, and Economic Ideas: Economic Crisis and the Rise and Fall of Keynesianism.' *International Studies Quarterly* 61(2): 269–83.

Friedman, M. (1968). 'The Role of Monetary Policy.' *American Economic Review* 58(1): 1–17.

Friedman, M. (1970). 'A Theoretical Framework for Monetary Analysis.' *The Journal of Political Economy* 78(2): 193–238.

Goldberg, M. A. (2013). 'The Fed's Dual Mandate: One Too Many.' *Review of Banking and Financial Law* 33(1): 343–80.

Haltam, R., and Weinberg, J. A. (2017). 'Does the Fed Have a Financial Stability Mandate?' *Economic Brief, No. 17-06*, Federal Reserve Bank of Richmond.

Hibbs, D. (1977). 'Political Parties and Macroeconomic Policy.' *American Political Science Review* 71: 1467–87.

Hibbs, D. (1987). *The American Political Economy*. Cambridge, MA: Harvard University Press.

Hopkin, J., and Blyth, M. (2019). 'The Global Economics of European Populism: Growth Regimes and Party System Change in Europe.' *Government and Opposition* 54(2): 193–225.

Kaplan, S., and Shim, S. (2024). 'Global Contagion Risk and IMF Credit Cycles: Emergency Exits and Revolving Doors.' *Regulation and Governance*. Available at: https://onlinelibrary.wiley.com/doi/10.1111/rego.12562.

Kaya, A., Golub, S., Kuperberg, M., and Lin, F. (2019). 'The Federal Reserve's Dual Mandate and the Inflation-Unemployment Tradeoff.' *Contemporary Economic Policy* 37(4): 641–51.

Lambert, L. (2011). 'Republicans Question Fed's Dual Mandate.' *Reuters*, October 4.

Miller, M. H., Weller, P. A., and Zhang, L. (2002). 'Moral Hazard and the U.S. Stock Market: Analyzing the Greenspan Put.' *Economic Journal* 112: C171–86.

McNamara, K. R. (2002). 'Rational Fictions: Central Bank Independence and the Social Logic of Innovation.' *West European Politics* 25(1): 47–76.

Puzzanghera, J. (2013). 'Obama Explains What He Wants in Next Federal Reserve Chairman.' *L.A. Times*, July 29.

Roberts, A. S. (2020). 'The Pandemic Exposes an Ailing US Governance Mode.' *Current History*, November: 310–16.

Samuelson, P. A., and Nordhaus, W. D. (1995). *Economics*. 15th edition. New York: McGraw-Hill Book Company, Inc.

Stiglitz, J. E. (2009). 'The Anatomy of a Murder: Who Killed the Economy?' *Critical Review* 21(2–3): 329–39.

Taylor, J. B. (2011). 'End the Fed's Dual Mandate and Focus on Prices.' *Bloomberg*, September 16.

Tinbergen, J. (1952). *On the Theory of Economic Policy*. 2nd edition. Amsterdam, Holland: North Holland Publishing Company.

Toloui, R. (2020). 'How do the Federal Reserve's New Tools Really Work?' *Policy Brief*. Stanford Institute for Economic Policy Research (SIEPR).

Corruption, state capture, and policymaking

7 Anticorruption challenges in Argentina

Natalia A. Volosin

Corruption in Argentina is an endemic, structural, or otherwise enduring public policy problem. Perceptions of corruption in Argentina have been steadily increasing both in absolute and relative terms vis-à-vis its South American neighbors, mostly in tandem with Bolivia (although they improved a bit between 2017 and 2020).[1]

Susan Rose-Ackerman's preventive-institutional theory is the best approach to address it. This conception can be summarized in her statement that corruption is a symptom of disease, not the disease itself, which is why "anticorruption strategies should seek to improve the efficiency and fairness of government and to enhance the efficiency of the private sector."[2]

Rose-Ackerman's institutional analysis argues that tolerance toward corruption that seems to exist in certain societies is not necessarily an expression of acceptance, but rather of resignation and fear of reprisal.[3] She and Bonnie Palifka explain that "even if ordinary citizens find payoffs necessary to survive, they disapprove of corruption. Such behavior is not viewed as a positive cultural feature."[4]

Furthermore, they say, "[c]orruption is not the inevitable result of history and culture,"[5] because even deeply embedded and self-reinforcing social norms can (and must) change. The theory holds that cultural acceptance may change if the hidden costs of corruption are exposed.[6] Moreover, the opportunities for illegal deals, and the incentives and abilities to monitor potential corrupt activities can be significantly affected through major institutional reform.

Rose-Ackerman's approach to corruption is based on the assumption that "[a] high level of corruption indicates that something is wrong with the state's underlying institutions and incentives; it signals a need for structural reform – not just more vigorous law enforcement."[7] Of course, "it is impossible to associate abstract political systems unproblematically with levels of corruption."[8] However, each regime should be analyzed considering "the ability of wealthy organized groups to obtain legal influence and the attitude of the general population toward the public provision of private benefits."[9] Given this assumption, policies that focus exclusively on limiting corruption "are unlikely to be effective."[10] Since "corruption is a symptom of underlying institutional weaknesses,"[11] policies should be directed at changing those shortcomings, which for Rose-Ackerman means changing "the competitiveness of the political system and … the discretion given to elected politicians."[12]

DOI: 10.4324/9781003416234-9

Following this approach, Argentina's history of corruption reveals that institutional weaknesses have been crucial over time. Political instability, authoritarianism, lack of checks and balances, patrimonialism, hyper-presidentialism, and corporatism have influenced the country's corruption-building processes for 200 years, while pervasive corruption has in turn increased these structural deficits.

Rose-Ackerman and Palifka elaborate a typology to "distinguish among four stylized cases that stress the competitive relationship between (private sector) bribers (who pay bribes) and (public sector) bribees (who receive bribes) as reflected in their power relationships."[13] It should be noted, though, that:

> The relative power of government officials and private interests may, in practice, be difficult to sort out. The extremes are kleptocracy, on the one hand, and state capture by powerful private interests, on the other. In some cases, concentrated power exists on both sides, and we have a bargaining situation similar to a bilateral monopoly in the private market.[14]

From its inception, Argentina has been steadily building an extremely well-oiled corruption apparatus whereby power shifted from the private sector to government officials, beginning with state capture (colony–1989) only interrupted by a short kleptocratic period (1827–52), and moving first to a bilateral monopoly (1989–1999) and then to a modern kleptocracy during Néstor Kirchner and Cristina Fernández de Kirchner's administrations (2003–15). This structural device, comprised of both public and private parts, was immune to both economic policy, global tendencies, and even local political trends.

But Argentina's case also reveals that, in a context of structurally sustained corruption, the political economy of reform and its associated hindrances are as significant as reform itself. There is no reform without addressing its political feasibility. In Argentina, the corruption device proved resistant to the liberal democratic transition (1983–89) and to deliberate attempts to curtail it (1999–2001 and 2015–19).

The 1999–2001 period, which followed Carlos Menem's highly corrupt ten-year administration, resulted in a first pro-reform fiasco. History repeated itself (only worse) after 12 years of Kirchnerism, with a second pro-reform fiasco that moved the device back to its state capture typology (2015–19) and that, through some real human-rights violations in judicial proceedings tainted by political influences, yielded an anticorruption backlash (2019–present), currently at play, that draws on the concept of "lawfare" to argue that anticorruption reform abused the law and judicial proceedings by turning them into weapons to overthrow pro-poor governments.

This chapter adopts a political-economy perspective and uses that historical narrative to identify four underlying hindrances for reform: public-private biases, Berensztein's paradox, the Chinese Trap, and the cultural-criminal approach. Then, it faces the pessimistic present and draws five lessons that Argentina and other structurally corrupt environments (as well as international agents of change) should keep in mind while hoping to generate a new anticorruption wave.

Argentina's brief history of corruption (and anticorruption)

To understand corruption in Argentina, it is useful to distinguish three historical periods (state capture, bilateral monopoly, and kleptocracy) and two anticorruption fiascos. While I have elsewhere studied these in depth,[15] in what follows I summarize them so as to better understand the lawfare backlash that the country is currently facing, and to draw general political-economy lessons that may help other structurally corrupt environments.

From state capture to kleptocracy and beyond (Colony–2019)

Until 1983, Argentina was a colony and then a nation dominated by state capture and corporatism. The Spanish crown was unable to set the fundamental elements of control of corruption. Smuggling, tax evasion, commercial monopolies and privileges, forgery of moneys, and all sorts of illegalities directed at rent seeking activities had a double structural nature. They extended throughout the Río de la Plata and were embedded in the formal and informal organization of political, economic, and social power.

A group of privileged settlers was turned into a dominating economic and political class that persisted long after independence, and state capture grew stronger after the 1810 revolution. Writing in 1906, Estanislao Zeballos argues that "the entire Nation works for two dozen families and their clients, who enjoy unlimited official favors."[16]

Interestingly enough, Argentina's golden age (1850–1930) was a crucial part of this process. The country went from the 1810 revolution to a kleptocratic interregnum by the famous *caudillos* (1827–52), failed state building efforts beginning with the 1853 Constitution, and decades of electoral fraud, violence, coups (in 1930, 1943, 1955, 1962, 1966, and 1976), political instability, authoritarianism, corporatism, and a complete lack of checks and balances.[17]

The state capture feature survived every economic model, taking rents from land distribution, external debt, local wars, customs, privatizations to form the agro-export infrastructure, external debt, financial speculation, public companies, sale of utilities to foreign interests, import–substitution–industrialization privileges, public procurement, and the incipient privatizations of the 1970s.

After seven years of terror by the last military dictatorship, in 1983 Unión Cívica Radical (UCR) candidate, Raúl Alfonsín, took office as the first democratically elected president since 1973. Although not free from a few corruption allegations, the government attempted to contain the structural state capture system that had prevailed since colonial times.

Alfonsín deliberately sought to deconstruct the corporatism that the country had been building for decades, but he was challenged by interests from the military, right-wing religious interests, some sectors of the press who had flourished during the military rule, private firms, and trade unions. Unfortunately, the government was only able to successfully counteract the military, and to a certain extent.

The new government was also quite concerned with the public counterpart of corporatism (the presidential system), especially due to its connections with political instability, which social scientists have been studying since the mid-1980s. In 1985, Alfonsín created the Council for the Consolidation of Democracy, chaired by Carlos Nino, to study the country's institutions and propose reforms to definitely achieve the consolidation of democracy. The Council's conclusions[18] exposed the dangers of the presidential system, and recommended the adoption of semi-presidentialism which divided executive functions between the President and a Prime Minister, subject to the legislature's confidence. Unfortunately, Alfonsín was himself a victim of the system, quitting office amidst a hyper-inflationary crisis in May 1989, six months before the end of his term.

Carlos Menem was elected president in 1989. During Menem's presidency, hyper-presidentialism was critical in the state's move toward a corrupt bilateral monopoly. Consistent with Rose-Ackerman and Jana Kunicova's model showing that presidential systems are more susceptible to corruption,[19] Menem's administration made use of extraordinary powers and an unprecedented concentration of normative authority, appointment discretion, and unchecked financial management and procurement systems to extract illegal rents.

Unlike previous state capture scenarios, Menem's extreme concentration of power led to an equal concentration of bribees. As Vitelli explains, although many corrupt deals exposed convergence between officials and private negotiators, "access was not free," but "focused on the presidential or even ministerial inner circle, which thus guaranteed the extraction of bribes and future rents."[20]

An aggressive weakening of external and internal accountability facilitated widespread corruption. This was achieved through the packing of the Supreme Court and the appointment of other pliant judges after supposed judicial "reforms" that allowed Menem to appoint more than 200 judges. Some were hand-picked federal magistrates in charge of investigating corruption.

After ten years of intense corruption scandals, in 1999 Fernando de la Rúa, through an alliance between the UCR and the Frepaso, a party formed in 1993 by small left parties and peronists who opposed Menem's neoliberal policies, took office. The Alianza came to power amidst a vigorous anticorruption campaign.

De la Rúa's government introduced small anticorruption policies, such as the creation of the Anticorruption Office (OA) within the Ministry of Justice, which had both investigative and policy-making functions. The OA pressed charges against Menemist officials, and the same judges who had protected them for ten years realized that the political winds had changed. In 2001, Menem was imprisoned for a corruption scandal related to the illegal sale of weapons to Croatia and Ecuador.

But the Alianza did nothing to change the underlying structural deficits, and the administration's political capital was lost when, in June 2000, a journalist revealed that peronist senators had received bribes from two leading members of government to pass a labor law reform required by the International Monetary Fund to approve a loan. A criminal investigation was launched and the Labor Minister was accused of being responsible for the payoffs. In October, the Vice-President resigned, claiming that De la Rúa had not taken decisive action into what happened.

This was the beginning of the end for the government. In December 2001, two months after losing the mid-term elections, De la Rúa resigned in the midst of a huge economic and financial crisis marked, as hyper-presidentialism predicts, by political instability and violence. In two days, more than 30 people were killed during public protests and lootings throughout the country.

The Alianza's failure to enact real anticorruption change was not without consequences. After five transitional administrations, including three successive presidents in a few days, presidents Néstor Kirchner (2003–07) and his wife Cristina Fernández de Kirchner (2007–15) moved the country's structural corruption closer to a kleptocracy.

The Kirchners were fortified by Menem's hyper-presidential corruption experience and by the new extraordinary powers amassed by the executive during the transitional governments in the face of the economic and social crisis. Within such an institutional setting, and with the private sector's increasing dependence on the state for survival, the Kirchners' administrations were marked by numerous corruption scandals. The schemes were for the most part related to procurement (particularly public works) and involved new business players who took public funds while being close associates of the governing couple.

Numerous corruption scandals during this period suggest that bribers were much more widespread than before, while bribees were concentrated at the top. Moreover, private newcomers were close associates of the Kirchners and their powerful Planning Minister, who concentrated every large business including transport, public works, housing, energy, oil, gas, mining, water, and sanitation.

The paradigmatic example of the kleptocratic move was the notebooks case. In 2018, a journalist revealed that he had been given copies of eight notebooks written during ten years (2005–15) by Oscar Centeno, the personal driver to the Planning Ministry's second man, identifying thousands of bribes taken by high-level officials from the country's most renowned business players. Many of the indicted businessmen and officials were detained and took pleas.

The Kirchners' private assistants and their personal accountant acknowledged to having taken bags with money from Buenos Aires to Santa Cruz Province (where the couple lived). The pilot that used to fly the Kirchners in official planes to the province also said that both they and their private secretaries traveled with bags that were not scanned and that came back empty. More than 50 people, including Cristina Fernández herself, are facing oral trial.

The 2015 presidential elections ended 12 years of Kirchnerism. Mauricio Macri won the presidency through a political alliance called Cambiemos (Let's Change) with the UCR and with integrity champion and the Kirchner's nemesis Elisa Carrió. Macri was the son of Francisco Macri, owner of one of the fastest-growing conglomerates during the bureaucratic-authoritarian times (1976–83), benefited with numerous privatizations in the bilateral monopoly period (1989–99), and part of the public works club in the modern kleptocratic stage (2003–15).

Within a regional anticorruption revival, the presidential campaign was filled with transparency rhetoric and promises. But, just as the Alianza had failed to accomplish any real change after Menem's bilateral monopoly, Macri's period was unsuccessful.

Almost immediately after Macri took office, ongoing investigations against former officials were re-activated, and major political leaders were imprisoned under corruption charges, including Cristina Fernández's Planning Minister and her Vice-President. Cristina Fernández herself was indicted – and has been recently convicted – on corruption charges related to public works.

The judiciary (that had been mostly complicit with impunity for 12 years) reacted to the fact that, as is usually the case after unending scandals, by 2015 corruption was at the top of public concerns. The government's influence on the judiciary was significant. While some iniquitous magistrates were removed or somehow tamed, others prevailed and their past was rapidly forgotten and forgiven. During Macri's administration, the multiple charges against Cristina Fernández (her husband had died in 2010) and her inner circle moved forward. While most files were based on clear suspicions of corruption, others allowed Kirchnerites to decry that they were being subject to political persecution. Moreover, some abuses of jurisdictional authority enabled magistrates to extend preventive imprisonments beyond constitutional boundaries.

Many people, fed up with Kirchnerite corruption scandals, celebrated imprisonments, most likely because for decades they had seen that massive corruption never corresponded with convictions. However, the rule of law suffers just as much with impunity as with due process violations. Moreover, abuses during this period helped raise support for the anticorruption backlash that would follow.

Macri's government did not exhibit a systematic anticorruption program. A few days after taking office, the President amended the OA's regulatory decree, transforming it into a Secretary and suppressing the requirement that its Director had to be an attorney. Accordingly, he appointed Laura Alonso as head of the office. Alonso had ended her term as House representative for Macri's party 15 days before and was famous for saying that she could fall in love with him. In 2019, a few months before leaving office, Alonso acknowledged that she did not and would not prosecute any case against her government's officials so that no one could accuse her office of complicity.

Meanwhile, there were several corruption and conflicts of interest allegations. President Macri and other high-level servants were accused of serious conflicts of interest, including his Energy Minister, his Finance Minister, his Deputy Chief of Staff and his Farmer Minister. Macri and others were involved in the scandals known as Panama Papers and Paradise Papers, and his family members were accused in relation to the famous Odebrecht case, which also involved the head of the Intelligence Agency (AFI), whose whole budget he suspiciously turned into a state secret.

The lawfare backlash (2019–present)

In December 2019, the Kirchners regained power, with Alberto Fernández (former Chief of Cabinet to both Néstor and Cristina Kirchner) as President, and

Cristina Fernández as Vice-President. In his assumption speech before Congress, the President said that there had been undue prosecutions and arbitrary detentions induced by Macri's administration and silenced by the press. He used the concept of "Nunca Más" (never again), related to systematic human-rights violations during the last dictatorship. Many spoke of an impunity pact between him and Cristina.

The President also announced a pack of bills to introduce a wholesale reform of the criminal federal judiciary, the intervention of the AFI and the annulment of Macri's decision regarding secret funds. "Never again to democracy's basements," he said. The AFI's reform was the only thing that the government managed to accomplish.

In 2020, Alberto Fernández formed a committee of experts to study reforms to the Supreme Court, the Attorney's Office and the Judicial Council. The committee made several proposals, none of which were passed into law. Later on, amidst a crisis between the government and the Supreme Court over several rulings (including one that ruled the Kirchner's 2006 reform to the Judicial Council unconstitutional), Alberto Fernández backed an attack on the court's members. Public manifestations were made asking the court's four members to resign[21] and Kirchnerite senators introduced a bill to pack it by enlarging it to 25 justices.

Fernández's administration also appointed as head of the OA a former prosecutor with non-hidden sympathies for the Kirchners,[22] who right from the start issued a resolution resigning the OA's private prosecutor role in every major case against Cristina Fernández, in which the Office had been working since Macri's times.[23] The Financial Intelligence Unit (UIF) did the same thing, refusing to press charges against Cristina Fernández and her close associates.[24]

The criminal federal judiciary went back to business as usual. Criminal charges against Kirchnerist officials began to fade away, while those affecting Macri and his officials were initially boosted. Most who had been imprisoned were freed, and many who had been indicted or sent to trial were acquitted or even charges were dismissed without trial. The pendulum swung again, though, and began helping Macri after Alberto Fernández's Government lost the mid-term elections in 2021. Moreover, Cristina Fernández was convicted on corruption allegations in 2022.

The current period is marked by a strong anticorruption backlash that draws on the concept of "lawfare" to argue that the regional surge of anticorruption judicial activism abused the law by turning it into a weapon to destroy left-wing leaders through groundless accusations and imprisonments supported by media interests who construct public verdicts outside the courts. The judges, they say, took the role that the military had played in the twentieth-century coups.

To be sure, the lawfare card is nothing but a euphemism for Argentina's structural lack of judicial independence, which the Kirchners have both benefited from and suffered. However, the discovery of some real abuses by the judiciary in the 2015–19 period, and of suspicious activities by Macri's executive officials to illegally influence judicial decisions (most notably through the illegal production and use of intelligence information)[25] has not helped the anticorruption discourse.

It is currently difficult to even speak of the fight against corruption in Argentina without being connected to human-rights violations. Political anticorruption champions, once seen as honest and trustworthy, have lost all credibility by backing up the excesses of Macri's government and its own corruption. The anticorruption agenda is perceived as conservative, right-wing oriented, and even part of an imperialist conspiracy against supposedly pro-poor administrations in the region. This means that the few progressives still standing after far-right outsider Javier Milei took office have no incentives whatsoever to embrace it. And, to be sure, people are not really interested in the subject anymore considering other urgencies such as the pandemic, the war in Ukraine, and the local economic debacle.

The political economy of (no) reform

The historical analysis of corruption and anticorruption outlined here exposes four interconnected limitations of the political economy of reform in Argentina, which might be useful for other structural environments. I call these the public-private biases, Berensztein's paradox, the Chinese Trap, and the cultural-criminal approach.

First, anticorruption discourse and reform are tainted by public-private biases. Contemporary reactions to creole *Mani Pulite*[26] scenarios faced by countries such as Argentina provide a stimulating entry point and help to explain the current lawfare backlash. It began with arguments made almost a decade ago by Brazilian sociologist and political scientist Emir Sader. He claimed that the elitist, oligarchic, racist, antinationalist political right uses (sometimes real) corruption as a pretext when, in truth, military and neoliberal governments have led to the biggest corruption cases in history, especially through privatization.[27] The right, Sader says, has managed to align the judiciary and the private media, so that the polls (which they produce as well) "show corruption as the most important issue, not social inequality nor the hegemony of speculative capitals over the Brazilian economy."[28]

Cristina Fernández de Kirchner made similar claims when a judge started to investigate her on corruption charges after Macri won the election. She argued that popular political movements are always accused of grave crimes associated with abuse of power and embezzlement as an excuse to hide adjustment plans and policies that sweep away social conquests.[29] Her most determined advocates followed through, claiming that "the coordination among the destitution and harassment processes against Dilma, Lula, and Cristina can be affirmed due to concurrence, international context, and sympathy by the same national and international actors."[30]

These supporters, once champions of investigative journalism and anticorruption campaigns during Menem's administrations,[31] started to claim that "the simultaneous suspension of Dilma in Brazil and the prosecution of Cristina here are the highest points of an anti-political offensive that uses corruption as a pretext."[32]

After being indicted for the cover-up of the 1994 terrorist attack against the Jewish organization AMIA bombing through a disputed legal proceeding that ended up with dubious preventive imprisonments, Cristina Fernández and her supporters introduced the concept of "lawfare," which Sader had employed to describe

Brazil.[33] To this end, they follow Charles J. Dunlap Jr., a retired major general and law professor at Duke, who defines lawfare as "the strategy of using – or misusing – law as a substitute for traditional military means to achieve an operational objective."[34] Conservatives used the concept to attack human-rights advocates who resorted to the courts to question state abuses emerging from the global war on terror.[35] That use of the term was nothing like Cristina Fernández's claim that anticorruption is a right-wing excuse to overthrow populist administrations.

But the whole argument is misguided. First, corruption in the region, and in the world for that matter, is neither new nor ideologically selective. The multiple scandals affecting neoliberal governments during the 1990s (Carlos Menem in Argentina, Alberto Fujimori in Peru, and Fernando Collor de Mello in Brazil, among others) suffice to prove this point.

Second, even if leftist governments in Latin America have historically faced corporatist and concentrated interests from the media, the military, multinational or even imperialistic groups, this does not excuse real corruption. Sader himself points out that there has been no control over cases of misappropriation, and highlights that absolute transparency in the administration of public funds should be a sacred, golden rule for the left.[36] There may be instances of political use or abuse of anticorruption rhetoric, but neither corruption nor anticorruption have an inherent partisan or ideological nature. China's massive crackdown on corruption should be enough proof of this.[37]

Still, Sader's rationale raises another point: the bogus dispute over whether corruption should be attributed to the public sector or, *instead*, to private sector practices. Irma Sandoval Ballesteros calls the first argument the "public sector" bias, which she claims is central in contemporary approaches to corruption.[38] The public sector bias sees the state as "the principal site of inefficiency, inefficacy and waste," so that "corruption is equated with the bribery of or extortion by a public agent, elected official or politician."[39] According to Johann Graf Lambsdorff, these theories claim that excessive government intervention, market restrictions, and a burdening bureaucracy are the most significant causes of corruption, so that "[c]orruption is then nothing else but a symptom of inadequate state intervention."[40] The public sector bias against corruption was the key to Carlos Menem's neoliberal policies in Argentina during the 1990s.

The public sector bias confronts a private sector bias that demands just as much attention, especially in countries where private rent seeking and abuse by the worst face of global capital are common. In a Senate hearing in 1976, George Ball, President Kennedy's unsuccessful critic of the Vietnam War, said:

> The vast volume of speeches, pamphlets, and advertising copy and propaganda leaflets extolling the virtues of free enterprise are cancelled every night when managements demonstrate by their conduct that a sector of multinational business activity is not free; it is bought and paid for. … [W]hen our enterprises stoop to bribery and kickbacks, they give substance to the communist myth – already widely believed in Third World countries – that capitalism is fundamentally corrupt.[41]

Of course, things have changed since the end of the Cold War. However, former Secretary of State Madeleine Albright's 1999 claim that "corruption is not capitalism's natural product, but its perversion"[42] is still not widely shared. The notion that capitalism is inherently corrupt is common among left-wing and progressive parties both in Argentina and elsewhere. Furthermore, recent global scandals involving offshore havens, Wall Street firms, multinational companies, and some of the most powerful businesses and political rulers in the world[43] contribute to make the point that the private sector has more to do with corruption than was previously acknowledged.

Former President Cristina Fernández de Kirchner exemplified this with great clarity. In a public letter, she claimed that:

> When a public official receives money, it is because someone from the private sector gave it to them. This is one of corruption's structural patterns in both Argentina and universal history. The other pattern is infinitely deeper yet, and has much more dire consequences: the establishment of political and economic projects that relinquish national wealth, indebt the country, and plunge millions of Argentines into poverty.[44]

But the debate between public and private sector corruption, or between modernization and neo-Marxist theory, presents a false dilemma. Corruption is not about how big or small a public or private sector is, neither in theory nor in the particular context of Argentina. Rather, the causes of corruption should be looked for in both the state *and* the market in a systemic way, as a whole. Alex Cuadros' reference to politics and public contracts as "an essential symbiosis" representing two of the oldest ways of getting rich in Brazil[45] could easily be a reference to Argentina.

The second permanent hindrance for reform is Berensztein's paradox. As Rose-Ackerman and Palifka explain, sound anticorruption change needs more than good ideas, moral commitment, and strong leadership: "[p]ast practice creates inertia. It is often easiest to go on as before – especially because the beneficiaries of the status quo will struggle against change. .... The challenge is to identify structural factors, apart from charismatic leadership, that create favorable conditions for reform."[46]

However, that may not be enough in a structurally corrupt environment. Rose-Ackerman and Palifka rightly point out that "[p]owerful politicians must believe that reform is in their interest," but they also acknowledge that "[t]his often occurs in response to pressures by influential private groups who decide that reform will benefit them."[47] The problem is that influential private groups might not really benefit from reform if they are a privileged part of the system.

Similar limitations arise from scandals and crises. Rose-Ackerman and Palifka use Berensztein's image, developed by the author to explain tax reform, in the anticorruption context.[48] The paradox explains how situations of scandal or crisis usually have a mixed impact on reform. On the positive side, they raise citizen demands, which, in turn, force politicians to act, advocating new policies or making reform proposals. However, the same need to rapidly satisfy social pressure makes incumbents react without much consideration for technical inputs, sustainability, or even critical mass.

The third hindrance to reform is the Chinese Trap: corruption scandals can force reform to restore public confidence, but an entrenched public-private dynamic will preclude any support for regime-undermining changes, which may be precisely what is needed. Fu Hualing's depiction of Xi Jinping's crackdown against corruption in China is useful to understand this point:

> While a perceived pervasive, endemic corruption undermines the legitimacy of a regime, a successful anticorruption campaign can allow a regime to recover from a crisis of legitimacy ....
>
> ... Political leaders in China have found it expedient to use anti-corruption campaigns to remove their political foes, to rein in the bureaucracy and to restore public confidence in their ability to rule. ....
>
> In an authoritarian state that experiences a high level of corruption, an anticorruption campaign is a delicate political battle that addresses two significant concerns. The first concern is to orchestrate the campaign so that it is regime-reinforcing instead of regime-undermining.[49]

Although Hualing writes in the context of an authoritarian regime, the concept of a government forced to reform but concerned with not jeopardizing its own survival is equally useful for a locked-in corrupt environment. If corruption is so entrenched within the public and private sectors that it cannot be significantly reduced without radical change of underlying institutional weaknesses, then incumbents and powerful private interests may oppose reform for being regime undermining.

Fourth, as a consequence of the three other hindrances, governments facing social outrage tend to focus on criminal prosecution actions against past corruption, and good governance facades to legitimize their own misdeeds through cosmetic variances of popular institutional reforms.[50]

The plot thickens if these *Mani Pulite* actions are themselves manipulated by an apparently pro-reform government to obtain electoral benefits at the expense of constitutional due process and at the same time to shield its own corruption from prosecution. If these "excesses" are uncovered, as happened with Argentina's second pro-reform fiasco (2015–19), the country may face an anticorruption backlash that makes meaningful reform not only difficult but almost impossible.

In Argentina, this hindrance comes as a cultural-criminal approach. Rose-Ackerman and Palifka explain that the cultural argument takes two forms.[51] The first is related to cultural differences in the meaning of "corruption": some societies may consider a bribe what other societies would take as an acceptable and maybe even normatively required gift. Anthropological studies on corruption make this argument.[52] The second form recognizes the perils of corruption, "but believe[s] that the only route to reform is through a thorough-going change in prevalent social norms."[53]

Argentina's prevalent approach to corruption is cultural in this second sense. It holds that corruption is merely a moral or cultural problem that stems from practices inherited from colonial times or learned afterwards, but that are unchangeable without revolutions of difficult or impossible reach. Mariano Grondona's seminal 1993 work is illustrative of the still prevalent cultural approach.[54] Grondona tracks corruption to a cultural mistake made by the governing elite that ruled during the prosperous 1880s. This fault was the imbalanced prosperity of the elite, which went from aristocratic to oligarchic, leaving the masses in ethical perplexity and disregarding the need to transmit an ethical value system to them.[55]

With this diagnosis, the solution is quite straightforward: a moralizing reaction. Grondona mentions the 1992 impeachment under corruption charges of Brazilian President Collor de Mello, former anticorruption champion as mayor of Maceió and Governor of Alagoas. The author holds that Brazil is an unprincipled country where, during the 1950s, the supporters of São Paulo's mayor Adhemar de Barros answered corruption allegations with the motto "*Adhemar rouba, mas faz*" (Adhemar steals, but gets things done) due to his huge infrastructure projects.[56] Even with this past, Grondona argues that when it came to light that Collor de Mello had himself been involved in illegal deals, "hundreds of thousands of citizens, shocked by moral indignation, invaded the streets asking for their President's impeachment."[57]

Within this general appeal to a moralizing reaction, Grondona proposes to fight corruption through cultural or moralistic tools, including massive anticorruption mobilizations and "the instruction of public officials through a morality or administrative ethos similar to that of other non-economic careers such as that of priests or doctors."[58] He also recommends ethical and civic education and the election of an "honest" President and governors who can push for anticorruption efforts.[59]

But this solution is obviously no solution at all. How do we realistically build a moralistic or administrative ethos similar to priests' and doctors' (even assuming it is a good one)? How will today's civic education help us reduce corruption in the near future? What does "honest" mean, how do we identify honest candidates, and how will honest people be able to subvert an inherently corrupt system?

The very example that Grondona uses to illustrate his moralizing reaction theory proves how vain morality can be when it comes to fighting corruption. Think of the situation in Brazil surrounding the *Lava Jato* operation, as well as President Dilma Rousseff's impeachment.[60] Even acknowledging dubious actions by judge Sergio Moro, who imprisoned Lula da Silva to secure Jair Bolsonaro's victory and become his Justice Minister, the case still shows that Brazil has the same pro-corruption institutional deficits that it did when Collor de Mello was accused of using Petrobras and other sources of public contracts to extract illegal payoffs from the private sector.[61] The moralizing protests and the impeachment process did not mean anything in the absence of structural change over the institutional deficits that gear corruption.

The cultural approach concludes that Argentines are either corrupt or tolerant of corruption. There is thus not much to do besides waiting for a moral revolution and, in the meantime, using the criminal law system. But the criminal law solution is as distracting as it is ineffective.

This is, in part, because corruption is particularly difficult to prove due to its covert nature and some judges are themselves corrupt and defense attorneys are experts in delaying procedures. All of this is true, and it certainly contributes to pessimistic determinism. As early as 2012, a study by Argentina's Attorney General's Office showed that criminal cases for corruption related offenses demand an average of 11 years, that it took a decade for a case to be ready for trial, and that the abuse of appellate review options and legal nullities by defense attorneys resulted in many of these cases ending because the statute of limitations ran out even before the accused could be brought to trial.[62]

However, even if criminal courts were honest and efficient, they would still be unable to reduce corruption in any significant way because, by its very nature, the criminal system is triggered *ex post facto*, when damages have already occurred. And because damages are not only economic, being late is almost the same as nothing. The cultural-criminal approach to corruption is an easy way out for governments to exercise *gattopardismo* ("everything must change so that nothing changes").[63]

Lessons from the Argentine Trap

In Argentina, the four anticorruption hindrances detailed in the previous section preclude real change. Reform is either absent due to determinism or only directed at *ex post* sanctioning. Structural approaches are out of the question, and thus corruption's underlying institutional deficits remain intact. This has always been the case, at least since the democratic transition. But the current situation is more disturbing. It is not just that the country is not really doing anything to prevent corruption, but rather that it is facing a backlash against anticorruption reform. This Molotov cocktail is what I call "The Argentine Trap."

If we go back to Rose-Ackerman's triad (opportunities for corruption, incentives, and abilities to control), what's left is a strainer full of holes through which corrupt deals can easily persist and a structure of crossed incentives and abilities. Those with sufficient capabilities, especially in terms of resources (horizontal accountability agencies)[64] have no incentive to monitor corruption because their political survival depends on their complicity. The Anticorruption Office's ridiculous actions in almost every administration is but one example. And those with enough incentives (social accountability agents such as NGOs and scholars) have insufficient resources (let alone legal powers) to pursue real change.

Moreover, amidst the lawfare backlash and Javier Milei's shock therapy to the devastating economic crisis, there is not much social support for or interest in anticorruption programs. Still, while we wait for momentum to surge again (and it will), it would be wise to remember a few lessons that we should have already learned from applying an institutional approach to Argentina's corruption, and that other structurally corrupt environments might also find useful.

First, deeply embedded institutional weaknesses most likely demand full-fledged reforms or structural changes to constitutional and private sector provisions and practices that will most likely never happen. And if they do, they will be manipulated by the forces that manage change in a structurally corrupt system so that either the strainer's holes become larger or that the so-called reforms only limit those who attempt effective reforms. So, be alert.

Second, this does not mean that we should instead support the piecemeal reform of pressing institutional weaknesses. Again, the beneficiaries of the status quo will use your activist discourse to perfect their rent seeking and extraction devices. Small change is only meaningful if supporters can successfully weaponize it in the short term to achieve regime-undermining reform. If not, better do nothing. Just raise awareness and wait.

Third, attempt sector-based analyses. People might not care about big transparency and efficiency arguments, but they will react if reformers can show, say, how corruption in the energy sector affects public utility rates.

Fourth, make the human-rights connection. This will be much more useful for the pursuit of broad institutional reform than all-encompassing anticorruption or transparency programs. A human-rights strategy can seek to measure and disclose corruption's hidden social cost and to integrate vulnerability criteria into the fight (a crucial step considering its disproportionately negative effect on vulnerable groups).

Local, regional, and international litigation and monitoring tools can motivate incumbents to support structural change. This will serve to identify concrete victims (defying the conventional view of corruption as a victimless crime), empower those entitled to make legal claims, and create new possibilities for action, such as remedial measures and non-repetition guarantees. These actions have a huge preventive potential because they can force specific policy goals on governments.

Fifth, aid agencies, multilateral banks, and influential scholars should please, please, please stop funding public anticorruption programs in places like Argentina. The money will be used to dress up the incumbent regime in anticorruption clothes while enlarging the strainer's holes. Just stop it. You are not helping. If you want to do good, fund NGOs and academia, though only if they are adopting the other four lessons (and especially if they understand how sectorial-based programs and human-rights advocacy relate to meaningful anticorruption reform). But be aware! In a place like this, showing off governmental support when applying for international funds should be a source of suspicion, not success. In case of doubt, take your money elsewhere, or go for direct pro-poor relief. Just please, please stop legitimizing anticorruption yada yada.

Notes

1 See Transparency International's Corruption Perceptions Index from 1995 to 2022. *See* Transparency International, Corruption Perceptions Index, available at www.transparency.org/en/cpi/2022 (last visited Apr. 18, 2023).

2 Susan Rose-Ackerman, The Political Economy of Corruption – Causes and Consequences, *Viewpoint*, Apr. 1996, at 4.

3 *See* Susan Rose-Ackerman, *Corruption and Government. Causes, Consequence and Reform,* 91 (Cambridge University Press 1999) [hereinafter *Corruption and Government*].

4 Susan Rose-Ackerman and Bonnie J. Palifka, *Corruption and Government: Causes, Consequences and Reform*, 236 (Cambridge University Press, 2nd ed. 2016) (1999).
5 Ibid. at 266.
6 *See Corruption and Government*, *supra* note 3, at 91–92.
7 Rose-Ackerman and Palifka, *supra* note 4, at 15.
8 *Corruption and Government*, *supra* note 3, at 130.
9 Ibid.
10 Susan Rose-Ackerman, Governance and Corruption, in *Global Crisis, Global Solutions*, 301, 309 (Bjørn Lomborg ed., Cambridge University Press 2004) [hereinafter *Governance and Corruption*].
11 Ibid.
12 *Corruption and Government*, *supra* note 3, at 130.
13 Rose-Ackerman and Palifka, *supra* note 4, at 277. The typologies are kleptocracy, bilateral monopoly, mafia-dominated states, and competitive bribery.
14 Susan Rose-Ackerman, Introduction and Overview, in *International Handbook on the Economics of Corruption*, at xiv, xx (Susan Rose-Ackerman ed., Edward Elgar 2006).
15 For a comprehensive study, see Natalia A. Volosin, *Corruption in Argentina: Towards an Institutional Approach* (Routledge 2019).
16 Quoted in Léon Pomer, *La Corrupción, una Cultura Argentina* [Corruptionm, an Argentine Culture] 113 (Leviatán 2004) (Arg.). The translation is mine.
17 The term *corporatist* is used here not in reference to open, participatory policy-making processes but in a specific sense familiar to Latin American countries and, in particular, to Argentina, whereby interest groups carved their place under the shadow of authoritarian rule. *See* Carlos S. Nino, Transition to Democracy, Corporatism and Constitutional Reform in Latin America, 44 *U. Miami L. Rev.* 131 (1989).
18 *See Consejo para la Consolidación de la Democracia, Reforma Constitucional: Dictamen Preliminar del Consejo para la Consolidación de la Democracia* (Eudeba 1986) (Arg.); and *Consejo para la Consolidación de la Democracia. Reforma Constitucional: Segundo Dictamen del Consejo para la Consolidación de la Democracia* (Eudeba 1987) (Arg.).
19 Jana Kunicová and Susan Rose-Ackerman, Electoral Rules and Constitutional Structures as Constraints on Corruption, 35 *Brit. J. of Pol. Sci.* 573 (2005).
20 *See* Guillermo Vitelli, *Negocios, Corrupción y Política. Las Repeticiones de la Argentina.* [Business, Corruption, and Politics. Argentina's Repetitions] 475 (Prendergarst 2006) (Arg.). The translation is mine.
21 *See Dos marchas reclamarán la renuncia de los jueces de la Corte Suprema*, Télam (Arg.), May 4, 2022, available at www.telam.com.ar/notas/202205/591476-corte-suprema-marcha-renuncia-jueces.html.
22 *See* Mariel Fitz Patrick, *Félix Crous, nuevo titular de la Oficina Anticorrupción: "Hay jueces que se parecen más a monarcas que a funcionarios de un sistema democrático moderno,"* Infobae (Arg.), Jan. 25, 2020, available at www.infobae.com/politica/2020/01/25/felix-crous-nuevo-titular-de-la-oficina-anticorrupcion-hay-jueces-que-se-parecen-mas-a-monarcas-que-a-funcionarios-de-un-sistema-democratico-moderno/.
23 *See La Oficina Anticorrupción dejó de ser querellante en las causas contra Cristina Kirchner y sus hijos*, Infobae (Arg.), May. 14, 2020, available at www.infobae.com/politica/2020/05/14/la-oficina-anticorrucpion-dejo-de-ser-querellante-en-las-causas-contra-cristina-kirchner-y-sus-hijos/; Patricia Blanco, *A días del alegato, la Oficina Anticorrupción renunció a la querella en el juicio por la obra pública contra Cristina Kirchner*, Infobae (Arg.), Jun. 14, 2022, available at www.infobae.com/politica/2022/06/14/a-dias-del-alegato-la-oficina-anticorrupcion-renuncio-a-la-querella-en-el-juicio-por-la-obra-publica-contra-cristina-kirchner/.
24 *See* Martín Angulo, *Obra pública en Santa Cruz: la UIF pidió la absolución de Cristina Kirchner,* Infobae (Arg.), July 11, 2022, available at www.infobae.com/politica/2022/07/11/obra-publica-en-santa-cruz-la-uif-no-acuso-a-cristina-kirchner-y-pidio-la-absolucion-de-todos-los-acusados/.

25 *See* Natalia A. Volosin, En las cloacas de la política: politización y cuentapropismo de la inteligencia argentina 298 *Revista Nueva Sociedad (N.U.S.O.)*4 (2022) (Arg.).

26 The *Mani Pulite* (clean hands) was a wholesale criminal prosecution launched at the beginning of the 1990s in Italy against former prime ministers, over 500 legislators, and several thousand public officials for political and bureaucratic corruption. The scandal yielded a severe political crisis and changed Italy's party system dramatically, but did not produce any real change to the "internal 'structures of governance' of corrupt transactions." *See* Alberto Vannucci, The Controversial Legacy of 'Mani Pulite': A Critical Analysis of Italian Corruption and Anti-Corruption Policies, 1 *Bull. Italian Pol.* 233, 236 (2009).

27 *See* Emir Sader, Op-Ed., Derechas gemelas, *Página*12 (Arg.), Feb. 27, 2015, *available at* www.pagina12.com.ar/diario/elmundo/4-266982-2015-02-27.html.

28 Emir Sader, Op-Ed., *De perseguido a candidato*, PÁGINA 12 (Arg.), Mar. 11, 2016, *available* at https://www.pagina12.com.ar/diario/elmundo/4-294295-2016-03-11.html. The translation is mine.

29 *See* Cristina Kirchner presentó un escrito y recusó a Bonadio: dijo que el Gobierno busca que vaya presa, *La Nación* (Arg.), Apr. 13, 2016, available at www.lanacion.com.ar/politica/cristina-kirchner-indagatoria-juez-claudio-bonadio-causa-venta-dolar-futuro-nid1888864/.

30 Horacio Verbitsky, Op-Ed., Usos de la corrupción, *Página* 12 (Arg.), May 15, 2016, available at ww.pagina12.com.ar/diario/elpais/1-299404-2016-05-15.html. The translation is mine.

31 *See* Horacio Verbitsky, *Robo para la Corona. Los Frutos prohibidos del Árbol de la Corrupción* [Steal for the Crown. The Forbidden Fruits of Corruption's Tree] (Planeta 1991) (Arg.).

32 Verbitsky, *supra* note 30. The translation is mine.

33 *See Qué es el "lawfare", la palabra que usó Cristina para criticar a la Justicia en su primer discurso en el Senado en 2017*, Clarín (Arg.), Dec. 27, 2017, available at www.clarin.com/politica/lawfare-palabra-uso-cristina-criticar-justicia-primer-discurso-senado-2017_0_Hy-cRr-Qz.html. *See also* Emir Sader, Op-Ed., La guerra jurídica, Página 12 (Arg.), Oct. 14, 2017, available at www.pagina12.com.ar/69019-la-guerra-juridica.

34 Charles J. Dunlap Jr., Lawfare Today: A Perspective, 3 *Yale J. Intl. Aff.* 146, 146 (2008).

35 *See, e.g.*, Nicola Perugini and Neve Gordon, Lawfare and the Threat of Human Rights, *Huffington Post,* available at www.huffingtonpost.com/nicola-perugini/lawfare-and-the-threat- of_b_7819282.html.

36 *See* Emir Sader, Op-Ed., Las crisis de la izquierda latinoamericana, *Página* 12 (Arg.), Feb. 27, 2016, available at www.pagina12.com.ar/diario/elmundo/4-293340-2016-02-27.html.

37 See James Leung, Xi's Corruption Crackdown. How Bribery and Graft Threaten the Chinese Dream, *Foreign Aff.*, May/June 2015, at 32, available at www.foreignaffairs.com/china/xis-corruption-crackdown. *See also* Fu Hualing, Wielding the Sword: President Xi's New Anti-Corruption Campaign, in *Greed, Corruption and the Modern State. Essays in Political Economy* 134 (Susan Rose- Ackerman and Paul Lagunes, eds., Edward Elgar 2015).

38 *See* Irma E. Sandoval-Ballesteros, From "Institutional" to "Structural" Corruption: Rethinking Accountability in a World of Public-Private Partnerships 3 (Edmond J. Safra Center for Ethics, *Harv. U., Working Papers*, No. 33, Dec. 20, 2013).

39 Ibid. at 5.

40 Johann Graf Lambsdorff, *The Institutional Economics of Corruption and Reform. Theory, Evidence, and Policy* 2 (Cambridge University Press, 2007) (referring to theorists such as David Bayley, Joseph Nye, Samuel Huntington, Nathaniel Leff, Theodore Morgan, Gregory Mankiw, Alberto Ades, and Rafael Di Tella).

41 *Foreign and Corporate Bribes: Hearings Before the S. Comm. on Banking, Housing and Urban Affairs*, 94th Cong. 41-42 (1976) (statement of George Ball, Lehman Bros.).
42 Statement quoted in Nora Boustany, Anti-Vice Vice Presidents, *Wash. Post*, Feb. 26, 1999.
43 Among others: the Panama and Paradise Papers, the FIFA scandal, Bernard Madoff's collapse, Lehman Brother's bankruptcy, Enron, the *Lava Jato* in Brazil, and Siemens' unprecedented bribery scandals.
44 Statement quoted in *Cristina Elisabet Kirchner: "El dinero que José López tenía en su poder alguien se lo dio y no fui yo"*, INFOBAE (Arg.), Jul. 12, 2016, http://www.infobae.com/noticias/2016/06/16/cristina-elisabet-kirchner-el-dinero-que-jose- lopez-tenia-en-su-poder-alguien-se-lo-dio-y-no-fui-yo/. The translation is mine.
45 Alex Cuadros, He Steals, but He Gets Things Done, *Slate*, July 14, 2016, *available at* ww.slate.com/articles/business/moneybox/2016/07/how_paulo_maluf_and_other_billionaire_builders_corrupted_brazilian_politics.html.
46 Rose-Ackerman and Palifka, *supra* note 4, at 415.
47 Ibid. at 416.
48 Ibid. at 429 (quoting Sergio Berensztein).
49 Hualing, *supra* note 37.
50 *See* Kalle Moene and Tina Søreide, Good Governance Facades, in *Greed, Corruption, and the Modern State. Essays in Political Economy*, *supra* note 37, at 46.
51 *See* Rose-Ackerman and Palifka, *supra* note 4, at 233.
52 *See*, *e.g.*, Akhil Gupta, Blurred Boundaries: The Discourse of Corruption, the Culture of Politics, and the Imagined State, 22 *Am. Ethnologist* 375–402 (1995) (examining the discourses of corruption in India).
53 *See* Rose-Ackerman and Palifka, *supra* note 4, at 233.
54 *See* Mariano Grondona, Historia de la corrupción [History of Corruption], in *La Corrupción* [Corruption] (Mariano Grondona ed., Planeta 1993) (Arg.).
55 Ibid. at 14–15.
56 *See* ibid. at 16. For an explanation of the "rouba, mas faz" issue, see Eugênio Bucci, Rouba, mas faz obra social, *Epoca* (Braz.), Oct. 9, 2015, available at http://epoca.globo.com/colunas-e-blogs/eugenio-bucci/noticia/2015/10/rouba-mas-faz-obra-social.html.
57 Grondona, *supra* note 54, at 17. The translation is mine.
58 Mariano Grondona, Medidas contra la corrupción [Anticorruption Measures], in *La Corrupción*, *supra* note 54, at 60.
59 Ibid.
60 The "*Lava Jato*" (Car Wash) is the popular name given to Brazil's corruption scandal involving the diversion of funds and extraction of bribes from contracts adjudicated through the country's oil company Petrobras. The case involves high-level officials from Lula da Silva and Dilma Rousseff's Worker's Party (PT), and coalition parties that paradoxically acted to impeach Rousseff.
61 *See* Brasilio Sallum Junior, o Impeachment de Fernando Collor [Fernando Collor's Impeachment] (*Editora* 34, 2015) (Braz.).
62 *See* Oficina de Coordinación y Seguuimento en Materia de Delitos contra la Administración Pública et al., los Procesos judiciales en Materia de Corrupción. Los Tempos del Proceso. Estado de Situación. [Legal Proceedings in Matters of Corruption. Processing Times. State of the Situation.] (Arg.) (2012), www.mpf.gob.ar/procelac-ap/files/2013/10/Los-procesos-judiciales-en-materia-de-corrupción.pdf.
63 Giuseppe Tomasi di Lampedusa's novel "The Leopard" famously portrayed Sicilian aristocracy's cynicism before the revolution with this statement. *See* Giuseppe Tomasi de Lampedusa, *Il Gattopardo* (Feltrinelli 1958) (Italy).
64 *See* Guillermo O'Donnell, Notes on Various Accountabilities and Their Interrelations, in *Enforcing the Rule of Law: Social Accountability in the New Latin American Democracies* 334, 334 (Enrique Peruzzotti and Catalina Smulovitz eds., University of Pittsburgh Press, 2006).

8 Good news? Latin American corruption scandals and the COVID-19 pandemic

Bonnie J. Palifka and Manuel Balán

The COVID-19 pandemic generated a crisis on many different key dimensions in Latin America, including a crisis of governance. In the first few months after the pandemic began in 2020, numerous corruption scandals hit the news. For example, in Mexico, the State of Hidalgo purchased 21 overpriced and defective ventilators from the son of the Director of the Federal Electrical Commission (Angulo, 2020a). In Ecuador, body bags were purchased at 13 times their normal price, and the police found thousands of face masks and coronavirus tests at the personal residence of former President Abdalá Bucaram (Kitreoff & Toj, 2020). In Brazil, 22 new investigations were opened between February and June of 2020 involving overpriced face masks, tests, mobile hospitals, and undelivered ICU beds (G1, 2020). In 2021, massive vaccination-related scandals broke out in Peru and Argentina, where people close to power (including the Peruvian President himself, Martín Vizcarra) received early doses of the vaccine through influence peddling (BBC, 2021; La Nación, 2021). The emergence of corruption scandals amidst the pandemic was hardly surprising, as corruption is widely considered a systemic problem in most Latin American countries.

Against this backdrop, the COVID-19 pandemic created a shock that introduced a set of new opportunities for corruption (Transparency International, 2021a; Rose-Ackerman, 2021), particularly in the health sector given the urgent needs for personal protective equipment (PPE), ventilators, other hospital equipment, and, eventually, vaccinations. This systemic shock was similar across countries, as the pandemic—by definition—affected the whole world with very few partial and only temporary exceptions (e.g., Uruguay had almost no COVID-19 cases until December of 2020), and real or feared scarcities developed. Yet, despite a similar shock, corruption scandals did not emerge everywhere: some published multiple allegations of wrongdoing over several news cycles, while others had little if any news on corruption. Perhaps fewer scandals are an indication of lower levels of corruption, but research has shown that the conversion from corruption to scandal is far from automatic and that there are other forces at play that explain how corruption becomes scandalous (Balán, 2011).

Corruption scandals are typically (and correctly) associated with corruption, but in order for them to come to light, some anticorruption institutions are also necessary. The first step is usually to increase transparency through Freedom-of-Information

DOI: 10.4324/9781003416234-10

Acts (FOIAs), freedom of press guarantees, and mechanisms like public procurement platforms. Once these are in place, investigative journalists can take advantage of them to uncover suspicious or clearly corrupt activity. Thus, developing countries may experience worsening corruption perceptions as these institutions begin to take shape. As the institutions develop further and become more effective, transparency is leveraged into accountability, and perceived corruption levels fall. FOIAs are more closely associated with reduced corruption when media outlets more actively cover corruption (Cordis & Warren, 2014). Historically, national and local corruption scandals have led to reform in the United States, the United Kingdom, and elsewhere (Rose-Ackerman & Palifka, 2016). Furthermore, press coverage of corruption has influenced electoral outcomes (Ferraz & Finan, 2008; Gentzkow, Glaeser & Goldin, 2006). Thus, corruption scandals are an important part of the long political journey from entrenched, systemic corruption to corruption as an exceptional occurrence (Johnston & Fritzen, 2021).

Because we study media coverage of corruption scandals, we do not cover official oversight mechanisms, but some news outlets do cover apparently well-working accountability institutions. Examples include investigations against at least 19 governors and 17 mayors in Colombia, resulting in the removal of at least one governor (Angulo, 2020a), and Brazilian investigations in at least 14 states, involving fraudulent contracts and the deviation of funds (G1, 2020).[1]

This chapter uses a mixed methodology, combining a statistical cross-country analysis that analyzes the extent to which there has been variation in corruption scandals during the pandemic throughout Latin America with a closer look at a few scandals that show the mechanisms at play. We argue that for acts of corruption to become public, anticorruption institutions—transparency, press freedom, and strong civil society—are necessary. In order to assess this argument, the chapter explores the role of transparency and oversight institutions in affecting the number of corruption-related news items in 36 Latin American and Caribbean countries in 2020. Our results suggest that corruption and transparency, especially in conjunction, contribute to more corruption-related news stories in the COVID-19 context, even when controlling for such coverage in the previous five years. The regression analysis is complemented with an analysis of several COVID-related corruption scandals. Scandals are a symptom of corruption, but also of institutional strength, and as such, a step toward greater accountability.

The first section analyzes the effect of the pandemic on corruption levels, building on a body of literature that links emergency situations, such as natural disasters, with corruption. The following section explores the relationship between corruption and scandals, showing that public information about corruption is far from an automatic process. Then we present the empirical analysis, providing details on methodology and sources of data, and reviewing the main findings. We then complement the statistical analysis with a closer look at COVID-19 related scandals in Mexico, Colombia, Peru, Ecuador, El Salvador, and Guatemala, shedding light on the causal mechanisms at play in the emergence of these scandals. The final section discusses the implications of the analysis.

Emergency and corruption

The COVID-19 pandemic presented a complex context for countries in the region. Although some leaders tried to downplay the dangers posed by the pandemic (McCoy, 2020), sooner or later in every country economic activity had to stop on a dime, health care services were stressed to their limits, and policymakers were forced to shift their attention to the multiple social and economic consequences of the pandemic (Cannon, 2020). For most people, this was an unprecedented situation, where lives were upended, and people's routines deeply affected (ibid.). Despite official measures taken against the pandemic, poverty, extreme poverty, and inequality rose rapidly, erasing between one and two decades of progress (CEPAL, 2021). Yet, in many ways, the conditions generated by the pandemic were comparable to those that prevail during extreme natural disasters and other emergencies (de Michele & Cruz Vieyra, 2020). Thus, we draw a parallel between the COVID-19 pandemic and other emergencies to analyze the impact that these situations have on corruption. In short, and as the literature shows, emergencies provide a broad window of opportunity for increased corruption. Following the literature on corruption and natural disasters, we identify three interrelated mechanisms that can result in increased corruption: (1) increased discretion in spending decisions, (2) increased public spending, and (3) easing of controls and reduced transparency. Given these effects, we argue that the pandemic embodied a shock that increased the opportunities for corruption across countries in the region.

Increased discretion

Emergencies, in particular health emergencies, generate an urgent need for certain products, which in the case of the COVID-19 pandemic included personal protective equipment, ventilators, ICU units, disinfectants, and alcohol, among others (Ranney et al., 2020). In addition, some governments distributed basic consumption packages to vulnerable populations that were out of work (Angulo, 2020b). This pressing need justified the use of expedited public contracting processes, departing from traditional norms by avoiding formalities that can delay the process by ensuring publicity and requiring multiple bids for contracts over a certain monetary value (Duri, 2021). Under expedited processes, spending and public procurement become significantly more discretionary, leaving public officials with room to maneuver in order to address pressing needs. However, speed and increased discretion, while often necessary, also generate more opportunities for corruption, such as collusion among bidding firms that do not have to compete and can increase prices and earnings unchecked, the request or offering of bribes in exchange for inflated prices, and an overall increase in other types of graft and rent seeking (ibid.). These mechanisms mirror the analysis carried out by Escaleras & Register (2016), who show that natural disasters lead to an increase in opportunistic corruption.

To make matters worse, Garcia (2019) and Radin (2016) show that the health care system is particularly vulnerable to corruption, even in normal times. As de Michele & Cruz Vieyra (2020) point out, "Problems of information and competitiveness make the sector particularly vulnerable to corruption—including fraud in hospital construction, drug approval processes, medicine prescriptions, beneficiary enrollment, and the private resale of supplies from public hospitals." The overall vulnerability of the health sector in the region became clear soon after the pandemic hit, both through the many scandals regarding public procurement of essential products, and through the very limited capacity of the health sector to address pressing needs for health services (Teremetskyi et al., 2021).

Increased spending

Aside from changing public procurement processes, emergencies also generate a growing need for public expenditure. On the one hand, emergencies generate specific needs for products that are required to address the consequences of the emergency, which imply increased spending for the provision of key items. On the other hand, emergencies invariably affect at-risk populations disproportionately, generating a need for financial relief for low-income sectors (Nikolova & Marinov, 2017). Regardless of whether the funds come from abroad in the form of humanitarian aid or from newly allocated public spending, increased spending generates a windfall that creates a growing opportunity to appropriate newly available resources (ibid.). It is through this mechanism that corruption spikes in the wake of emergencies and natural disasters, as demonstrated in Bulgaria (Nikolova & Marinov, 2017), the US (Lesson & Sobel, 2007, 2008), Brazil (Brollo, Perotti, & Tabellini, 2013), Vietnam (Nguyen, 2017), and cross-nationally (Yamamura, 2014). The findings hold across the different types of emergencies analyzed in these articles, ranging from natural disasters more generally to a specific focus on earthquakes, floods, or hurricanes.

Easing of controls and reduced transparency

Another effect of emergencies is that both governments and the private sector reduce operations, declaring that certain activities are essential while shutting down whole sectors deemed not essential (Cannon, 2020). One sector that is usually among the last to return to normal is the work of government control agencies explicitly tasked with monitoring the work of other public agencies. To put it bluntly, control agencies are not considered essential services in Latin America nor elsewhere. Moreover, this is the case both for area-specific control agencies tasked with overseeing the provision of public services, and for agencies with broader control mandates (such as Anti-Corruption Offices, Ombudsman, and General Auditing Offices) and Courts and the Judiciary more broadly. Other bodies (e.g., the legislature) that perform a wider set of activities leave control and monitoring aside, to focus on others deemed more essential.

In at least ten countries in the region, administrative activity such as judicial proceedings, audits, and the right to information provided by FOIA laws were suspended temporarily. Thus, the institutions responsible for fulfilling requests enjoyed extended or indefinite deadlines, although the transparency institutions in Argentina and Guatemala were exempted from the suspensions (Global Right to Information Rating, 2020). The overall effect is one in which most, if not all, controls of public sector work are eased and deemed secondary, leaving those making decisions unchecked for significant periods of time.

In contrast, several countries created portals specifically to promote transparency in COVID-19-related procurement and to receive reports of corruption. Examples include "Ecuador Transparente en Tiempos de COVID19" (FGE, 2020) and Colombia's "Herramienta de Control Ciudadano COVID-19" (Colombia Compra Eficiente, 2020). At least 20 countries in Latin America and the Caribbean received support from the IMF; of these, 14 were required to take anticorruption measures, such as publishing contracts and beneficial ownership information, and conducting audits of COVID-related spending (Transparency International, 2020). Despite these official commitments to full transparency, however, as vaccines became available, some countries designated procurement contracts for vaccines as classified, exempting them from these transparency requirements. In El Salvador, the Centro de Asesoría Legal Anticorrupción (ALAC) submitted a freedom of information request regarding COVID-19 tests, but the contracts were officially kept from public disclosure for two years (Cea, 2021). Mexico has kept vaccine contracts from public view for five years, despite the president's promise of transparent procurement (Olmos, 2021).

Aside from the causal link that reveals higher levels of corruption as the result of emergencies, corruption also aggravates the negative impact of emergencies and exacerbates the human cost of disasters (Escaleras, Anbarci & Register, 2006). This causal effect makes sense, insofar as corruption diverts scarce funds from their intended purpose, resulting in subpar responses to emergency situations. Hence there is a pressing need for studies that analyze responses to corruption in contexts of public emergencies, such as the COVID-19 pandemic.

Corruption and scandals

Although the emergency created by the COVID -19 pandemic produced increased opportunities for corruption and, very likely, higher levels of corruption in most countries, we show that pervasive corruption scandals emerged in some places while in other countries there was little to no news on cases of corruption related to the pandemic. Although media coverage of corruption has been used in the past as an indicator of overall levels of corruption (Di Tella & Franceschelli, 2011; Morris, 1991), the connection between corruption and scandal is far from linear (Balán, 2011). In order for the media to cover news on corruption a few elements are essential, such as access to government information (transparency), the ability to publish news that may be damaging to powerful political figures (freedom of the press), and a level of societal demand for such news (civil-society oversight). In other words, while the publication of news on corruption may seem to indicate to some that more corruption is taking place, it can actually be reinterpreted as good news, insofar as such publication can become a first step in holding corrupt actors accountable.

Therefore, the link between corruption and corruption scandals needs to be understood in all its complexity in order to correctly interpret the implications of scandals. In high-corruption contexts, news of corruption may not circulate due to governmental control of media sources, while in low-corruption contexts, there may be little to report. It is precisely in mid-level cases, both in terms of corruption and in terms of development, where corruption scandals may take place, and where such scandals can become useful information to achieve accountability and eventually prevent future acts of corruption. The analysis that follows examines scandals in this light, focusing on the factors that can explain higher and lower levels of scandal amidst an emergency that is ripe for corruption across the board.

Empirical analysis

In our empirical analysis, we examine how corruption, transparency, and civil-society oversight (civic engagement and freedom of the press) are related to the quantity of news about corruption. Specifically, based on the arguments laid out above, we shed light on the following hypotheses:

H1: Other things equal, countries with higher levels of corruption have more news items about corruption scandals.
H2: For a given level of corruption, countries with higher levels of transparency have more news items about corruption scandals.
H3: For a given level of corruption, countries with greater oversight have more news items about corruption scandals.
H4: Countries with both higher levels of corruption and higher levels of transparency have more news items about corruption scandals.
H5: Countries with both higher levels of corruption and greater oversight have more news items about corruption scandals.
H6: The combination of higher corruption, higher transparency, and greater oversight results in more news items about corruption scandals.

Methodology and data

To test the effects of corruption, transparency, and civil-society oversight on the publication of corruption-related news during 2020, we used OLS regression analysis on a series of stepwise models based on hypotheses H1–H6. Each model includes population as a control variable, using the logic that larger countries—and especially federations—have more opportunities for corruption scandals to occur. We also include the average number of news articles about corruption in the five years prior to 2020, with the expectation that countries with an established press willing to expose corruption scandals will be more likely to publish such stories during the pandemic. Therefore, our models consider the effects of higher corruption, transparency, and oversight, accounting for underlying journalistic anticorruption enthusiasm. Although we acknowledge that additional controls might be desirable, with only 36 observations parsimony is essential.

In order to conduct the analysis, we used the following data sources (selected, in part, for their full coverage of the region):

News2020: news items for 2020 with the keyword "corruption" in Latin American Weekly Reports, LAWR (LatinNews, 2021), a database of relevant weekly news from every country in Latin America and the Caribbean. The report presents a digest of the most important news from the region, in English, prepared by the staff of LatinNews for those interested in Latin America (LatinNews, 2022).

NewsAve: news items with the keyword "corruption" in Latin American Weekly Reports, LAWR (LatinNews, 2021) for 2015–2019.

Corruption: the World Bank's 2019 Control of Corruption Indicator (CCI), which is a composite index of (mostly expert) perceptions of corruption (World Bank, 2020). The CCI is reported on a scale from approximately -2.5 to 2.5, and also as a percentile rank; countries with higher numbers on either scale are countries that are better at controlling corruption. We used the percentile rank so that all numbers are positive, and reversed the scale, so that higher numbers represent more corruption, by subtracting the indicator for each country from 100. We chose this measure rather than the more popular Corruption Perceptions Index (Transparency International, 2021b) because the CCI covers all countries in Latin America and the Caribbean. Both measures use similar methodologies and are closely correlated with each other.

Transparency: the 2019 TRACE risk matrix Transparency domain, a composite indicator that measures government transparency (TRACE, 2019). It is expressed as a risk measure so that higher numbers represent greater risk (less transparency), so we reversed this measure by subtracting it from 100.

Oversight: the 2019 TRACE risk matrix Oversight domain, a composite indicator that measures press freedom and civil-society engagement—or rather, limits on them (TRACE, 2019). As with the Transparency domain, we reversed the scale so that higher numbers represent greater oversight.

Population: the country population, as reported by the United Nations (2019), recorded in thousands of inhabitants. We took the natural log of the population.

Table 8.1 provides the descriptive statistics for our variables. On average, six articles per country were published in 2020, but this belies a large variance. Twelve of the 36 countries had no corruption news in 2020. (Of these, eleven have lower-than-average corruption and nine have better-than-average oversight, but they are split regarding transparency.) These same countries had no corruption news published on LAWR during 2015–2019. Two countries, Belize and Jamaica, had corruption news for the first time in 2020. Annual news about corruption was higher before the pandemic than during 2020, possibly because journalists also faced limitations during quarantines. We should also take into account that Brazil, with the maximum annual corruption news, documented the wide-ranging Lava Jato and Odebrecht scandals during that period. The next highest, Peru (with 31.4) and Mexico (30.2), also experienced major corruption scandals between 2015 and 2019.

Corruption varies widely in Latin America, with Barbados, Uruguay, and Aruba scoring better than at least 85 per cent of countries, and Venezuela and Haiti in the

Table 8.1 Descriptive statistics

	Obs.	*Mean*	*Std. Dev.*	*Min.*	*Max.*
News2020	36	6.3333	7.9929	0	28
NewsAve	36	6.8833	12.1720	0	61
Population (1,000s)	36	18,101.31	40,806.63	53	212,559
lnPopulation	36	7.8864	2.3559	3.9703	12.2670
Corruption	36	50.3823	24.3230	11.5385	95.6731
Transparency	36	49.5556	14.7672	22	78
Oversight	36	65.1944	13.8271	29	89

Source: Authors' calculations

Table 8.2 Correlation coefficients

	news2020	*NewsAve*	*Corruption*	*transparency*	*oversight*
news2020	1.0000				
NewsAve	0.8394***	1.0000			
Corruption	0.6005***	0.3392**	1.0000		
transparency	0.0110	0.2124	-0.5608***	1.0000	
oversight	-0.3832**	-0.1219	-0.7052***	0.5356***	1.0000
population	0.7312***	0.9245***	0.2391	0.2457	-0.1066

Notes: ** statistically significant at the 95% level *** statistically significant at the 99% level

Source: Authors' calculations

most corrupt decile. In terms of transparency, Chile, Colombia, and Uruguay rank best and Venezuela, Nicaragua, and Suriname worst. The countries with the best journalistic and civil-society oversight are Puerto Rico, Costa Rica, and Uruguay, while the worst are Venezuela, Cuba, and Nicaragua. Note that, in general, Latin American countries have better oversight than transparency, according to the TRACE matrix.

Table 8.2 displays the correlation coefficients for the principal variables. There is considerable correlation among the variables. Notably, the average number of news articles (NewsAve) and transparency are correlated with fewer of the others. Importantly, NewsAve is uncorrelated with both transparency and oversight. The significant correlations are of the expected signs; specifically, more corruption is associated with more news items, less transparency, and less oversight.

A closer look at the data reveals that, for the most part, corruption moves in the opposite direction to transparency and oversight: only five countries with above-average corruption also have above-average transparency, while six countries are below average on both. On the other hand, thirteen countries have high corruption and low transparency; twelve are low on corruption and high on transparency. The relationship between corruption and oversight follows a similar pattern. Therefore, these data largely reflect the degree of institutional development.

Findings

To identify whether corruption, transparency, and oversight contributed to more or fewer corruption news items during 2020, we ran regressions using OLS estimation with robust standard errors (Table 8.3).[2] The robust and highly significant coefficients on news average demonstrate that countries with an established journalistic tradition of publishing news about corruption were more likely to uncover corruption during the pandemic. Even accounting for this, however, more corrupt countries were more likely to publish more corruption-related news in 2020 (models 1 and 2), until we take into account both transparency and oversight (models 3–6). Neither transparency nor oversight seems to make a difference when controlling for the other factors.

The interacted terms are introduced in models 4–6. With these terms, the coefficients on corruption become insignificant. Instead, the combination of higher corruption and greater transparency is significant and positive in regressions (6), and (7), while the combination of high corruption and high oversight results in fewer news items, according to model (5) only. Transparency alone also turns negative and highly significant in model (5). These non-intuitive results may reflect the underlying correlations among the covariates, so in Table 8.4 we regressed 2020 news on the controls and each variable or interacted term, in turn.[3]

Even when taking the variables one at a time (Table 8.4), transparency and oversight have negative coefficients, significant at the 95 per cent level. Therefore, neither transparency nor oversight is picking up the effects of higher corruption. On the contrary, countries with better transparency or oversight published fewer news articles related to corruption in 2020. Looking at the interacted terms (models 10–12), only the combination of corruption and transparency has the expected sign: countries with both higher corruption and stronger transparency standards were more likely to publish news about corruption in 2020.[4]

We set out to prove that countries with higher transparency are more likely to publish news about corruption. We found that the story is much more complex. The combination of high corruption and greater transparency (models 5 and 10) is, indeed, associated with more corruption news articles. Other combinations, however, such as high corruption and high oversight, or combining all three variables of interest, yielded insignificant results or significantly negative coefficients. Thus, our hypotheses H1 and H4 are most strongly supported by our results, but these relationships are far from conclusive. A larger sample size might yield more robust results.

Cases

This section discusses a number of specific corruption scandals that emerged during the COVID-19 pandemic. This analysis serves two main purposes. The cases provide concrete examples of the types of corrupt schemes that emerged during the first months of the pandemic, particularly as they related to public procurement processes of PPE, ventilators, and other medical equipment. At the same time, the cases help to illustrate the mechanisms analyzed in the statistical analysis. In concrete terms, we can see that the effects of transparency and oversight do not

Table 8.3 Regression results. Dependent variable: News2020

Variable	*(1)*	*(2)*	*(3)*	*(4)*	*(5)*	*(6)*
Corruption	0.0882***	0.1000***	0.0772	-0.0718	0.1311	-0.0154
	(0.02778)	(0. 0336)	(0.0493)	(0.1650)	(0.1486)	(0.3534)
Transparency		0.0209	0.0318	-0.1134	-0.3056***	-0.4007
		(0.0449)	(0.0388)	(0.1184)	(0.1057)	(0.4842)
Oversight			-0.0652	-0.0901	0.2283	0.2151
			(0.0697)	(0.1009)	(0.1370)	(0.3867)
Corruption*Transparency				0.0028	0.0079***	0.0147*
				(0.0025)	(0.0025)	(0.0074)
Corruption*Oversight					-0.0066***	-0.0032
					(0.0021)	(0.0046)
Transparency*Oversight						0.0023
						(0.0059)
Transparency*Oversight* Corruption						-0.0001
						(0.0001)
News average	0.3939***	0.3897***	0.3941***	0.3602***	0.3408***	0.3619***
	(0.1083)	(0.1099)	(0.1121)	(0.1184)	(0.1052)	(0.1002)
ln Population	0.7327**	0.6634**	0.5676*	0.8662*	0.6865	0.5075
	(0.2806)	(0.2822)	(0.3283)	(0.4872)	(0.4120)	(0.4229)
N	36	36	36	36	36	36
R^2	0.8349	0.8355	0.8415	0.8536	0.8860	0.8951

Robust standard errors. * Statistically significant at the 90% level. ** Statistically significant at the 95% level. *** Statistically significant at the 99% level.

Source: Authors' calculations.

Table 8.4 Testing individual variables one by one. Dependent variable: News2020

Variable	*(7)*	*(8)*	*(9)*	*(10)*	*(11)*	*(12)*
Corruption	0.0882***					
	(0.02778)					
Transparency		-0.0819**				
		(0.0393)				
Oversight			-0.1217**			
			(0.04974)			
Corruption*Transparency				0.0020**		
				(0.0009)		
Corruption*Oversight					0.0009	
					(0.0006)	
Transparency*Oversight*Corruption						0.0000
						(0.0000)
News average	0.3939***	0.3992***	0.3972***	0.3349***	0.3675***	0.3627***
	(0.1083)	(0.1218)	(0.1164)	(0.1101)	(0.1165)	(0.1251)
ln Population	0.7327**	1.3007***	1.0308***	0.8839**	1.1103***	1.3185***
	(0.2806)	(0.356)	(0.2950)	(0.3862)	(0.3963)	(0.4220)
N	36	36	36	36	36	36
R^2	0.8349	0.8108	0.8279	0.8192	0.8032	0.7899

Notes: Robust standard errors. * Statistically significant at the 90% level. ** Statistically significant at the 95% level. *** Statistically significant at the 99% level.

Source: Authors' calculations

necessarily go hand in hand. We begin with a case study of Mexico, followed by examples of scandals in Colombia, Peru, Ecuador, El Salvador, and Guatemala. These cases were not selected to represent the whole region, but rather provide concrete illustrations of the types of cases and causal dynamics discussed above.

Mexico

In January 2021, Mexico City was identified as "the most lethal global capital" of the pandemic (Anderson, 2021). Mexico's president, Andrés Manuel López Obrador, initially minimized the COVID-19 threat, holding (mask-less) public events throughout the country and keeping schools and businesses open until late March 2020, by which time the virus had gained momentum in the general population. An estimated 326,612 excess deaths[5] occurred in 2020 (Palacio-Mejía et al., 2021), on par with the 350,831 COVID-related deaths in the United States (which has double the population) in the same year (Centers for Disease Control and Prevention, 2022). Over a million formal jobs were lost between March and June 2020 (Martínez, 2020), and the impact on the informal sector was very large. The public policy response was tepid, at best, with no unemployment insurance for unemployed workers and insufficient social support programs. Doctors and medical staff suffered from a lack of PPE, sometimes forced to provide their own face masks or reuse those provided. Some Social Security hospital staff were fired for denouncing these conditions and corruption (Álvarez, 2020).

Mexico has an exemplary FOIA, created under pressure from journalists (Michener, 2010), and ranks second internationally on the Right To Information (RTI) Index (Access !Nfo and Centre for Law and Democracy, 2019). Its public procurement transparency platform, COMPRANET, was established in the 1990s and has been a model for other countries in the region (Palifka & Cuellar Lasso, 2024). The 2001 *Toallagate* scandal is an early and excellent example of the combined power of transparency portals and investigative journalism (Oppenheimer, 2001). Despite these impressive credentials, however, perceptions of corruption deteriorated rapidly from 2008 to 2018, as the country descended into a vicious spiral of corruption and organized crime (Palifka, 2020). López Obrador was elected on an anti-corruption platform.

The health sector had long suffered from corruption in procurement in the form of fake invoices from phantom companies; López Obrador's solution was to centralize medical purchases, which did not address the underlying problem and caused shortages. On March 27, he signed a proclamation relaxing public procurement protocols for medical supplies (Tello Arista, 2020).

Civil society responded with its own oversight mechanisms. Transparencia Mexicana and Tojil, both civil-society organizations, combined forces to create #SusanaVigilancia, a program to keep track of transparency in COVID-related procurement, justice, debt, and official oversight activities (Transparencia Mexicana, 2020). The Transparency and Anti-Corruption Initiative of the Tecnológico de Monterrey University created a website to receive reports of cases of corruption involving access to medical care or test results, public procurement, and (later) vaccines (ITAC and Derechos Humanos, 2021). Users reported "coyotes" (intermediaries) posted outside hospitals, offering admission for 1,500 pesos (about USD65) per week, the theft of medical supplies, and extortion to receive test results (Estrada and Guerrero, 2020). However, both the #SusanaVigilancia campaign and the reporting site seem to have lost momentum after June 2020.

On May 1, 2020, the investigative journalism organization Mexicanos Contra la Corrupción y la Impunidad (MCCI) published a report based on reviewing all the public procurement contracts for ventilators in Mexico. The report revealed that the most expensive ventilators (85 per cent more expensive than the least expensive) had been purchased by the Social Security (IMSS) hospital system in Hidalgo state, from Cyber Robotics Solutions, a firm owned by León Bartlett, the son of Manuel Bartlett, who is the head of the Federal Electricity Commission (Sánchez Ley & Olmos, 2020a). As a result, the Secretariat of Public Affairs opened an investigation and the contract was canceled (Sánchez Ley & Olmos, 2020b); the IMSS Hidalgo director and three other IMSS employees were suspended for the duration of the investigation (Sánchez Ley, 2020); and Cyber Robotics Solutions was debarred for two years and fined over two million Mexican pesos (about USD100,000) (El Universal, 2020). The fate of the suspended public servants is unclear. This was the most polemic case of corruption due to the connection to a member of López Obrador's cabinet, but there were many more cases of overpriced contracts, unfulfilled contracts, and phantom firms.

This case reveals the way that journalists are able to take advantage of procurement transparency to compare costs and discover anomalies. It further shows how a journalistic investigation can lead to at least some accountability. The remaining cases are explained in less detail, as examples of corruption news published in the region.

Colombia

In Colombia, the state took a more proactive role in anticorruption. The "Herramienta de Control Ciudadano COVID-19" (Colombia Compra Eficiente, 2020) allows citizens and authorities to review contracts and provides an e-mail address to report cases of corruption.

The General Comptroller denounced overpricing of up to 60 per cent in the procurement of ambulances in the Department of Putumayo (Angulo, 2020a; Fiscalía General de la Nación, 2020). The governor at the time, Buanerges Florencio Rosero Peña, was investigated and argued that usual procedures of transparency were not in force during the pandemic emergency, a point that was dismissed by the investigators (Fiscalía General de la Nación, 2021). Although he was initially removed from office and investigated, he was reinstated nine months later, as delays in the process precluded a more thorough investigation of the facts underlying the accusations (Caracol, 2021).

The General Comptroller also denounced overpricing in the purchase of food and soap, destined to be distributed to poor populations in a number of jurisdictions (Acosta, 2020). Some items, such as hand sanitizer, were purchased for over five times their market price (ibid.). The allegations had two dimensions, one associated with price gauging and the other with the distribution of goods for political ends. Despite an array of accusations, no funds were recovered and no public officials or private actors were charged with crimes.

Peru

In the Province of Sánchez Carrión, the Director of the Health Network denounced the provincial government for distributing hand sanitizer, liquid soap, and other cleaning supplies purchased at multiple times the market value (RPP Noticias, 2020). Moreover, the purchased products lacked the proper health approvals, and they were both ineffective and potentially harmful to users.

Similarly, there were multiple cases of corruption in the provision of goods and financial aid to low-income families (Gestión, 2020a). Recipients received fewer products than they should have, and only a portion of the funds that were approved. Investigators raided the family homes of 35 police officers accused of being implicated in the scheme (Gestión, 2020b).

Police officers were subject to another accusation. In procurement contracts for masks and disinfectant for police use, suppliers sold equipment that not only was overpriced but also was not meant for human use (Gestión, 2020c).

Ecuador

Prosecutors uncovered a criminal organization selling body bags to hospitals at 13 times the market price. The criminal ring included former president Abdalá Bucaram and his family members, according to prosecutors (Angulo, 2020a; Solano, 2020). Despite the seemingly overwhelming evidence that included finding thousands of masks and COVID-19 tests in Bucaram's personal residence, both he and his family were released due to insufficient evidence (DW, 2021). The case is still pending, having been delayed by legal hiccups several times and, most recently, postponed at the request of the defense (El Universo, 2023a).[6]

In another case, former and current municipal health secretaries from the municipality of Quito were implicated in the alleged embezzlement linked to the purchase of COVID-19 tests, along with the Mayor of Quito, Jorge Yunda (El Periódico, 2021). Yunda was removed from his post and was ordered to stay in the country (Primicias, 2021). But the judicial investigation stalled and had to restart in May 2023 (El Universo, 2023b). As in Colombia, government food-aid baskets were purchased at inflated prices: the Comptroller found that the kits contained products valued at USD95, but the purchase price was USD151. Rice was overpriced 67 per cent; beef and tuna were also overpriced. Especially suspicious was the fact that the contract was signed on April 1, with a supplier that had only entered the market on March 21 (Angulo, 2020b).

Guatemala

The Ministry of Health purchased overpriced drugs, at an over-valuation of over 50 per cent (Aristegui Noticias, 2020). In April 2020, the Anti-Corruption Prosecutor confirmed that the Public Ministry was reviewing ten complaints involving corruption in the acquisition of medical supplies to fight the pandemic (ibid.).

The Ministry of Health condemned the fact that fake and useless COVID-19 tests had been provided by Kron Científica e Industrial Sociedad Anónima (Pérez, 2021). Paperwork was falsified to make it appear as if the tests had first passed through the Ministry of Health's warehouses (ibid.). The Anti-Corruption Attorney (*Fiscalía contra la Corrupción*) has accused the firm criminally. Juan Pablo Arocha, the firm's representative and also a subject of the investigation, expressed a willingness to cooperate and repay the value of the contract; six thousand of the thirty thousand defective tests have been replaced. Ronaldo Estrada Rivera, the former employee of the Ministry of Health who signed the purchase contract, is also under investigation (Escobar, 2021). Two years later, no charges have been brought—the Public Ministry claims to be awaiting mutual legal aid from the United States—and the evidence is not available to the public. A representative of the civil-society organization Acción Ciudadana (Citizen Action) indicated that in post-CICIG[7] Guatemala, "most corruption cases are on pause, and the [Public Ministry] has focused on criminalizing the operators of justice" (Ola, 2023).

El Salvador

El Salvador is a case of rapidly deteriorating institutions. The International Commission against Impunity in El Salvador (CICIES)[8] uncovered a set of overvalued government COVID-19 related purchases from companies owned by public officials (Alemán, 2020). They shared their findings with the prosecutor's office. Allegations included three public officials selling overpriced masks to the Ministry of Health; Ministry of Health purchases of rubber boots from a company linked to the Minister of Health; and the purchase of medical supplies from questionable companies (Cáceres, 2020).

Separately, the Court of Audit denounced corruption in the purchase of food packages for low-income households (Flores, 2020). The Ministry of Agriculture rejected requests for information and the case went away without any concrete consequences or verified official information (ibid.).

Subsequently, the legislature, controlled by the party of the sitting president, approved a law that guarantees immunity for all public officials and private contractors involved in the provision of medical and health related supplies for the pandemic (Alvarado, 2021a), and canceled the CICIES convention with the Organization of American States (Alvarado, 2021b).

***

These cases demonstrate the power and limitations of civil society and journalism as ways to hold the corrupt accountable in times of crisis. Mexico had strong laws and transparency mechanisms in place since long before 2020, but official oversight was suspended and civil-society organizations stepped in, taking advantage of procurement transparency portals to reveal cases of overpricing. There was eventually some accountability in the form of canceled contracts and debarment. In contrast, Colombia's Comptroller's office worked quickly and aggressively, early on providing a portal for citizens to report cases of corruption and following through with the Prosecutor General's office. Prosecutors and other officials in Peru and Ecuador were similarly involved in uncovering allegedly corrupt dealings, but prosecutions there have been less successful. At the other extreme, Guatemala and El Salvador have canceled their respective justice contracts with international organizations and been hostile to journalists. Suffering the deterioration of institutions, their authorities have opened some cases without concluding them; furthermore, in El Salvador, those involved in COVID-19 procurement are now legally protected against prosecution, prolonging and expanding the lack of accountability.

Conclusions

The COVID-19 pandemic took most governments and societies by surprise. After the early months, Latin America became the region most affected, as a lack of clear public policies contributed to high case and mortality rates. The global state of emergency created supply–demand imbalances and urgent competition between governments trying to acquire ventilators, PPE, body bags, and mobile hospital units. This situation expanded existing loopholes and opened up new opportunities for corruption, fraud, and price gauging.

In a state of zero transparency and press censorship, such cases would remain hidden and enjoy impunity. While we acknowledge that publishing corruption scandals does not lead inevitably to justice, we argue that such scandals must be part of the long political fight that can lead a society to lower corruption and better governance. Furthermore, although transparency is not a cure for corruption, it facilitates the publication of corruption scandals, for example, by enabling investigative journalists to examine public contracts.

The countries of Latin America and the Caribbean have widely varying levels of corruption, transparency, and civil-society oversight. In this chapter, we have demonstrated empirically that a combination of high corruption and more transparency is a better predictor of corruption news than either phenomenon alone. It appears that government transparency makes it possible for the media to investigate problematic government activities. However, oversight of government, measured as a composite of press freedom and civil-society engagement, had no independent effect on corruption scandals that interest the media. That index, however, includes a heterogeneous collection of underlying factors, so it does not seem to be picking up cross-country differences in the strength of investigative journalism. In our case studies, we detail some of the scandals that took place and examine the ways that transparency and civil society combine to bring corruption scandals to light. The challenge remaining in many countries in the region is to strengthen institutional capacity, so that transparency leads not only to greater visibility of corruption, but to true accountability.

Notes

1 Brazil's Office of the Comptroller has been hailed as a success story (Recanatini, 2011).
2 All analysis was carried out using Stata 13. We also attempted Probit regressions, but they were uninformative.
3 We also tested separating the Oversight variable into its two subdomains: press freedom and civil society oversight. However, we had access to these subdomains for 2022 only. The correlation coefficient between Oversight in 2020 and Oversight in 2022 is 0.92; the correlation coefficient between the two subdomains is 0.94. We ran the equivalents of models (3) and (6). In the former, neither subdomain yielded a significant coefficient. In the latter, the coefficient on the interaction between transparency and civil society was negative and significant at the 0.1 level—nothing more.
4 Running these regressions using only countries that published at least one corruption-related news item in 2020 yielded similar results, except that the coefficient of 0.0016 on Corruption*Oversight was significant at the 95% level of confidence.
5 Excess deaths are the best estimate available because there were no COVID tests at first; then tests were not applied universally; and in many instances, deaths occurred from other causes because the hospitals were full of COVID patients.
6 Although he has not been brought to justice in Ecuador, Bucaram and his immediate family have been placed on the "designated" list by the U.S. government, which bars them from legal entry into the U.S., for "significant corruption" during his presidency (U.S. Department of State, 2022).
7 The CICIG (Comisión Internacional Contra la Impunidad en Guatemala, [International Commission against Impunity in Guatemala]) was an international organization formed by a convention between the United Nations and the Guatemalan state. From 2007 to 2019, the CICIG helped to train, expand, and professionalize criminal investigative capacity; built cases for the Attorney General to prosecute; and drafted policy proposals. It was generally seen as a model for other countries with high levels of impunity. In 2017, finding himself under scrutiny, then-president Jimmy Morales announced his intention not to renew the convention; in 2018 he named a new Attorney General, who proceeded to file charges against anti-corruption judges, magistrates, and prosecutors. Many of these have fled Guatemala rather than face imprisonment.
8 The CICIES was founded in 2019, at the beginning of the Bukele presidency. It was inspired by the success of the CICIG, but underwritten by the Organization of American States instead of the United Nations. It lasted less than two years. Civil society organizations are concerned that the Bukele government has "dismantled all the transparency and accountability institutions" (Avelar, 2023).

References

Access !Nfo and Centre for Law and Democracy (2019) Global Right to Information Rating. Available at: https://www.rti-rating.org/wp-content/uploads/2019/09/Historical-RTI-Data-29Sept2019.xlsx (accessed June 5, 2021).

Acosta LJ (2020) "$5 Cans of Tuna: Colombia Corruption Thrives during Coronavirus Outbreak." *Reuters*, April 14. Available at: https://www.reuters.com/article/us-health-coronavirus-colombia-corruptio/5-cans-of-tuna-colombia-corruption-thrives-during-coronavirus-outbreak-idUSKCN21W2RC (accessed June 5, 2021).

Aleman M (2020) "Fiscalía salvadoreña investiga compras durante la pandemia." *AP News*, November 11. Available at: https://apnews.com/article/noticias-4547cd1e01d05b0a142 42e2f3aa5bc63 (accessed June 5, 2021).

Alvarado J (2021a) "Asamblea otorga inmunidad a funcionarios de Bukele por compras durante la pandemia." *El Faro*, May 5. Available at: https://elfaro.net/es/202105/el

_salvador/25462/Asamblea-otorga-inmunidad-a-funcionarios-de-Bukele-por-compras-durante-la-pandemia.htm (accessed June 5, 2021).

Alvarado J (2021b) "Bukele sepulta su principal promesa de campaña, la Cicíes." *El Faro*, June 5. Available at: https://elfaro.net/es/202106/el_salvador/25526/Bukele-sepulta-su-principal-promesa-de-campa%C3%B1a-la-Cic%c3%ADes.htm (accessed June 5, 2021).

Álvarez E (2020) "Médicos y Autoridades del IMSS Revisarán Casos de Suspensión o Despidos." *MVS Noticias*, June 5. Available at: https://mvsnoticias.com/noticias/nacionales/medicos-y-autoridades-del-imss-revisaran-casos-de-suspension-o-despidos/ (accessed June 5, 2021).

Anderson B (2021) "Ciudad de México es la Capital Global Más Letal Durante la Pandemia de Covid." *La-Lista*, January 11. Available at: https://la-lista.com/ciudad-de-mexico/2021/01/11/ciudad-de-mexico-es-la-capital-global-mas-letal-durante-la-pandemia-de-covid (accessed January 11, 2021).

Angulo EM (2020a) "La oscura mina de oro en la que se convirtió la compra de equipos por la pandemia en Latinoamérica." *France24*, May 8. Available at: https://www.france24.com/es/20200508-corrupcion-insumos-m%C3%A9dicos-covid19-pandemia (accessed June 19, 2020).

Angulo EM (2020b) "Una plaga de corrupción consume los fondos para los 'kits de alimentos Covid-19'." *France24*, May 15. Available at: https://www.france24.com/es/20200515-corrupci%C3%B3n-kits-alimentos-pandemia-covid19-ecuador-colombia (accessed June 19, 2020).

Aristegui Noticias (2020) "Investigan corrupción en sector salud de Guatemala ante Covid-19." *Aristegui Noticias*, April 22. Available at: https://aristeguinoticias.com/undefined/mundo/investigan-corrupcion-en-sector-salud-de-guatemala-ante-covid-19/ (accessed June 5, 2021).

Avelar B (2023) "Bukele Anuncia una Nueva 'Guerra' contra los Corruptos y la Creación de Otra Cárcel en El Salvador." *El País*, June 2. Available at: https://elpais.com/internacional/2023-06-02/bukele-anuncia-una-nueva-guerra-contra-los-corruptos-y-la-creacion-de-otra-carcel-en-el-salvador.html (accessed August 15, 2023).

Balán M (2011) "Competition by Denunciation. The Political Dynamics of Corruption Scandals in Latin America." *Comparative Politics* 43(4): 459–476.

BBC (2021) "Coronavirus en Perú: 4 claves para entender el escándalo de las vacunas que causa indignación en el país." *BBC News*, February 17. Available at: https://www.bbc.com/mundo/noticias-america-latina-56101527 (accessed June 5, 2021).

Brollo F, Nannicini T, Perotti R and Tabellini, G (2013) "The Political Resource Curse." *American Economic Review* 103(5): 1759–1796.

Cáceres, M (2020) "Ministro de Salud compró $225,000 en insumos médicos a empresa de su familia." *elsalvador.com*, July 11. Available at: https://www.elsalvador.com/noticias/nacional/ministro-salud-alabi-compro-insumos-medicos-familia/732087/2020/ (accessed June 5, 2021).

Cannon, B (2020) "COVID-19 in Latin America: Uneven Responses, Uneven Impacts, Shared Challenges." In Carmody P, McCann G, Colleran C and O'Halloran, C (eds.), *COVID-19 in the Global South, Impacts and Responses*. Bristol University Press, 105–113.

Caracol (2021) "Rosero Peña retomó su cargo como gobernador del Putumayo." *Caracol*, August 17. Available at: https://caracol.com.co/emisora/2021/08/17/neiva/1629232917_251442.html (accessed August 24, 2023).

Cea, M (2021) "Alac Pide Desclasificar Información sobre Pruebas de COVID-19 y Paquetes Agrícolas." *La Prensa Gráfica*, May 25. Available at: https://www.laprensagrafica.com/elsalvador/Alac-pide-desclasificar-informacion-sobre-pruebas-de-covid-19-y-paquetes-agricolas-20210525-0053.html (accessed May 29, 2021).

Centers for Disease Control and Prevention (2022) *2020 Final Death Statistics: COVID-19 as an Underlying Cause of Death vs. Contributing Cause*. Available at: https://www.cdc.gov/nchs/pressroom/podcasts/2022/20220107/20220107.htm (accessed August 30, 2023).

CEPAL (2021) *Social Panorama of Latin America 2020*. Santiago, Chile: ECLAC.
Colombia Compra Eficiente (2020) "Herramienta de Control Ciudadano COVID-19." Available at: https://app.powerbi.com/view?r=eyJrIjoiMGQ5YTkwNzItZWVhMC00ZTgxLWJmYzgtODE1NWE0ZGZmNDVkIiwidCI6IjdiMDkwNDFlLTI0NTEtNDlkMC04Y2IxLTc5ZDVlM2Q4YzFiZSIsImMiOjR9 (accessed June 5, 2021).
Cordis AS and Warren PL (2014) "Sunshine as Disinfectant: The Effect of State Freedom of Information Act Laws on Public Corruption." *Journal of Public Economics* 115: 18–36.
De Michele R and Cruz Vieyra J (2020) "How Transparency Can Save Lives in the Coronavirus Crisis." *Americas Quarterly*, April 2. Available at: https://www.americasquarterly.org/article/how-transparency-can-save-lives-in-the-coronavirus-crisis/ (accessed June 5, 2021).
Di Tella R and Franceschelli I (2011) "Government Advertising and Media Coverage of Corruption Scandals." *American Economic Journal: Applied Economics* 3: 119–151.
Duri J (2021) "Corruption in Times of Crisis." Transparency International. Available at: https://knowledgehub.transparency.org/helpdesk/corruption-in-times-of-crisis (accessed June 5, 2021).
DW (2021) "Ecuador: sobreseen a Dalo Bucaram en caso de supuesta corrupción." *DW*, May 14. Available at: https://www.dw.com/es/ecuador-sobreseen-a-dalo-bucaram-en-caso-de-supuesta-corrupci%C3%B3n/a-57524324 (accessed June 5, 2021).
El Periódico (2021) "Fiscalía puede imputar al alcalde de Quito por corrupción al comprar PCR." *El Periódico*, February 11. Available at: https://www.elperiodico.com/es/internacional/20210211/fiscalia-imputar-alcalde-quito-corrupcion-11511910 (accessed June 5, 2021).
El Universal (2020) "Función Pública Sanciona a Empresa de Hijo de Bartlett." *El Universal*, July 7. Available at: https://www.eluniversal.com.mx/nacion/sancionan-hijo-de-bartlett-por-venta-de-ventiladores (accessed June 5, 2021).
El Universo (2023a) "Por Cuarta Ocasión se Difiere Audiencia de Juicio por Caso de Pruebas de COVID-19 que Involucra a Expresidente Abdalá Bucaram." January 6. Available at: https://www.eluniverso.com/noticias/seguridad/por-cuarta-ocasion-se-difiere-audiencia-de-juicio-por-caso-de-pruebas-de-covid-19-que-involucra-a-expresidente-abdala-bucaram-nota/ (accessed August 15, 2023).
El Universo (2023b) "Tribunal de Juicio del caso por peculado contra Jorge Yunda y otros formaliza con la nulidad que la etapa de juzgamiento vuelve a cero." May 24. Available at: https://www.eluniverso.com/noticias/politica/tribunal-de-juicio-del-caso-por-peculado-contra-jorge-yunda-y-otros-formaliza-con-la-nulidad-que-la-etapa-de-juzgamiento-vuelve-a-cero-nota/ (accessed August 24, 2023).
Escaleras M, Anbarci N and Register C (2006) "Public Sector Corruption and Natural Disasters: A Potentially Deadly Interaction." Department of Economics, College of Business, Florida Atlantic University Working Papers 6005.
Escaleras M and Register C (2016) "Public Sector Corruption and Natural Hazards." *Public Finance Review* 44(6): 746–768.
Escobar I (2021) "Pruebas falsas: Kron Científica e Industrial dice estar dispuesta a devolver Q7.3 millones al Estado." *Prensa Libre*, March 3. Available at: https://www.prensalibre.com/guatemala/politica/pruebas-falsas-kron-cientifica-e-industrial-dice-estar-dispuesta-a-devolver-q7-3-millones-al-estado-breaking/ (accessed June 5, 2021).
Estrada A and Guerrero C (2020) "Cuánta Corrupción se ha Denunciado en Tiempos de COVID-19?" *Animal Político*, June 18. Available at: https://www.animalpolitico.com/blog-invitado/cuanta-corrupcion-se-ha-denunciado-en-tiempos-de-covid-19/ (accessed June 18, 2020).
Ferraz C and Finan F (2008) "Exposing Corrupt Politicians: The Effects of Brazil's Publicly Released Audits on Electoral Outcomes." *The Quarterly Journal of Economics* 123(2): 703–745.
FGE (2020) "Ecuador Transparente en Tiempos de COVID19." Available at: https://www.fiscalia.gob.ec/buzon-de-transparencia (accessed June 5, 2021).

Flores R (2020) "Corte de Cuentas de la República con Auditoría a Medias a Paquetes Alimentarios." *La Prensa Gráfica*, July 22. Available at: https://www.laprensagrafica.com/elsalvador/Corte-de-Cuentas-de-la-Republica-con-auditoria-a-medias-a-paquetes-alimentarios-20200721-0080.html (accessed June 5, 2021).

Fiscalía General de la Nación (2020) "El expediente de la Fiscalía contra el Gobernador de Putumayo." November 13. Available at: https://www.fiscalia.gov.co/colombia/hechos-concretos/el-expediente-de-la-fiscalia-contra-el-gobernador-de-putumayo/ (accessed June 5, 2021).

Fiscalía General de la Nación (2021) "Fiscalía acusó al gobernador de Putumayo por presuntas irregularidades en la compra de 10 ambulancias medicalizadas." February 11. Available at: https://www.fiscalia.gov.co/colombia/corrupcion/fiscalia-acuso-al-gobernador-de-putumayo-por-presuntas-irregularidades-en-la-compra-de-10-ambulancias-medicalizadas (accessed June 5, 2021).

G1 (2020) "Wilson Lima é o 3º Governador Alvo de PF em Investigação sobre Combate ao Coronavírus; veja todas." *globo.com*, June 10. Available at: https://g1.globo.com/bemestar/coronavirus/noticia/2020/06/10/veja-operacoes-da-pf-sobre-coronavirus.ghtml (accessed June 30, 2020).

García P (2019) "Corruption in Global Health: The Open Secret." *The Lancet* 394: 2119–2124.

Gentzkow M, Glaeser EL and Goldin C (2006) "The Rise of the Fourth Estate: How Newspapers Became Informative and Why it Matte." In Glaeser EL and Goldin C (eds.), *Corruption and Reform: Lessons from America's Economic History*. Chicago: National Bureau of Economic Research, 187–122.

Gestión (2020a) "Fiscalía interviene en local del Minsa por presuntas irregularidades en compra de mascarillas N-95." *Gestión*, April 30. Available at: https://gestion.pe/peru/coronavirus-peru-fiscalia-interviene-en-local-del-minsa-por-presuntas-irregularidades-en-compra-de-mascarillas-n-95-contraloria-general-de-la-republica-covid-19-nndc-noticia/?ref=gesr (accessed June 5, 2021).

Gestión (2020b) "Allanan viviendas de policías presuntamente vinculados a compras irregulares en emergencia." *Gestión*, July 17. Available at: https://gestion.pe/peru/coronavirus-peru-allanan-viviendas-de-policias-presuntamente-vinculados-a-compras-irregulares-durante-la-pandemia-del-covid-19-cuarentena-estado-de-emergencia-nndc-noticia/?ref=gesr (accessed June 5, 2021).

Gestión (2020c) "Fiscalía investiga 15 denuncias a nivel nacional por compras sobrevaloradas para PNP." *Gestión*, May 3. Available at: https://gestion.pe/peru/politica/coronavirus-peru-fiscalia-investiga-15-denuncias-a-nivel-nacional-por-compras-sobrevaloradas-para-policia-nacional-pnp-covid-19-nndc-noticia/?ref=gesr (accessed June 5, 2021).

Global Right to Information Rating (2020) "COVID-19 Tracker." Available at: https://www.rti-rating.org/covid-19-tracker/ (accessed June 1, 2021).

Iniciativa de Transparencia y Anticorrupción (ITAC) and Derechos Humanos y Litigio Estratégico Mexicano (2021) *denunciacorrupcion.mx*. Available at: https://denunciacorrupcion.com/ (accessed June 5, 2021).

Johnston M and Fritzen SA (2021) *The Conundrum of Corruption: Reform for Social Change*. London and New York: Routledge.

Kitreoff N and Mitra T (2020) "Latin America's Virus Villains: Corrupt Officials Collude with Price Gaugers for Body Bags and Flimsy Masks." *The New York Times*, June 20. Available at: https://www.nytimes.com/2020/06/20/woaciónsicas/coronavirus-latin-america-corruption.html (accessed June 21, 2020).

La Nación (2021) "Horacio Verbitsky contó que llamó a Ginés González García y fue vacunado en el Ministerio de Salud." *La Nación*, February 19. Available at: https://www.lanacion.com.ar/politica/polemica-horacio-verbitsky-conto-llamo-gines-gonzalez-nid2607158/ (accessed June 5, 2021).

LatinNews (2021) *Latin American Weekly Reports*. Available at: https://www.latinnews.com (accessed June 5, 2021).

LatinNews (2022) *About Us*. Available at: https://www.latinnews.com/about-us.html (accessed August 25, 2022).

Leeson PT and Sobel RS (2007) "The Impact of FEMA on US Corruption: Implications for Policy." *Mercatus Policy Comment* 8.

Leeson PT and Sobel RS (2008) "Weathering Corruption." *The Journal of Law and Economics* 51(4): 667–681.

McCoy T (2020) "Brazil Ignored the Warnings. Now, while Other Countries Fret over a Second Coronavirus Wave, It Can't Get Past its First." *The Washington Post*, June 16. Available at: https://www.washingtonpost.com/world/the_americas/brazil-bolsonaro-coronavirus-cases-deaths-reopening-second-wave/2020/06/15/3282d27e-ae4b-11ea-856d-5054296735e5_story.html (accessed June 17, 2020).

Martínez MP (2020) "COVID-19 Ha Generado Un Millón 113,677 Despidos." *El Economista*, July 13. Available at: https://www.eleconomista.com.mx/empresas/Covid-19-ha-generado-un-millon-113677-despidos-20200713-0012.html (accessed June 5, 2021).

Michener G (2010) *The Surrender of Secrecy: Explaining the Emergence of Strong Access to Information Laws in Latin America*. Ph.D. Dissertation, University of Texas at Austin, Austin.

Morris S (1991) *Corruption & Politics in Contemporary Mexico*. Tuscaloosa: University of Alabama Press.

Nguyen Q (2017) "Do Natural Disasters Open a Window of Opportunity for Corruption?" *The Journal of Development Studies* 53(1): 156–172.

Nikolova E and Marinov N (2017) "Do Public Fund Windfalls Increase Corruption? Evidence from a Natural Disaster." *Comparative Political Studies* 50(11): 1455–1488.

Ola AL (2023) "Investigación por Pruebas COVID-19 Falsas que Adquirió Salud No Prospera." *Prensa Libre*, January 28. Available at: https://www.prensalibre.com/guatemala/comunitario/investigacion-por-pruebas-covid-19-falsas-que-adquirio-salud-no-prospera/ (accessed August 15, 2023).

Olmos R (2021) "México Pide Vacunarse, pero Oculta Hasta por Cinco Años Contratos de las Vacunas." *Mexicanos Contra la Corrupción y la Impunidad*, April 29. Available at: https://contralacorrupcion.mx/mexico-oculta-contenido-contratos-vacunas-covid (accessed May 31, 2021).

Oppenheimer A (2001) "El 'Toallagate', Modelo de Lucha Anticorrupción." *La Nación*, June 26. Available at: https://www.lanacion.com.ar/el-mundo/el-toallagate-modelo-de-lucha-anticorrupcion-nid315404 (accessed November 16, 2019).

Palacio-Mejía L, Wheatley-Fernández JL, Ordóñez-Hernández I, López-Ridaura R, Gatell-Ramírez HL, Hernández-Ávila M and Hernández-Ávila JE (2021) "Estimación del exceso de mortalidad por todas las causas durante la pandemia del Covid-19 en México." *Salud Pública de México* 63(2). Available at: https://doi.org/10.21149/12225 (accessed August 30, 2023).

Palifka BJ (2020) "Corruption, Organized Crime and the Public Sector in Mexico." In Graycar A (ed.), *Handbook on Corruption, Ethics and Integrity in Public Administration*. Cheltenham, and Northampton, MA: Edward Elgar, 274–288.

Palifka BJ and Cuellar Lasso D (2024) "Public Procurement and Corruption in Mexico." In Williams-Elegbe S and Tillipman J (eds.), *Routledge Handbook of Public Procurement Corruption*. Abingdon and New York: Routledge.

Pérez S (2021) "Guatemala: Denuncian compra de pruebas falsas de COVID-19." *AP News*, February 21. Available at: https://apnews.com/article/noticias-0f35e9e9cb8cdf1bfb3127a6d26ab614 (accessed June 5, 2021).

Primicias (2021) "La gestión de Yunda al frente del Municipio de Quito fue cuesta abajo." *Primicias*, June 4. Available at: https://www.primicias.ec/noticias/sociedad/yunda-quito-municipio-remocion-errores/ (accessed August 24, 2023).

Radin D (2016) "Why Health Care Corruption Needs a New Approach." *Journal of Health Services Research & Policy* 21(3): 212–214.

Ranney ML, Griffeth V and Jha AK (2020) "Critical Supply Shortages–The Need for Ventilators and Personal Protective Equipment during the Covid-19 Pandemic." *The New England Journal of Medicine* 382(18): e41(1)–e41(3).

Recanatini F (2011) "Anti-Corruption Authorities: An Effective Tool to Curb Corruption?" In Rose-Ackerman S and Søreide T (eds.), *International Handbook on the Economics of Corruption, Volume Two*. Cheltenham and Northampton, MA: Edward Elgar, 528–569.

Rose-Ackerman S (2021) "Corruption and COVID-19." *Eunomía. Revista en Cultura de la Legalidad* 20: 16–36.

Rose-Ackerman S and Palifka BJ (2016) *Corruption and Government: Causes, Consequences, and Reform*, 2nd edition. Cambridge: Cambridge University Press.

RPP Noticias (2020) "La Libertad: Hospital de Huamachuco distribuyó alcohol en gel, jabón líquido y lejía sin registro sanitario." *RPP Noticias*, April 29. Available at: https://rpp.pe/peru/la-libertad/coronavirus-peru-trujillo-hospital-de-huamachuco-distribuyo-alcohol-en-gel-jabon-liquido-y-lejia-sin-registro-sanitario-noticia-1261958?ref=rpp (accessed June 5, 2021).

Sánchez Ley L (2020) "IMSS Suspende A 4 Funcionarios por Compra de Ventiladores a Bartlett." *Mexicanos Contra la Corrupción y la Impunidad*, May 28. Available at: https://contralacorrupcion.mx/imss-suspende-funcionarios-ventiladores-bartlett/ (accessed June 5, 2021).

Sánchez Ley L and Olmos R (2020a) "Hijo de Bartlett Vendió al Gobierno el Ventilador COVID-19 Más Caro." *Mexicanos Contra la Corrupción y la Impunidad*, May 1. Available at: https://contralacorrupcion.mx/hijo-bartlett-ventilador-covid-19/ (accessed June 5, 2021).

Sánchez Ley L and Olmos R (2020b) "IMSS-Hidalgo rechaza ventiladores del hijo de Bartlett por no cumplir con requerimientos contratados." May 13. Available at: https://www.animalpolitico.com/2020/05/imss-hidalgo-rechaza-ventiladores-hijo-bartlett/ (accessed June 5, 2021).

Solano, G (2020) "Ex-Ecuador president detained in COVID-19 corruption raid." Available at: https://abcnews.go.com/International/wireStory/ecuador-president-detained-covid-19-corruption-raid-71052269 (accessed June 5, 2021).

Tello Arista I (2020) "3 Momentos de Corrupción en el Sistema de Salud." *El Universal*, July 24. Available at: https://www.eluniversal.com.mx/opinion/irene-tello-arista/3-momentos-de-corrupcion-en-el-sistema-de-salud (accessed July 25, 2020).

Teremetskyi V, Duliba Y, Kroitor V, Korchak N and Makarenko O (2021) "Corruption and Strengthening Anti-corruption Efforts in Healthcare during the Pandemic of Covid-19." *Medico-Legal Journal* 89(1): 25–28.

TRACE (2019) TRACE Bribery Risk Matrix. Available at: https://www.traceinternational.org/trace-matrix (accessed June 5, 2021).

Transparencia Mexicana (2020) "A 100 Días de #SusanaVigilancia, ¿Qué Riesgos Siguen Latentes en COVID-19?" *Transparencia Mexicana*, June 29. Available at: https://www.tm.org.mx/susanavigilancia-balance100dias-covid19/ (accessed June 30, 2020).

Transparency International (2020) "IMF COVID-19 Anti-Corruption Tracker." September 20. Available at: https://www.transparency.org/en/imf-tracker (accessed June 5, 2021).

Transparency International (2021a) "Prevención de la Corrupción en las Operaciones Humanitarias." Available at: https://images.transparencycdn.org/images/2010_HandbookHumanitarianOperations_ES.pdf (accessed June 5, 2021).

Transparency International (2021b) "Corruption Perceptions Index 2020." Available at: https://www.transparency.org/en/cpi/2020/index/nzl (accessed June 5, 2021).

United Nations Department of Economic and Social Affairs (2019) "Population Dynamics, 'World Population Prospects 2019'." Available at: https://population.un.org/wpp/Download/Files/1_Indicators%20(Standard)/EXCEL_FILES/1_Population/WPP2019_POP_F01_1_TOTAL_POPULATION_BOTH_SEXES.xlsx.

U.S. Department of State (2022) “Designation of Former Ecuadorian President Bucaram for Involvement in Significant Corruption.” Available at: https://www.state.gov/designation-of-former-ecuadorian-president-bucaram-for-involvement-in-significant-corruption/ (accessed August 15, 2023)

World Bank (2020) “Worldwide Governance Indicators.” Available at: https://info.worldbank.org/governance/wgi/Home/downLoadFile?fileName=wgidataset.xlsx (accessed June 5, 2021).

Yamamura E (2014) “Impact of Natural Disaster on Public Sector Corruption.” *Public Choice* 161(3–4): 385–405.

9 Politicization of international anticorruption law

Kevin E. Davis

In July 2019, U.S. President Trump attempted to persuade Ukrainian President Zelensky to investigate Joe Biden, and Biden's son Hunter Biden, for corruption. This affair, which led to Trump being impeached before the end of the year, provides a classic example of an attempt to politicize international anticorruption law. If President Trump's wish had been granted the incident would have represented two distinct forms of politicization: a politician influencing the law enforcement process and enforcement officials influencing the political process. This chapter considers the questions of what legal rules govern, and ought to govern, these kinds of interactions between legal and political processes.[1]

Answering these questions engages two recurring themes in Susan Rose-Ackerman's scholarship. First, what is the appropriate relationship between legal and political actors?[2] Second, what role should foreign actors play in combating political corruption in any given country?[3] Exploring these themes in a volume in her honor seems only fitting.

The dominant view in international anticorruption law condemns political influence of anticorruption enforcement that has cross-border effects but appears to condone anticorruption enforcement actions that influence foreign political processes. The analysis below points to a more nuanced approach. The basic argument is that international interactions between law enforcement and political processes should be evaluated in terms of legitimacy as well as effectiveness and that the results of such an evaluation will be highly contingent. The analysis pulls together two strands in the literature on international anticorruption law that usually remain separate. One strand contains debates on the effectiveness and legitimacy of international anticorruption enforcement practices aimed at political actors in other societies.[4] A second strand considers the regulation of political intervention in international anticorruption enforcement actions.[5] Beyond international anticorruption law, the argument here is consistent with a broader literature that documents and justifies variation across Western democracies in how they structure the relationship between prosecutors and domestic politics.[6]

This chapter begins by defining politicization of anticorruption enforcement to encompass both international lobbying and international enforcement, that is to say, both the influence of politicians on anticorruption enforcement and the influence of anticorruption enforcement on political activity. The next section outlines mechanisms for controlling each form of influence, in both domestic and international

DOI: 10.4324/9781003416234-11

law. The third section discusses the extent to which those mechanisms constrain politicization of anticorruption enforcement with international dimensions. The following section discusses how international lobbying and enforcement ought to be regulated and evaluates alternatives to the currently dominant approach, including the proposal for an International Anti-Corruption Court. The final section concludes.

Forms of politicized anticorruption enforcement

There are at least two ways in which law enforcement can be politicized. First, political actors can seek to influence law enforcement. Second, law enforcers can influence the political process. The first form of politicization involves political influence of enforcement while the other involves political influence through enforcement. For convenience, we will call these forms of politicization *lobbying* and *enforcement* respectively. Lobbying and enforcement whose effects cross international borders will be referred to as *international lobbying* and *international enforcement*. We are only concerned here with lobbying by political actors, as opposed to, say, private actors, and enforcement that has significant political ramifications. However, to avoid cumbersome terminology the restriction to activities with political dimensions will remain implicit.

Lobbying and enforcement may be interrelated. Most notably, political actors may attempt to induce law enforcement agencies to target other political actors in order to alter the balance of power in their favor. Alternatively, enforcement agencies may target politicians in order to advance their own political agendas. President Trump's interactions with the Ukrainian government involved interrelated forms of international lobbying and enforcement. Trump was clearly a politician, Joe Biden was his leading political opponent, and Trump's aim was to influence the decisions of Ukrainian law enforcement agencies and thereby affect the outcome of the U.S. presidential election due to take place in November 2020.[7] Since the Bidens were both U.S. nationals, if Ukraine had opened an investigation of them it would have involved an instance of international enforcement prompted by international lobbying.

These are not isolated examples. For instance, President Trump was not the only U.S. politician to try to influence Ukraine's anticorruption enforcement. Joe Biden actually beat him to the punch. In 2016, while he was Vice-President of the United States, Biden spearheaded efforts on the part of the Obama administration to have the Ukrainian government dismiss Viktor Shokin, the country's prosecutor general.[8] The U.S. and its allies – including the European Union, international financial institutions and Ukrainian reformers – accused Shokin of blocking cases against his political allies. The Ukrainian Parliament voted overwhelmingly to dismiss Shokin after Biden reportedly threatened to withhold $1 billion worth of loan guarantees for Ukraine.[9] Biden's conduct was what President Trump tried to induce Zelensky to investigate.

There are also historical examples of U.S. anticorruption enforcement actions that have influenced political events in other countries. One famous example involved United Brands, a firm that played a prominent role in Latin American politics for much of the 20th century on account of its dominance of banana production. In 1975, the U.S. Securities and Exchange Commission accused United Brands of paying a $2.5 million dollar bribe to Honduran officials and the firm later pleaded guilty to a criminal charge of conspiracy to commit wire fraud. The revelations led to the ouster of the president of Honduras in a military coup.[10] The United Brands affair was one of several corruption scandals in this time period that motivated the adoption of the U.S. Foreign Corrupt Practices Act of 1977 (FCPA).[11]

A more recent example of the politicization of international anticorruption law is Operation Car Wash ("*Lava Jato*" in Portuguese), a large enforcement operation initiated by enforcement agencies in Brazil which led to parallel enforcement operations in the U.S. (and elsewhere) and allegations that the U.S. agencies unduly influenced their Brazilian counterparts.[12] The initial focus of Car Wash was a group of Brazilian construction companies that paid bribes to obtain contracts from Petrobras, a large oil company partially owned by the Brazilian state. Luiz Inácio Lula da Silva ("Lula"), the former president of Brazil, was convicted of receiving bribes from one of the construction companies, Odebrecht. Although the conviction was eventually overturned, in the interim Lula was barred from running for president. This created a political vacuum that undoubtedly benefited Jair Bolsonaro, eventual winner of the 2018 presidential election. Four years later, the recently exonerated Lula ran against and narrowly defeated Bolsonaro.

Car Wash also had political ramifications outside of Brazil.[13] The investigation expanded beyond dealings with Petrobras to cover a wide range of additional misconduct, including bribes paid by Odebrecht in other countries in Latin America and Africa. The Odebrecht corruption scandal implicated officials at the very highest levels of government, including the last five presidents of Peru and former presidents in Bolivia, Ecuador, El Salvador, and Panama. The officials implicated in the scheme were typically ousted, upsetting the political balance of power in their respective countries. Years after the operation concluded, the aftershocks continue to reverberate through Latin American politics.

Domestic law mechanisms for depoliticizing anticorruption enforcement

Lobbying and enforcement are susceptible to different types of control mechanisms. Each type of control can be further divided into mechanisms that *prohibit* the relevant form of politicization and those that *protect* the targets of politicization. There is considerable variety within each of these classes of control mechanisms.

Consider the mechanisms that prohibit or protect against lobbying. Prohibitions apply to politicians who might seek to exert influence. For example, in the Westminster system of government, the Attorney General is an elected member of Parliament appointed by the Prime Minister but is solely responsible for decisions on whether to authorize criminal prosecutions, and members of cabinet are prohibited from putting the Attorney General "under pressure."[14] By contrast, the alternative way of addressing lobbying, protection of enforcement officials, generally is accomplished by limiting the ability of political actors to dismiss enforcement officials or to control the budgets or mandates of their agencies. For instance, in Brazil, although the head of the Ministério Público is politically appointed, individual prosecutors within the agency are selected through a competitive examination, earn tenure after two years on the job, and are protected from being demoted or having their salaries reduced.[15] Moreover, the agency presents its own budget to the legislature.[16]

In some situations, the existence of multiple enforcement agencies, a condition sometimes referred to as "institutional multiplicity", serves as another form of protection against lobbying. This is only plausible in situations where it is safe to assume that multiple agencies are unlikely to all succumb to undesirable influences at the same time.[17] Under these conditions, institutional multiplicity can be an effective way of preventing politicians from blocking anticorruption enforcement. However, institutional multiplicity does nothing to thwart lobbying in situations where a single agency is capable of blocking other agencies' enforcement actions. Moreover, institutional multiplicity can facilitate rather than thwart politicization when, as in the case of President Trump, a politician's aim is to initiate rather than to block an enforcement action. In this scenario, the more enforcement agencies there are to influence, the greater the odds of success.

A distinct class of mechanisms prohibit or protect against enforcement. Prohibitions represent the most direct approach and are used extensively in U.S. federal law. U.S. Department of Justice policy states that "politics must play no role in the decisions of federal investigators or prosecutors regarding any investigations or criminal charges."[18] U.S. federal law also prohibits all federal employees from engaging in partisan political activity while on duty or while using federal government property.[19] Sometimes even actions that might have the effect of altering the balance of political power are prohibited, regardless of their purpose. For instance, the U.S. Department of Justice has a longstanding rule against taking any investigative steps or making any overt disclosures that may affect an election in the two or three months prior to the election.[20]

Another approach to addressing enforcement is to protect political actors. For example, in Paraguay, legislators can only be arrested or prosecuted with the approval of a two-thirds majority of the members of the legislative chamber to which they belong.[21] Ministers and presidents can only be prosecuted after being impeached by two-thirds majorities of both legislative chambers, and former presidents enjoy these protections for life.[22] Meanwhile in Brazil, federal politicians benefit from the *foro privilegiado*, a right to be criminally prosecuted only before the country's Supreme Court in proceedings initiated by the politically appointed prosecutor general.[23]

Countries vary in the combination of measures they use to regulate the interaction between law enforcement and politics. For instance, in U.S. federal law many of the norms that limit political influence upon criminal prosecutions and bar prosecutions that will have political effects are not legally binding, and while U.S. politicians enjoy several forms of immunity, none is likely to shield them from liability for corruption.[24] The Brazilian legal system takes a very different approach: limits on political influence and provisions for immunity are constitutionally enshrined. However, there appears to be no legally binding prohibition on prosecutions that will affect elections. Each country's approach has the potential to strike a different balance between shielding law enforcement and the political process.

International law mechanisms for depoliticizing anticorruption enforcement

International law, at least as set out in the two leading anticorruption conventions, provides substantial safeguards against lobbying but does relatively little to limit enforcement.

The United Nations Convention against Corruption ("UNCAC") and the OECD Convention on Combatting Bribery of Foreign Public Officials in International Business Transactions ("OECD Convention"), generally stress the need for measures that insulate anticorruption enforcement institutions from political pressures.[25] Article 36 of the UNCAC requires state parties to have specialized bodies charged with enforcement of anticorruption laws which "shall be granted the necessary independence, in accordance with the fundamental principles of the legal system of the State Party, to be able to carry out their functions effectively and without any undue influence." In addition, the UNCAC Implementation Review Group has concluded that Article 30(3) of the Convention, which requires prosecutorial discretion to be exercised to maximize effectiveness, also requires prosecutors' discretionary decisions to be made independently from members of the executive.[26]

The OECD Convention deals with insulation of enforcement agencies from political influence even more explicitly than the UNCAC. Article 5 of the OECD Convention provides that investigation and prosecution of foreign bribery "shall not be influenced by considerations of national economic interest, the potential effect upon relations with another State or the identity of the natural or legal persons involved," three of the main considerations likely to motivate political actors to exert pressure on enforcement officials.[27] The state parties' official commentary on this article explains, "in order to protect the independence of prosecution, [prosecutorial] discretion is to be exercised on the basis of professional motives and is not to be subject to improper influence by concerns of a political nature."[28]

In contrast with the protections afforded to enforcement officials, international law provides public officials little protection against enforcement. The relevant body of international law is the law of official immunities, which confers immunity upon certain public officials against law enforcement actions brought by foreign states. Those immunities have a very limited scope.[29] Under customary international law, heads of state, heads of government and ministers of foreign affairs enjoy "personal" immunity from legal actions in other states, but only during their term in office and so long as the immunity is not waived by their home state. In addition, all state officials enjoy immunity from liability in foreign states for acts performed in an official capacity even after the end of their term, except where they have committed certain violent international crimes. This second form of immunity, sometimes known as functional immunity, also can be waived by the state of the relevant foreign official. More importantly, many courts and commentators have concluded that corrupt acts do not qualify as acts performed in an official capacity, suggesting that functional immunity does not protect foreign officials against prosecution for corruption.[30]

Constraints on international lobbying and enforcement

In general, both domestic and international law appear to place more constraints on international lobbying than upon international enforcement, but the constraints upon international lobbying are far from complete. In other words, it seems that the law often provides enforcement agencies with some protection against being influenced by foreign political actors but generally allows political processes to be influenced by foreign enforcement agencies. I express these conclusions about the state of the law tentatively, however, because I have not conducted an exhaustive analysis of the subject.

My tentative conclusion rests on several points. To begin, prohibitions on lobbying do not necessarily apply to attempts to influence foreign enforcement actions. For example, it was reasonably clear that President Trump would have violated longstanding norms – though perhaps not legally binding rules – if he had tried to persuade the U.S. Department of Justice to investigate the Bidens for corruption. However, no one suggested that President Trump breached U.S. norms simply by trying to influence Ukrainian enforcement agencies. The basis for his impeachment was *how* he tried to influence the Ukrainians, in other words, by what means and to what end. He was impeached for trying to influence the Ukrainians in ways that threatened the U.S. political process and U.S. national security.[31]

The main constraints on international lobbying are provided by domestic and international laws that protect enforcement agencies from political influence. However, in spite of the lofty language of the international anticorruption bodies, those protections often seem to be imperfect. For example, Ukraine's domestic law provided only limited protection against U.S. efforts to influence anticorruption enforcement. In 2015, under pressure from international actors, the country began to reform its anticorruption framework in order to, among other things, enhance enforcement agencies' independence from political influence. But in 2019, when President Trump placed his fateful call to President Zelensky, the reforms were not yet complete. A few months later European authorities reported that additional measures were still required to guarantee the independence of the anticorruption agency, judges, and prosecutors.[32]

Enforcement agencies in some countries may receive more protection from lobbying than agencies in the Ukraine, but there are many countries in which independence is not guaranteed. This is true even among members of the OECD Convention that enforce their laws against foreign bribery most vigorously. The best data on this topic comes from the OECD Working Group on Bribery, which evaluates countries' compliance with the OECD Convention's rules on enforcement of laws against foreign bribery. In recent years, the OECD Working Group has raised concerns about the independence of enforcement officials in several state parties to the Convention, including France and the United Kingdom, both of which are relatively vigorous enforcers of laws against foreign bribery.[33]

The fact that multiple countries' enforcement agencies can pursue cases of transnational corruption will sometimes override the effects of political influence on transnational anticorruption enforcement, much as it does in the domestic sphere. Specifically, even if one country refrains from enforcement on account of political considerations, the effect of its restraint might be undone by another country's enforcement action. For example, in late 2006 the Director of the Serious Fraud Office of the United Kingdom decided to discontinue an investigation into corrupt dealings on the part of BAE Systems Plc in relation to a massive defense contract with the government of Saudi Arabia. The decision was made with the support of the Attorney General, to whom the Director reported, and in response to pressure from the government of Saudi Arabia, the Prime Minister, and the Foreign and Defence Secretaries. The decision was controversial, but the UK's highest court, which at that time was the House of Lords, found that the conduct of the Director and the Attorney General, including their consultations with members of cabinet, was consistent with applicable principles of British law.[34] Nevertheless, the U.S. proceeded with its own investigation of BAE and in 2010 BAE pleaded guilty to various charges and was sentenced to pay a $400 million criminal fine.[35] The effect of the U.S. action was to negate the effects of international lobbying on the part of both the U.K. and Saudi governments, even though that lobbying was permitted under British and (I presume) Saudi law.

Turning to international enforcement, although the topic warrants further research, constraints on the use of anticorruption enforcement to influence political processes across borders appear to be quite limited. To begin, even when countries, such as the U.S., prohibit enforcement agencies from taking political considerations into account, it is unclear whether those prohibitions bar consideration of the impact on foreign political processes. In the case of the U.S., it is difficult to resist the conclusion that some U.S. enforcement actions actually have been intended to influence foreign political processes.[36] A case in point is the 2020 indictment of Venezuelan President Nicolás Maduro Moros, who was indicted along with several other officials in his government on charges of drug trafficking and, for some officials, corruption.[37] The indictment made no explicit reference to political considerations, but it was announced just over one year after the U.S. decided not to recognize Maduro as head of state, and just one month after President Trump referred to Maduro as "an illegitimate ruler, a tyrant who brutalizes his people," and promised that his "grip on tyranny will be smashed and broken."[38] In the course of announcing the indictment, the Attorney General of the United States declared, "Maduro and the other defendants have betrayed the Venezuelan people and corrupted Venezuela's institutions. While the Venezuelan people suffer, this cabal lines their pockets with drug money and the proceeds of their corruption. This has to come to an end."[39]

The indictment of President Maduro also shows that cross-border enforcement can limit the effects of protections that political actors enjoy under domestic law, particularly if the enforcing state does not recognize the legitimacy of the relevant politician's regime. Whatever protection from prosecution Maduro enjoyed under domestic law in Venezuela,[40] or under international law in states that continued to recognize him as head of state, did not prevent the U.S. from indicting him in a U.S. court.[41]

Cross-border enforcement also may serve to pressure foreign institutions to limit the scope of protection they provide. That was arguably the effect of the U.S. government's prosecution of Juan Orlando Hernández, who was elected president of Honduras in 2013 and 2017, and left office at the beginning of 2022. In 2019, a U.S. court convicted Hernández's brother, Juan Antonio, of being a large-scale drug trafficker and sentenced him to life imprisonment plus 30 years after he was arrested in Miami. Almost immediately after leaving office, Juan Orlando Hernández became a member of the Central American Parliament, a position that reportedly entitled him to immunity in the states represented in the Parliament.[42] Nonetheless, the U.S. quickly filed a request to have Hernández extradited to face charges that he took millions of dollars in bribes in exchange for facilitating shipments of cocaine through Honduras and shielding the traffickers. Interestingly, the Supreme Court of Honduras refused to block the government from complying with the extradition request.[43] It is unclear whether Hernández did in fact enjoy immunity from prosecution in Honduras that was properly removed by the Supreme Court or whether the initial reports that he enjoyed immunity were mistaken.[44] In any event, the effect of the U.S. prosecution was to reset previous understandings of the limits of immunity for similarly situated Honduran politicians.

How to regulate international lobbying and enforcement

So far we have considered what constraints are placed on international lobbying and enforcement, but it is also worth asking what constraints ought to be imposed. The OECD Working Group opposes international lobbying but encourages international enforcement. Since the members of the Working Group consist of the some of the most economically powerful states in the world, its views are naturally quite influential. However, the merits of this aspect of the OECD paradigm – to use a phrase I have adopted in other writing – are contestable.[45]

Alternative approaches to regulation of the politicization of anticorruption law can be evaluated in terms of both their likely effectiveness in protecting the public interest in controlling corruption and their legitimacy.[46] Legitimacy depends, in part, on effectiveness, but it also depends on whether all affected interests are represented in the decision-making process. This framework implies that the roles played by politicians and law enforcement agencies ought to depend on factors such as relative expertise, impartiality, and accountability. Viewed in this way it is difficult to arrive at any firm conclusion about how to regulate the politicization of anticorruption law.

From the perspective of an institutional designer, political actors and enforcement agencies bring different strengths and weaknesses to anticorruption law. Political actors' great strength is that they typically represent and are accountable to a segment of the domestic population. However, politics inevitably involves partisan conflict and individual politicians are unlikely to be impartial when groups with which they are affiliated clash with other groups. It also is difficult to ensure that politicians have expertise relevant to anticorruption law, at least without narrowing the portion of the population they represent. By contrast, in principle it should not be difficult to design enforcement agencies with expertise that is superior to that of politicians. It is also commonplace – at least outside the United States, where elected prosecutors, judges, and sheriffs abound – for enforcement agencies to be subject to restrictions on lobbying and other safeguards designed to limit the influence of partisan interests. However, absence of external influence does not guarantee impartiality, since agents may develop political biases independently. Moreover, measures designed to ensure the expertise and impartiality of enforcement agencies tend to reduce their representativeness and accountability.

In the face of these competing considerations, different jurisdictions may justifiably adopt different approaches to regulation of lobbying and enforcement.[47] In restricting lobbying and tolerating enforcement, the OECD paradigm prioritizes expertise and impartiality over ensuring that enforcement practices reflect the views of all affected parties. There is no self-evident justification for that set of priorities.

In fact, the analysis of how to regulate *international* lobbying and enforcement is particularly indeterminate. At first glance, the legitimacy of international lobbying may seem questionable because those whose interests are being represented are not members of the population to whom the enforcement agency is formally accountable. In other words, President Trump and the Saudi government did not represent the interests of Ukrainians or British people when they lobbied Ukrainian and U.K. enforcement agencies respectively. At the same time, each case demonstrates that international lobbying provides a channel for an enforcement agency to hear from people who are formally outside of its political community but may, nonetheless, be affected by its decisions. Providing that kind of communication channel is not illegitimate.

To see this, suppose that President Trump had a genuine and well-founded belief that Joe Biden had engaged in corruption in Ukraine, a fact which if true would almost by definition threaten the integrity of the U.S. political system. In this scenario it would be perfectly legitimate for President Trump and President Zelensky to try to persuade Ukrainian anticorruption agencies to take the threat seriously, and for the agency to take those views into consideration. Analogous arguments could be made in the BAE case about the lobbying by the Saudi government if there were genuine grounds for concern about the effects in Saudi Arabia of proceeding with the investigation (for the general public, as opposed to just a set of corrupt officials and their allies). In these cases, tolerating international lobbying enhances the legitimacy of the enforcement process. Therefore, the task for an institutional designer is to assess whether these scenarios are likely, given the limited expertise and inevitable partiality of political actors.

Analysis of how to regulate international enforcement is similarly indeterminate. In places where domestic anticorruption agencies have limited capacity and political corruption runs unchecked, international enforcement typically allows foreign enforcement agencies to bring greater expertise and impartiality to bear on the problem and so is likely to have positive ramifications. At the same time, foreign enforcement agencies typically will not represent themselves as accountable to the people most significantly affected by their actions, and may well act in ways contrary to many people's interests. This suggests that international enforcement risks being ineffective and illegitimate if local anticorruption agencies are reasonably effective, democratic political processes are capable of checking political corruption, or enforcement actions favored by foreign enforcement agencies impose high costs on local actors. In these situations, giving affected local actors some sort of authority to limit international enforcement might be appropriate.[48]

Operation Car Wash illustrates why the merits of international enforcement can be contestable. On the one hand, Car Wash allowed a set of relatively expert foreign enforcement agencies to contribute to the fight against corruption in countries where corruption was by all accounts widespread. On the other hand, the enforcement actions sparked by the interventions of the U.S. and Brazilian agencies were extremely costly for the countries affected. The costs were not limited to the political effects outlined above. In Brazil, the reputational taint and threat of liability hanging over many of the construction companies led to paralysis of the sector and a credit shortage, with knock-on effects for many other sectors. One study estimated the losses to the Brazilian economy at 2% of the country's GDP in 2014 and 5% in 2015.[49] Meanwhile, in other Latin American countries, the proceedings against Odebrecht sparked by Car Wash had similar economic effects. In Peru, for example, the International Monetary Fund estimated that Car Wash-related delays in investment reduced economic growth in 2017 by 0.8% of GDP.[50] Perhaps unsurprisingly, there was considerable public backlash against Operation Car Wash in both Brazil and Peru.[51] These outcomes should give institutional designers pause before they uncritically endorse international enforcement.

The argument sketched above calls into question the merits of the proposed International Anti-Corruption Court's approach to international lobbying and enforcement, which essentially adheres to the OECD paradigm.[52] The current proposal contemplates an international body with both prosecutorial and adjudicative functions that would be capable of targeting high-level political actors while remaining as insulated as possible from political influence. The institution appears to be designed to score highly in terms of expertise and impartiality but is unlikely to be representative of or accountable to affected populations.

Conclusion

In an interconnected world, anticorruption law frequently has political consequences that cross international borders. Two important manifestations of this tendency, which are often interrelated, are international lobbying of anticorruption enforcement agencies by politicians and international anticorruption enforcement that has political ramifications. Further research is required to both document and evaluate the legal mechanisms that prohibit or protect against these practices. The preliminary assessment above suggests that the law tends to restrict international lobbying but tolerate international enforcement. The analysis above also suggests that the merits of the dominant approach are highly contingent, turning on factors such as the relative expertise of local and foreign enforcement agencies and politicians, as well as whose interests each set of actors represents.

There are many possible alternatives to the status quo in the regulation of international lobbying and international enforcement. One is to favor the regulatory approach adopted by the jurisdiction whose actors are being influenced. This would mark a significant change in the rules concerning international enforcement, since it would entail respecting domestic rules such as grants of immunity that serve to protect politicians accused of corruption. This could be justified by reference to legal principles such as international comity and respect for sovereignty.[53] Yet another option is a balancing test, which tolerates international lobbying and enforcement only when factors such as relative expertise, impartiality and accountability weigh against respecting the political processes likely to be affected. Under this approach, not only would foreign politicians respect local prohibitions on lobbying, foreign enforcement agencies would respect local prohibitions on enforcement and grants of immunity so long as the local rules do not appear to have been the products of dysfunctional political processes. There are also intermediate approaches. For example, countries could be encouraged to apply the same rules to international lobbying and international enforcement that they apply to purely domestic forms of lobbying and enforcement.

Another set of possible interventions aim to enhance the expertise of political actors engaged in international lobbying or the legitimacy of enforcement agencies engaged in international enforcement. For example, Steven Koh argues that U.S. federal prosecutors involved in transnational enforcement should be even more insulated from the influence of the executive branch than at present but ought to educate themselves on and take greater account of U.S. foreign policy interests, which include minimizing resentment on the part of the inhabitants of foreign countries.[54]

In light of the complexity of the relevant issues, scholars and policymakers should be open to exploring these and other alternative ways of regulating politicization of international anticorruption law. In the meantime, it may be unwise to codify the dominant approach in an institution with as broad a mandate as the proposed International Anti-Corruption Court.

Notes

1 I am grateful to Arthur Filho and Susan Rose-Ackerman for comments and conversations about a draft of this chapter, to Youssef Aziz for research assistance, and to the Filomen D'Agostino and Max E. Greenberg Research Fund at NYU School of Law for financial support. A preliminary version benefitted from the discussion at the Boston College Law School Roundtable on Global Criminal Justice.

2 Rose-Ackerman (2021).
3 Rose-Ackerman & Palifka (2016), pp. 446–490.
4 Davis (2019).
5 See, e.g., Rose-Ackerman & Billa (2007), Davis (2023).
6 Langer & Sklansky (2017), Reddy et al. (2013).
7 U.S. House of Representatives, Committee on the Judiciary (2019), pp. 83–93.
8 Cullison (2019).
9 Andrew E. Kramer, "Ukraine Ousts Viktor Shokin, Top Prosecutor, and Political Stability Hangs in the Balance," *New York Times*, March 29, 2016, www.nytimes.com/2016/03/30/world/europe/political-stability-in-the-balance-as-ukraine-ousts-top-prosecutor.html?smid=url-share.
10 Davis (2019), p. 37.
11 Davis (2019), pp. 34–37.
12 Davis et al. (2023); Fishman et al. (2020).
13 Davis et al. (2023).
14 *Krieger v. Law Soc'y of Alberta*, [2002] 3 S.C.R. 372 (Can.).
15 Constitution of the Federative Republic of Brazil, Arts. 127, 128.
16 Ibid., Art. 127.
17 Davis (2021).
18 Loretta E. Lynch, Election Year Sensitivities, Memorandum, April 11, 2016.
19 Hatch Act, 5 U.S.C. § 7323(a) and § 7324(a).
20 Ryan Goodman, "Bill Barr's Hidden Truths About Justice Department's Rule of Forbearance in an Election," *Just Security*, August 31, 2020, www.justsecurity.org/72243/bill-barrs-hidden-truths-about-justice-departments-rule-of-forbearance-in-an-election/.
21 Republic of Paraguay, Political Constitution of 1991, Art. 191.
22 Ibid., Arts. 189, 225, 241.
23 Constitution of the Federative Republic of Brazil Arts. 53, 102 I(b). State prosecutors may file non-criminal cases against federal politicians for certain kinds of corruption, which may result in fines and suspension of political rights. Lei No. 14,230/2021 (Braz.).
24 Koh (2021), pp. 772–776.
25 2003, 2349 UNTS 41; 37 ILM. 4 (1998).
26 United Nations Office on Drugs and Crime (2017), p. 113.
27 OECD Convention, Article 5.
28 Commentaries on the Convention on Combating Bribery of Foreign Public Officials in International Business Transactions, adopted by the Negotiating Conference on 21 November 1997, para. 27.
29 Foakes (2014); United Nations (2022).
30 United Nations (2022), p. 213.
31 U.S. House of Representatives, Committee on the Judiciary (2019) , Article I.
32 Council of Europe, Group of States Against Corruption, Compliance Report: Ukraine, Fourth Evaluation Round, adopted by GRECO at its 84th Plenary Meeting (Strasbourg, 26 December 2019), GrecoRC4(2019)28 https://rm.coe.int/fourth-evaluation-round-corruption-prevention-in-respect-of-members-of/16809d768c, pp. 6–7, 14–30.
33 Three reports of the OECD Working Group on Bribery: Phase 4 Report: France (2021), pp. 59–61; Phase 4 Report: United Kingdom (2017), pp. 34–36, 37–43; Phase 4 Two-Year Follow-up Report: United Kingdom (2019), pp. 7–8. See also OECD Working Group on Bribery, "Brazil must immediately end threats to independence and capacity of law enforcement to fight corruption" (2019); "OECD will follow Canadian proceedings addressing allegations of political interference in foreign bribery prosecution" (2019); Phase 4 Report: Japan (2019), pp. 46–51; Phase 4 Report: Korea (2018), pp. 45–47; Phase 4 Report: Czech Republic (2017), pp. 31–33. On relative levels of enforcement (2018–2021) see Transparency International (2022, 8).

34 *R (On the Application of Corner House Research and Others) v. Director of the Serious Fraud Office*, [2008] UKHL 60, paras 42, 54.
35 U.S. Department of Justice, "BAE Systems PLC Pleads Guilty and Ordered to Pay $400 Million Criminal Fine", March 1, 2010, available at www.justice.gov/opa/pr/bae-systems-plc-pleads-guilty-and-ordered-pay-400-million-criminal-fine.
36 For a balanced discussion of the evidence see Koh (2021).
37 U.S. Department of Justice, "Nicolás Maduro Moros and 14 Current and Former Venezuelan Officials Charged with Narco-Terrorism, Corruption, Drug Trafficking and Other Criminal Charges," March 26, 2020, available at www.justice.gov/opa/pr/nicol-s-maduro-moros-and-14-current-and-former-venezuelan-officials-charged-narco-terrorism.
38 Rashbaum et al. (2020).
39 Barr (2020).
40 The Venezuelan constitution does not confer immunity upon the President, but it does give the Supreme Court exclusive authority to preside over the prosecution of the President. Constitución de la República Bolivariana de Venezuela, Art. 266.2.
41 *U.S. v. Noriega*, 117 F.3d 1206 (11th Cir. 1997).
42 Palencia (2022).
43 Poder Judicial de Honduras, "Pleno De Magistrados Declara No Ha Lugar Recurso De Apelación Del Ex Presidente Juan Orlando Hernánde," available at www.poderjudicial.gob.hn/Paginas/BolPJ24022022.aspx.; Suazo & Kurmanaev (2022).
44 It is unclear to me whether deputies of the Central American Parliament enjoy immunity in their home state beyond whatever immunity is granted to the state's own parliamentary deputies, and Honduras does not grant immunity to legislators. *Tratado Constitutivo del Parlamento Centroamericano*, Art. 22, available at https://parlacen.int/assets/pdf/Parlacen-Tratado%20Constitutivo.pdf; LADB Staff (2004).
45 Davis (2019).
46 Davis (2019).
47 Reddy et al. (2013).
48 Davis (2019), pp. 229–231.
49 Nozaki (2018).
50 De Michele et al. (2018), p. 2; International Monetary Fund (2018), p. 21.
51 Davis et al. (2023); Da Ros & Taylor (2022); Baraybar & Gonzalez-Ocantos (2022).
52 Wolf (2018).
53 See, for example, the reference to respect for the principle of sovereign equality in Article 4 of the UNCAC.
54 Koh (2021), pp. 772–781.

References

Baraybar, Viviana & Ezequiel Gonzalez-Ocantos. "Prosecutorial Agency, Backlash and Resistance in the Peruvian Chapter of Lava Jato," in S. Botero, D. Brinks & E. Gonzalez-Ocantos (Eds.), *The Limits of Judicialization: From Progress to Backlash in Latin America* (pp. 314–340). Cambridge University Press, 2022.

Barr, William P. "Attorney General William P. Barr Delivers Remarks at Press Conference Announcing Criminal Charges against Venezuelan Officials," March 26, 2020, https://www.justice.gov/opa/speech/attorney-general-william-p-barr-delivers-remarks-press-conference-announcing-criminal.

Cullison, Allan. "Bidens in Ukraine: An Explainer," *Wall Street Journal* (September 22, 2019).

Da Ros, Luciano & Matthew Taylor. "Kickbacks, Crackdown, and Backlash: Legal Accountability in the Lava Jato Investigation," in S. Botero, D. Brinks & E. Gonzalez-Ocantos (Eds.), *The Limits of Judicialization: From Progress to Backlash in Latin America* (pp. 242–265). Cambridge University Press, 2022.

Davis, Kevin E. "Anti-Corruption Law and Systemic Corruption: The Role of Direct Responses," *Revista Direito GV* 17 (2021): e2129.

———. *Between Impunity and Imperialism: The Regulation of Transnational Bribery*. Oxford University Press, 2019.

———. "International Regulation of Law Enforcement" (unpublished draft, February 10, 2023).

Davis, Kevin E., Marta Machado, Raquel de Mattos Pimenta & Mariana Prado. "Inclusive Experimentalism in Transnational Law Reform: Lessons From Operation Car Wash," unpublished draft, 2023.

De Michele, Roberto, Joan Orial Prats Cabrera & Isaías Losada Revol. *Effects of Corruption on Public–Private Partnership Contracts: Consequences of a Zero-tolerance Approach* (2018), http://dx.doi.org/10.18235/0001355.

Fishman, Andrew, Natalia Viana & Maryam Saleh. "'Keep it Confidential' The Secret History of U.S. Involvement in Brazil's Scandal-Wracked Operation Car Wash," *The Intercept* (March 12, 2020), https://theintercept.com/2020/03/12/united-states-justice-department-brazil-car-wash-lava-jato-international-treaty/.

Foakes, Joanne. *The Position of Heads of State and Senior Officials in International Law*. Oxford University Press, 2014.

International Monetary Fund. *Peru: Staff Report for the 2018 Article IV Consultation* (June 18, 2018), https://www.imf.org/en/Publications/CR/Issues/2018/07/25/Peru-2018-Article-IV-Consultation-Press-Release-Staff-Report-and-Statement-by-the-Executive-46099.

Koh, Steven Arrigg. "The Criminalization of Foreign Relations," *Fordham Law Review* 90 (2021): 737–787.

LADB Staff. "Immunity Curtailed in Honduras," (2004), https://digitalrepository.unm.edu/noticen/9222.

Langer, Máximo & David Alan Sklansky. "Epilogue: Prosecutors and Democracy – Themes and Counterthemes," in M. Langer & D. A. Sklansky (Eds.), *Prosecutors and Democracy: A Cross-National Study* (pp. 276–299). Cambridge University Press, 2017.

Nozaki, William. *Jornal GGN*, "Os impactos econômicos da Operação Lava Jato e o desmonte da Petrobras," August 27 2018, https://ineep.org.br/os-impactos-economicos-da-operacao-lava-jato-e-o-desmonte-da-petrobras/.

OECD Working Group on Bribery. "Brazil Must Immediately End Threats to Independence and Capacity of Law Enforcement to Fight Corruption" (13/11/2019), https://www.oecd.org/corruption/brazil-must-immediately-end-threats-to-independence-and-capacity-of-law-enforcement-to-fight-corruption.htm.

———. *Implementing the OECD Anti-Bribery Convention, Phase 4 Report: France* (adopted 9 December 2021).

———. *Implementing the OECD Anti-Bribery Convention, Phase 4 Report: Japan* (adopted 27 June 2019).

———. *Implementing the OECD Anti-Bribery Convention, Phase 4 Two-Year Follow-up Report: United Kingdom* (adopted 6 March 2019).

———. *Implementing the OECD Anti-Bribery Convention, Phase 4 Report: Korea* (adopted 13 December 2018).

———. *Implementing the OECD Anti-Bribery Convention, Phase 4 Report: Czech Republic* (adopted 15 June 2017).

———. *Implementing the OECD Anti-Bribery Convention, Phase 4 Report: United Kingdom* (adopted 16 March 2017).

———. "OECD will Follow Canadian Proceedings Addressing Allegations of Political Interference in Foreign Bribery Prosecution" (11/03/2019), https://www.oecd.org/corruption/oecd-will-follow-canadian-proceedings-addressing-allegations-of-political-interference-in-foreign-bribery-prosecution.htm.

Palencia, Gustavo. "Hours Out of Office, Honduras Ex-President Gains Immunity through Regional Post," *Reuters*, January 27, 2022, https://www.reuters.com/world/americas/hours-out-office-honduras-ex-president-gains-immunity-through-regional-post-2022-01-28/.

Rashbaum, William K., Benjamin Weiser & Katie Benner. "Venezuelan Leader Maduro Is Charged in the U.S. with Drug Trafficking," *New York Times*, April 13, 2020, https://www.nytimes.com/2020/03/26/nyregion/venezuela-president-drug-trafficking-nicolas-maduro.html.

Reddy, Karthik, Moritz Schularick & Vasiliki Skreta. "Immunity," (October 31, 2013). CESifo Working Paper Series No. 4445, https://ssrn.com/abstract=2348067 or http://dx.doi.org/10.2139/ssrn.2348067

Rose-Ackerman, Susan. *Democracy and Executive Power: Policymaking Accountability in the US, the UK, Germany, and France*. Yale University Press, October 2021.

Rose-Ackerman, Susan & Benjamin Billa. "Treaties and National Security," *New York University Journal of International Law & Politics* 40 (2007): 437–496.

Rose-Ackerman, Susan & Bonnie J. Palifka. *Corruption and Government: Causes, Consequences, and Reform*. 2nd ed. Cambridge University Press, 2016.

Suazo, Joan & Anatoly Kurmanaev. "Honduran Supreme Court Ratifies U.S. Extradition Request of Ex-President," *New York Times*, March 28, 2022.

Transparency International. *Exporting Corruption (2022): Assessing enforcement of the OECD Anti-Bribery Convention* (2022), https://images.transparencycdn.org/images/2022_Report-Full_Exporting-Corruption_English.pdf .

United Nations. *Report of the International Law Commission Seventy-third Session* (18 April–3 June and 4 July–5 August 2022), A/77/10.

United Nations Office on Drugs and Crime. *State of Implementation of the United Nations Convention against Corruption: Criminalization, Law Enforcement and International Cooperation*, Second edition (2017).

U.S. House of Representatives, *Impeachment of Donald J. Trump President of the United States, Report of the Committee on the Judiciary, House of Representatives, together with Dissenting Views, to Accompany H. Res. 755*, H.R. Rep 116-346, December 15, 2019.

Wolf, Mark L. "The World Needs an International Anti-corruption Court," *Daedalus* 147 (2018): 144–156.

10 Scope and precision in the laws against corporate bribery

Kalle Moene and Tina Søreide[1]

Corruption is both a moral and a legal category. Those involved seek personal benefits at the expense of political goals irrespective of whether these goals are legitimate or not. Thus, "[c]orruption can advance either nefarious or noble aims" – it "violates the rules of the game through payoffs from unethical actions that may or may not be consistent with state policy" (Rose-Ackerman, 2018). Legal corruption, therefore, is far from a contradiction in terms, but rather a serious problem in many countries (Kaufmann and Vicente, 2011).

The distinctions are not semantic. By reserving corruption-related terms to the harmful mechanisms at play, it becomes possible to take enforcement actions. In this chapter, we consider 'the most actionable' definitions of corruption, emphasizing trade-offs between being comprehensive and being precise. We consider acts where those involved should be held legally responsible. If enforcement fails, political inaction or the inability to curb the problem becomes evident. A legal definition includes only what governments define as corrupt – including governments whose leaders themselves lack integrity. With a sufficiently narrow definition, there might be no legal corruption at all, while the problem is just as present.

In this chapter, we investigate the application of strict and narrow definitions of corruption compared with less strict but more comprehensive definitions. We explore whether intolerance of corruption requires a clear view of what one does not tolerate. The flip side of this 'more means less hypothesis' suggests that defining corruption more broadly may result in weaker regulation and control, despite the anti-corruption ambition it appears to reflect.

We focus on how the definition of corruption varies across jurisdictions and what it means for societies' ability to control the crime. Because countries define corruption differently, thus making meaningful country comparison difficult, we, instead, study one specific form of corruption: foreign bribery. Specifically, we narrow this focus to study how the enforcement of foreign corporate bribery legislation affects firms' inclination to bribe. Does a broader scope of liability mean less definitional clarity? Does it matter if enforcement happens through court proceeding or negotiated settlement? If so, how does the clarity of the definition of corruption affect the enforcement process? And, if there is variation in the quality of countries' definitions of bribery and liability, does it reflect common perceptions of good or bad governance?

DOI: 10.4324/9781003416234-12

Varieties of corporate liability for bribery

Airbus, Siemens, Alstom, Herbalife, VimpelCom, Telia, BAE, Ericsson, Rolls Royce, Petrobras, Yara all are examples of corporations subjected to one or more enforcement actions for foreign bribery.[2] In such cases, the offenses crossed borders, often via complex corporate and financial structures. These crimes are difficult to observe and prove according to criminal law standards.

As the responsible individuals are part of organizations, they are often protected from criminal liability because of the difficulty of determining individual culpability. Under these circumstances, the criteria for liability and the details of the jurisdiction's definition of foreign bribery are decisive for the enforcement system's ability to act on the crime. It is not clear, however, which types of liability are the most important for successful enforcement.

Domestic enforcement of bribery abroad

There is substantial variation across countries in the regulation and enforcement of corporate criminal liability. While international conventions against corruption, such as the United Nations Convention against Corruption and the OECD Anti-Bribery Convention, could leave the impression of harmonization in jurisprudence and joint international ambition in law enforcement, many governments apply a narrower scope of liability than what the text of the conventions suggests. In addition, corporate crime is an under-developed concept in many jurisdictions. Criminal law scholars have found it difficult to align it with criminal law values (Laufer, 2008; Pieth, 2020). Many practitioners welcome new trends toward 'failure to prevent' regulations, placing a larger burden of proof on the defendants. Yet, scholars warn against movements away from the basic criminal law requirement that those accused and punished must be the ones responsible for the crime (Ashworth, 2018).

These features help us to understand why there is substantial cross-country variation in foreign bribery enforcement activity. By 2019, the United States had been responsible for 66% of all completed foreign bribery cases, while nearly all the other such cases had been pursued in Europe (TRACE, 2020). The picture is in flux. European countries were in 2019 responsible for more than half of ongoing foreign bribery investigations, but countries in other regions also began to pursue such cases. By 2019, however, one-third of the countries that made foreign bribery illegal around year 2000, had not enforced the legislation in one single case (Transparency International, 2020).

Enforcement practices and the level of sanctions differ as well. Even if the size of penalties for bribery is a core criterion for deterrence,[3] it is not central to our discussion. The form of enforcement practice is more relevant because it influences the de facto definition of criminal liability for bribery. Especially important is how countries, increasingly, enforce corporate bribery cases by offering non-trial resolutions (OECD, 2019a).[4] A few countries, such as Austria, Belgium, and Japan, still enforce corporate liability by trial only, but in other countries there is a clear trend toward accepting non-trial solutions. Such enforcement has proved to be faster and more flexible for prosecutors who offer incentives for firms that self-report their offenses and cooperate with law enforcers.[5] This is why the OECD Working Group on Bribery (also called the WGB), endorses the use of non-trial resolutions (Ivory and Søreide, 2020).[6]

Settlement-based enforcement, however, limits the relevant case law, even if it leads to a higher number of enforcement cases. Enforcement agencies tend to share far fewer facts about a case when solved by settlement compared to cases concluded by trial. As a result, it becomes harder for the public to know the exact difference between legal and illegal practices. At the same time, firms in the same jurisdiction will learn little about the criteria for compliance with anti-corruption laws. Furthermore, whereas the offender's bargaining power under the circumstances should make no difference to the result of court proceedings, in many circumstances it will determine the outcome of settlement-based enforcement. Thus, it is possible and important to distinguish jurisdictions from one another, especially in how they define foreign bribery.

Dimensions of corporate liability for bribery

The definition of corporate liability for bribery depends on what acts are included and how precisely they are stipulated. Conceptually, therefore, the liability in foreign bribery cases depends on both scope and clarity. Scope, in this context, refers to the categories of organizations, acts, and circumstances covered by the legislation. More categories mean greater scope. The clarity of the liability refers to the precision with which the law lists the criteria for liability and the categories of players. A two-dimensional characterization of the liability based on these aspects allows us to simplify the notion of country-by-country variation by sorting liability into four classes, described in Figure 10.1.

What feature of corporate liability in foreign bribery cases is the most important for law enforcement? Which of the two weaknesses poses the greatest impediment to an efficient anti-corruption agenda, a narrow scope or vaguely defined liability? How will these flaws impede enforcement? And consequently, what strategy should reform-friendly governments use to improve their prosecutors' ability to pursue foreign bribery cases? Clearly, definitions that fall into category B are best able to promote a law's enforceability, while category C-definitions are the worst. It is the two remaining categories, A and D, that are difficult to rank,

		Scope	
		Narrow	*Broad*
Clarity	*Clear*	**A.** Enforcement made difficult by limited scope of acts.	**B.** Highly enforceable foreign bribery legislation.
	Unclear	**C.** Difficult to enforce foreign bribery legislation.	**D**. Enforcement impeded by the difficulty of proving liability.

Figure 10.1 Categories of corporate liability for bribery.

Source: Authors

and in need of further scrutiny. The underlying mechanisms play a significant role.

For instance, for a given level of precision in the foreign bribery definition, a broader scope of the definition is always better for society if we can rely on the premise that (i) acts are criminalized only within the limits of what constitute harmful business practice, and (ii) criminalized acts never encompass honest and development-friendly activities. If precision declines when the scope increases, however, there are two separate and rather divergent possibilities for enforceability. They depend on whether a broader scope is accompanied by what we denote (i) a "safety-first behavior" or (ii) "a safety-last behavior."

In the case of *safety first*, more uncertain limits of the law instigate a more careful law-abiding behavior by firms and their counterparts in government. This effect is likely if the consequences for those detected and found guilty are severe, even if the law is a bit unclear about exactly which acts lead to the consequences. The risk of bad consequences might induce agents to err on the safe side, staying on the right side of the law by a substantial margin.[7] In this case, a broader scope combined with imprecise descriptions of liability, such as a movement from category B to D, in Figure 10.1, can make actors *more cautious*. If so, a broader scope at the expense of precision implies a more efficient enforcement system, reducing firms' inclination to pay bribes.

The case of *safety last,* in contrast, refers to a situation where offenders are aware of how the uncertain limits of liability protect them from prosecution. For example, the lack of precision in the definition of liability may allow corporations to evade vicarious responsibility while they also manage to shield responsible employees from the personal consequences of detection. For such employees, the imprecise definition of liability may intensify the temptation to secure personal gains from their corporation's successful bribery, for example through compensation systems and career promotions, but also kickbacks from business partners. In this case, a broader scope at the expense of precision may fail to reduce bribery. The legal gray zone serves as an invitation to bend the rules, and to stretch the interpretation of what is accepted business practice. The *safety last* scenario weakens the law's enforceability. A broader scope of the legal definition, at the expense of precision – a movement from category C to D in Figure 10.1 – may intensify the problem of foreign bribery.

Another nuance is the ability of authorities to curb rule bending and stretching through enforcement and court proceedings. If authorities are unable to do so, a broad and imprecise definition of liability may induce firms to cut deals that a less ambiguous definition of liability would deem illegal. If several firms headquartered in one country share such a perception of the legislation, the members of the business community may well begin to condone and defend foreign bribery on a general basis. If so, a broader yet imprecise definition of such liability intensifies the problem it is meant to curb.

New forms of venal business practice raise additional challenges. A broader scope of liability, combined with a lower level of precision, would then not adversely affect how actors behave. With newly detected methods of conducting bribery, a broadening of the law's scope for the sake of including these practices does not worsen the bribery problem. The benchmark in this case is a situation with no regulation of the new forms of bribery, and therefore, a broader scope of a still imprecise legal definition does not intensify the bribery problem. Also, there is no reason to believe that the introduction of a new imprecise regulation automatically reduces the level of precision of existing regulations.

As seen, we find that there are circumstances where a broader scope of liability at the cost of weaker precision may improve law enforcement – for instance in "safety-first" circumstances. Yet, for a given scope of liability, lower precision weakens the enforceability of the law – it reduces the ability to sanction and deter corporate bribery.

Scope, precision, and the form of enforcement[8]

Generally, improving the precision of the foreign bribery regulation for a given scope of liability has the same qualitative implications regardless of whether the authorities enforce by non-trial resolution (such as negotiated settlement) or trial. Likewise, the consequences of an extended scope of liability, for a given level of precision, will not depend on the enforcement mode. Irrespective of the specific definition of liability, settlement-based enforcement may improve the deterrence of bribery. For a given budget, it allows the enforcement system to pursue more cases per year. A higher frequency of enforcement cases implies more frequent reminders of the illegality of the act and the possible consequences of enforcement, and thus, settlement-based enforcement may serve as a better corrective against the temptations to bribe, compared to trial-based enforcement. For several reasons, however, there is also a risk that enforcement by settlement adds to the problems associated with an unclear foreign bribery definition.

First, under settlement-based enforcement, an imprecise definition of liability tends to strengthen the corporate defendant's bargaining position vis-à-vis the prosecutor. The prosecutor's offer of a non-trial resolution requires approval by the defendant for the agreement between the two to replace trial proceedings. A less precise definition of liability makes the outcome of an imagined court case less predictable, leading to higher expected gains from out-of-court settlements for both sides. While both parties gain, however, unclear liability, combined with the prosecutor's heavy burden of proof, might benefit the corporate defendants the most. Their bargaining power goes up as they can more safely let time pass. While an important worry might be the emergence of new information about the bribery, such as whistleblower-based information or details brought up by journalists, this worry decreases the less precise the legal definition of liability. When the law is imprecise, such new information is less likely to make a difference. That makes it safer for the defendant to wait and allow the prosecutor's settlement offer to reach a level it will accept, while the risk of having the case brought to trial is less of a worry.

Second, an imprecise definition, combined with settlement-based enforcement, means the prosecutor holds broad discretionary authority. In this setting, discretionary authority will not necessarily improve the prosecutor's bargaining powers. Quite the contrary, the discretion may leave the prosecutor less able to withstand the corporate offender's demands. As in any bargain, the stronger the counterpart, the more easily one is inclined to accept an inferior result. Likewise, the stronger the corporate defendant, the more inclined is the prosecutor to reduce the settlement penalty in exchange for a conclusion of the case. However, the prosecutor's opportunity and inclination to offer 'soft treatment' depends on the agency's discretionary authority and the aspects on which it is evaluated. According to the IBA survey, most countries that permit settlements do so informally in largely unregulated and unchecked manners, allowing prosecutors the flexibility they desire (Makinwa and Søreide, 2018). With respect to evaluation, enforcement agencies typically are considered more successful the larger the number of cases resolved, with less attention paid to fair procedure in each case. Settlement-based enforcement speeds up the enforcement of cases, while the consequences of allowing negotiated outcomes of criminal law investigations are less understood (Hawley, King and Lord, 2020; Transparency International, 2020). Under the circumstances, enforcement agencies may be inclined to concede if their concessions increase the number of successful prosecutions, while the corporate offenders accept penalties that, in practice, are little more than a regular tax on doing business in certain markets.

Third, a broader scope and lower precision of liability for foreign bribery, combined with settlement-based enforcement, allow governments to enforce the law inconsistently. Governments can point to a higher number of enforcement cases, and at the same time, treat corporate offenders variably. This is convenient for officials who want to be seen as acting against crime without punishing large corporations too aggressively. Since the true amount of foreign bribery is unobservable, elected officials in fact can 'have their cake and eat it too' – in the sense that they evade the difficult trade-off between shielding and sanctioning important corporations for the profit-motivated crimes they commit abroad. The use of settlement-based enforcement allows elected officials to gain recognition for their commitment to international anti-bribery efforts, even if their actions de facto condone foreign bribery and protect many corporate offenders from heavy penalties (Tullock and Rowley, 2005; Søreide, 2016, Ch 6). This double political gain is more likely when the scope of the law is broad, and the precision is low.

Considering these three mechanisms in combination, we find enforcement of foreign bribery legislation through the largely unregulated use of settlement-based enforcement, combined with imprecise definitions of foreign bribery, allows governments far more flexibility than precise regulation and enforcement by trials. As a result, firms may find that bribery in international markets is less risky, even if the use of non-trial resolutions increases the number of enforcement actions.

Type I and type II errors in the law enforcement against corporate corruption

As should be clear from the discussion above, in the enforcement of laws against corporate corruption both type I and type II errors may occur: corrupt corporations may go free (type I); law-abiding corporations may be found guilty (type II). Most likely type I errors dominate because the scope of the law is bound to be incomplete, and the definition of corporate misconduct is rarely precise.

In all cases, we are interested in the probability that the offender is held responsible. To be precise, let the vector Y describe what is illegal according to prevailing norms. Foreign bribery is, thus, an element in Y, denoted y_i. For our purpose, we assume that y_i captures a common idea of what people associate with foreign bribery, for example reflecting views in civil society, the press, and international organizations, such as the OECD, the United Nations, and the World Bank.

Further, let the vector S describe the *scope* of the law as compared to the prevailing norm, whereas its elements, s_i ζζ0,1ζ, denote the scope of the legal definition with respect to crime *i*. When s_i is close to unity, the de jure liability nearly overlaps with the prevailing norm, and when s_i approaches zero, what citizens consider crime is legal by the law. Accordingly, we should expect that s_i is strictly below 1. The scope of the legal definition is normally narrower than people's perception of the crime.

Finally, let the vector P reflect the *precision* of the law, which elements are denoted p_i ζζ0,1ζ. When the concepts of the law are vague and imprecise, a corporation cannot be punished effectively: low precision in the description of what qualifies as bribery (p_i approaching zero) makes it more difficult for enforcement agencies to prove criminal responsibility.

There is variation across jurisdictions in the importance of legal precision. Some enforcement agencies manage to pursue cases of foreign bribery despite a weak definition, while others seem to exploit the legal imprecision to skip such cases, in some instances because their governments want to shield corporate offenders from sanctions.[9] Legal imprecision either allows generous sanction discounts or, in contrast, boosts enforcers' ability to pursue potential misconduct. We seek to capture this difference in terms of the vector Z, whose elements, $z_{i,}$ indicate a rebate if positive and an over-charge if negative. If z_i is close to zero, the lack of precision does not impede investigation and enforcement. One reason could be that the jurisdiction in question places more weight on the purpose of the law relative to the letter of the law. If z_i is close to y_i, however, the imprecision implies gaps in law enforcement as the letter of the law means more than its purpose. If z_i is negative, imprecision gives the court unwarranted discretion where neither the letter nor the purpose of the law restrains the judgment.

Now, an observed act of potential foreign bribery can be represented by the scalar x_i. A higher value of x_i means that the act appears cleaner. In any case, the act qualifies for investigation in most citizens' view if x_i is an element in Y. Whether the act will also be found illegal according to law, depends on whether x_i is an element in $s_i\left[y_i-\left(1-p_i\right)z_i\right]$, where we have incorporated the way low precision p_i can grant the potential offender a high expected vagueness rebate (relative to the norm y_i) when z_i is positive, and an expected vagueness over-charge (relative to the norm y_i) when z_i is negative.

Clearly, the precision and the scope of law are rarely exact measures. In practice both are subject to interpretation by courts or to opaque appraisals when cases end with non-trial resolution – as is typically the case in corporate bribery cases. The ensuing uncertainty around the limit values of p_i and s_i can be captured by incorporating stochastic error terms. With additive error terms the probability that an act x_i of suspected corporate bribery is found de facto illegal is then the same as the probability that

$$x_i < s_i\left[y_i - (1-p_i)z_i\right]$$

We can use this expression to characterize the two classical errors in decision-making:

Type I error, that corrupt corporations go free, can be represented as follows: the offender is guilty according to the norm, hence $x_i < y_i$, but the court says not-guilty so $x_i > s_i\left[y_i - (1-p_i)z_i\right]$. As seen, the type I error is then associated with a high vagueness rebate together with a low scope and a low precision of the corruption law.

Type II error, that law-abiding (or norm-abiding) corporations may be found guilty, can be represented as follows: the offender is not guilty according to the norm, hence $x_i > y_i$, but the court says guilty so $x_i < s_i\left[y_i - (1-p_i)z_i\right]$. These two inequalities can only hold simultaneously when the court over-charges ($z_i < 0$). When this is the case, the type II error is associated with a high scope and a low precision.

As seen, both type I and type II errors are more likely under laws with low precision. The fear of becoming a victim of a type II error, therefore, can be an example of safety-first behavior: corporations err on the safe side in case the low precision of the law might lead to a false conviction for being corrupt. By contrast, corporations speculating in a type I error in the enforcement of law, exemplify what we called safety-last behavior: corporations then become more tempted to be corrupt because they expect the low precision of the law will prevent them from being convicted.

Related to this discussion, we can also ask: what levels of s_i and p_i would maximize the probability that the offender is treated in a fair manner? Clearly, the answer is the level that guarantees that the suspected corporation is found guilty if and only if $x_i < y_i$. This outcome can be reached only in the unconstrained case with a full scope and a complete precision, $s_i = p_i = 1$. However, constraints in the governance of law enforcement make this circumstance less relevant for policy purposes.

The most worrisome concern is the likelihood of a negative relationship between scope and precision. If in fact the precision p_i depends negatively on the scope s_i, the optimal scope of the law may be less than $s_i = 1$ since a high scope can imply a low precision, and thus, a high implicit vagueness rebate that might lower the probability of impeachment.

In our stylized representation, however, consider the special case of $z_i < 0$, that is, the case where, given the vagueness over-charge, the probability of conviction increases with the imprecision of the law. A negative relationship between scope and precision then means that the probability of impeachment goes up with a definition of liability that combines a broad scope with low precision. To argue that this would be 'optimal', however, one must not only trust the unbound judgment of the court, but also be unconcerned about type II errors.

How do scope and precision covary in practice?

The classification of jurisdictions according to their definition of foreign corporate bribery requires information about the scope and clarity of their laws. Below we illustrate some regularities, using a stocktaking report on "the features of the systems for liability of legal persons found in the 41 Parties to the Anti-Bribery Convention" which contains comprehensive information for our purpose (OECD, 2016: 3).

The benefits of the report are the details on holding perpetrators responsible for foreign bribery under each country's laws. The information was gathered in one time period, using the same 'round' of country evaluations by the OECDs Working Group on Bribery.[10] The report gives a proper snapshot of the status in 2016. The downside is the ease with which such information may become outdated.

The report presents details about the scope and clarity of bribery definitions. It addresses many different aspects of corporate liability, including criteria for the liability of legal persons and their dependence on the types of legal persons covered, standards of liability, what acts trigger liability, and requirements with respect to the natural persons involved in the crime. In addition, it addresses whether the presence of a compliance system precludes liability, the relevance of intermediaries (consultants), and various questions with respect to sanctions. For each of the aspects considered, the report records the scope of liability and finds it unclear if difficult to determine. The information is presented in a manner that makes it easy to count the number of areas covered by liability and the number of areas for which the legislation is imprecise. Based on that information[11] we prepared a table with scores given to countries depending on their system for holding corporate offenders liable for bribery. This table facilitated the preparation of a simple index, the Bribery Liability Index (BLI) which is simply the arithmetic mean of indicators developed from the information presented in the report, with the information on each indicator normalized for the purpose and given equal weight. The scaling records higher scores the broader the scope of liability and the more precise the liability. See the Appendix for more details.

Table 10.1 presents the index score for each jurisdiction included in the sample, including the scores on scope and clarity, and thus the information required for the Bribery Liability Index (BLI).

The table shows that several of the most active enforcers have the most functional definitions of liability for corporate bribery, including United States, the Netherlands, Germany, and the United Kingdom. However, those who hardly enforce this legislation are spread all over the list.

Considering the four categories in Figure 10.1, countries that appear closest to category A (better score on clarity than scope) are Sweden, Portugal, Ireland, and

Table 10.1 Countries included in the sample and their Bribery Liability Index score. The BLI score is the average of scope and clarity

Country	*Scope*	*Clarity*	*BLI*
US	.94	.87	.90
Canada	.80	.89	.85
Netherlands	.79	.80	.85
Germany	.80	.88	.84
Colombia	.85	.80	.82
UK	.72	.78	.75
Norway	.76	.66	.71
Portugal	.65	.76	.71
Italy	.68	.72	.70
Chile	.69	.69	.69
Czech Rep.	.63	.74	.68
NewZealand	.68	.64	.66
Iceland	.78	.52	.65
Slovakia	.72	.57	.64
Denmark	.72	.48	.60
Slovenia	.66	.53	.59
Hungary	.68	.49	.58
South Korea	.57	.48	.57
Austria	.62	.53	.57
Australia	.54	.60	.57
Luxembourg	.64	.49	.56
Spain	.56	.56	.56
Belgium	.58	.53	.55
Israel	.63	.46	.55
Latvia	.64	.45	.55
Poland	.64	.45	.55
Japan	.60	.49	.55
Finland	.62	.44	.53
Turkey	.58	.48	.53
Mexico	.56	.49	.53
Ireland	.45	.60	.53
Sweden	.45	.60	.53
France	.54	.50	.52
Switzerland	.46	.54	.50
Estonia	.47	.41	.44
Greece	.53	.35	.44

Source: Authors

the Czech Republic; examples of countries in category B (clear and broad liability) are the United States, Canada, Netherlands, Germany, and Colombia; examples of countries in category C (unclear and narrow liability) are Switzerland, Estonia and Greece, and examples of countries in category D (better score on scope than clarity) are Iceland, Denmark, and Poland.

Countries' scores on clarity and scope exhibit a strong correlation. Figure 10.2 shows the correlations, where scope is measured on the horizontal axis and clarity

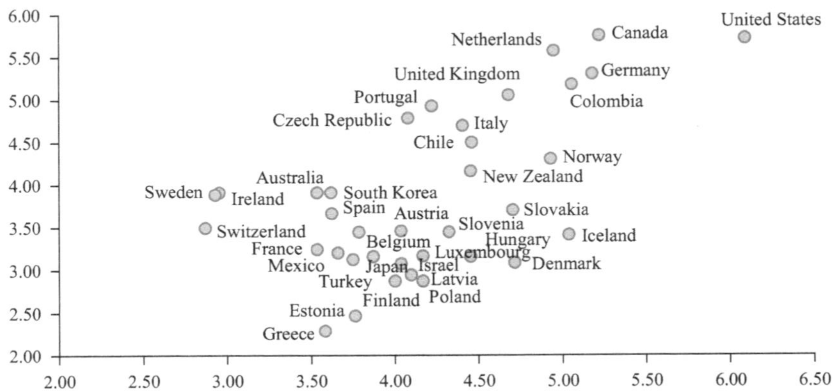

Figure 10.2 Liability with respect to scope (horizontal axis) and clarity (vertical axis).

Source: Authors

on the vertical. The figure shows there might be little cause for concern about the danger that a wide scope of the liability implies a low precision. The strong positive correlation between scope and clarity (or precision) indicates they move closely together. The pattern seems to be that the more ambitious countries are in terms of securing broad liability for corporate bribery, the better they are at describing the criteria for liability in a precise way as well.

Do scope and precision reflect good governance?

To see whether jurisdictions that perform well in terms of its bribery liability, perform well on other governance indicators too, we calculated some simple correlations. We then calculated the correlations between BLI scores and publicly available data on countries' legal system, their economy, and political system. As expected, there is a clear correlation between countries' bribery liability score and the number of completed enforcement actions for foreign bribery, which is noteworthy, even if the number of enforcement actions is read simply as an indicator of the jurisdiction's proven ability and inclination to pursue cases once they are detected.[12] Similarly, countries with a high BLI score tend to have more ongoing investigations, they impose more sanctions on both individuals and firms, and they allocate more funding for their enforcement agencies.[13] However, these serious enforcers do not allow their prosecutors broader freedom for negotiating cases with corporate offenders. In fact, there is a negative correlation between BLI score and both de jure and de facto prosecutor independence.[14] The result indicates that prosecutors' discretionary authority is not directly related to the matter of high scope and high precision, and therefore, a concern about vagueness over-charge is still warranted.

As foreign bribery is attached to commercial activity the associations with trade-related variables are of special interest. Are countries that are largely dependent on international trade less inclined to hold 'their firms' liable for foreign bribery? The relationship is not so obvious. On average, countries with a high BLI score have a larger economy and bigger populations, according to World Bank Development Indicators. According to OECD National Accounts Statistics, they are more engaged in trade, both imports and exports.

Considering trade in both goods and services, countries with a high BLI score have fewer trade restrictions and fewer barriers to entry in their own societies, found using the OECD Services Trade Restrictiveness Index. In this respect, the countries that are the most open to trade have the more functional definition of corporate bribery. This association does not rule out the possibility that some governments condone bribery if their commercial sector is dependent on securing contracts abroad.

In fact, once we consider trade as a percentage of GDP, the correlation with the BLI score is negative, suggesting that the most *trade-dependent* countries have a less enforceable definition of foreign bribery than countries that are *trade-friendly* in terms of their trade-promoting policies.[15] Hence, a trade-oriented political agenda does not seem to provide an intuitive reason for an inadequate anti-bribery regulation. When it comes to variations depending on important commercial sectors in society, expressed by OECD National Accounts Statistics, we find countries whose GDP level relies heavily on financial intermediation services (in terms of size of economy with respect to GDP) have a lower BLI score, whereas countries at the forefront with respect to technology/science, and those with a large public administration, have higher BLI scores, which means, they operate with more enforceable definitions of corporate liability for foreign bribery.

In various ways, the associations we emphasize indicate that 'good things go together'. For instance, we find that countries with a higher BLI score have less inequality. It does not matter how the disparities are measured (Gini-coefficient, Palma ratio, P90/P10 ratio, or the presence of inequality-reducing inheritance taxes all produce similar correlations[16]). Higher BLI scores are also associated with higher employment rates (OECD National Accounts Statistics), lower labor market insecurity (OECD Better Life Index), and tax policies. Countries with hardly any corporate taxes (as reported by KPMG Corporate Tax Insights) are also among the countries with the weakest definition of liability for foreign corporate bribery, as captured by the BLI score.

Regarding political system, we find countries that score well in terms of how formal stakeholder engagement is part of the development of primary laws and subordinate regulations also perform better in terms of their ability to hold corporations liable for bribery, i.e., they have a higher BLI score. The variable "formal stakeholder engagement" is a component of the OECD's Better Life Index and calculated as a composite estimate of various measures established to secure consultation and engagement ahead of new primary laws as well as subordinate regulations.[17] With respect to indicators of the quality of democracy more generally, such as political participation, electoral process, and civil liberties, country performance correlates positively with the BLI score (using data from the OECD's

Better Life Index). Consistently with such correlations, press freedom, as presented by *Reporters without Borders,* is better secured in countries with a high BLI score. Journalists are safer in countries that have defined foreign bribery in a way that facilitates law enforcement.

In sum, the correlates of liability in foreign bribery, as captured by the BLI, indicate how both scope and clarity in the jurisdictions' definitions of foreign bribery go together with a high score on a range of good governance indicators. Countries that are governed well simply seem to prefer a functioning approach to corporate liability in foreign bribery cases, suggesting that good policies go together with good politics including with respect to international commitments. But the opposite is also true; a weak approach to corporate liability in foreign bribery is associated with weaknesses in governance and bad policies.

The politics of scope and precision

Imprecision in the legal definition of corporate foreign bribery easily impedes efficient enforcement, irrespective of the definition's scope. As in many countries today, the use of non-trial resolutions relative to trials intensifies the consequences of poorly defined liability. Rather than curbing firms' inclination to pay bribes abroad, flexible law enforcement with an imprecise definition may intensify the problem.

If this conclusion is correct, and if our index reflects current regulatory realities, it must (in the light of Table 10.1) be more important for countries like Iceland, Denmark, and Poland to improve the clarity of their definitions of bribery, than for Ireland, Portugal, Sweden, and the Czech Republic to broaden the scope of their law. Countries that resemble category C in Table 10.1, Switzerland, Estonia, and Greece, might have an even greater potential for improvement, yet in this area of regulation, the need for reform is generally much greater among non-OECD countries, for which we have no similar data.

Considering the likelihood of reform, we should keep in mind that foreign bribery legislation is an area of regulation where *realpolitik* may trump governments' ambitions to promote international development. One clear indicator of such profit-oriented opportunism is the large share of *passive enforcers*, consisting of export-oriented countries that made foreign bribery illegal two decades ago, yet to date, have completed no, or very few, enforcement cases. The group of passive enforcers includes countries like Japan, Russia, Turkey, Finland, India, China, Poland, Belgium, Hungary, Mexico, Ireland, and South Korea (Transparency International, 2020). Examples of governments that strongly endorse doing business with highly corrupt autocratic regimes, and elected officials who interfere in enforcement actions, point in the same direction. UK Prime Minister Tony Blair's intervention to halt the investigations of corruption in BAE's arms export to the Saudi regime is a case in point. To defend his blunt intervention, Blair emphasized "real and immediate risk of collapse in UK/Saudi security, intelligence, and diplomatic cooperation" (Feinstein, 2011: 141–142; see also Rose-Ackerman and Billa, 2008).

The politics of foreign bribery enforcement has some alarming trends. It has become too simple to act as an advocate for anti-corruption, while at the same time, vigorously promoting commercial ambitions in the defense sector, production of non-renewable natural resources, or large infrastructure projects in countries with too weak barriers against corruption, for example with generous offers of export credit support (Hawley, 2003).[18] A report by the Basel Institute of Governance shows that governments of the 20 largest economies fail consistently in approving and implementing anti-corruption initiatives promoted by the private sector, as presented by the largest business organizations, the B20 (Wannenwetsch, 2020).

Such signals suggest we have no reason to believe that a weak definition of corporate liability for foreign bribery is a matter of coincidence. The correlations between features of good governance and a high BLI score make it tempting to suspect that some governments with a weak bribery liability definition fail intentionally in their international anti-corruption ambitions. These correlates tell us that a weak definition of foreign bribery goes together with restrictions on press freedom and civil society, weak standards with respect to law reform, high income inequality, and a lower inclination to tax corporations. At the same time, we have seen how easily governments inclined to condone foreign bribery may conceal their true intentions by pointing to the broad scope of corporate liability in foreign bribery cases, while remaining silent about how this liability is combined with an imprecise definition of corporate liability. There is a considerable 'vagueness-rebate', it seems, as exemplified by a largely unregulated use of non-trial resolutions for corporate offenders. When political leaders in a loud voice emphasize the scope of liability, and a low voice when they call for law enforcement, we may well face an attempt to establish an international anti-corruption façade behind which foreign bribery may thrive (Moene and Søreide, 2015).

Conclusion

What characterizes the most 'actionable definitions' of corruption? Should countries go for a more precise definition of liability or a definition with a broader scope? What are the trade-offs for reform-friendly governments? By zooming in on countries' regulation and enforcement of foreign bribery, we have explained how, for a given scope of liability, lower precision in the definition of liability always impedes the enforcement system's ability to sanction and deter corporate bribery.

We have shown how low precision in the definition of corporate bribery can go together with type II errors that let corporate criminals go free, implicitly inviting more corporate crime, in this analysis deemed a 'safety last' principle. Also, low precision can go together with type I errors that evict innocent corporations, thus leading to over-deterrence, in the sense that firms choose to stay away from legitimate business deals if too worried they will be suspected of bribery, in our analysis, acting in line with a 'safety first' principle. If the theorized mechanisms reflect reality, the insights ought to have implications for governments' regulation of corporate bribery, and in particular, the current expansion in the use of non-trial resolutions. While this form of enforcement may increase the number of enforcement cases, it is important for enforcement systems to apply precise definitions of wrongdoing and avoid dilution of case law.

To shed light on the empirical relevance we draw on OECD material, and on that basis, we rank 36 jurisdictions with respect to the scope and precision of their definition of corporate liability in bribery cases. We find substantial variation across jurisdictions and show that countries that perform well in terms of their corporate bribery definition, perform well on a range of other governance indicators too, and they are better able to enforce corporate liability. A broad scope of liability together with a high precision of the law easily make criminalization of foreign bribery appear more functional than it is.

Appendix: The Bribery Liability Index

As explained in the text, the construction of the BLI is based on information from the OECD (2016) stocktaking report on corporate liability, specifically: Table 3. *Type of legal person covered*; Table 4. *What acts are covered by liability*; Table 5. *Standard of liability/strictness of vicarious liability (VL)*; Table 6. *Compliance defense*; Table 8. *Liability for related firms/partners*; Table 10. *Successor liability*; and Table 11. *Jurisdiction over legal persons*.

For each table we plotted the scope per country, i.e., what is included in the jurisdiction's liability and the lack of clarity in terms of question marks reflecting that it is difficult to tell. Table 5 was relevant for scope only, while apart from that table, all the tables were used for both dimensions of the BLI.

The OECD report covers well the spectrum of relevant 'components'. Composing the index, we applied the most straightforward approach, that is, the arithmetic mean. We gave each component equal weight because we cannot justify why one would be more important than another. We then scaled them so that 'more is better'. That means, the broader the scope of liability the 'better' the definition, and likewise, the clearer its contents, the higher the score on our bribery liability estimate. Eventually, we normalized each sub-indicator (i.e., scope and clarity) so that regardless of the amount of underlying information, the score would be a figure between 1 and 7. Even if there are six indicators on scope and seven on clarity, clarity and scope have the same weight for the BLI.

The OECD stocktaking report that contains all the information applied for the construction of the Bribery Liability Index is openly available on the OECD website.

Notes

1 We thank Susan Rose-Ackerman and Peter Solmssen for useful comments.

2 These firms have all been subject to enforcement by the US Department of Justice, and facts about the cases are available on its website: www.justice.gov/criminal-fraud/enforcement-actions

3 For discussion about sanctions in corruption cases, see Rose-Ackerman (2010), Garrett (2014), Chapter 6 of Rose-Ackerman and Palifka (2016), Søreide (2016) and Arlen (2020).
4 For the result of a survey of enforcement practices in corporate bribery cases across 66 countries, see Makinwa and Søreide (2019).
5 See Arlen (2012), Arlen and Kahan (2017), Makinwa and Søreide (2020). Note also, the benefits one hopes for, such as incentives for self-reporting, are difficult to achieve in practice because many governments fail to offer predictable benefits, they are not sufficiently open about their enforcement practices, and not able to protect corporate offenders from double jeopardy (Low and Prelogar, 2020; Oded, 2020).
6 See the OECD website for the working group's revised recommendations, the 2021 OECD Anti-Bribery Recommendation.
7 'Safety first' behavior resembles risk aversion but is not the same. A risk averse leader may either stay away from bribery because of the risk of sanctions, or, pay bribes out of fear for losing out in business because competitors pay bribes, thus be more inclined to commit crime (Søreide 200X). Risk aversion is a deviation from rationality, whose impact depends on the concern in question. By 'safety first' we refer instead to the rational adaptation of the business community to the regulatory reality.
8 The arguments in this paper draw heavily on a theoretical analysis we did on a similar theme (Moene and Søreide, 2021).
9 Søreide (2016, Ch. 3) reviews OECD country evaluation reports and discusses variation across countries when it comes to their apparent willingness to enforce their foreign bribery legislation.
10 The evaluations are all available at the OECD anti-bribery website: www.oecd.org/daf/anti-bribery/countrymonitoringoftheoecdanti-briberyconvention.htm
11 Tables 3–6, 8, 10 and 11 of the OECD WGB stocktaking report.
12 Enforcement data in this context are not weighted against factors such as the size of the economy or a country's private sector's exposure to bribery risk. Such weighting is difficult because the ratio between the number of underlying cases and other factors is unknown. The bigger the difference between actual bribery cases and the number of enforcement cases, the less relevant the ratio between these figures becomes. In this context the figure reflects a jurisdiction's proven ability and inclination to pursue cases once they are detected, regardless of other country characteristics.
13 Based on simple regressions with enforcement data (OECD, 2019b), TRACE (2020), and Gibney (2019).
14 Based on simple regressions run against data on prosecutor independence provided by Van Aaken, Feld and Voigt (2010), who define prosecutor independence as the extent to which a prosecutor can carry out his or her duties without interference from external forces, particularly political actors. They create an index of public prosecutor independence (PPI) reflecting formal independence, appointment procedure, security of tenure, and budgetary autonomy.
15 The negative correlation between BLI and trade as a percentage of GDP captures the fact that the most trade-dependent countries have other governance challenges as well. None of the correlations show causality.
16 All indicators provided by OECD National Accounts Statistics, and higher inheritance tax (by Tax Foundation Tax Foundation: https://taxfoundation.org/estate-and-inheritance-taxes-around-world/)
17 According to the OECD website https://stats.oecd.org/Index.aspx?DataSetCode=BLI, this indicator describes the extent to which formal stakeholder engagement is built in the development of primary laws and subordinate regulations. The indicator is calculated as the simple average of two composite indicators (covering respectively primary laws and subordinate regulations) that measure four aspects of stakeholder engagement, namely i) systematic adoption (of formal stakeholder engagement requirements); ii)

methodology of consultation and stakeholder engagements; iii), transparency of public consultation processes and open government practices; and iv) oversight and quality control that refers to existence of oversight bodies and publicly available information on the results of stakeholder engagement. The stakeholder engagement indicator has been computed based on responses to the 2017 OECD's regulatory indicators survey for OECD countries as well as Colombia and Costa Rica, and to the OECD-IDB Survey on Regulatory Policy and Governance 2015 for Brazil. Respondents to all surveys were government officials. The scores for primary laws refer exclusively to processes for developing primary laws initiated by the executive. There is no score for primary laws for the United States, where all primary laws are initiated by Congress, and Brazil. In the majority of countries, most primary laws are initiated by the executive, except for Mexico and Korea, where a higher share of primary laws are initiated by parliament/ congress (respectively 66% and 87%).

18 A recent OECD recommendation suggests the risk of corruption attached to export credit agencies still needs to be addressed by several governments (see the Recommendation of the Council on Bribery and Officially Supported Export Credits, OECD/LEGAL/0447, as adopted by the OECD Council on Wednesday 13 March 2019).

References

Arlen, Jennifer. 2020. The potential promise and perils of introducing deferred prosecution agreements outside the US. In T. Søreide and A. Makinwa (eds.), *Negotiated Settlements in Bribery Cases*. Edw. Elgar Publishing.

Arlen, Jennifer, and Marcel Kahan. 2017. Corporate governance regulation through nonprosecution. *The University of Chicago Law Review*, 84(1): 323–387.

Ashworth, Andrew. 2018. A new generation of omissions offences? *Criminal Law Review*, 5: 354–364.

Feinstein, Andrew. 2011. *The Shadow World – Inside the Global Arms Trade*. Penguin.

Garrett, Brandon L. 2014. *Too Big to Jail*. Harvard University Press.

Gibney, Nicolas. 2019. Does size really matter? A study of banking sector size as it relates to money laundering and anti-money laundering enforcement. Thesis for the master degree at The Norwegian School of Economics (open access: https://openaccess.nhh.no/nhh-xmlui/handle/11250/2609822).

Hawley, Susan. 2003. *Turning a Blind Eye: Corruption and the UK Export Credits Guarantee Department*. London: Corner House.

Hawley, Susan, Colin King, and Nicholas Lord. 2020. Justice for whom? The need for a principled approach to Deferred Prosecution Agreements in England and Wales. In T. Søreide and A. Makinwa (eds.), *Negotiated Settlements in Bribery Cases*. Edward Elgar Publishing, 309–346.

Kaufmann, Daniel, and Pedro C. Vicente. 2011. Legal corruption. *Economics & Politics*, 23(2): 195–219.

Laufer, William S. 2008. *Corporate Bodies and Guilty Minds: The Failure of Corporate Criminal Liability*. University of Chicago Press.

Low, Lucinda, and Brittany Prelogar. 2020. Incentives for self-reporting and cooperation. In T. Søreide and A. Makinwa (eds.), *Negotiated Settlements in Bribery Cases: A Principled Approach*. Edw. Elgar.

Makinwa, Abiola, and Tina Søreide. 2018. *Structured Criminal Settlements: Towards Global Standards in Structured Criminal Settlements for Corruption Offences*. The International Bar Association (IBA).

Moene, Kalle, and Tina Søreide. 2015. Good governance facades. In S Rose-Ackerman and P Lagunes (eds.), *Greed, Corruption, and the Modern State*. Edw. Elgar Publishing.

Mungiu-Pippidi, Alina. 2015. *The Quest for Good Governance: How Societies Develop Control of Corruption*. Cambridge University Press.
Oded, Sharon. 2020. The DOJ's anti-piling on policy. Time to reflect? In T Søreide and A Makinwa (eds.), *Negotiated Settlements in Bribery Cases: A Principled Approach*. Edw. Elgar.
OECD. 2016. *The Liability of Legal Persons for Foreign Bribery: A Stocktaking Report*. Paris: OECD.
OECD. 2019a. *Resolving Foreign Bribery Cases with Non-Trial Resolutions: Settlements and Non-Trial Agreements by Parties to the Anti-Bribery Convention*. Paris. OECD.
OECD. 2019b. *2018 Enforcement of the Anti-Bribery Convention Investigations, Proceedings, and Sanctions*. Paris. OECD.
Pieth, Mark. 2020. Negotiating settlements in a broader law enforcement context. In T Søreide and A Makinwa (eds.), *Negotiated Settlements in Bribery Cases: A Principled Approach*. Edw. Elgar.
Rose-Ackerman, Susan. 2018. Corruption & purity. *Daedalus*, 147(3): 98–110.
Rose-Ackerman, Susan. 2010. The law and economics of bribery and extortion. *Annual Review of Law and Social Science*, 6: 217–238.
Rose-Ackerman, Susan, and Benjamin Billa. 2008. Treaties and national security. *NYU Journal of International Law and Politics*, 40: 437–496.
Rose-Ackerman, Susan, and Bonnie J. Palifka. 2016. *Corruption and Government: Causes, Consequences, and Reform*. 2nd edition. Cambridge University Press.
Rotberg, Robert I. 2019. *The Corruption Cure: How Citizens and Leaders can Combat Graft*. Princeton University Press.
Rothstein, Bo, and Jan Teorell. 2008. What is quality of government? A theory of impartial government institutions. *Governance*, 21(2): 165–190.
Søreide, Tina. 2016. *Corruption and Criminal Justice*. Edw. Elgar Publishing.
TRACE. 2020. *2019 Global Enforcement Report*. Annapolis: TRACE International.
Transparency International. 2020. *Exporting Corruption. Progress Report 2020: Assessing enforcement of the OECD Anti-Bribery Convention*. Berlin: Transparency International.
Tullock, Gordon and Charles Kershaw Rowley. 2005. *The Social Dilemma: Of Autocracy, Revolution, Coup d'etat, and War*. Vol. 8. C.K. Rowley (ed.). C.K. Liberty Fund Inc.
Van Aaken, Anne, Lars P. Feld, and Stefan Voigt. 2010. Do independent prosecutors deter political corruption? An empirical evaluation across seventy-eight countries. *American Law and Economics Review*, 12(1): 204–244.
Wannenwetsch, Scarlet. 2020. The G20's responsiveness to B20 anti-corruption recommendations 2010–2017 Part I: Baseline report. Basel: Basel Institute of Governance.

11 The corruption-FDI nexus in the global defense industry

Nancy Hite-Rubin

The corruption-FDI nexus in the Global Defense Industry

Corruption in the defense sector and in the international arms trade is uniquely pervasive.[1] One surprising finding is that arms procurement by "corrupt" countries strongly predicts increasing foreign direct investment (FDI) inflows during the post-Cold War era (Drezner and Hite-Rubin 2014; Hite-Rubin 2015). During the same time that the Global Defense Industry (GDI) sales shifted toward politically risky markets, corrupt governments attracted *more* FDI when they increased arms imports and defense budgets (Hite-Rubin 2023). This is concerning because high corruption within these states, along with greater rent-seeking and security risks, brought on by rising military spending and arms imports, is a recipe for "development in reverse" (Collier et al. 2003). Unfortunately, this empirical correspondence is robust and significant, demonstrating a military-FDI link, that grows stronger the more "corrupt" the country is perceived to be. As consequential as this state-level statistical correspondence appears to be, it has not yet been causally identified.

My goal in this chapter is to explore the causal mechanisms that underlie this puzzling trend using an interdisciplinary approach.[2] It is important to emphasize from the outset that corruption is neither the independent nor the dependent variable in this study. The data indicate that the interplay of defense expenditures and arms imports vis-à-vis FDI is *mediated* by corruption. Empirically, the complex phenomenon labeled "corruption" is captured imperfectly through an annual index that measures the degree to which experts believe that corrupt principal-agent interactions distort public power and delegitimize institutions within a particular country. Corruption can be thought of as an equilibrium or a "syndrome", where a state's index score predicts the existence of an array of "corrupt" attributes (Johnstone 2005). The presence and severity of corruption within a country fundamentally alters the functioning of markets and institutions. As such, all engagements of both transnational economic actors and domestic governments are mediated by corruption. The prevalence of entrenched corruption threatens the profitability of multinational corporations (MNCs), constrains the decision making of domestic states, and influences which entities attract foreign capital and how. As endemic corruption distorts market efficiency and allocation, the role of legal prices in market exchange diminishes, and investments are more uncertain due to political risk.

DOI: 10.4324/9781003416234-13

The military-FDI link is a compelling topic for inquiry, given that systemic corruption typically thwarts rather than facilitates FDI. In theorizing the military-FDI link, one must first clarify what the empirical variables represent. Military expenditures and arms imports are state-level variables and exclude non-state actors and private security spending.[3] The GDI is not an empirical variable, but a term to describe the organizations and MNCs that produce and sell military equipment and services primarily for national defense. Every nation state has a defense sector and furnishes weapons and military systems through a combination of domestic production and foreign procurement. The "military expenditures" variable represents the annual economic burden of each country on everything from barbed wire to fighter jets, salaries to military aid, operations to contracted fees. The "arms imports" variable is an estimate of the volume of major conventional arms delivered in the calendar year and includes transfers of second-hand weapons, significant components, and licensed production. The military expenditures and arms imports variables both indicate how intensely countries are engaged with the GDI, where every stage of production from R&D, to financing, materials, production, and repair is as fragmented and transnational as the automotive industry (Brauer 2011).

The International Arms Trade is unlike any other. Defense procurement is notoriously associated with corruption due to the secrecy, complexity, high cost, and the interrelationships between public goods provision, politics, and commercial interests.[4] Defense contracting is further complicated by the globalization of production, the sensitivity of transferable technologies, joint venture partnerships, and third-party subcontracting over politically risky and long time-horizons. The WTO Agreement on Government Procurement (GPA) exempts defense trade[5] from free-trade requirements, allowing secrecy and countertrade practices to thrive in international defense procurement. Post-Cold War shifts in security and military spending priorities mean that large US, UK, and EU defense firms[6] compete heavily in a highly lucrative 'buyer's market'. The center of gravity of the GDI has shifted toward buyers with endemic corruption (Hite-Rubin 2023). The increasing prevalence of defense offsets agreements, which are countertrade measures stipulated in defense contracts, is arguably the result of the same market imperfections that render defense procurement so susceptible to corruption. Systematic data on these "reciprocal agreements that are a condition of sale for defense exports" (Schoeni 2023, p. 343) are impossible to collect. Yet, multiple studies indicate that offsets are high value and include diverse stipulations that accommodate the buying country's demands.

This chapter considers four hypotheses that could explain the defense spending-FDI link. The first section explains the robust correspondence of military spending and FDI in greater detail. The following section explores two hypotheses that connect domestic security expenditures to macroeconomic growth. First, the "geoeconomic favoritism" hypothesis, espoused by critics of US military retrenchment (Brooks et al. 2012; Drezner 2013), is considered. This hypothesis emphasizes the role of state power, namely the US's economic and military primacy, in advancing its interests in the face of economic globalization. Yet, geoeconomic favoritism cannot explain why it is that military spending and arms imports of great powers actually leads to attracting less, rather than more, FDI inflows (Drezner and Hite-Rubin 2016). The second hypothesis posits that the military-FDI correlation implies causation. The notion that military expenditures are directly beneficial to economic growth, inclusive of FDI inflows, is the subject of over 30 years of empirical research in defense economics. However, the macro-econometric growth scholarship lacks cogent identification strategies and is based on highly problematic underlying assumptions. These analyses rely on a "guns vs. butter" heuristic, falsely asserting rational, competitive markets that are trading 'normal' goods. Both the "security channel" and the "geoeconomic favoritism" explanations for a military-FDI nexus rely on the false premise that military spending and GDI sales are akin to 'buying peace'. This section concludes that neither the 'security channel' or the 'geoeconomic favoritism' hypotheses can explain this research puzzle.

The latter part of the chapter clarifies how GDI sales and linked activities uniquely affect corrupt states. I develop two theories, referred to as hypotheses 3 and 4, to explain the empirical military-FDI link. Under hypothesis 3, the military-FDI link results from the prevalence of defense offsets where FDI is one of the stipulations made in contracting GDI sales to corrupt states. By focusing on the geopolitics of US-Foreign Military Sales (FMS), I introduce a conceptual framework to show how offset packages are codetermined by buyers' and sellers' priorities, preferences, and tolerance for risk. Since the US FMS program sells more arms to the "riskiest nations" than its "low risk" allies (Thrall and Dorminey 2018), risk mitigation must occur at the contracting level. Therefore, indirect offset arrangements in the form of FDI are more frequently contracted with non-allied or fragile states where they are necessary to make a sale. The US Department of Defense administers such "gray area" deals with FDI offset provisions which are less hazardous than direct offset arrangements, such as defense coproduction and technology transfer. Furthermore, corrupt countries are more inclined to require indirect offsets, given their amenability to rent seeking and patronage disbursement. Through this offset mechanism, GDI deals in politically risky markets create the military-FDI link.

International investors view corruption as a consequential form of 'political risk' that devalues FDI by increasing uncertainty and costs.[7] Yet, although government corruption generally stifles FDI and harms economic growth (Mauro 1995), there are exceptions where FDI is impervious to political risk calculations. Hypothesis 4 is that firms in the GDI are 'risk loving'. The characteristic illiberal trade impacts, firm-specific business advantages, and corruption externalities create the military-FDI link. At the first level, the investments bundled together as defense-offset FDI are a form of countertrade that is written off as part of the GDI sale and thus does not face competitive-market pressures. Additionally, major GDI firms are further advantaged because of the institutional infrastructure and business assets built over decades of defense-offset contracting in politically risky markets. Finally, GDI engagements with corrupt states create market distortions and corruption externalities that further undermine the political economy and FDI attractiveness. Therefore, the military-FDI link is strongest in the most corrupt countries since 'risk loving' GDI engagements have the highest comparative advantage over 'normal' FDI in these high-risk markets.

The chapter concludes with the next steps in this research project. These include ways to operationalize the third and fourth hypotheses for empirical testing.

The military-FDI link

The econometric results presented in my prior publications demonstrate that the relationship between military spending and FDI hinges significantly upon perceptions of corruption.[8] These results can be understood by showing that the military-FDI link is strongly indicated through a technique called marginal effects analysis (ME). ME is often used to interpret how a main effect is affected by the presence of a moderating variable (Busenbark et al. 2022). The marginal effects analysis depicted in Figure 11.1 indicates that the military-FDI link is stronger the more corrupt the state is, where corruption is represented on the x-axis; from most corrupt 0, to least corrupt, 6. Importantly, the figure demonstrates the relationship among three variables: FDI, military spending, and corruption scores. The 'military-FDI link' is the relationship between military spending and subsequent FDI and is plotted on the y-axis. This main effect is mapped across corruption levels (the moderating variable) on the x-axis. The corruption measure employed comes from Political Risk Group's (PRS) International Country Risk Guide (ICRG) corruption index score for the degree to which "corruption within the political system … [represents] a threat to foreign investment", determined annually.

The downward sloping curve in Figure 11.1, demonstrates that for the global time series analysis, a statistically significant military-FDI link is strongest when and where corruption is highest. The marginal effect of military spending on FDI slopes downward and crosses the x-axis at corruption scores of roughly 3.5 and higher ('lower corruption'). This moderating effect of corruption on a country's military expenditure-FDI profile is striking. On the left side, we see that for the most corrupt states an increase in military spending predicts significant

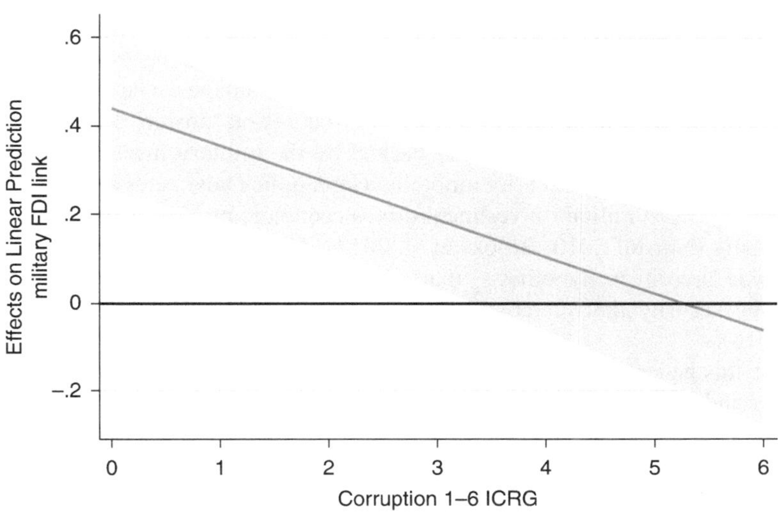

Figure 11.1 Marginal effects of military expenditures on FDI inflows by corruption level.

Source: Author and Drezner and Hite-Rubin (2014, unpublished paper).

increases in FDI inflows. The flow of foreign capital appears to chase military spending into the world's most corrupt domestic markets at double the rate that it flows into moderately corrupt countries. Military spending is most tied to FDI for countries where foreign investments are arguably the most political risky. This finding is also consistent with additional analyses utilizing the SIPRI arms import variable which demonstrates that both arms imports and military spending follow the same curious trend, drawing FDI into exceedingly corrupt states (Drezner and Hite-Rubin 2014; Hite-Rubin 2015).

Global security, defense economics and FDI (examining hypotheses 1 and 2)

Political-economic consideration of the interdependence of foreign investment and military expenditure is older than classical economics itself. Mercantilist pamphlets by Gerard de Malynes and Edward Misselden, elaborated in the writings of Thomas Mun, invoke the primacy of military power as fundamental to foreign trade and investment, and vice versa. In the early capitalist period, mercantilists sought a symbiotic relationship with monarchies to open new markets abroad. These writings assert that the capacity to carry out wars, to project military capacity, to establish and defend foreign investment was the *raison d'état* for the state. In other words, a military-FDI feedback loop lies at the very base of mercantilism.

The existence of a military-FDI feedback loop is no longer so evident and basic. In early-stage capitalism nation states acted unilaterally and international institutions, such as the World Trade Organization, United Nations, and International Monetary Fund, were unthinkable. Yet, the logic of neorealism has a subtle throughline to modern economic imperialism. Just as mercantilists emphasized the monarch's role in securing foreign treasure, so too do some modern scholars and policy hawks provide rationales for outsized military spending to establish geopolitical dominance and command foreign market advantages. The neorealist tradition in International Political Economy (IPE) focuses on 'power' determined by economic strength, which is critically backed by the military investments of superpowers, namely the US security umbrella. Here, policy advocates and scholars argue that outsized military investment drives economic prosperity within the global economy (Norrlof 2010; Brooks et al. 2012). These views coalesce to the 'geo-economic favoritism hypothesis' that military predominance implies political-economic security that thereby attracts investment and net economic gain (Drezner 2013).

However, this geoeconomic favoritism hypothesis is refuted via empirical testing (Drezner and Hite-Rubin 2016). If anything, Drezner and Hite-Rubin's global empirical analysis of the relationship between military expenditures and FDI provides evidence of a 'peace dividend' among superpowers in the post-Cold War era. Furthermore, empirics demonstrate that for countries scoring as least 'corrupt', marginal increases in defense products are significantly tied to *decreasing* FDI inflows (Hite-Rubin 2015). This artifact of imperialism, a military-FDI correspondence, does not hold for the original superpowers who now comprise the

'Global North'. Rather, antithetically it is the 'South' where military expansion is linked to greater FDI inflows. The more corrupt a state is perceived to be, *ceteris paribus*, the greater the likelihood that the purchase of foreign defense products is followed by FDI inflows. The military-FDI connection pivots on the axis of corruption, not 'power', thereby undercutting the geo-economic favoritism hypothesis.

Guns, butter, and growth macroeconomics

Why then, does this echo of economic imperialism, a robust and positive feedback loop across military expenditures and foreign investment, hold only for corrupt and fragile states? Early IPE scholarship emphasized the relationship between military expenditure and economic growth, which is inclusive of FDI. The earliest empirical tests employed simple bivariate OLS regression and produced contradictory results.[9] By the late 1990s empirical literature on the relationship between military power and economic growth shifted from political science primarily to defense economics journals.

The past 30 years of empirical study into the relationship between military expenditure and economic growth has not yielded a consensus (Azam 2020; Dunne and Smith 2020). The empirical studies on the 'guns vs. butter' debate employ cross-country regression analysis with varied specifications.[10] There is a growing dissatisfaction with supply and demand growth models that do not consider the political and strategic determinants of military expenditures, such as threat (Dunne et al. 2008). The dominant empirical methods from defense economics treat military spending as an exogenous input. Therefore, they model military expenditures as influencing economic growth directly through either investment or production factor channels.

Recent empirical contributions tackle the non-linearity challenge by utilizing 'threat of conflict' as a mediating variable. Aziz and Khalid's 2019 paper on the FDI impacts of military spending illustrates the theoretical fragility of much of the empirical defense economics literature. Although acknowledging the value of incorporating noneconomic variables into the defense economics literature, a few critiques are in order. First, their analysis requires a model for FDI inflows.[11] Second, their measure of 'threat' is dubious, and the assumption that threat is quelled directly by military spending is flawed. The authors misinterpret their ME analysis as causal and suggest that states spend "a sufficient amount on military resources in order to attract and sustain higher FDI inflows" (Aziz and Khalid 2019, p. 248). In contrast, my work aims to develop an empirical strategy for identifying the causal mechanism undergirding the robust correlations in the data (Hite-Rubin 2015; Hite-Rubin 2023). To claim from statistically robust observational findings that corrupt governments should ramp up militarily to attract FDI would be erroneous and unethical.

Defense economists recognize that identification is a major issue that persists despite efforts to account for heterogenous estimands (Dunne and Smith 2020). Recent studies tackling non-linearities provide better empirical fit but do not allow strong causal claims. The point, however, is not to denigrate the economists who integrate political science constructs into their macro-econometric model specifications. Rather, one should welcome them to "a field in which everyone is painfully aware that theoretical concepts sometimes have weak empirical analogues and where data collection is often error-ridden, highly aggregated, or otherwise problematic." Hence, the bar for confirming theories with regression analysis should be very high (Wilson and Butler 2007, p. 119). This is a point of cautious optimism for more interdisciplinary studies and fruitful application and interpretation of such quantitative methodology.

Military spending isn't buying peace

The 'geoeconomic favoritism' theory of neorealist IPE echoes the defense economists' explanation for a military-FDI link. Both hypotheses connect military capability to economic reward. However, geoeconomic favoritism is grounded in IR's neorealism theories, where the relationships between military capabilities and security threat are highly contextualized and complex. Furthermore, their hypothesis is constructed around the claim that the US's position as the military hegemon confers direct economic advantages, such as FDI inflows into the US. Alternatively, defense economists rely upon a 'security channel' hypothesis that military spending brings security as a direct and universal effect. This implicit assumption that more military expenditure, more arms, more defense equals greater security, *ceteris paribus*, is well illustrated by Dunne 2012–

> An important issue in empirical work is the identification problem that results from the fact that we observe military spending and growth changing and both are influenced by security threats. If the economic determinants of growth are constant, but there are variations in the security threat, a negative relationship between military expenditure and output will be observed. On the other hand, if the threat is constant but the economic variables are changing, a positive relationship between military expenditure and output will be observed. This can be used to explain some country experiences with different combinations of growth and military expenditure.
>
> (Dunne 2012, p. 550)

The assumption that military expenditure consistently implies greater security is problematic. While it is hardly controversial that countries increase military expenditure in the face of security threat (Nordhaus et al. 2012), the interdependencies and dynamics are highly varied. These macroeconomics papers rely upon the simplification that military expenditures, 'guns', are comparable to economically rational goods, 'butter'. In these model specifications, 'security threat; is treated as a latent variable that coherently explains demand for military expenditure, which in turn purchases threat reduction. Military spending does not quell security threat in the same way that butter makes a cake. There are myriad reasons for why a security channel should not be as straightforward and symmetric as Dunne's hypothetical above. Military expenditure does not purchase normal goods within rational markets.

National defense is the quintessential public good, it is non-rivalrous and non-excludable (Cooter and Ulen 2000). Military expenditures are determined by political institutions which are highly influenced by bureaucratic organizations, standard operating procedures, and political constituencies and "thus decreases in spending do not necessarily follow a decline in international threats" (Cappella et al. 2017, p. 794). As public goods, defense spending is codetermined with social spending, tax revenue, debt, and the money supply (Carter et al. 2021). Military expenditures include current and capital spending on a broad portfolio of defense activities, personnel, and procurement. Both the composition of military budgets and level of spending vary dramatically across countries and marginal fluctuations in defense spending are arguably more contingent upon policy processes and political preferences than threat.[12] The inherently political aspect of military spending is further influenced by non-threat factors such as business cycles, credit constraints, foreign aid, trade costs, and the globalization of production.[13] The existence of threat, both international and internal, although certainly important, does not track coherently to marginal differences in defense spending across countries.

The burgeoning subfield of global security research demonstrates the importance of various non-threat determinants of military expenditures. The level of military spending is an intrinsically political decision that is filtered through institutional factors and political-economic constraints. Relatedly, the 'security channel' completely ignores corruption. This is a problem since military spending levels, expenditure allocation, and defense procurement transactions are particularly susceptible to corruption (Cole and Tran 2011; Hite-Rubin 2015; Perlo-Freeman 2018). Military expenditures purchase 'credence goods', which entail such complexity and informational uncertainty, that their value is unclear even after consumption.[14] The secrecy, complexity, uniqueness, and high profit margins of defense procurement all mean that corruption risks are pervasive. High corruption is tied empirically to higher military expenditures and procurement, as a portion of GDP (Gupta et al. 2001; Lopes da Silva 2022). Furthermore, some argue that military expenditures are motivated more by rent-seeking opportunism than security or threat considerations (Holden et al. 2016).

A serious weakness of the 'security channel' explanation for a military expenditure-growth nexus, is the assertion that military expenditures quell security threats. General market equilibrium pricing assumptions neglect the fact that national defense is both a credence and public good, and that the defense industry is beset by factors that make corruption more likely. Military expenditures do not buy blanket security because military expenditures affect the level of threat. The endogeneity of threat and military expenditures manifests in the phenomena of arms races and arms proliferation. [15] Furthermore, there is compelling evidence on the way rising military expenditures adversely affect security and mechanisms by which foreign aid results in unintendedly higher military expenditures and conflict risks. [16]

Defense spending does not have a linear correspondence with the international threat environment (Cappella Zielinski et al. 2017). Government spending decisions in the face of varied threats (internal and external) are contingent upon regime characteristics and politics. It is therefore unsurprising that defense-growth nexus research whose models rely entirely on 'threat' as a mediator are underwhelming in terms of statistical power and are not causally identified.[17] Bayesian model averaging and forecasting analysis demonstrates the weakness of 'threat' measures relative to institutional and economic predictors in determining the level of military expenditures (Böhmelt and Bove 2014). The theoretical concept of threat, proxied in global data sets as internal and external conflict propensity, does not track well with military spending levels. The 'security channel' assumption that underpins much of the Defense Economics growth literature does not account for the complexity of defense spending and political risk.

Global security, FDI, and political risk (proposing hypotheses 3 and 4)

Neither geoeconomic favoritism nor security channel theories can solve the empirical puzzle indicated in Figure 11.1. What, then, is achieved by *not* explaining the military-FDI link? There are two key lessons. First, defense spending and the international arms trade are not amenable to neoclassical assumptions of the price mechanism and competitive markets. Second, politics and non-market mechanisms powerfully motivate military expenditure and arms sales. The GDI is uniquely positioned to drive vast sums into economic activities that would collapse within a competitive marketplace. The military-FDI link arguably results from politically embedded GDI transactions made within corrupt markets.

Geopolitics and the non-market features of GDI sales together form an illiberal *invisible hand* that uniquely influences the political economy of corrupt countries. To explain this military-FDI link, I turn to two complementary hypotheses. The first considers geopolitical drivers of foreign military arms sales to corrupt states and argues that such deals have a greater propensity for exorbitant, indirect offsets that are counted in total FDI inflows. Second, I argue that the GDI's illiberal market features render it a 'risk loving' industry that has competitive advantages in conflict-prone and corrupt markets. Although FDI is generally stifled by political risk, defense-linked investments are propped up by offset provisions and market distortions. These two complementary mechanisms, hypotheses 3 and 4, create the military-FDI link that is strongest where corruption is highest.

Geopolitics of foreign military sales

Both the decision to export and to procure foreign defense goods and services are largely influenced by geopolitics. According to neorealist theorizing, states strategically either seek 'balancing' alliances against an emerging threat or turn to 'bandwagoning' and ally with the disrupter of the status quo. Stephen Walt's balance of threat theory hypothesizes when weak states yield to bandwagoning to the detriment of the status quo, and interstate security (Walt 1990). An empirical analysis of alliance behavior tests for conditions in which small or weak states bandwagon with revisionist states, and finds that poor bureaucratic capacity, civil conflict, and geographic proximity to threat are significant determinants (Carter 2022).[18] Political leaders of corrupt countries are more prone to militaristic posturing to consolidate power and/or patronage enrichment. It is thematic in

PE-GS, that weak states are characterized by corruption-induced security risks that heighten the risk of bandwagoning and other geopolitical instability. Thus, to maintain international stability and security, Carter espouses a form of deep military engagement familiar in security studies –

> It is imperative that status quo powers recognize this dynamic early and aid in state building and joint operational (military, law enforcement and bureaucratic) exercises to root out the problem at its core, reducing domestic security threats and making these weak states internally strong enough to resist the revisionist threat.
>
> (Carter 2022, pp. 22–23).

Thus, geopolitics motivates arms spending and GDI transfers to corrupt states. Corrupt and failing states are seen as threatening to US interests and global security, given their susceptibility to forming dangerous alliances with revisionist states. There seems to be a misconception that the US sells only to allies. The reality is that the US-led GDI employs arms sales as a mode of influence and statecraft universally. Calls for preemptive and/or expansive state-building measures and joint operational engagement certainly entail increased military expenditures and arms flows. Increases in military expenditures of 'potential enemies' significantly predicts increases in domestic military expenditure (Dunne et al. 2008). This phenomenon of structurally motivated militarization[19] occurs on a spectrum from dyadic arms races on one extreme, to less obvious build ups of defense procurement within a region, alliance, or network.

GDI commercial activities are highly contingent upon international relations and serve multiple foreign policy objectives. Both balancing and 'bandwagoning' involve military alliances, where two or more states formally agree to cooperate militarily in the face of military threats. The criterion for a "military alliance" is a "commitment for cooperative action in the event of conflict" and contains variable features, such as leasing territory, arms sales, military aid, basing, border delimitation, intelligence sharing, logistics/supplies etc. (Leeds 2022, p. 7). Regardless, of whether balancing and 'bandwagoning' are employed, military alliances lead to higher military expenditures, foreign arms procurement, and transfers. These structurally motivated increases in militarization are met with increased MNE activity that is profitable for the GDI. Overall, the aggregate impact is an increase in state-level military expenditures and arms imports. In general, alliances promote intra-alliance security provisions and structurally motivate further spending by adversaries. Alliances promote efficiency gains, but the net impact of alliance-driven gains in joint military expenditures and increased arms sales is notoriously difficult to estimate (Kinne and Kang 2023). Global trends make it clear that post-Cold War military spending and GDI sales are rising (Wezeman et al. 2021). And in addition to traditional military alliances, a new form of defense cooperation – formal weapons cooperation agreements (WCAs) – have significantly increased the international flow of weapons (Kinne 2016). Formal military alliances and WCAs both provide institutional platforms for motivating and facilitating GDI sales.

The US's historical investment in defense R&D helps to explain its current GDI dominance and its leverage in using arms sales and defense offsets agreements for geopolitical aims (Flamm 1999). US-foreign arms sales and military aid are often applied to help manage the balance of power. The two channels used by the US are, first, efforts to strengthen the military capabilities of allies and second, to gain geopolitical leverage (Thrall and Dorminey 2018). Under the US's grand strategy, arms sales and transfers are regularly employed for enhancing military posture, engaging in great power competition, and dealing with idiosyncratic international security threats (CRS 2022). In practice, although the geopolitical underpinning of defense contracts varies enormously, the US defense firms profit from defense sales whatever their motivation.

The GDI is profit seeking wherever it operates, and there is little indication that corruption risks or state fragility deter the global trade in weapons and military services. US firms dominate the GDI in terms of foreign sales and the international presence of MNCs through inter-firm agreements, subcontracting, joint ventures, mergers, and acquisitions (Beraud-Sudreau et al. 2020). All US sales and contracts are managed by the DoD and shaped by US geopolitical strategy and regulations in an obtuse manner akin to Soviet central planning (Hartley 2007). US firms made a near record of $110.9 billion in government to government offers in 2020 under the Foreign Military Sales (FMS) program, which accounts for the bulk of US arms sales (Hartung and Yousif 2021). According to TI international, most sales are made to countries classified as having high or very high-risk markets.[20] The US's defense contractors market power within the GDI means that it could refuse to deal with highly corrupt buyers (Caverley 2017). But despite its market dominance, the US is second only to Russia in the volume of arms sales to highly corrupt countries (Fish and Man 2016).

Between 2002 and 2016, the US government transferred conventional weapons to 167 nations with an estimated value of $197 billion (Thrall and Dorminey 2018). Dollar estimates for confirmed US weapons sales are likely conservative because sales contracts are secretive and there are no legal requirements for reports of arm sales deliveries, services, or contractual offsets.[21] SIPRI bypasses this challenge by tracking and estimating the physical volume of major conventional weapons transferred into countries. Neither source publishes systematic information on defense offsets, which often exceed the value of the initial sale and are ubiquitous in foreign defense sales (Magahy et al. 2012). Little is known about these countertrade contracts because defense offsets are exempt from WTO free-trade compliance rules. The corruption risks in defense offsets are rife, and the lack of transparency and accountability concerning offsets shifts the burden onto the purchasing government's taxpayers (Schoeni 2023). Defense offsets are often required to make a sale, with the express motivation of appeasing domestic audiences by 'offsetting' the burden of defense procurement spending with more desirable benefits. Purchasing governments often mandate or request defense offsets, which results in higher sales prices, harmful market distortions, and discriminatory policies (Markowski and Hall 2014; Collins 2018).

Defense offsets are a transparency loophole that undermines the WTO's vision of open global markets, and they are a magnet for corruption risks. GDI firms compete in a buyer's market where purchasing states sometimes value offset deals more highly than economical procurement costs when evaluating competing bids (Dehoff et al. 2014). Figure 11.2, prepared by the US Bureau of Industry and Security (BIS) illustrated the kinds of contractual obligations occurring within defense-offset arrangements. Note that the terms "investment" and "other" may have no connection to the defense equipment purchased.[22] To attain a competitive edge, major defense firms enter offset obligations with foreign governments, which have been estimated by Avascent, an industry consulting firm, to reach a cumulative of $500 billion from 2012 through 2016 (Avascent 2012). Everything from training mechanics in Finland to investing in a shrimp farm in Saudi Arabia is not disclosed. Defense firms also invest substantial sums in establishing and marketing offset packages. US companies appear exempt from notification requirements for expenses such as political contributions, marketing fees, and commissions related to defense offsets (Goodman 2020). Ann Markusen, who served as Senior Fellow at the Council of Foreign Relations (1995–2002) and the Presidential Commission of Arms Trade Offsets (2000–01) describes the transaction costs GDI firms incur to win lucrative foreign sales:

> major firms have set up extensive offset operations, manned by self-made deal-makers whose work is essentially that of a trading company – evaluating offset demands [by foreign governments], marketing offset products, building plants in or working with potential foreign suppliers, searching for saleable technologies, training foreign firms' managers and engineers, identifying sources of credit, bargaining with buyers over commitments and

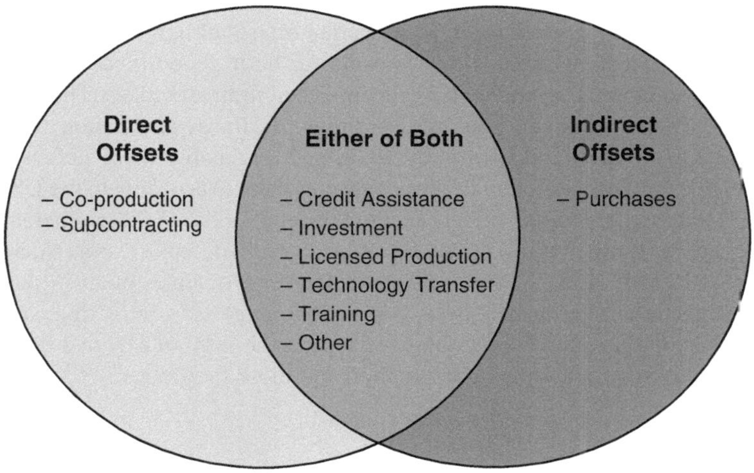

Figure 11.2 US commerce categorization of defense-offset compensation practices.

Source: US Bureau of Industry and Security (BIS), Offsets in the Defense Trade, 2021, p. 39.

> performance, trading offset credits and debits, and accomplishing paperwork … the transaction costs involved in fulfilling them is currently running between 7 and 10 percent of the value of the arms sale.
>
> (Markusen 2011)

Markusen's description of US defense suppliers acting like modern trading companies illustrates the expansiveness of GDI engagement with the purchasing state. Although US companies are legally compelled to follow national laws while operating in foreign markets, as codified by the Foreign and Corrupt Practices Act (FCPA), the complexity and opacity of offset agreements provides a considerable gray area for US defense firms.

Importantly, offsets agreements are not illegal bribes, and the practice does not explicitly defy international law[23] or anti-corruption regimes. The criteria for what can be stipulated in an offset package are seemingly boundless,[24] and what is known about defense offsets in practice is that the contracts are reflective of the unique preferences of the purchasing government. It is apparently impossible to infer defense-offset provisions from either SIPRI arms transfer volumes or publicly released sales data. However, the corruption risks in defense-offset contracting are likely highest for corrupt countries[25] and both US GDI sales and offset stipulations are moderated by the degree of corruption of the purchasing country. Which leads to the following hypothesis:

H3: *US GDI sales vis-à-vis corrupt countries are more likely to involve defense offsets that are credited as FDI inflows.*

Hypothesis 3 states that that the military-FDI link is an artifact of defense-offset arrangements made in the commission of US GDI sales to corrupt countries. The argument is that both 'supply' and 'demand' factors in US sale negotiations with corrupt countries prompt lucrative sales with opaque offsets obligations that are met by FDI. This conjecture stems from considering both geopolitical factors related to US arms sales and the rent-seeking incentives of indirect offsets. Though it appears that the "United States has sold weapons to almost any nation that wanted to buy them" (Thrall and Dorminey 2018, p. 3), arguably these defense acquisitions map onto wildly different defense-sale contracts. According to the US Department of Commerce, indirect offsets accounted for 59.94% of the estimated total value of (reported) offset transactions related to foreign defense export sales between 1993–2019 (BIS 2021). Direct offsets in the form of investment in the acquiring country's defense industrial base, coproduction and subcontracting can also result in FDI stimulus. However, indirect offsets, in the form of FDI to a firm unrelated to the defense procurement are common and more fungible.

Supply-side mechanisms for offset-driven FDI

The US Conventional Arms Transfer policy (CAT) provides a directive framework for government agencies to evaluate potential arms transfers. The National

Security Memoranda issued by each presidential administration on CAT provides insight on the geopolitical drivers of GDI sales and defense contracting. Benefits to security, foreign policy, industrial competitive and financial benefits of arms sales are set against considerations of security risks for proliferation, international humanitarian law, sensitive technology, and end-use violations. The latest memorandum, issued on February 23, 2023, by the Biden administration, is the first to contain the word "corruption".

Although there is no systematic data on the offset packages that accompany US arms deals, some supply-side variables apparently factor into the content:

- Alliance members, US security partnerships.
- Defense industrial cooperation and competitive advantage.
- Degree of assurance for sensitive technology.
- Strategic and foreign policy influence.
- Commercial profit.
- Security, legal and reputational risk of procurement/engagement.

These factors are arguably as consequential to the contractual terms of the sale, as they are to the approval process. The first five variables are interrelated and frequently espoused as the rationale for promoting global security via arms sales/transfers. These objectives are balanced against a risk assessment for security implications, legal liability, and reputational harm. Though there is ample evidence that the US does not discriminate in selling to highly corrupt and fragile states, some risk mitigation likely happens at the contracting level.

Procurement contracts for sales or transfers to allies facing a common security threat are presumably very different from those negotiated with a "counterbalancing" country. US DoD is unlikely to give clearance for sales to non-allied and volatile states if they also include offset agreements with benefits such as defense coproduction, licenses, and defense technology transfer. Given such geopolitical risks, these sales are more likely to include offset credit arrangements, awarded with vague investments in non-defense-related sectors under the pretense of advancing economic development. If the US firm earns offset credits by piecemeal investments in civilian enterprises, the arrangements carry considerable corruption risks. However, the opaque, highly complex foreign contracting process provides arm's length distance that enables the US GDI to participate in these payments with minimal legal exposure.

The US's stance on defense offsets is that they "are economically inefficient and trade distorting", and government agencies are prohibited from "encouraging, entering directly into, or committing U.S. firms to any offset arrangement in connection with the sale of defense articles or services to foreign governments".[26] Yet, the Foreign Military Sales (FMS) program of the DoD does set ground rules for offset obligation payments, indicating an "odd arrangement" by which the US is both ambivalent and tacitly facilitating these deals (Schoeni 2023). Indeed, "U.S. defense contractors have informed U.S. Government agencies, including BIS, that offsets are usually necessary in order to make defense sales" (BIS 2021, p. 1). In a 'buyer's' market where U.S. defense firms and political interests are keen to make a sale, it seems likely that firms will use offsets unrelated to the buyer's defense sector. Because 'corruption' has not been an explicit concern in the official directive for conventional arms transfers (CAT) until this year, the higher corruption risks of indirect offsets containing FDI are unlikely to stand in the way of a highly lucrative sale.

Defense offsets are not just a contractual burden; they also give a competitive advantage to dominant companies. The means used to develop, market, negotiate, and implement these complex, multifaceted offset packages are valuable trade secrets.[27] I argue that GDI firms leverage defense offsets to make sales to risky states by deprioritizing corruption risks in purchasing states. Offset benefits such as defense coproduction, technology transfers, and defense industrial collaboration are replaced with more fungible financial benefits that result in FDI. Obscured offset stipulations for investments for the vague purposes of "economic development" have strong ethical implications and are corruption 'red flags'. Yet, the ubiquity of these indirect offsets indicates that the tangible risks and liabilities for firms must have been outweighed by commercial reward.

Demand-side mechanisms for offset-driven FDI

As previously argued, when countries raise military expenditure for foreign defense procurement, they are not buying peace. US GDI arms agreements are not discrete purchases of normal goods procured from competitive markets. Arms deals are highly specialized and politically embedded, bringing the buyer and seller into a long-term foreign policy relationship. Importantly, foreign governments are not purchasing an item – they are participating in a military sale that usually includes a defense-offset package. Corrupt countries, particularly those with corruption problems specific to defense, will demand larger and indirect offset packages as a sale precondition. The more corrupt the purchasing country, the more that interest in rent-seeking and patronage opportunities will override other demand-side features of the GDI sale.

Foreign defense procurement decisions are filtered through domestic institutional factors and political-economic constraints. Defense-industry offsets and/or the primary defense article purchased vary significantly across countries. Security threats alone cannot explain US-GDI purchases because they are trumped by geopolitical motivations and rent-seeking potential. The purchasing country allocates military expenditures to purchase a credence good and engages in a contractual relationship. Defense-offset packages, negotiated with the purchasing government, add further complexity and informational uncertainty. The rationales for engaging in foreign defense procurement with GDI firms operating under the US rules are highly specific to each country. Nevertheless, there are some demand-side considerations integral to defense-offset demands. They are a mixture of:

- Defense industrial specialization.
- Alliance and/or strategic partnership.

- Counterbalancing, 'bandwagoning' – seeking US backed security.
- Symbolic interests – buying big shiny things, national pride.
- Security considerations.
- Price and quality – of 'credence' good.
- Corruption; rent seeking and patronage opportunities.

Defense offsets are priced into the contract, meaning that the purchasing country is paying for offset stipulations with domestic military expenditures. Offset provisions entail "any type of non-monetary compensation that a procuring government requires an exporting firm to provide as a condition of the sale" (Petersen 2011, p. 485).

The final negotiated offset package reveals a good deal about the relative priority that the country places upon the factors listed above. However, this is a two-way negotiation, and US DoD constrains what ultimately is included in a defense offset. Thus, US firms offer defense-related offsets, such as coproduction, knowledge sharing, and technology transfer, to allies when demand is high and geopolitical risks are low. Conversely, when geopolitical risks are high, the buyer country has less leverage for defense-related offset demands. Thus, non-US allies, facing political instability and corruption challenges are more likely to demand offsets as 'sweeteners' that take the form of FDI.

My conjecture that corrupt countries prefer FDI-heavy offset packages is not a blanket indictment of all such civilian investment projects. The argument is that such ventures pose a moral hazard that makes corruption far more likely. Indirect offset stipulations arguably provide the most opportunity for ill-gotten gains and patronage. Unlike a bribe, which would be a direct financial transfer in exchange for a defense sale, FDI is not illegal. It is not a legal liability for a US defense firm to put investment funds into an underperforming scheme that disburses patronage to "promote economic development". Furthermore, offset arrangements often use credit swaps in which off-the-books negotiations can be untraceable.

Although systemic data on offsets are not available, one can infer general trends and 'red flags' from case studies. For example, in 1992 the Finnish Defense ministry selected McDonnell Douglass to buy 64 FA-18 Hornet fighter-bombers over four rival aircraft bids in a $3 billion- deal, with a 100% defense offset minimum.[28] The Finnish defense ministry had a heavy hand in designing the required offsets that were directed toward coproduction, skills training, and defense-industrial collaboration. The Finnish government conducted its first official offset audit, showing that over the first six of the ten-year offset period, 88% of commitments were fulfilled, involving roughly 600 offset projects (Sköns 2011). The offset package demands of the Finish ministry were intended to work as an insurance mechanism so the Finnish defense industrial sector could "keep their flying ability as high as possible" and drastically reduce future maintenance costs (Kanniainen and Lehtonen 2019). Yet, this rosy account is contradicted by the Finnish national audit report showing that only 16% of offsets were directed to the defense sector, defense-offset administration costs were between $100–200 million, and that fulfillment statistics were unreliable (Sköns 2011).

It would be informative to compare the defense offsets for the 1992 Finnish fighter jet purchase to other comparable US-GDI aircraft sales to more endemically corrupt countries. However, the transparency needed for such direct comparison is elusive for the very reasons it is needed. The greater corruption is a mediating force, the more likely it is that arms purchases will require high offset values that inflate the sale price. The supply and demand features outlined here codetermine the diversity of offset provisions. Heightened geopolitical risk concerns and rent-seeking opportunism make FDI in defense offsets more likely. Corruption in defense procurement distorts both allocational and spending efficiency, which translates to bloated military budgets, distorted markets, wasteful projects and far worse. The World Peace Foundation (WPF) *Compendium of Arms Trade Corruption* found corruption in defense offsets to be integral for at least 11 of their 40 cases. Extra investigative attention and civil society pressure is needed to bring understanding and accountability to these countertrade stipulations.[29] Although incentives and opportunity do not guarantee corruption for every transaction, moral hazard all but guarantees that corruption increases. Furthermore, indirect offsets that act as investment for civilian projects arguably have the least security rational for secrecy and the most to be gained from transparency.

Political risk and FDI

Political risk is a salient factor of the business environment which determines FDI.[30] Empirical studies conceptualize political risk in terms of conflict propensity and corruption and generally find it to impede FDI.[31] Hypothesis 3 argues that supply and demand features codetermine that GDI sales to corrupt countries are more likely to have defense-offset benefits paid out as FDI. This mechanism is the first part of the story. Hypothesis 4 extends the argument to claim that the GDI is arguably a 'risk loving' industry buoyed by the illiberal market of defense contracting and the comparative advantages GDI firms have in conflict-prone, corrupt states. The military-FDI link becomes more prominent on the axis of corruption because of the relative scarcity of 'normal' FDI.

H4: *GDI is a 'risk loving' industry, where FDI connected to GDI engagement is resilient to political risks posed by conflict propensity and corruption.*

Recent empirical research finds exceptions to the blanket assertion that conflict and security threats stifle FDI. These studies produce "counter intuitive findings" for specific sectors, industry attributes, and/or characteristics of the sending country.[32] My research on the military-FDI link contributes to this literature. The GDI defies competitive-market expectations because it is an illiberal industry. First, the GDI does not sell normal goods in rational, competitive markets. It sells credence goods and long-term, politically embedded engagements. Thus, foreign defense procurement is not akin to buying units of peace. The decision to export or procure foreign defense articles is geopolitically driven and governments are the principals in the exchange. Thus, GDI is uniquely encased by non-market factors that are wholly unrelated to typical investment uncertainty.

Defense offsets are not free-market transactions. Competitive global markets dictate that the more corrupt and conflict prone a country is, the lower the expected returns on capital investment. But political risk factors are not consequential for defense-offset investments in the same ways as 'normal' FDI. 'Buy-back' investment stipulations if made a precondition for a GDI sale are absorbed into the sale price. The impact of this illiberal countertrade is to subsidize the GDI-linked investment, which is market distorting. Purchasing governments with a protectionist orientation to defense-related industries, i.e., 'security nationalism', aggressively intervene to advantage GDI investments. Both the GDI-sale subsidy and higher levels of government intervention can inefficiently redirect domestic industries and supply chains. Defense offsets that take the form of coproduction and defense-industrial investments divert skilled labor and expertise away from civilian sectors (Abdelbaki and El-Sherbiny 2022). Indirect offsets, that is, contract stipulations to benefit non-defense-related entities, have even broader anticompetitive impacts. As the Finnish case study showed, indirect offset project investments were less economically successful, and it was unclear how much of the project's returns resulted from the countertrade subsidy (Sköns 2011).

Corruption amplifies the anticompetitive and costly impacts of FDI linked to defense offsets. If investment funds are channeled to a project for non-competitive reasons, it disadvantages other enterprises and misallocates human and financial capital. In the extreme, indirect offset investments are worse than a cost-inefficient subsidy from the military expenditures of the purchasing country. Offset contracts enable the transfer of hidden funds invested for vague purposes, providing considerable opportunity for ill-gotten gains and patronage disbursement. Defense offsets are a worrying source for rent-seeking incentives that may propel GDI sales in corrupt countries (Hite-Rubin 2015). Therefore, the military-FDI link is most prominent in highly corrupt states because the GDI's risk loving engagement in these states itself increases corruption. GDI driven offsets can result in a toxic codependency where defense acquisitions become a key source for FDI, while 'normal' FDI is deterred by exacerbated political risk.

Although political risk is measured as a country-specific phenomenon, much of the variation in the impact of political risk on investment occurs at the firm level (Henisz and Zelner 2003). International business studies, utilizing firm-level data, illuminate mechanisms by which FDI may defy political risk. Such papers show how MNC's experiential learning from conflict provides an intangible benefit that makes further investment into conflict-prone settings more likely and profitable. According to these studies, experiential learning from the MNC's survival of "high-risk–high-return" engagement gives the firm strategic advantages and reputational capital. This is consistent with evidence that major defense companies view their offset practices as valuable trade secrets that can leverage complex defense contracts. In risk-prone countries, MNCs with experience can internalize their strategic assets around managing risk in a way that eventually positions them to expand over the long term (Oh and Oetzel 2017, p. 729). The largest GDI companies, such as Lockheed Martin Corp, Boeing, BAE Systems and Thales, have all developed such intangible benefits. These firm-level benefits extend to GDI parent companies but are especially important for GDI-linked activities such as subsidiaries, joint ventures, subcontracts, and offset investment projects.

The GDI is political risk loving, in part because of the legal-institutional infrastructure established by the world's largest defense firms. The GDI has legal-institutional and geopolitical advantages that enable these MNCs to participate in profitable contracts in the face of extreme political risk. It is very valuable to have a successful track record for structuring defense offsets that meet the preferences of ethically dubious decision makers in highly corrupt and unstable regimes. US GDI firms have invested heavily in sophisticated compliance programs to prevent and mitigate liability for anti-corruption violations (Tilipman and Surampudi 2023). The benefits of such compliance investments and know-how, however, extend beyond reducing legal liability; they are a cultivated business asset. In the wake of 1980s procurement scandals, a small number of very large US GDI firms have built reputational capital from their highly complex, expensive, and proprietary defense contracting infrastructure. Evolutionary changes in the US's defense contracting rules are argued to have an anticompetitive impact on the defense market while still leaving blind spots in anti-corruption measures (Yukins 2023, p. 391).[33] Thus the large, remaining GDI MNCs have oligopolistic advantages that further aid 'doing business' in corrupt and conflict-prone markets.

The reasons that the GDI is risk loving extend beyond those outlined here. GDI-linked investments have an advantage in politically risky markets chiefly because they are a form of illiberal trade. Over time, the major defense firms have leveraged these non-market benefits and business experiential learning. This resulted in the modern GDI that sells highly complex bundles of goods, services, and counter investments predominately to risky states. GDI transactions extend far beyond the primary defense sector and affect the political economy and business environment of the purchasing state. All GDI-linked activities, such as subcontracting, coproduction arrangements, transnational supply chains, holding and investment companies, and offset FDI to unlisted firms and projects, are risk loving because of these illiberal market advantages. Corruption supercharges the anticompetitive, wasteful, and destabilizing impact of the GDI on the purchasing country's political economy and, thus, further enhances the GDI's risk loving advantage. Thus, the link between major arms procurement and subsequent FDI, grows stronger the higher the level of corruption.

Conclusion

This chapter underscores how the global defense industry (GDI) is a politically embedded and anticompetitive industry that consequentially exacerbates corruption. The GDI is different than any other industry because secrecy and countertrade practices are tolerated in international arms procurement. Supply and demand-side incentives codetermine that defense-offset FDI features most potently in GDI sales to corrupt countries. Defense-offset FDI is bundled into the GDI agreement and is therefore insulated from market competition. At best, these countertrade practices are less efficient and market distorting. At worst, defense-offset FDI is a vehicle for ill-gotten gains and patronage disbursement. My goal is to improve our understanding of how these GDI commercial engagements risk exacerbating corruption, distorting markets, and undermining political economies.

The GDI has produced a military-FDI link that is strongest when and where corruption is highest. The military-FDI link is an observational finding from global empirical study of post-Cold-War data. The next step is to test my hypotheses that the military-FDI link is brought about by GDI sales, mediated by country-level corruption. Because it is impossible to systematically observe defense offsets and GDI sales, empirical testing must locate an alternative variable that influences the military to FDI effect. I am constructing an arms embargo database for US, EU, and UN embargo regimes as a key to unlocking the empirical puzzle. Hypotheses 3, and then arguably 4, can be tested by employing arms embargoes as an instrumental variable.[34] When the US imposes a country wide arms embargo on a country in a specific year, the flows of US-foreign military sales and defense-offset FDI projects are cut off. This mechanism accounts for the majority of GDI sales, and the other major GDI suppliers of offset FDI are beholden to EU, UN, and UK weapons embargoes.

In suggesting an empirical test of my theoretical proposal, my aim is neither to condemn nor to exonerate the GDI. The interrogation of the military-FDI link moves beyond the headlines of massive corruption scandals to better address the systemic impacts of the GDI. The GDI is propelled, in large part, by demand from institutionally weak and developing nations creating major security and development concerns (Hite-Rubin 2023). The optimistic view that the defense offsets facilitate growth by encouraging FDI into risky markets seems unfounded (Hite-Rubin 2015). This chapter provided a rationale for believing that defense-offset FDI and other GDI engagements are likely harmful to the political economy of highly corrupt states. As these sales and linked engagements are only expected to rise, this is where our scrutiny ought to be directed.

Notes

1 See (Gupta et al. 2001; Auriol 2006; Schoeni and Vestner 2023); for corruption research focusing on the defense sector, arms trade and/or industrial procurement: Stockholm International Peace Research Institute (SIPRI); Transparency International (TI); see also Center for Ethics and Rule of Law (CERL) the University of Pennsylvania and the World Peace Foundation (WPF) Tufts University.

2 Akin to how corruption research spans across disciplines, the relevant literature and theory do not fit squarely into one explanatory box. It is arguably both opportune and overwhelming that this project draws practical relevance and theoretical insights from academic research spanning the fields of international law, international relations, political economy, international business and defense economics.

3 The "military expenditures" variable is the annual national defense budget for a given state, collected by Correlates of War Project (COW). The "arms imports" variable is from Stockholm International Peace Research Institute (SIPRI) Arms Transfer Database. SIPRI's "arms import" variable is a volume estimate for "major conventional weapons" received by a particular state, within a calendar year. This includes licenses, weapons systems, production components but does not include what the UN classifies as "small arms and light weapons" (SALW) such as guns and ammunition.

4 Transparency International (TI) has identified 10 key corruption risk areas in international defense contracting and reports on the known behaviors and features of major defense industrial companies along these dimensions. See the Defence Companies Index on Anti-Corruption and Corporate Transparency (DCI), available June 7, 2023 at: https://ti-defence.org/dci/risk-categories/

5 The WTO's Agreement on Government Procurement (GPA) includes an exemption in Article III, "relating to the procurement of arms, ammunition or war materials, or to procurement indispensable for national security or for national defence purposes" (WTO 2012).

6 China and Russia are observers to the WTO's GPA, and negotiating accession as of 2002 and 2013, respectively. SIPRI reports that in 2021 Chinese defense firms captured 18% of arms sales market and Russia 3%. GDI competition is generally referenced as occurring among NATO allies, with the US consistently dominating over 50% market share.

7 On how investors respond to corruption as "political risk" see: Henisz and Zelner 2003; Straub 2008; Bekaert et al. 2015.

8 See (Drezner and Hite-Rubin 2014; Hite-Rubin 2015).

9 Chowdhury 1991; Kusi 1994; Mintz and Stevenson 1995.

10 These empirical works can be categorized by methodological approach: employing cross-country regression analysis with varied specifications, with 'supply side' macroeconomic specifications, or with 'demand side' macroeconomic specifications.The supply side (Feder-Ram) versus demand side (Keynesian) models are based on divergent economic theories and therefore employ distinct model specifications, with different explanatory variables. The Feder-Ram approach estimates production inputs and theorizes a military expenditure-growth connection in terms of military expenditures purportedly enhancing the economy via industrial spillover, technological progress, civilian productivity, and export effects. The Keynesian view contends that demand for goods and services drives economic growth and thus tests for either a 'multiplier' or 'crowding out' effect of military spending upon macroeconomic growth.

11 There is a consensus around major FDI determinants that their integration into baseline model specifications is necessary (Tokunaga, Masahiro, and Ichiro Iwasaki 2017; Zander 2021). Greater concern for the functional form of the statistical model and its relationship to testable theory is critical. The obvious concern of ignoring the economics of 'traditional' or 'gravity' models for FDI determinants is first omitted variable bias, serial correlation, erroneous coefficient estimates and poor fit, in the sense that very little variance in the dependent is correctly attributed to explanatory variables.

12 (Böhmelt and Bove 2014; Whitten and Williams 2011; Cappella Zielinksi et al. 2017).

13 For influences on military expenditures see business cycles (Cappella Zielinksi et al. 2017), credit constraints (DiGiuseppe 2015; Shea 2016), foreign aid (Collier and Hoeffler 2007; Kono and Montinola 2013), trade costs (Seitz et al. 2015).

14 On "credence" goods see Dulleck et al. (2011).

15 Of several works see (Sample 1997; Collier and Hoeffler 2007).

16 See Collier and Hoeffler (2007); Kono and Montinola (2013); Seitz et al. (2015); Holden et al (2016).

17 Furthermore, the coefficients can be substantially biased when the proportion of observations within interaction variable groups is unequal (Słoczyński 2022), as is the case is with conflict propensity.

18 Carter posits that weak states often enter military alliances with aggressor states, i.e., 'bandwagoning', to quell internal instability as well as for economic opportunism.

19 Anticipated shifts in the 'balance of power' (BOP) in the international system are the primary justification for weapons transfers.

20 2021 TI DS – Between 2013 and 2017, nine of the top ten global importers were rated as being at high or very high risk of defense sector corruption.

21 The US is the only major GDI exporter known to publish statistics at this time (Schoeni 2023).The Security Assistance Monitor (SAM) is the first and only resource to house publicly available, official data on arms sales and security assistance. Congress must be notified about FMS sales that fall above a certain threshold, while direct commercial sales are generally considered proprietary and only a high-level summary of approved export authorizations is provided via Department of State Section 655 reports. There are no statutory requirements for deliveries to be reported, so data on final sales is scant (Security Assistance Monitor).

22 The US Bureau of Industry and Security (BIS) provides an open-ended description of the kinds of contractual obligations that may be contained in defense offset arrangements. Defense offsets are classified as either "direct" if they are to the defense article being procured, and otherwise "mixed" or "indirect". BIS categorizes offset transactions as: "co-production, technology transfer, subcontracting, credit assistance, training, licensed production, investment, purchases, and other".

23 According to WTO's Agreement on Government Procurement (GPA) Article XXIII, procurements that the acquiring country views as "necessary for the protection of its essential security interests" are exempt from the GPA general ban on offset agreements.

24 According to the US Defense Procurement and Acquisition Policy, the term 'offset' refers to: " the entire range of industrial and commercial benefits provided to foreign governments as an inducement or condition to purchase military goods or services, including benefits such as co-production, licensed production, subcontracting, technology transfer, in-county procurement, marketing and financial assistance, and joint ventures (Defense Offsets Disclosure Act of 1999, Pub. L. 106–113, section 1243(3)". For further information on countertrade and offsets, see 'FAQs' issued by the Global Offset and Countertrade Association at www.globaloffset.org/faqs.php, or read about offsets on the EPICOS website at www.epicos.com/Portal/Main/AerospaceDefence/ICOffset/Pages/default.aspx. For more information about the US law, see Defense Procurement and Acquisition Policy (DPAP), www.acq.osd.mil/dpap/sitemap.html.

25 That is not to say that national corruption, defense sector, and procurement contracting corruption are equivalent. Transparency International (TI) provides extensive research on state-level corruption and corruption in defense, including issuing a Government Defence Anti-corruption Index See also. (Fish and Man 2016).

26 Defense Production Act Amendments of 1992 (Pub. L. 102-558, Title I, Part C, § 123).

27 According to BAE systems, around 80 countries have official offset requirements, and the company's efforts to plan, negotiate, and deliver defense offsets are an important component of its business development. Several leading GDI firms have similar communications indicating the ubiquity of defense offsets and touting their firm's competitive advantage in this complicated domain www.baesystems.com/en/sustainability/governance/oversight/policy-summaries/offset-policy

28 www.nytimes.com/1992/05/08/world/finland-in-3-billion-deal-for-64-mcdonnell-douglas-combat-jets.html According to BIS 2007 survey and report, Finland's Department of Defense required 100% offsets. The report also indicated that over the period of 1993 to 2005, the actual offset ratio of sales was also 100% as calculated by dividing the offset value by the export value.

29 A promising technique is to randomly sample GDI sales for investigation and then to extrapolate relative corruption hazards by population parameters.

30 Political risk is a salient factor of the business environment which determines FDI (Henisz et al. 2010).

31 For review of empirical research on conflict risks effect on FDI (Blair et al. 2022). Much of this work demonstrates that corruption has the net effect of stifling foreign investment (Mauro 1995; Zander 2021).

32 Research papers finding MNC investment to be counterintuitive to political risk aversion, base findings that are contingent upon primary sector (Blair et al. 2022) industry

attributes (Barry 2018; Bussy and Zheng 2023); characteristics of the originating investor (Driffield et al. 2013); and civil war economies (Pinto and Zhu 2022; Maher 2022)

33 However, I disagree with Yukins that barriers to market entry for new weapons sellers are problematic.

34 Put crudely, a valid IV is something that impacts FDI (the dependent variable) only indirectly through military expenditures and/or arms imports (the independent variable). More formally, for a single endogenous regressor – the IV variable Z (arms embargo status 0|1) instruments arms imports X in the scalar regression model model y = x+u if (1) Z is uncorrelated with the error u; and (2) Z is correlated with the regressor x.

Additional confirmation of instrument relevance and exogeneity are also required.

See chapter 10 of Stock, James H., and Mark W. Watson (2003), *Introduction to Econometrics*. Boston, MA: Addison Wesley.

Bibliography

Abdelbaki, Hisham, and Amr E. M. El-Sherbiny. 2022. "The Causal Relationship between Corruption, Military Expenditures and Economic Growth in Egypt." المجلة المصرية للدراسات التجارية 50–201: (4)46

Auriol, Emmanuelle. 2006. "Corruption in Procurement and Public Purchase." *International Journal of Industrial Organization* 24(5): 867–85.

Avascent. 2012. *The Half Trillion Dollar Challenge: Designing Offset Strategies to Build Reputation, Promote Development*. http://www.avascent.com/wp-content/uploads/2013/02/Avascent-Offsets-2-White-Paper.pdf.

Azam, Muhammad. 2020. "Does Military Spending Stifle Economic Growth? The Empirical Evidence from Non-OECD Countries." *Heliyon* 6(12): e05853.

AzamAziz, Nusrate, and Usman Khalid. 2019. "Armed Conflict, Military Expenses and FDI Inflow to Developing Countries." *Defence and Peace Economics* 30(2): 238–51.

Barry, Colin M. 2018. "Peace and Conflict at Different Stages of the FDI Lifecycle." *Review of International Political Economy* 25(2): 270–92.

Bekaert, Geert, Campbell R. Harvey, Christian T. Lundblad, and Stephan Siegel. 2015. "Political Risk and International Valuation." Working paper.

Béraud-Sudreau, Lucie et al. 2020. *Mapping the International Presence of the World's Largest Arms Companies*. Stockholm International Peace Research Institute.

BIS. 2021. *Offsets in Defense Trade Twenty-Fifth Study*. U.S. Department of Commerce Bureau of Industry and Security. Conducted Pursuant to Section 723 of the Defense Production Act of 1950, as Amended. https://www.bis.doc.gov/index.php/documents/pdfs/2788-twenty-fifth-report-to-congress-7-21/file.

Blair, Graeme, Darin Christensen, and Valerie Wirtschafter. 2022. "How Does Armed Conflict Shape Investment? Evidence from the Mining Sector." *The Journal of Politics* 84(1): 116–33.

Böhmelt, Tobias, and Vincenzo Bove. 2014. "Forecasting Military Expenditure." *Research & Politics* 1(1): 1–8.

Brauer, Jurgen. 2011. "Economic Aspects of Arms Trade Offsets." In *Arms Trade and Economic Development: Theory, Policy, and Cases in Arms Trade Offsets*, Studies in defence economics, eds. Jurgen Brauer and Paul Dunne. London and New York: Routledge, Taylor & Francis Group.

Brooks, Stephen G., G. John Ikenberry, and William C. Wohlforth. 2012. "Don't Come Home America: The Case Against Retrenchment." *International Security* 37(3): 7–52.

Busenbark, John R., Scott D. Graffin, Robert J. Campbell, and Eric Young Lee. 2022. "A Marginal Effects Approach to Interpreting Main Effects and Moderation." *Organizational Research Methods* 25(1): 147–69.

Bussy, Adrien, and Huanhuan Zheng. 2023. "Responses of FDI to Geopolitical Risks: The Role of Governance, Information, and Technology." *International Business Review*: 102136.

Cappella Zielinski, Rosella, Benjamin O. Fordham, and Kaija E. Schilde. 2017. "What Goes Up, Must Come Down? The Asymmetric Effects of Economic Growth and International Threat on Military Spending." *Journal of Peace Research* 54(6): 791–805.

Carter, Brittnee. 2022. "Revisiting the Bandwagoning Hypothesis: A Statistical Analysis of the Alliance Dynamics of Small States." *International Studies* 59(1): 7–27.

Carter, Jeff, Heather L. Ondercin, and Glenn Palmer. 2021. "Guns, Butter, and Growth: The Consequences of Military Spending Reconsidered." *Political Research Quarterly* 74(1): 148–65.

Caverley, Jonathan D. 2017. "Slowing the Proliferation of Major Conventional Weapons: The Virtues of an Uncompetitive Market." *Ethics & International Affairs* 31(4): 401–18.

Chowdhury, Abdur R. 1991. "A Causal Analysis of Defense Spending and Economic Growth." *Journal of Conflict Resolution* 35(1): 80–97.

Cole, Shawn, and Anh Tran. 2011. "Evidence from the Firm: A New Approach to Understanding Corruption." In *International Handbook on the Economics of Corruption. Volume 2*, eds. Susan Rose-Ackerman and Tina Søreide. Cheltenham and Northampton, MA: Edward Elgar.

Collier, Paul, and World Bank, eds. 2003. *Breaking the Conflict Trap: Civil War and Development Policy*. Washington, DC; New York: World Bank; Oxford University Press.

Collier, Paul, and Anke Hoeffler. 2007. "Unintended Consequences: Does Aid Promote Arms Races?" *Oxford Bulletin of Economics and Statistics* 69(1): 1–27.

Collins, David. 2018. "Government Procurement with Strings Attached: The Uneven Control of Offsets by the World Trade Organization and Regional Trade Agreements." *Asian Journal of International Law* 8(2): 301–21.

Congressional Research Service. 2022. "Great Power Competition: Implications for Defense—Issues for Congress." November 8. https://crsreports.congress.gov.

Cooter, Robert, and Thomas Ulen. 2000. *Law and Economics*. 3rd ed. Reading, MA: Addison-Wesley.

Dehoff, Kevin, John Dowdy, and O Sung Kwon. 2014. *Defense Offsets: From 'Contractual Burden' to Competitive Weapon*. Mckinsey & Company. https://www.mckinsey.com/industries/public-and-social-sector/our-insights/defense-offsets-from-contractual-burden-to-competitive-weapon.

DiGiuseppe, Matthew. 2015. "Guns, Butter, and Debt: Sovereign Creditworthiness and Military Expenditure." *Journal of Peace Research* 52(5): 680–93.

Drezner, Daniel W. 2013. "Military Primacy Doesn't Pay (Nearly As Much As You Think)." *International Security* 38(1): 52–79.

Drezner, Daniel W., and Nancy Hite-Rubin. 2014. "Does Military Spending Attract (Corrupt) Foreign Investment? An Empirical Investigation." Working paper prepared for presentation at the American Political Science Association annual meeting, Washington, DC, August.

Drezner, Daniel W., and Nancy F. Hite-Rubin. 2016. "Does American Military Power Attract Foreign Investment?" In *Sustainable Security*, eds. Jeremi Suri and Benjamin Valentino. Oxford University Press, 51–72. https://academic.oup.com/book/2679/chapter/143110659.

Driffield, Nigel, Chris Jones, and Jo Crotty. 2013. "International Business Research and Risky Investments, an Analysis of FDI in Conflict Zones." *International Business Review* 22(1): 140–55.

Dulleck, Uwe, Rudolf Kerschbamer, and Matthias Sutter. 2011. "The Economics of Credence Goods: An Experiment on the Role of Liability, Verifiability, Reputation, and Competition." *American Economic Review* 101(2): 526–55.
Dunne, John Paul. 2012. "Military Spending, Growth, Development and Conflict." *Defence and Peace Economics* 23(6): 549–57.
Dunne, J. Paul, Sam Perlo-Freeman, and Ron P. Smith. 2008. "The Demand for Military Expenditure in Developing Countries: Hostility vs Capability." *Defence and Peace Economics* 19(4): 293–302.
Dunne, J. Paul, and Ron P. Smith. 2020. "Military Expenditure, Investment and Growth." *Defence and Peace Economics* 31(6): 601–14.
Fish, Katie, and Michelle Man. 2016. *Licence to Bribe? Reducing Corruption Risks around the Use of Agents in Defence Procurement.* Transparency International. http://ti-defence.org/wp-content/uploads/2016/06/Licence-to-Bribe-web.pdf.
Flamm, Kenneth. 1999. *Trends and Challenges in Aerospace Offsets.* Washington, DC: National Academies Press. http://www.nap.edu/catalog/6315 (June 13, 2023).
Goodman, Colby. 2020. *Holes in the Net: US Arms Export Control Gaps in Combatting Corruption.* Transparency International.
Gupta, Sanjeev, Luiz de Mello, and Raju Sharan. 2001. "Corruption and Military Spending." *European Journal of Political Economy* 17(4): 749–77.
Hartley, Keith. 2007. "Chapter 33 The Arms Industry, Procurement and Industrial Policies." In *Handbook of Defense Economics*, eds. Todd Sandler and Keith Hartley. Elsevier, Amsterdam,1139–76.
Hartung, William D., and Elias Yousif. 2021. *U.S. Arms Sales Trends.* Center for International Policy.
Henisz, Witold J., and Bennet A. Zelner. 2003. "The Strategic Organization of Political Risks and Opportunities." *Strategic Organization* 1(4): 451–60.
Henisz, Witold J., Edward D. Mansfield, and Mary Ann Von Glinow. 2010. "Conflict, Security, and Political Risk: International Business in Challenging Times." *Journal of International Business Studies* 41(5): 759–64.
Hite-Rubin, Nancy. 2015. "Chapter 9: A Corruption, Military Procurement and FDI Nexus?" Cheltenham: Edward Elgar Publishing. https://www.elgaronline.com/view/edcoll/9781784714697/9781784714697.00016.xml.
———. 2023. "The Nexus of Arms Embargoes, Corruption, and Foreign Investment." In *Ethical Dilemmas in the Global Defense Industry*, eds. Daniel E. Schoeni and Tobias Vestner. New York, NY: Oxford University Press.
Holden, Paul et al. 2016. *Indefensible: Seven Myths That Sustain the Global Arms Trade.* London: Zed Books Ltd.
Johnston, Michael. 2005. *Syndromes of Corruption: Wealth, Power, and Democracy.* Cambridge: Cambridge University Press.
Kanniainen, Vesa, and Juha-Matti Lehtonen. 2019. "Offset Contracts as an Insurance Device in Building the National Security." *Defence and Peace Economics* 30(1): 85–97.
Kinne, Brandon J. 2016. "Agreeing to Arm: Bilateral Weapons Agreements and the Global Arms Trade." *Journal of Peace Research* 53(3): 359–77.
Kinne, Brandon, J., and Stephanie N. Kang. 2023. "Free Riding, Network Effects, and Burden Sharing in Defense Cooperation Networks." *International Organization* 77 (2):405–39.
Kono, Daniel Yuichi, and Gabriella R. Montinola. 2013. "The Uses and Abuses of Foreign Aid: Development Aid and Military Spending." *Political Research Quarterly* 66(3): 615–29.
Kusi, Newman. 1994. "Economic Growth and Defense Spending in Developing Countries." *Journal of Conflict Resolution* 38(1): 152–59.
Leeds, Brett Ashley. 2022. *Alliance Treaty Obligations and Provisions (ATOP) Codebook.* Department of Political Science Rice University. http://www.atopdata.org.

Lopes da Silva, Diego. 2022. "Political Accountability and Military Spending." *Defence and Peace Economics* 1–18. DOI: 10.1080/10242694.2022.2129128

Markowski, Stefan, and Peter Hall. 2014. "Mandated Defence Offsets: Can They Ever Deliver?" *Defense & Security Analysis* 30(2): 148–62.

Markusen, Ann. 2011. "Arms Trade as Illiberal Trade." In *Arms Trade and Economic Development: Theory, Policy, and Cases in Arms Trade Offsets*, Studies in defence economics, eds. Jurgen Brauer and Paul Dunne. London and New York: Routledge, Taylor & Francis Group.

Mauro, P. 1995. "Corruption and Growth." *The Quarterly Journal of Economics* 110(3): 681–712.

Mintz, Alex, and Randolph T. Stevenson. 1995. "Defense Expenditures, Economic Growth, and The 'Peace Dividend': A Longitudinal Analysis of 103 Countries." *Journal of Conflict Resolution* 39(2): 283–305.

Nordhaus, William, John R. Oneal, and Bruce Russett. 2012. "The Effects of the International Security Environment on National Military Expenditures: A Multi-country Study." *International Organization* 66(3): 491–513.

Norrlof, Carla. 2010. *America's Global Advantage: US Hegemony and International Cooperation*. Cambridge: Cambridge University Press.

Oh, Chang Hoon, and Jennifer Oetzel. 2017. "Once Bitten Twice Shy? Experience Managing Violent Conflict Risk and MNC Subsidiary-level Investment and Expansion." *Strategic Management Journal* 38(3): 714–31.

Perlo-Freeman, Samuel. 2018. "Arms, Corruption, and the State: Understanding the Role of Arms Trade Corruption in Power Politics." *The Economics of Peace and Security Journal* 13(2): 37–46.

Petersen, Carol Dawn. 2011. "Defense and Commercial Trade Offsets: Impacts on the U.S. Industrial Base Raise Economic and National Security Concerns." *Journal of Economic Issues* 45(2): 485–92.

Sample, Susan G. 1997. "Arms Races and Dispute Escalation: Resolving the Debate." *Journal of Peace Research* 34(1): 7–22.

Schoeni, Daniel E. 2023. "Some Ethical Dimensions of Defense Offsets." In *Ethical Dilemmas in the Global Defense Industry*, Ethics national security rule law series, eds. Daniel E. Schoeni and Tobias Vestner. New York, NY: Oxford University Press.

Schoeni, Daniel E., and Tobias Vestner, eds. 2023. *Ethical Dilemmas in the Global Defense Industry*. Ethics National Security Rule Law Series. New York, NY: Oxford University Press.

Security Assistance Monitor. "SAM Data Guide for U.S. Arms Sales." https://securityassistance.org/arm-sales/ (June 28, 2023).

Seitz, Michael, Alexander Tarasov, and Roman Zakharenko. 2015. "Trade Costs, Conflicts, and Defense Spending." *Journal of International Economics* 95(2): 305–18.

Shea, Patrick E. 2016. "Borrowing Trouble: Sovereign Credit, Military Regimes, and Conflict." *International Interactions* 42(3): 401–28.

Sköns, Elisabeth. 2011. "Evaluating Defense Offsets: The Experience in Finland and Sweden." In *Arms Trade and Economic Development: Theory, Policy, and Cases in Arms Trade Offsets*, Studies in defence economics, eds. Jurgen Brauer and Paul Dunne. London and New York: Routledge, Taylor & Francis Group.

Słoczyński, Tymon. 2022. "Interpreting OLS Estimands When Treatment Effects Are Heterogeneous: Smaller Groups Get Larger Weights." *The Review of Economics and Statistics* 104(3): 501–9.

Straub, Stéphane. 2008. "Opportunism, Corruption and the Multinational Firm's Mode of Entry." *Journal of International Economics* 74(2): 245–63.

Thrall, A. Trevor, and Caroline Dorminey. 2018. "Risky Business. The Role of Arms Sales in U.S. Foreign Policy." *Cato Institute Policy Analysis* no. 836.

Tillipman, Jessica, and Vijaya Surampudi. 2023. "The Compliance Mentorship Program: Improving Ethics and Compliance in Small Government Contractors." In *Ethical Dilemmas in the Global Defense Industry*, Ethics national security rule law series, eds. Daniel E. Schoeni and Tobias Vestner. New York, NY: Oxford University Press.

Tokunaga, Masahiro, and Ichiro Iwasaki. 2017. "The Determinants of Foreign Direct Investment in Transition Economies: A Meta-Analysis." *The World Economy* 40(12): 2771–831.

Walt, Stephen M. 1990. *The Origins of Alliances*. Ithaca and London: Cornell University Press.

Wezeman, Pieter, Alexandra Kuimova, and Siemon Wezeman. 2021. *Trends in International Arms Transfers, 2020*. Stockholm International Peace Research Institute. https://sipri.org/sites/default/files/2021-03/fs_2103_at_2020.pdf.

Wilson, Sven E., and Daniel M. Butler. 2007. "A Lot More to Do: The Sensitivity of Time-Series Cross-Section Analyses to Simple Alternative Specifications." *Political Analysis* 15(2): 101–23.

Whitten, Guy D., and Laron K. Williams. 2011. "Buttery Guns and Welfare Hawks: The Politics of Defense Spending in Advanced Industrial Democracies." *American Journal of Political Science* 55(1): 117–34.

WTO. 2012. "Agreement on Government Procurement." (GPA 2012) April 15, 1994, Marrakesh Agreement Establishing the World Trade Organization, Article III. https://www.wto.org/english/docs_e/legal_e/rev-gpr-94_01_e.htm#articleIII.

Yukins, Christopher R. 2023. "Mandatory Disclosure: How Anti-Corruption Measures Can Affect Competition in Defense Markets." In *Ethical Dilemmas in the Global Defense Industry*, Ethics national security rule law series, eds. Daniel E. Schoeni and Tobias Vestner. New York, NY: Oxford University Press.

Zander, Tobias. 2021. "Does Corruption Matter for FDI Flows in the OECD? A Gravity Analysis." *International Economics and Economic Policy* 18(2): 347–77.

12 State capture matters

Considerations and empirics toward a worldwide measure

Daniel Kaufmann[1]

With the Soviet planned economy in decline, by 1991 President Mikhail Gorbachev embarked on 'glasnost' (opening up) and 'perestroika' (restructuring). This twin set of policies led to a request for technical assistance from the IMF and the World Bank. The World Bank set up a technical assistance unit for the Soviet Union. I was the first staff to join. We headed to Moscow.

During one long work spell, we ventured out of the hotel and went to Red Square, facing the Kremlin. It was a frigid Christmas Day, 1991. We witnessed an historical development: the Soviet flag was being lowered, replaced by the flag of the Russian Federation. Gorbachev then resigned and turned over his presidential powers to Boris Yeltsin, who became the first president of the Russian Federation. By the next day, the Soviet Union formally ceased to exist when the presidents of Ukraine, Belarus, and Russia, the founding members of the Soviet Union, met to dissolve it formally. Ukraine's independence was approved *de jure* and recognized by the international community. A historical transition had been set in motion.

Soon thereafter, I headed to Kyiv, Ukraine, as the first head of the World Bank mission to the newly independent country. As an economist, working for a development bank, the expectation was that my exclusive focus would be on traditional economic matters, anticipated to be critical during the early stages of the transition. These included mammoth macro-economic challenges, which, mindful of the inadequacy of the conventional economic notion of "stagflation" for Ukraine at the time, I characterized at the time as "hyper-depression" – the combination of hyper-inflation and a sharp fall in economic activity.

There were other challenges as well. Emblematic of the legacy of the Soviet planned economy, the notion of 'the market' was in its infancy, at best. For starters, as World Bank staff, we needed to find an office and residential housing. But there was no real estate market yet. We had to have an audience with a high official in the Ministry of Real Estate – one of over 70 soviet-legacy ministries, which were akin to accounting units.

Our meeting was brief. It did not go well at all. The senior ministry official had brought his lawyer to our meeting and presented me with a brief document they had readied for an anticipated quick signature. In it, I was supposed to commit to deposit tens of thousands of dollars in a private account in Vienna in exchange for his agreement to provide offices to rent to the World Bank, as well as residential accommodation. With my interpreter, who ascertained that nothing was being lost

DOI: 10.4324/9781003416234-14

in translation and that I was effectively being asked to commit to paying a bribe, we abruptly left the meeting. Not long after, we made a formal complaint to the office of the prime minister.

The episode was a rude reminder that traditional economic tools on their own were not going to take us very far. I was wedded to the power of evidence. With the nudging of a young reformist minister of the economy in Ukraine, who was also concerned about corruption, and the collaboration of colleagues and local surveyors, we organized a set of periodic small surveys of firms in Ukraine and Russia to assess the climate for business and delve into the issue of corruption. Such surveys provided us with a list of "bribe fees" for both countries for a plethora of public government services, such as obtaining various permits, a phone line, a loan, and the like. The substantial prevalence and extent of established payoffs across the spectrum – on average the amounts were about twice as high in Russia compared to the Ukraine – whether linked to trade, financial or other regulations, suggested a systemic issue. The bribe I had been asked for was not an isolated incident.

Yet in traditional economic circles, attention to corruption was either seen as not belonging to our field of inquiry, or even frowned upon, viewed as a 'soft' niche, not subject to the analytical rigor and empirical testing of traditional economic matters. In fact, in the early stages of our work I did get a reprimand from the World Bank's chief legal counsel regarding undertaking initiatives related to corruption, which at the time were regarded as off-limits by the institution, its statutes being interpreted as a domestic political matter back then, and, thus, unrelated to the economic development mandate of the institution. Undaunted, my instinct that corruption did matter – including for economics and growth – prompted me to persist with the empirical work. Further, I scoured the literature for rigorous writings on the topic.

That is when I found the legal-economic writings of an eminent academic, Professor Susan Rose-Ackerman. It gave me a crucial intellectual lifeline and strengthened my conviction that my faraway quest was far from quixotic. Well beyond her influence on my intellectual enrichment, Susan's pioneering work on corruption has left an impressive legacy, reflected in her writings over many decades, and those of generations of students and scholars whom she taught and influenced.

Among her specific contributions to the field that influenced me was the application of a principal-agent framework to the study of corruption, the role of institutions in corruption outcomes, and the unbundling of the generic notion of corruption into "grand" vs. "petty" corruption. As important, her multidisciplinary approach, particularly traversing law, economics, and public policy, as well as her global perspective in studying the corruption phenomenon in both industrialized and emerging economies, also left an indelible mark.[2]

Susan's notion of grand corruption, referring to high-level corruption involving the political and government leaders, and its major cost to society, had increasing resonance as I got to know better the reality of Russia and Ukraine. With a twist: by then Russia, Ukraine, and other post-Soviet states were on a troubling path toward oligarchic corruption, where increasingly powerful members of the private elite were exerting undue influence on politicians and governments that were transitioning to democracy.

It was in this transitional economy context that I met Joel Hellman, an expert on Russia working then at the European Bank for Reconstruction and Development (EBRD). We argued that for economies in transition focusing largely on public-sector-led administrative forms of corruption missed the point. Instead, we shared the view that powerful non-state actors played a lead role in unduly influencing the state. We also believed in the power of evidence-based research and embarked on a joint World Bank/EBRD survey of economies in transition for all former socialist countries from central and eastern Europe and the former Soviet Union (CEE/FSU).

The rest of this chapter builds on that basis to discuss the notion of state capture and some of its historical antecedents. Following that introductory background, the chapter reviews empirical efforts to measure this phenomenon. I suggest that, in contrast to conventional notions of corruption, state capture has not been subject to systematic global cross-country measurement, even though some valuable regional and country-specific measures have been gathered at particular points in time.

Subsequently, and mindful of challenges and the need for caution in embarking on a global measure of state capture, I present an approach to develop such a global proxy, based on a simple conceptual framework and a few existing global data sources. The construction of such an index based on this simple methodology and the sources results in a global State Capture Index for 172 countries, spanning over a quarter century. The approach taken, as well as the results, suggest that such a global over time measure may offer value added, pointing to insights that emerge from a comparison between the State Capture Index and a conventional measure of corruption. I conclude with salient considerations and implications for the study of state capture ahead.

On the notion of state capture and its antecedents

State capture in (early) transition. Drawing, among others, from Susan's writings which suggested that corruption was a multi-dimensional concept which distinguished between various types and manifestations, Hellman and I proposed a particular variant at the intersection of grand corruption and the undue power of influential non-state actors. We labeled it *state capture* (Hellman, Jones and Kaufmann, 2000).

We regarded state capture as a phenomenon where powerful non-state actors were able to *shape* the societal (public) rules of the game for their private benefit, in contrast to conventional and largely transactional notions of administrative or bureaucratic corruption, where actors manipulate the *implementation* of the given rules of the game for their benefit. Under that view, firms tended to be seen as operating within a given set of rules and thus were seen as 'takers' of the business environment provided by state regulations, whereas under a state capture lens, powerful business leaders could be major 'shapers' of the business environment.

Importantly, and also deviating from traditional and legalistic notions of corruption, we posited that state capture could take place via legal means. In large measure, this could literally and figuratively take place by 'construction', because the relevant laws, not necessarily serving the public interest, may have been shaped by captors in the first place (Kaufmann and Vicente, 2011).

There is a difference 'in kind', rather than merely of 'degree', between shaping the rules of the game – state capture –, versus simply taking them as given, and then getting around them for one's own transactional benefit – administrative corruption. The difference has major potential implications: the societal cost of the former may easily be orders of magnitude higher than that of the latter. The vast body of empirical work utilizing existing measures of corruption indicates that the cost to society of administrative corruption is already large, suggesting that the cost of state capture may be massive where capture prevails.

Fast forward. Over the past two decades, many scholars have contributed significantly to the evolution of the study of state capture. The details on the full scope and richness of the evolution of the field and the literature, which can be found in various dimensions, among others, in David-Barrett (2023), David-Barrett, Kaufmann and Ceballos (2023), and De Greiff et al. (2023), is beyond the scope of this contribution. In brief, and not doing justice to its many rich details and variants, the study of state capture has entailed four noteworthy developments over recent decades.

First, the concept has expanded to encompass more fields of inquiry, and, in particular, the growing treatment of the phenomenon by many political scientists and others in the social sciences, well beyond the field of economics. Hence, even if politics did feature our early writings, granular political dimensions have been increasingly studied.

Second, and related, there has been an expansion in the scope of actors engaging in capture. In particular, many scholars have considered state actors as captors as well, contrasting our initial work whose focus was on non-state actors, especially powerful private firms. The study of state actors engaging in capture meant that either state leaders and/or politicians, as well as political parties, were also regarded as captors.

Third, over time there was a more detailed unbundling of all the potential 'objects of capture', the so-called 'captees', comprising institutions, policies, regulations, and laws, as well as an added emphasis on understanding the processes resulting in capture.

Fourth, the evolution of work on state capture over the years led to studies well beyond the initial focus on empirical research limited to a group of transition economies, to also include detailed scholarly research at the organizational and subnational level within specific countries. Further, there has been an expansion into the applied policy field, where commissions of experts have been convened to write about policy responses[3] to capture, including prevention strategies, and where country leaders and policy-makers have also become increasingly involved.[4]

Illustrating these expansions as applied to practical policy debates, a state capture framework – rather than a traditional corruption lens – has been used to investigate a major national corruption scandal in South Africa, involving the Gupta family and ex-President Jacob Zuma.[5] Further, Brazil's Lava Jato scandal involving the Odebrecht private construction empire and Petrobras, the National Oil Company, was such a compelling and complex case of a corrupt network with state capture elements which also captured the public's imagination and was turned into a popular political TV drama series describing how capture worked in practice, called 'O Mecanismo' (The Mechanism).[6]

Importantly, there have been significant empirical contributions to the field, which we review below, covering different approaches to measuring state capture or its proxies, particularly at the country, subnational, and even organizational levels. Illustrating the growing interest in and relevance of measuring state capture, the International Anti-Corruption Academy recently convened a group of experts on the topic, where various approaches to measurement were showcased, and a summary report was published.[7]

Fast rewind. Although our writings with Hellman over two decades ago may have played a role in advancing the notion of 'state capture', this development did not take place in a vacuum or without antecedents. To the contrary.

Path-breaking work on the related notion of regulatory capture had taken place decades earlier thanks to the seminal work of George Stigler, a Nobel Prize economist, who authored the influential paper on "The Theory of Economic Regulation" in 1971.[8] A few years earlier Mancur Olson, in his book *The Logic of Collective Action* (1965), argued that special interest groups and elites can manipulate state institutions for their benefit. And earlier still, outside the field of economics, Gabriel Kolko addressed the influence of corporate interests on regulatory agencies in the United States, presaging the notion of regulatory capture.[9]

Back in history, instances of a concept similar to state capture can be traced back to ancient Rome, where influential individuals and factions often sought to influence and control the Roman Senate and other government bodies for their own interests. The Roman historian Sallust, in his work *The Jugurthine War*, described how the Roman Republic faced corruption and the manipulation of political institutions by powerful individuals during the Jugurthine War (c. 112–105 BC).

Even further back in time, a case can be made that the tale of the ancient nobility of the Greek region of Attica, the Eupatridae, was a case of capture, morphing from a monopolized version to a more 'competitive' (elite) type, around 700 BC. The Eupatridae, meaning 'offspring of noble fathers' or 'the well-born', exerted exclusive influence and power, both in administration and in justice, during the time of limitation of the monarchy. Yet the rule of law changes introduced by Draco and subsequently the major 'democracy' reforms (by ancient standards) adopted by Solon, circa 600 BC, opened voice, influence and offices to any citizen with a certain amount of landed property. This introduced a form of 'competitive capture', effectively eliminating the monopolistic political influence by the Eupatridae because wealthy citizens of other classes obtained access as well.[10]

Completing a full circle of sorts, and recalling that the powerful 'captors' that we witnessed a few decades ago in post-Soviet Russia and Ukraine were quickly labeled as 'oligarchs', it is noteworthy that the notion of oligarchy derives from Ancient Greek, Oligarkhía, meaning 'rule by few'. It was in fact no other than Aristotle, around 350 BC, who pioneered the use of the term as meaning 'rule by the rich', contrasting it with aristocracy, arguing that oligarchy was a perverted form of aristocracy. Tellingly, Winters (2011) cites Aristotle as writing that "oligarchy is when men of property have the government in their hands … wherever men rule by reason of their wealth, whether they be few or many, that is an oligarchy, and where the poor rule, that is a democracy".[11]

In sum, although the exact term 'state capture' may be a modern creation, similar notions and practices have existed for centuries, referring to the shaping and manipulation of national laws, regulations, policies, and institutions by the powerful for their own benefit at the expense of the public good. At a basic level, given what we know about the human condition, and the simple fact that humans have historically engaged in capturing as well as in forming the state, it can be argued that state capture may well be as old as the state.

Reviewing the empirical literature

There have been many studies aiming to measure state capture or related notions using a variety of approaches. Fieberlkorn (2019) and David-Barrett, Kaufmann and Ceballos (2023) provide overviews of efforts at the micro and national levels, as well as cross-country initiatives and also of potential data sources for future efforts. Here, we complement such treatments by focusing on selected studies at the country level, especially those involving multiple countries, as they are particularly relevant for an initiative to generate a worldwide State Capture Index.

As reviewed by Fiebelkorn, the 1999 Business Environment and Enterprise Performance Survey (BEEPS) was designed to assess the quality of governance across 21 countries in central and eastern Europe and the former Soviet Union from a firm-level perspective. The BEEPS survey[12] that Hellman and I put together was first carried out in 1999 under the auspices of the World Bank and the EBRD. It directly measured firm-level experiences with state capture in post-socialist economies and led to a number of research papers by us and by others as well.

Among the various forms of 'grand corruption' that we incorporated into the BEEPS to assess state capture were the sale of Parliamentary votes on laws to private interests; the sale of Presidential decrees to private interests; the mishandling of funds by the Central Bank; the sale of court decisions, and the contributions paid by private interests to political parties and election campaigns. Based on these responses by firms in economies in transition, we constructed at the time indices to measure the extent of state capture at different levels of government, deriving from them a composite index of state capture, calculated as the average proportion of firms reporting the prevalence of various manifestations of state capture.

The analysis of state capture across the region in transition revealed significant variation. By the late 1990s, some former soviet countries such as Russia, Ukraine, and Azerbaijan exhibited extremely high levels of state capture; countries in central/eastern Europe, such as those in the Baltics, had largely managed to avoid such a trap and were transitioning to competitive markets and a democratic polity.

The research also shed light on the large costs of capture, with non-influential firms in captured economies growing and investing at about one-half the rate of competitive firms in non-captured countries. Further, the evidence suggested that countries that had embarked on a transition with a more competitive polity and markets at the time tended to exhibit lower degrees of state capture, as reported by firms, though this telling association obviously does not prove causality.

Subsequently, utilizing the 2002 version of the BEEPS survey, we empirically explored a correlate notion and potential determinant of state capture, namely 'inequality of influence', for which we constructed an empirical proxy based on the responses by firms that we labelled *crony bias*. The measure served as a proxy for the extent to which firm managers reported that there were other actors with more clout than their own collective voice on shaping the basic rules of their business environment, specifically drawing on responses on the relative influence of firms in shaping of laws, rules and regulations (Kaufmann and Hellman, 2004).[13]

The extent of crony bias perceived by a firm is the difference between the firm's characterization of the influence of individuals or firms with close, personal ties to political leaders and the influence of its own business or trade association on recently enacted laws, rules, and regulations affecting their business. The firm-level crony bias scores were aggregated to construct country-level aggregates for the perceived inequality of influence.[14]

Another noteworthy source of data for a few years in the early 2000s was the Enterprise Opinion Survey of the World Economic Forum's (WEF) Global Competitiveness Report (GCR), where this author collaborated with the WEF to develop the survey instrument and performing data analysis. At the time, several questions on corruption and state capture were included in the survey (Kaufmann, 2003; Kaufmann and Vicente, 2011). The WEF survey for the GCR had a much larger country sample than the BEEPS, surveying at the time over 7,000 firms in over a hundred countries, allowing us to develop basic proxies of state capture and undue influence (including 'crony bias'). Yet, in the WEF survey the questions to firms on state capture were few, and were eventually discontinued in later years as the survey was shortened.[15]

A different strand of empirical measurement focused on collecting data to measure the extent of political connections by private firms. In particular, Faccio (2004) assembled a database of over 20,000 publicly traded firms in 47 countries. A company was defined as politically connected[16] if at least one of its one of its top officers (such as its CEO, chairman, president, VP), or a large shareholder was a head of state (i.e., president, king, or prime minister), a government minister or a member of the national parliament as of 1997. Faccio and co-authors find that politically connected firms are more likely to be bailed out than are their non-connected peers. Among bailed-out firms, those that are politically connected exhibit significantly poorer operating performance than their non-connected peers at the time of the bailout and over the following two years.

Using part of Faccio's data, Faccio, Masulis and McConnell (2006) explore how political connections influence the allocation of capital resulting from financial assistance to connected companies in economic distress. To investigate this, they studied 450 politically connected firms in 35 countries over the six-year period 1997–2002. Subsequently, Faccio (2010) analysed how connected firms differed from non-connected firms across a wide range of countries, finding that connected firms have higher leverage, pay lower taxes, and have stronger market power, yet exhibit poorer accounting performance.

The World Bank has also had its own enterprise surveys, which take place in dozens of countries over a multi-year period, covering thousands of firms in dozens of countries. Such surveys have also included questions about the extent to which the political influence of firms in shaping national policies affects their business. Among others, such data has been used by Desai & Olofsgård (2008) to study cronyism,[17] and by Hallward-Driemeier and Pritchett (2015), studying how firms do business in the developing world.

A recent valuable empirical initiative in the field, also covering a number of countries, is the State Capture Assessment Diagnostics (SCAD), carried out by the Centre for the Study of Democracy in Bulgaria (Stoyanov et al, 2019). The SCAD assesses the existence of state capture at the national, sectoral, and organizational levels, and consists of two main components: (i) Business State Capture Pressure, which assesses monopolization pressure and evaluates the effectiveness of anti-monopoly laws, and (ii) State Capture Enablers, assessing national-level institutional and environmental factors, such as media capture, administrative corruption, and the integrity, and impartiality of public institutions as well as the effectiveness of their anti-corruption policies. Data are collected through an online and anonymous survey of experts, and it also utilizes existing aggregate indicators, such as the Indices on Press Freedom and Rule of Law. It was piloted in five EU countries: Bulgaria, Romania, Spain, Italy, and the Czech Republic and further applied in the Western Balkans. The results indicate that Bulgaria is facing particularly high vulnerabilities in terms of business pressure and institutional enablers, closely followed by Romania.

Other scholars have also developed measures of political influence and connections for specific countries. Decades ago, Fisman (2001) used an innovative approach to measure political connections. He used rumors about the health of Indonesia's ailing President Suharto in his final years in office to infer the value of connections. Fisman identified episodes during which there were adverse rumors about Suharto's health and compared the returns of firms with differing degrees of political exposure, finding that the value of well-connected firms suffered, suggesting that a large percentage of a well-connected firms' value appeared to derive from political connections.

Indirectly, and more generically, some earlier papers had dealt with related empirical attempts to assess the benefits of political connectedness, starting with Anne Krueger's (1974) work focused on aggregate (rather than firm-specific) rent-seeking behavior and efficiency losses resulting from restrictive trade policies. Subsequently, for the U.S., political scientist Brian Roberts (1990) probed more directly, yet narrowly, into the valuation of a particular political connection by examining the effect of Senator Henry Jackson's unexpected death on his various constituent interests as well as the constituent interests of his successor on the U.S. Senate Armed Services Committee. Subsequently Blanes I Vidal et al. (2012) empirically studied the phenomena of revolving door lobbyists in the United States, which can be viewed as intermediate agents (and enablers) of state capture.

Papadimitri, Pasiouras, Pescetto and Wohlschlegel (2021) use data from U.S. commercial banks over the period 2000–2015 and show that their measure of political influence reduces a bank's probability of receiving a formal regulatory enforcement action. Similarly, Khwaja and Mian (2005) show that political firms borrow 45 percent more and have 50 percent higher default rates at government banks. Braham, de Peretti and Belkacem (2022) study the specific impact of political patronage on banks, having created a measure of political connections specific to the Middle East and North Africa (MENA) region.

In a rigorous in-depth empirical study for one vast country with multiple regions, namely Russia, Slinko, Zhuravskaya and Yakovlev (2005) evaluated the effects of special interests on the performance of firms with and without political influence. In that study, to measure firms' political power and a proxy for capture for each one of Russia's region, Slinko et al. employed a unique micro-level panel dataset on Russian regional laws and regulations that treat firms preferentially between 1992–2000. Firm-level political power was measured as the share of regional preferential treatments that go to a firm in the total number of regional preferential treatments for the five enterprises that received the largest number of preferential treatments that year.

Similarly, regional capture in Russia was measured in their study by the concentration of preferential treatments for the five enterprises that received the largest number of preferential treatments holding the total number of preferential treatments constant. Their study finds that political power generates substantial performance gains to firms both in the long and the short run, while capture hurts firms that hold no political power. At the regional level, capture negatively affects small business growth, the tax capacity of the state, and the share of social public expenditure.[18]

Focused on the United States, McCann et al. (2021) use state-level data on campaign finance, lobbying, industry size, ethics, and transparency to measure the degree to which the fifty-state executive, legislative, and judicial branches are at risk of capture by the dominant industries in the state. They compile 58 indicators that serve as indirect proxies of state capture between 2010 and 2020 from a variety of sources and describe the institutional features and processes that correspond to state capture in four categories: influence, obligation, and power; infiltration; weak ethics constraints; and transparency and visibility.

Studying aspects of state capture in Tunisia, Rijkers, Freund and Nucifora (2017) examined the relationship between entry regulation and the business interests of former President Ben Ali's family using firm-level data. Data on 220 firms owned by Ben Ali's family and confiscated in the aftermath of the Tunisian revolution were identified and paired with administrative tax data that contain information on gross output and profits, allowing for the identification of the relationship between investment policies and the business interests of Tunisia's politicians during the last decade and a half of Ben Ali's tenure. The findings pointed to the existence of capture, which benefited Ben Ali clan-owned businesses.

Taking a different approach to state capture, and focusing on Hungary, Fazekas and Tóth (2016) developed an analytical framework for gauging state capture based on micro-level contractual networks in public procurement. They construct a Corruption Risk Index in government contracting focusing on the behavior of individual organizations, specifically measuring the likelihood of corruption occurring in a tender, based on micro-level red flags, such as tight tender submission deadlines. The data are derived from Hungarian public procurement announcements from 2009–2012 covering multiple organizations and procurement brokers. Those densely connected clusters of high-corruption-risk organizations are denoted by the authors as the domain of state capture. More recently Fazekas et al (2023) have applied a similar framework in Bulgaria.[19]

Toward a global index of state capture

Rationale for advancing a global measure of state capture. The literature review pointed to multiple empirical efforts to measure state capture and closely related phenomena over the past quarter century. Most initiatives have either focused on a particular country or a few countries. Likewise, most – but not all – empirical initiatives have also been relatively narrow in terms of state capture themes, homing in on particular aspects, such as political connections by firms or irregularities in procurement. The narrower focus does enable one to probe in more depth the aspect of capture under study, yet it doesn't shed light on other aspects of capture likely to prevail as well, since state capture is an interconnected and encompassing phenomenon. Further, a specialized in-depth investigation is usually, at best, country-specific at a specific moment in time and, therefore, not compatible with very broad country coverage (or periodic monitoring over time).

Regarding efforts to include larger country coverage, the BEEPS surveys we undertook decades ago did cover all the former socialist countries in central and eastern Europe and the former Soviet Union. Yet, that initiative was strictly regional in nature with a limited set of relevant questions related to state capture. The subsequent initiative of which I was a part empirically assessed state capture, crony bias, and legal corruption in a larger set of countries. It relied on WEF-administered surveys and covered about one-half of the world's countries, yet it only allowed for a very small number of generic questions, and these questions were included in surveys only for a few years two decades ago.

In sum, there has not been a measure of state capture with broad coverage in space, time, and themes, and which could be periodically updated over time.

Of course, prior to embarking on an initial effort to construct a worldwide index, it is important to ask whether state capture – and measuring it – really matters. This is particularly relevant given the plethora of available measures of traditional notions of corruption, which may be seen as serving as a good enough proxy. Part of the answer in the affirmative lies in understanding the notion of state capture, as well as its outsized potential costs. It relates to the undue influence of vested interests in shaping the rules of the game – and not merely efforts to get around the transactional implementation of existing rules associated with conventional notions of corruption.

Hence, the societal cost is likely to be orders of magnitude higher than for conventional forms of corruption. Ssuch outsized 'cost's inflicted by state capture on society extend far beyond the economic realm, shaping of the rules of the game and institutions to benefit the powerful few: society also 'pays a heavy price' as rule of law, security, human rights, democracy, and accountability are undermined, and as society becomes increasingly unequal and divided.

Yet it could still be argued that the existing measures of corruption may provide a decent proxy for state capture, obviating the need for a new global measure. At the empirical level, this tenet should be subject to testing, which can only be done with comparable datasets on corruption and state capture. At the conceptual level, this line of thought can be challenged by the fact that state capture can encompass manifestations of mis-governance which are legal and may not be characterized as strictly corrupt, as well as the inverse: the myriad manifestations of corruption, whether petty or administrative, which do not constitute state capture.[20]

Further, conventional measures of corruption, by measuring traditional and easily measurable activities, such as reports of conventional bribery, are not good proxies for more complex forms of abusing power for personal benefit at the expense of the public good. Consequently, these more complex and subtler types of unethical practices, which may prevail in countries with more sophisticated institutions, may be underestimated by the emphasis on measurement-friendly illegal and administrative forms of corruption. Thus, having a measure of state capture may help shed light on the extent and implications of such possible biases and differences between both types of measures, providing insights and shedding light on the added value of a stand-alone measure of state capture.

Basic tenets and principles in creating a State Capture Index

The proposed approach, described below, while simple, is relatively broad in scope along three key dimensions, namely in space, time, and themes. In other words, we attempt to cover the vast majority of the world's countries, following their trajectory over almost three decades, and utilizing a relatively broad interpretation of state capture, while assessing distinct dimensions of capture. Specifically, we cover 172 countries, for which there is sufficient data, over the 1996–2022 period, and construct an index based on three major components, informed by 19 different relevant variables, drawn from various sources.

The three main components that constitute the State Capture Index cover three key realms, namely the rule of law – including the legal-judiciary dimension –, policy and polity – including the economic policy and political dimensions, and the (capture) enabling environment – including the extent of acute inequality and of vulnerabilities in major dimensions of national governance.

The first two realms are informed by a variety of carefully selected specific variables from the very large and robust dataset, Varieties of Democracy (V-Dem)[21], which we use to assess the specific capture of the law, polity, and policy, or more specifically, capture of the rule of law, in the first component, and of political access, public goods and policymaking, in the second. The third realm, the (capture-) enabling environment, is informed by national-level proxies from the Worldwide Governance Indicators (WGI)[22] for national governance, and from the World Inequality Dataset (WID) for inequality. This basic framework to empirically assess state capture (SC) is depicted in the diagrammatic Figure 12.1.

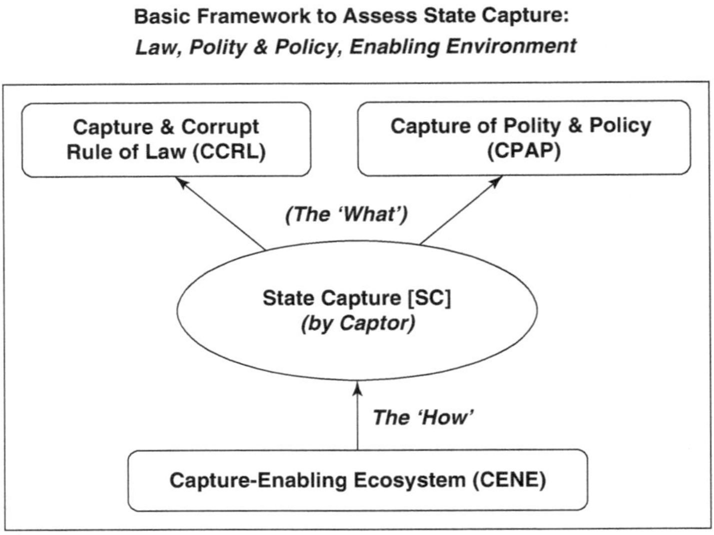

Figure 12.1 Basic framework for assessing state capture: Law, polity & policy, enabling environment.

Source: Prepared by author

Constructing the index

The State Capture Index (SCI) is constructed for 172 countries over the period 1996–2022. For some countries, some data were missing for some periods, so missing data were extrapolated utilizing near periods. With the complete dataset, for each input indicator, we calculated three-year averages starting in 1996, totaling nine periods. These averages were then normalized and converted to range from 0 (low capture) to 100 (high), and percentile ranks were calculated for each component.

The three main components of the State Capture Index and the variables comprising each component are listed in Table 12.1 and are as follows:

1: **CCRL – Corrupt and Captured Rule of Law**:

(1) CCRL = [Legislature corruption + Judicial corruption + High Court Lack of Independence + Executive Bribery and Corrupt Exchanges + Media corruption] / 5

This component is informed by five indicators from V-Dem, including corrupt legislature, judiciary, media, high-level executive and absence of high court independence. The average scores of the five indicators were then converted into percentile ranks.

2: **CPAP -- Captured Political Access and Policy**

(2) CPAP = [Power distributed by Socioeconomic position + (Disclosure of Campaign donation+ Election vote buying)/2 + Particularistic vs Public good + (Reasoned justification + Range of consult)/ 2] / 4

Table 12.1 SCI: Components, variables, sources and country coverage

SCI Component and sources	*Components and variables*	*No. of countries at source*
1. CCRL	**Captured & Corrupt Rule of Law**	
	1a. Legislature corruption	176
Source:	1b. High-level judiciary corruption	176
V-Dem	1c. High court lack of independence	176
	1d. Top/high-level corruption in executive	176
	1e. Media corruption	176
2. CPAP	**Captured Political Access and Public Goods**	
Source:	2a. Power distributed by socioeconomic position	176
V-Dem	2b. Disclosure of campaign finance	176
	2c. Election vote buying	176
	2d. 'Captured' (particularistic) 'public goods'	176
	2e. Policy reform justification by political elite	176
	2f. Range of consultation	176
CENE	**Capture Enabling Environment**	
	3a. Lack of voice and accountability	208
Source: WGI	3b. Lack of rule of law	211
	3c. Lack of r4egulatory quality	211
	3d. Extent of corruption	211
Source: WID	3f. Top 1% income distribution	172
	3g. Top 1% wealth distribution	170
	3h. Top 0.1% income distribution	172
	3d. Top 0.1% wealth distribution	170

Source: prepared by author

*The number of countries covered by the index is 172, which includes all countries for which the variables informing the Index were available. The exceptions were the cases of Belarus and Kosovo, which lacked data on wealth distribution, yet had data on income distribution (and for all other variables). Thus, for these pair of countries, the income distribution scores were used for the inequality calculations from WID.

The six variables informing the CPAP component were also drawn from V-Dem dataset,[23] and percentile ranks were computed.

3: **CENE -- Capture (or capturing) Enabling Environment**

(3) CENE = [% rank average WGI (VA + RQ + RL + CC) + % rank average (WIDY +WIDW)] / 2

WGI: Worldwide Governance Indicators, VA its Voice & Accountability indicator; RQ its Regulatory Quality indicator, RL its Rule of law indicator, and CC its Control of Corruption indicator.[24] WID: World Inequality Dataset,[25] WIDY: average of share of income by the top 0.1% and the top 1%; WIDW average of share of wealth by the top 0.1% and the top 1%.

Further, note that in calculating some of the components, as shown in equations 2 and 3 above, some of the constituent variables were first subject to aggregation and averaging at the subcomponent level, in instances when the disaggregated variables referred to a very similar aspect of capture (e.g. elections; governance indicators; inequality). By so doing we avoid unduly overweighting an aspect of capture merely due to the larger number of individual variables that were available to inform each component.

The (composite) State Capture Index was calculated as the simple average of the percentile ranks of the three components:

(4) SCI= [%rank of CRL + %rank of CPAP + %CENE] / 3

Empirical results

The full dataset emerging from constructing the SCI utilizing the various data sources, variables and aggregation method outlined above, covering the 1996–2022 period, can be accessed at https://r4d.org/resources/state-capture-index. The index data comprise nine averaged three-year periods during the 27-year time span. In addition to the composite SCI itself, it also includes the results for each of its constituent components. Here I showcase summary results discussing a set of charts, pointing to initial insights.

First, by reviewing the new dataset, we investigate the question whether the SCI measures end up being materially different from traditional corruption measures or, instead, are similar enough to question the notion that an empirical SCI measure may provide significant value added. Indeed, even if there are a priori conceptual differences between both notions, it could have been the case that for all practical purposes existing corruption indices may prove to be good enough proxies of state capture if statistically they turn out to be virtually indistinguishable.

We review and compare the data for both indicators, corruption and state capture, for the latest average three-year period available, 2020–2022, using the same 0–100 (percentile rank) scale, where 0 is absence of corruption/state capture; 100 is its maximum. At first sight, a visual comparison between both measures for the same set of roughly 70 countries, via the Control of Corruption indicator from the WGI (Figure 12.2) and the State Capture Index (SCI, in Figure 12.3), suggests a very similar pattern.

Yet, such comparison is akin to an optical illusion because the similar pattern arises from the construction of these charts, which are automatically ordered from lowest to highest corruption/capture score. The relevant question instead is whether the rank ordering is very similar or materially different between both measures.

For many countries the percentile rank is rather similar across both measures. Yet there are major non-trivial differences. Focusing on the most recent period, 2020–2022, for 78 countries (45 percent) out of all 172 in the sample there is a difference of at least 10 percentile point ranks between both measures (in either direction), and for 42 countries (26 percent of the full sample) the difference between both measures exceeds 15 percentile ranks.

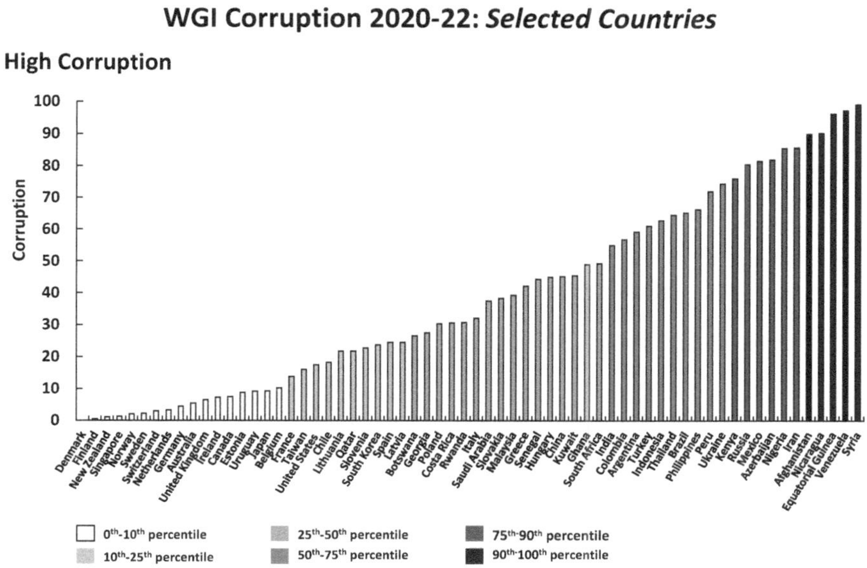

Figure 12.2 Worldwide Governance Indicator (WGI) for corruption 2020–22: Selected countries.

Source: Prepared by author

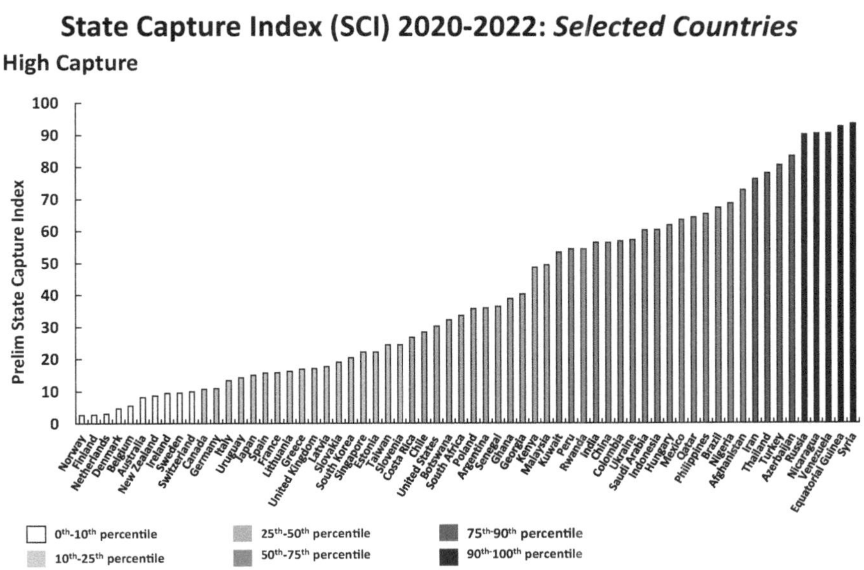

Figure 12.3 State Capture Index (SCI) 2020–2022: Selected countries.

Source: Prepared by author

Illustrating some of these differences, Figure 12.4 simultaneously depicts both measures for a select group of OECD countries.[26] Some countries that have traditionally been assessed as having very low corruption levels, such as the Nordic countries and the Netherlands, also score similarly low in terms of degree of state capture, according to the SCI. In countries, such as Canada and Uruguay, with relatively low levels of corruption, the degree of state capture is slightly higher, yet not high. In countries such as Slovakia and Greece, the middling degree of state capture contrasts with a substantially higher level of traditionally measured corruption. In stark contrast, in countries like the United States and Chile, with relatively low-to-middling levels of corruption, the degree of state capture is measured to be substantially higher, relatively speaking.

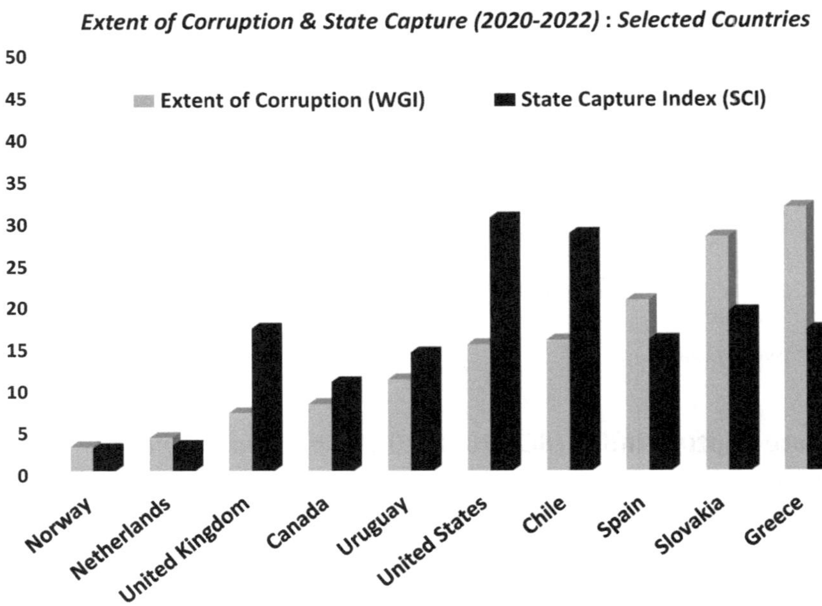

Figure 12.4 Extent of corruption & state capture (2020–2022): Selected countries.

Source: Prepared by author

Observing substantial deviations between indices of corruption and of state capture for many countries gives rise to the question of whether there are important differences for important groups of countries. Exploring whether there are differences for high-income countries compared with medium and lower-income countries is particularly relevant.

Global corruption indicators have been in existence for about three decades. As a 'poll of polls' – based on multiple single source measures – such efforts started with the Transparency International (TI) Corruption Perception Index (CPI) in 1995, followed by the corruption control measure (as one of six governance indicators) in the WGI. For decades, a persistent question was whether these traditional measures of corruption may underestimate the extent of the governance challenge in high-income countries, which overall rate relatively highly in these traditional measures, with some notable exceptions.

Tellingly, the gap between the scores of high-income countries and the emerging/developing countries shrinks when measuring state capture, as seen in Figure 12.5. This is not surprising, because both the notion and the measurement of state capture embrace manifestations of mis-governance which, while highly damaging, can be legal, and seemingly more nuanced than outright bribery or stolen public funds. The latter and coarser forms of corruption tend to feature prominently in the existing measures of corruption, partly due to legacy, partly because it is easier to ask about them and thus measure. By contrast, undue influence in shaping the rules of the game, particularly if done legally (or 'extra-legally', in 'gray areas'), which are harder to measure, may be the strategy of choice in some wealthier countries for elite captors, benefitting themselves at the expense of the public good.

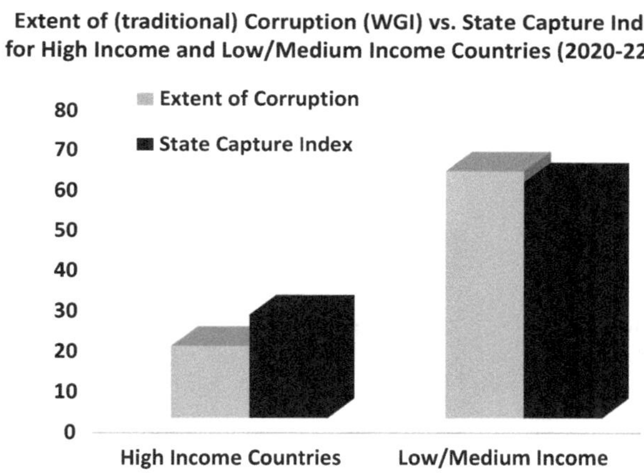

Figure 12.5 Extent of (Traditional) corruption (WGI) vs. State Capture Index (SCI) for high income and low/medium countries (2020–22).

Source: Prepared by author

It is also worth noting that the state capture score for high-income countries depicted in Figure 12.5 is an average across all industrialized countries. As we observed in the previous figure showcasing individual countries, there is substantial variance, implying that the extent of state capture itself and the gap between it and corresponding lower levels of traditional corruption can be very high for many countries, while lower, or reversed, for some others.

In many industrialized countries and some emerging economies where rule of law institutions are evolving, non-state actors may calculate that, given the higher risk of engaging in overtly illegal activities, it pays to ensure that the laws are shaped in such a way that their actions may not be strictly illegal according to current norms. Thus, they may invest in, as well as engage in, influencing polity, policy. and law, deviating from accepted ethical norms, to benefit privately at the expense of public welfare, yet at the same time avoiding legal jeopardy.

Unbundling the group average for all low- and medium-income countries into its regional groupings reveals significant variation across regions. Although, on average, high-income countries exhibit (relatively) higher degrees of capture on average than of traditional corruption, the reality appears to be more mixed across low/medium-income countries. As depicted in Figure 12.6, the (relative) extent of corruption is even higher than of the (still high) level of state capture in Latin America and the Caribbean as well as in Sub-Saharan Africa and – barely – South Asia. Conversely, the relative extent of state capture appears to be substantially larger than of traditional corruption in Emerging East Asia and somewhat larger in the Middle East and in the former Soviet countries (and slightly so in Central/ Eastern Europe).

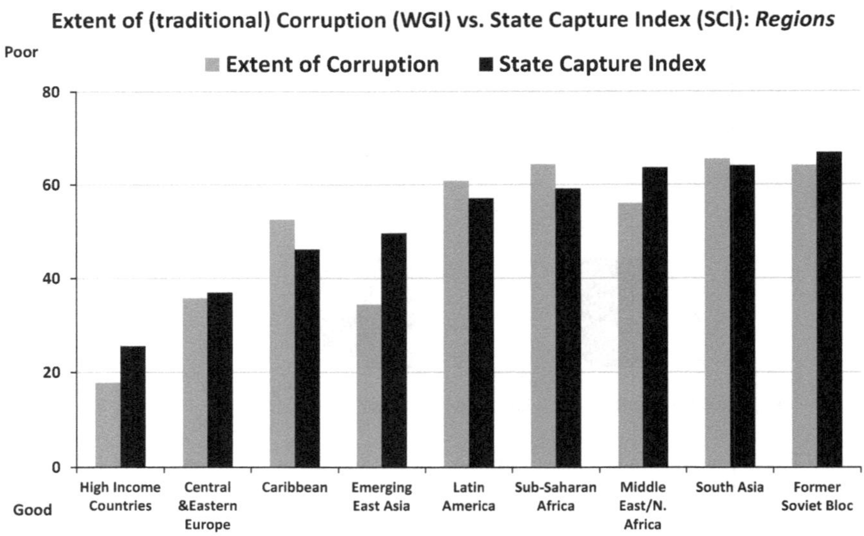

Figure 12.6 Extent of (traditional) corruption (WGI) vs. State Capture Index (SCI): Regions.

Source: Prepared by author

Beyond the differences between traditional measures of corruption and state capture for countries and regions around the world, the variation across regions in the extent of state capture is also noteworthy. On average, former soviet countries, South Asia and the Middle East exhibit very high levels of capture, while the next tier – albeit still a degree of capture – comprising Sub-Saharan Africa and Latin America is a notch down, with Emerging East Asia and the Caribbean one notch further down – relatively high capture –, and then Central/Eastern Europe exhibiting somewhat lower levels of capture.

Naturally, however, there is substantial variance within each group of countries as well, even if they share geography or income grouping, as we saw in the earlier Figure 12.4 which depicted a number of industrialized countries. Consequently, regional and income group averages ought to be interpreted with caution.

State capture regimes

Observing the fraught path of the post-Soviet transition toward democracy during the early 1990s, we advanced at the time a notion of state capture focused exclusively on non-state actors as the captor of the rules of the game, and within these on powerful private actors, such as the so-called oligarchs and powerful enterprises that had been recently privatized. As mentioned earlier, in recent decades, scholarship evolved toward a more encompassing notion of state capture embracing a much wider set of potential captors, and allowing for state actors also to be regarded as captors within a state capture framework. In so doing, autocratic leaders could be regarded as the key captor in their countries. In a sense, the early notion of state capture as the 'capture *of* the state' (by non-state actors) was expanded to allow for 'capture *by* the state' (by its leader and/or other state organs).

Since my aim in this contribution is to provide an initial worldwide empirical measure of state capture, I do not advance a comprehensive treatment of the validity and the pros and cons of embracing a much-expanded notion of state capture. Instead, for measurement purposes, I err on the side of inclusion, suggesting that, with the proper interpretative care taking into account differences in political regimes, it is also possible to arrive at a state capture proxy for non-democratic settings.

Such differentiation is warranted, since capture *of* the state is not the same as capture *by* the state. This is particularly relevant for any formulation of policy and institutional initiatives to address capture. Two countries may exhibit similarly high levels of state capture, yet if one country is a democracy and the other is not, with their divergent power dynamics and interplay between non-state and state actors, the implications for analysis and policy would also differ.

Concretely, for empirical purposes of the proposed SCI here, we included countries in the assessment of state capture irrespective of their 'democracy' status and did not differentiate between them in constructing the index, utilizing the same variables and criteria.

At the same time, while presenting the dataset for all countries, for purposes of further inquiry, we identify the type of political regime for each country, following the classification of political regimes by V-Dem's Regimes of the World (RoW). Showcasing all countries in the state capture index in a single chart, yet visually differentiating democracies from autocracies, Figure 12.7 depicts all rated countries, showing the scores for traditional corruption (according to the WGI measure, in the horizontal axis) and that for the state capture (SCI, vertical axis). Further, following the political regimes classification by V-Dem's Regimes of the World (RoW), the black dots represent (both the liberal and electoral) democratic countries, while the gray triangles depict (both the electoral and closed) autocratic countries.

The bundling of the types of democracies as well as the two types of autocracies into the simple distinction between democracies and autocracies simplifies the depiction of political regimes in the figure below 12.7, and roughly dovetails with the distinction we have made between capture *of* the state and capture *by* the state.

Showcasing the extent of (traditionally measured) corruption on the horizontal axis, and state capture on the vertical axis in Figure 12.7 permits visualizing the extent to which their relative measures empirically differ by observing how far they are from the 45-degree diagonal line, in either direction. Although many countries fall close to the diagonal line, many others do not. This backstops the illustration made for a select group of advanced countries in Figure 12.4. State capture is different from corruption.

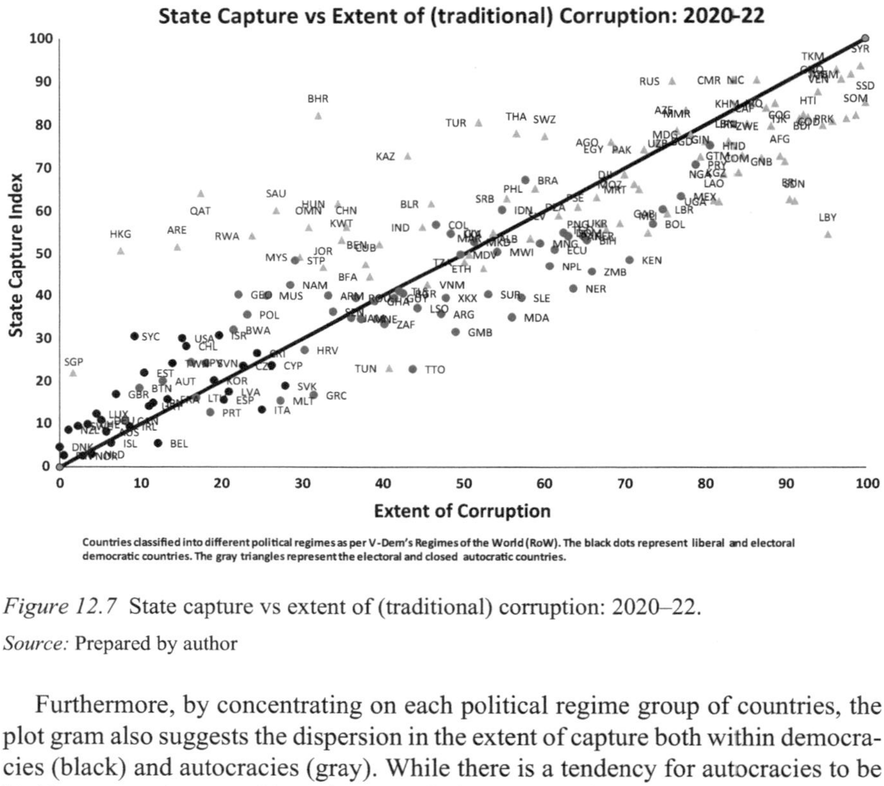

Figure 12.7 State capture vs extent of (traditional) corruption: 2020–22.

Source: Prepared by author

Furthermore, by concentrating on each political regime group of countries, the plot gram also suggests the dispersion in the extent of capture both within democracies (black) and autocracies (gray). While there is a tendency for autocracies to be highly captured – arguably at least partly by construction –, democratic countries exhibit highly varying degrees of state capture. In fact, it is noteworthy that even among many democratic, higher-income countries, as depicted in Figure 12.4, the extent of state capture varies significantly.

The disaggregation of state capture by regime type – democracy or autocracy, in particular – may also be warranted due to the likely existence of important dynamics linking capture with the evolution of varieties of democracy (or lack thereof) over time. In particular, a hypothesis worth exploring empirically is whether democratic countries subject to a higher (and growing) extent of state capture are more likely to traverse away from democratic institutions toward more autocratic ones. In fact, given such possible dynamics over time, the particular classification of a country shown for the current period snapshot in Figure 12.7 above would not have necessarily been the same at an early period.

Evolutions of state capture: Illustrative empirics

Significant differences in the extent of state capture across space obviously do not guarantee major differences across time within countries, since it may take considerable time for national institutions and rules of the game to evolve. Yet, it is of interest that over the time span of our dataset there are substantial changes for many countries, while there is relative stability for others. In fact, we find that in 61 countries (35 percent of the sample) the SCI has changed by at least ten points in either direction between the first and last periods. Further, many of the evolutions, when they happen, are not necessarily unidirectional; reversals do take place as well. Therefore, beyond the 61 countries that exhibit a large change between the first and last period, there are others that experienced large changes in the extent of state capture over the period of study in both directions due to reversals (and thus the difference between the initial and last period may not be large).

Showcasing some notable dynamics, the United States, Chile, and Uruguay, three countries in the Americas, are illustrated in Figure 12.8. Norway, with very low capture, is included as a benchmark. The United States has experienced a substantial increase in the measured extent of state capture since 1996, albeit not strictly linear, likely linked to the government in power in a given period. In this respect, the sharp upturn during the recent Trump presidency that started in 2017 is noteworthy, followed by an incipient reversal in more recent years following his tenure. Uruguay, an emerging economy, starting at low levels of state capture in

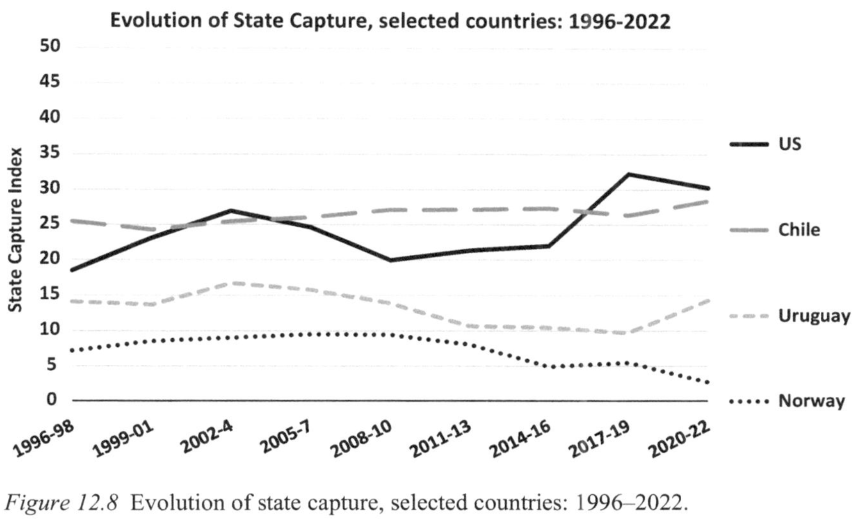

Figure 12.8 Evolution of state capture, selected countries: 1996–2022.

Source: Prepared by author

the 1990s, exhibits some decline over most of the period of study, ending at a substantially lower level than the mighty U.S. Chile has remained stable throughout the period in terms of state capture (at a much higher percentile rank relative to its corruption levels), having started at a higher level than the U.S. in the 1990s. Yet, the rise in state capture in the U.S. means that the latter caught up with Chile.

Moving to post-socialist economies and others in Eurasia, it is not surprising that the extent of state capture is rather high in many of them; it wasn't accidental that when they entered transition decades ago, we focused on them in our early work on state capture. The varying dynamics over time within each country are noteworthy.

As illustrated in Figure 12.9, countries such as Hungary and Russia exhibited substantial increases in the extent of state capture over the past few decades. Turkey also exhibits a sharp increase in recent decades, after an initial improvement of sorts in the earlier period.

In contrast, Ukraine, starting at a very high level similar to Russia in the mid-1990s, and still increasing and remaining high in subsequent periods, has seen its levels of state capture decline over the past decade or so. Armenia, even more acutely than Ukraine, exemplifies the existence of non-linear dynamics over time within a country, in this case featuring a positive reversal as well: following a sharp increase in state capture during the earlier periods, it undergoes a substantial decline during the latter period.

Contrasting the marked 'positive' reversal of Armenia (inverted V-shape), we observe the 'negative' (V-shape) reversal of Serbia during the full period – improvement in the extent of state capture in the earlier period, followed by a deterioration thereafter.

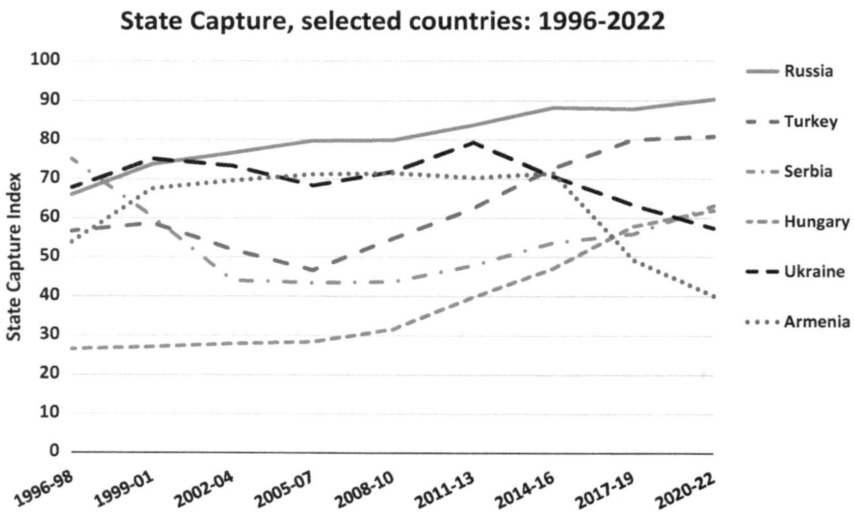

Figure 12.9 State capture, selected countries: 1996–2022.

Source: Prepared by author

These within-country shifting dynamics over time, including sharp reversals, challenge notions of path dependency, since the evidence suggests that there is no inexorable pre-determined path toward or away from state capture. This, in turn backstops the importance of having empirical tools to monitor the extent of state capture in each country over time.

Concluding considerations and thinking ahead

Inspiration for trying to measure governance phenomena in general, and state capture in particular, dates back to a century and half ago when Lord Kelvin (a.k.a. William Thompson), the inventor of the Celsius temperature scale, is said to have said 'if you cannot measure it, then it is not science' as well as 'if you cannot measure it, then you cannot improve it'.

Still, it will be up to students, scholars and practitioners to eventually determine whether a worldwide State Capture Index as proposed here, and variants thereof, can be useful and provide value added compared with existing empirical initiatives.

The review of the existing literature and data initiatives provided here suggested that there has been an empirical gap, particularly regarding initiatives to continuously monitor and measure state capture globally. The approach presented here suggests a path towards a periodic and global State Capture Index, comparable across countries and over time.

Given that this is an initial effort toward such a global index, as well as the general nature of the available data for governance and institutions, interpretative caution is in order. Scanning and studying a plethora of sources and variables available in the field of governance and institutions, careful identification and selection of sources and specific variables within each selected source took place. In doing so, we were mindful of their potential to assess a state capture-linked phenomena, and considered the extent of data availability over time and space for each candidate indicator. Yet, legitimate debate and consideration lie ahead regarding other potential sources and variables that one could integrate into the project. Likewise, the relatively simple approach to the implicit weights given to each variable and component could be subject to further review and sensitivity analysis.[27]

Further, as mentioned, any index construction in the governance field and in the social sciences is subject to margins of error, and the index presented here is no exception. In fact, phenomena such as state capture, or corruption or governance more broadly, are intrinsically (directly) unobservable from a statistical standpoint. This negates the possibility of ever reaching perfect measurement accuracy and necessitating reliance on proxies. This is what we have also attempted to do here, as in other related initiatives in the field.

This implies that interpretative caution regarding the empirical results and scores is in order. Typically, small differences over time or space of, say, less than 5–8 points on scales of 0–100 are not material. Yet, at the same time, after taking such imprecision into consideration, inferences can be made with care, particularly where differences are large. This suggests that, even exercising caution, the data can be useful – given the prevalence of large changes and differences over time and across countries.

Mindful of such caution, we found that the data do provide relevant insights, including on the relatively higher prevalence of state capture compared with traditional measures of corruption in many advanced economies, as well as non-trivial differences between both phenomena across regions of the world. At the same time, we found significant differences in the extent of state capture across countries, even within the same region and also within countries over time, with positive as well as negative evolutions, as well as reversals mid-way. This points to the potential relevance of having measurement tools at hand, such as the one proposed here, to monitor countries and to make comparisons across space and time.

More specifically, this type of global measurement initiative presents an opportunity to raise flags at a relatively early stage, potentially helping to avert a descent into full-fledged state capture. Identifying countries on a path to state capture, but not fully there yet, may lead to timely strategies and actions reversing such trends, preventing fuller capture. In governance, as in other fields, prevention typically enjoys a much higher payoff and is more feasible than attempts at belated remedial action, once the damage has been inflicted and the rot becomes entrenched. Hence, it may be especially valuable to focus on prevention in countries with 'middling' levels of capture, and particularly so if the capture trend is clearly pointing in the wrong direction.

Nonetheless, a global index of the type presented here is no substitute for more granular, in-depth, in-country diagnostic work. To the contrary, both the more aggregate/'macro' view, and the 'micro' view, ought to be seen as complementary. The aggregate approach has limits regarding the specific and concrete policy and institutional steps to mitigate capture that would be required at the national or subnational levels.

Regarding the potential usefulness of utilizing the SCI going forward, there are multiple research avenues, largely beyond the scope of this contribution. To illustrate, we can go back full circle to a couple of decades ago, when research pointed to a very large and strong causal effect of improved governance on country income per capita, while at the same time finding no evidence for such reverse effect. Indeed, contrary to widely held notions, we found that higher income per capita did not guarantee improved governance.

At the time, we speculated that a possible reason was that higher incomes occurred in two distinct settings, with potentially offsetting governance results: competitive countries growing robustly, on the one hand, and countries obtaining largely rents from natural resources (or foreign aid), on the other, which were more prone to capture. In captured settings, incomes may be higher for some time benefitting the few, yet governance may be deteriorating, in contrast with competitive countries growing more equitably.[28] Further research exploring the different income and development dynamics between captured and non-captured countries may offer further insights on the links between governance, incomes, and development outcomes.

Relatedly, the growth of interest in the state capture field is taking place at the same time as there is increasing concern and focus on inequality. The a priori links between the inequality of political and economic influence, state capture, and income inequality are evident. Research featuring data on state capture could shed further light on these links.

Furthermore, the framework advanced in this chapter, backstopped by suggestive empirical results, points to important differences between corruption and state capture, and raises the question of what's next in the study of the notion of state capture and which framework may offer a more promising approach. Let me suggest two alternative paths.

The first would no longer study state capture as if it were merely a subset of corruption (and within it, a subset of 'grand corruption'). The emphasis would be on cases where accepted ethical and social norms may indeed be violated and manipulated by powerful actors so that state capture takes place, even though the actions may not be strictly illegal according to the prevailing (and possibly captured) legal norms.

Under this scenario, there may be some overlap between corruption and state capture, yet there would also be many activities that unduly benefit elites at the expense of society, but which are not corrupt in the legal sense. Conversely, under this scenario, there would also be many transactions that may be regarded as corrupt which do not constitute state capture. Further, political economy approaches and tools would help deepen the understanding of drivers of state capture, such as the extent of inequality in political influence.

Rather than clearly separating the study of corruption from that of state capture, the second alternative would explicitly consider broadening the scope of what constitutes corruption, fully embracing the full essence in the notion of state capture. This path would first entail placing corruption more firmly under an ethical/social norms lens, rather than under a strictly legal or administrative framework, and then also considering the range of activities that may turn out to be legal yet unethical.

Importantly, this path would also imply the need to consider a re-interpretation, if not a reformulation, of the traditional definition of corruption. The prevailing notion of corruption as 'abuse of public office for private gain' has traditionally been seen as focusing on illegal activities ('abuse') by public officials ('public office') to enrich themselves ('private gain'). Although high-level politicians could be interpreted as those able to abuse 'public office', its lack of explicitness belittles the central role of the political elite in state capture and has tended to perpetuate the focus on bureaucrats and civil servants. More glaringly, the accepted definition of corruption essentially ignores the central role played by non-state actors in state capture, such as powerful private actors. And it does not address the question of whether the rules of the game are being shaped (or subverted) for the benefit of the elite, resulting in a high cost to society.

In brief, as an antithesis to a traditional notion of corruption, one could posit instead 'the privatization of public policy, polity and law' that benefits the powerful few at the expense of society. Such a reformulation could encapsulate the essence of state capture, contrasting it with traditional notions of corruption.

Another set of conceptual issues that warrant further work, and which may benefit from the framework advanced here, refers to the definitional debate around state capture, and, in particular, the inclusion of state actors as captors as well – thereby broadening the scope of state capture to include not just capture of the state, but also capture by the state. As mentioned, fully embracing such a definitional extension means that the boundaries of state capture would need to be set. This is because a limitless broadening of the scope of state capture would fail Popper's falsifiability test, due to the inability to determine the 'empty set', namely 'what is *not* state capture'. This, in turn, would weaken the state capture concept.

Further, and beyond the basic definitional debate, embracing such an expanded understanding of state capture would also necessitate an explicit differentiation between various regimes, notably between democracies and autocracies, because different institutional outcomes and policy responses would emerge, depending on which state capture regime afflicts the country.

Finally, a unified empirical framework to measure state capture worldwide, as we have advanced here, which explicitly accounts for regime differences, could help shed light on transitions within countries over time from one regime to another and further research into the question of whether increasing levels of state capture in fragile or transition countries, or even in others, increase the risk of eventual descent into autocracy.

In ending, we go back full circle to where we started on that frigid Christmas Day facing the Kremlin, as the Soviet Union ceased to exist, pondering in awe what it all actually meant, and what it augured. Then, over three decades ago, we started our work as Russia and other countries in the region were attempting to establish fledgling democracies. It is poignant to recap the words of Russia's current leader as he was starting his reign almost a quarter century ago:

> I only want to draw your attention straightaway to the fact that you have yourselves formed this very state, to a large extent through political and quasi-political structures under your control. So perhaps what one should do least of all is blame the mirror.
>
> – Vladimir Putin, in a meeting with Russia's business leaders, in July 2000[29]

Here we are today, on the other side of the mirror.

Notes

1 I thank Saba Yifredew for invaluable research assistance in this project, including in the extensive data work, in the preparation of charts, and in supporting the literature review. I am very thankful for the insightful comments and suggestions by Liz David-Barrett, Pablo de Greiff, Eduardo Engel and Susan Rose-Ackerman. She also provided inspiration and encouragement throughout the project. I also benefitted from the feedback of participants at the Conference in Honor of Susan Rose-Ackerman, held at Yale University on August 26–27, 2022 and suggestions participants of the State Capture workstream convened by the Center for Human Rights & Global Justice, New York University School of Law, as well as participants of the State Capture workshop at IACA. The material

and intellectual support by the governance group (and the Governance Action Hub) in Results for Development for this line of work, led by Mario Picon, is much appreciated as well.

2 Far from doing full justice to her many pathbreaking writings on the subject, among others, see Rose-Ackerman, S. (1978); Rose-Ackerman, S. (2001); Rose-Ackerman, S. (2008); Rose-Ackerman, S. (2010), and Rose-Ackerman, S., & B. J. Palifka. (1999).

3 A recent example is the State Capture workstream – which include academics and practitioners from around the world – of the Prevention Project, led by the Center for Human Rights & Global Justice at New York University School of Law, and its report *State Capture as Enabling Condition for Human Rights Violations* (De Greiff and Knapp 2024).

4 Tellingly, the judiciary leadership of South Africa, in investigating former President Jakob Zuma, adopted the framework of state capture, moving away from a traditional approach to corruption. In so doing, for their proceedings and hearings, they requested expert submissions on the subject antecedents and evidence from other countries. See our submission in Hellman and Kaufmann (2018). More generally and in-depth about the politics of state capture in South Africa, see Chipkin, et al. (2018). Further, the leadership of international financial institutions, such as the Inter-American Development Bank and the International Monetary Fund have requested external input into this phenomena, given that it was regarded as increasingly 'macro-critical'. Many academics around the world have also become increasingly inclined to write policy-oriented books, articles, and blogs on state capture risks in particular countries. For the United States, see, for instance, Johnson and Kwak (2011) focusing on the regulatory capture by elite Wall Street bankers, *13 Bankers: The Wall Street Takeover and the Next Financial Meltdown.* On the UK, see David-Bárrett (2022), as well as Innes' (2021) blog on the subject.

5 https://www.statecapture.org.za/

6 https://en.wikipedia.org/wiki/The_Mechanism_(TV_series).

7 www.iaca.int/measuring-corruption/measuring-state-capture/.

8 It is noteworthy that his Nobel Prize in Economics, awarded in 1982 "for his seminal studies of industrial structures, functioning of markets, and causes and effects of public regulation", was the first Nobel awarded to an economist whose primary appointment was in a business school.

9 Kolko (1963).

10 Chisholm (1911).

11 Winters (2011).

12 The sample of firms in each country was designed to be as representative as possible for the population of firms in a country and subject to various minimum quotas from each country. Firms were randomly sampled from business directories and respondents were asked similar questions to allow for cross-country comparisons. The BEEPS had features to ensure higher reliability and greater depth in assessing these challenges. Survey questions were based on the direct experience of firms rather than subjective comparisons across countries. Where possible, the survey offers numerical cardinal estimates of the phenomena at hand. (Fiebelkorn, 2019).

13 The specific question posed was "How much influence do you think the following groups actually had on recently enacted national laws, rules and regulations that have a substantial impact on your business?" Firms assessed their own influence and in direct succession were asked to compare the influence of a large set of other actors including: your domestic competitors, foreign firms, your business association, other business associations, dominant firms or conglomerates in key sectors of the economy (other than yours), labor unions, organized crime, regional or local government, military, international development agencies or foreign governments, and individuals or firms with close personal ties to political leaders.

14 Illustrating the use of the BEEPS survey to further research state capture, Bartlett (2021), among others, investigates the economics of state capture by analyzing the impact of

political connections on business performance in Southeast Europe. For this work a subsequent round of the BEEPS survey was used, focusing on nine countries. The BEEPS survey has also been used by a number of other authors to investigate empirically the association between state capture and other governance-related phenomena, such as in Bagashka (2014), who studies the effects of veto players on state capture and bureaucratic corruption in post-communist countries.

15 Based on this survey enterprise data by the WEF, and as a variant of the study of state capture, in Kaufmann and Vicente's "Legal Corruption" (2011), we presented a political economy model that integrated both corruption and the legal system attempting to explain patterns of legal and illegal corruption across a large group of countries.

16 Claessens, Djankov & Lang (2000).

17 More generally, there have been empirical studies on crony capitalism, as for instance in the compilation for the Middle East in Diwan et al, eds (2019)

18 It is noteworthy that this study allowed some examination of state capture during President Putin's first and second terms, which were marked by a significant shift in the relationship between the business and the state.

19 And yet another rather different approach to empirically assess capture, via a proxy, is taken by Andersen et al (2022), by estimating the extent to which incremental foreign aid to a country is associated with concurrent spikes in capital flight to financial centers abroad. Further, there are multiple rigorous studies that empirically explore other (albeit related) manifestations of misgovernance, such as patronage in Ghana (Brierley 2021), as well as Kruse et al (2021) on standards and political connections, among many others.

20 Indeed, as suggested, state capture is a broader and potentially more pernicious phenomenon than traditional forms of corruption and bribery. The latter tend to be transactional and focus on illegal payments and the diversion of funds associated with implementation of the rules of the game. This is in sharp contrast to state capture, which refers to the shaping of the rules of the game to benefit the few exerting undue influence at the expense of the citizenry. And state capture can take place without engaging in strictly illegal activities, since the laws may have been shaped and distorted so to protect the capturing elite. Thus, traditional measures of corruption miss many important components of state capture.

21 For access to V-Dem methodology and codebook, see Coppedge et al (2023a, 2023b, respectively).

22 For details on the WGI methodology, see Kaufmann, D., A. Kraay, & M. Mastruzzi. (2010), and for access to the data and related resources, at www.govindicators.org

23 Power distributed by socioeconomic position is a measure of political equality. It is concerned with the political effects of income and wealth inequality. Disclosure of campaign donations and electoral vote buying are concerned with the transparency and quality of elections. Particularistic vs. public goods, reasoned justification, and range of consult gauge the nature of deliberation and discourse in political communication. These gauge the extent and the nature to which political elites give public justifications, profile the nature of spending in the country as being clientelistic vs. public goods, and a measure of the range of consultation at elite level.

24 After computing the 3-year period averages for each country, the four components of the WGI, namely Voice and Accountability (VA), Regulatory Quality (RQ), Rule of Law (RL) and Control of Corruption (CC) were normalized to range from 0 to 100. These scores were reversed to range from good (0) to bad (100). These four components were then averaged and converted to percentile ranks to form the WGI part of CENE.

25 For technical details and data on the WID, see their World Inequality Report 2022, in Bajard et al (December 2021).

26 These are not randomly selected countries, but instead meant to illustrate some notable differences, as well as some similarities, among industrialized countries.

27 Noting that in fact experience suggests that instead of varying weights between included variables a far more important decision regarding 'weights' is likely to be any potential candidate variable so far excluded, which by construction gets zero weight.
28 Kaufmann and Kraay (2002).
29 Reported by Hoffman, D., on July 28, 2000, in the Washington Post.

References

Andersen, J. J., N. Johannesen, & B. Rijkers. (2022). Elite capture of foreign aid: Evidence from offshore bank accounts. *Journal of Political Economy*, 130(2), 388–425. https://www.journals.uchicago.edu/doi/abs/10.1086/717455?casa_token=1YQZVI21-G4AAAAA:qssVr-UD2ovkZTXLGwYH3DffGMhfcWOgQq1x_B18Ggf2XQ_KHrBcnOQmxdm6YIqbC_He54DA-7eXhw

Bagashka, T. (2014). Unpacking corruption: The effect of veto players on state capture and bureaucratic corruption. *Political Research Quarterly*, 67(1), 165–180. https://doi.org/10.1177%2F1065912913492584

Bajard, Felix, & Lucas Chancel Rowaida Moshrif. (2021). World inequality report 2022 technical notes for figures and tables. https://wir2022.wid.world/www-site/uploads/2021/12/WIR2022-Technical-Note-Figures-Tables-1.pdf

Bartlett, W. (2021). The performance of politically connected firms in South East Europe: State capture or business capture? LEQS Paper No. 171, LSE.

Blanes i Vidal, J., M. Draca, & C. Fons-Rosen. (2012). Revolving door lobbyists. *American Economic Review*, 102(7), 3731–3748.

Braham, R., C. Peretti, & L. Belkacem. (2022). On the measurement and extent of banks' political connection in the Middle East and North Africa Region. Comparative Economic Studies, Palgrave.

Brierley, Sarah. (2021). Combining patronage and merit in public sector recruitment. *The Journal of Politics*, 83(1), 182–197. https://doi.org/10.1086/708240

Chipkin, I., M. Swilling, H. Bhorat, M. Buthelezi, S. Duma, H. Friedenstein, & L. Mondi. (2018). *Shadow State: The Politics of State Capture*. Johannesburg: Wits University Press.

Chisholm, Hugh, ed. (1911). Eupatridae. In *Encyclopædia Britannica*, Vol. 9 (11th ed.). Cambridge University Press. Edinburgh

Claessens, S., S. Djankov, & L. H. P. Lang. (2000). The separation of ownership and control in East Asian Corporations. *Journal of Financial Economics*, 58pp. 81–112 .

Coppedge, Michael, John Gerring, Carl Henrik Knutsen, Staffan I. Lindberg, Jan Teorell, Kyle L. Marquardt, Juraj Medzihorsky, Daniel Pemstein, Lisa Gastaldi, Sandra Grahn, Josefine Pernes, Oskar Rydén, Johannes von Römer, Eitan Tzelgov, Yi-ting Wang, & Steven Wilson. (2023). V-Dem methodology v13. *Varieties of Democracy (V-Dem) Project*. https://www.v-dem.net/documents/26/methodology_v13.pdf

Coppedge, Michael, John Gerring, Carl Henrik Knutsen, Staffan I. Lindberg, Jan Teorell, David Altman, Michael Bernhard, Agnes Cornell, M. Steven Fish, Lisa Gastaldi, Haakon Gjerløw, Adam Glynn, Sandra Grahn, Allen Hicken, Katrin Kinzelbach, Kyle L. Marquardt, Kelly McMann, Valeriya Mechkova, Anja Neundorf, Pamela Paxton, Daniel Pemstein, Oskar Rydén, Johannes von Römer, Brigitte Seim, Rachel Sigman, Svend-Erik Skaaning, Jeffrey Staton, Aksel Sundström, Eitan Tzelgov, Luca Uberti, Yi-ting Wang, Tore Wig, & Daniel Ziblatt. (2023). V-Dem codebook v12. *Varieties of Democracy (V-Dem) Project*. https://www.v-dem.net/static/website/img/refs/codebookv12.pdf

David-Barrett, Elizabeth. (2022). *Is the UK Sliding into State Capture?*. https://journals.lwbooks.co.uk/renewal/vol-30-issue-2/abstract-9561/

David-Barrett, Elizabeth. (2023). State capture and development: A conceptual framework. *Journal of International Relations and Development*. https://doi.org/10.1057/s41268-023-00290-6

David-Barrett, Elizabeth, D. Kaufmann, & J. C. Ceballos. (2023). Measuring state capture. In *Insights Briefs Series No. 8*. IACA, Laxenburg. https://www.iaca.int/measuring-corruption/measuring-state-capture/

De Greiff P., M. Knapp (2024). *State Capture as Enabling Condition for Human Rights Violations*. Center for Human Rights & Global Justice, New York University School of Law, New York. Forthcoming.

Desai, R. M., & A. Olofsgård. (2008). Do politically connected firms undermine their own competitiveness? Evidence from Developing Countries (January 2008). *Brookings Global Economy and Development Working Paper*, (18). https://papers.ssrn.com/sol3/papers.cfm?abstract_id=1100114

Diwan, I., A. Malik, & I. Atiyas, eds. (2019). *Crony Capitalism in the Middle East: Business and Politics from Liberalization to the Arab Spring*. Oxford University Press. https://oxford.universitypressscholarship.com/view/10.1093/oso/9780198799870.001.0001/oso-9780198799870

Faccio, M. (2004). Politically connected firms. SSRN: https://ssrn.com/abstract=444960 or http://dx.doi.org/10.2139/ssrn.444960

Faccio, M. (2010). Differences between politically connected and nonconnected firms: A cross-country analysis. *Financial Management, Financial Management Association International*, 39(3), 905–928.

Fazekas, M., & I. J. Tóth. (2016). From corruption to state capture: A new analytical framework with empirical applications from Hungary. *Political Research Quarterly*, 69(2), 320–334.

Fazekas, Mihaly, Viktoriia Poltoratskaia, & Bence Tóth. (2023). Corruption risks and state capture in Bulgarian public procurement. Policy Research Working Papers. The World Bank. https://doi.org/10.1596/1813-9450-10444

Fiebelkorn, A. (2019). State capture analysis: How to quantitatively analyze the regulatory abuse by business-state relationships. World Bank Discussion Paper.

Fisman, Raymond. (2001). Estimating the value of political connections. *American Economic Review*, 91(4), 1095–1102.

Hallward-Driemeier, M., & L. Pritchett. (2015). How business is done in the developing world: Deals versus rules. *Journal of Economic Perspectives*, 29(3), 121–140.

Hellman, J. S., & Kaufmann, D. (2004). The inequality of influence. In *Building a Trustworthy State in Post-Socialist Transition* (pp. 100–118). New York: Palgrave Macmillan. https://link.springer.com/chapter/10.1057/9781403981103_6

Hellman, J. S., & D. Kaufmann. (2018). State capture in transition: Submission to the judicial commission of inquiry into allegations of state capture, corruption and fraud in the public sector including organs of state of South Africa. https://resourcegovernance.org/sites/default/files/documents/state-capture-in-transition.pdf

Hellman, J. S., G. Jones, & D. Kaufmann. (2000). Seize the state, seize the day: State capture and influence in transition economies. World Bank Working Paper and (2003) *Journal of Comparative Economics*, 31(4), 751–773. https://doi.org/10.1016/j.jce.2003.09.006

Hoffman, D. (2000). Putin aims to assure tycoons: Russian disavows pressure by police. *Washington Post*, July 28.

Innes, Abby. (2021). *Corporate State Capture in the UK*. LSE blog. https://blogs.lse.ac.uk/politicsandpolicy/corporate-state-capture/

Johnson, Simon, & James Kwak. (2011). *13 Bankers: The Wall Street Takeover and the Next Financial Meltdown*. Knopf Doubleday.

Kaufmann, D. (2003). Governance redux: The empirical challenge. World Economic Forum Global Competitiveness Report 2003–04. https://papers.ssrn.com/sol3/papers.cfm?abstract_id=541322

Kaufmann, D., & Aart Kraay. (2002). *Growth without Governance*. Economia. https://papers.ssrn.com/sol3/papers.cfm?abstract_id=316861

Kaufmann, D., & P. Vicente. (2011). Legal corruption. Economics and Politics. https://doi.org/10.1111/j.1468-0343.2010.00377.x

Kaufmann, D., A. Kraay, & M. Mastruzzi. (2010), The worldwide governance indicators: Methodology and analytical issues. World Bank Policy Research Working Paper No. 5430. Worldwide Governance Indicators (www.govindicators.org).

Khwaja, A. I., & A. Mian. (2005). Do lenders favor politically connected firms? Rent provision in an emerging financial market. *The Quarterly Journal of Economics*, 120(4), 1371–1411. https://doi.org/10.1162/003355305775097524

Kolko, G. (1963). *The Triumph of Conservatism: A Reinterpretation of American History, 1900–1916*. Chicago.

Krueger, Anne. (1974). The political economy of the rent-seeking society. *American Economic Review* pp. 291-303

Kruse, H. W., I. Martínez-Zarzoso, & L. Baghdadi. (2021). Standards and political connections: Evidence from Tunisia. *Journal of Development Economics*, 153, 102731. https://www.sciencedirect.com/science/article/pii/S0304387821001036

McCann, P. J. C., D. M. Spencer, & A. K. Wood. (2021). Measuring state capture. *Wisconsin Law Review*, 1141. https://heinonline.org/hol-cgi-bin/get_pdf.cgi?handle=hein.journals/wlr2021&section=43&casa_token=oTThrdYQA1gAAAAA:19ARKKHVsWBiHK5I34F1i6bcjhyuTpTiCkzzVXMcWZ-utUHVKZquhFzBJ0WBegNWOwgniEeMm1c

Olson, M. (1965). *The Logic of Collective Action*. Cambridge, MA: Harvard University Press.

Papadimitri, P., F. Pasiouras, G. Pescetto, & A. Wohlschlegel. (2021). Does political influence distort banking regulation? Evidence from the US. *Journal of Financial Stability*, 53, 100835. https://doi.org/10.1016/j.jfs.2020.100835

Rijkers, B., C. Freund, & A. Nucifora. (2017). All in the family: State capture in Tunisia. *Journal of Development Economics*, 124, 41–59. https://www.sciencedirect.com/science/article/pii/S0304387816300608

Roberts, Brian E. (1990). A dead senator tells no lies: Seniority and the distribution of federal benefits. *American Journal of Political Science*. Vol. 34, No. 1 (February 1990), pp. 31-58

Rose-Ackerman, S. (1978). The political economy of corruption. *Corruption and the Global Economy*, 31(60), 54. Academic Press. https://doi.org/10.1016/B978-0-12-596350-3.50005-3

Rose-Ackerman, S. (2001). Trust and honesty in post-socialist societies. *Kyklos*, 54(2–3), 415–443. https://onlinelibrary.wiley.com/doi/10.1111/1467-6435.00161

Rose-Ackerman, S. (2008). Corruption and post-conflict peacebuilding. *Ohio NUL Rev*, 34, 405. https://openyls.law.yale.edu/bitstream/handle/20.500.13051/4976/Corruption_and_Post_Conflict_Peace_Building.pdf?sequence=2&isAllowed=y

Rose-Ackerman, S. (2010). The institutional economics of corruption. In G. de Graaf, P. von Maravić, & P. Wagenaar (eds.), *The Good Cause: Theoretical Perspectives on Corruption* (1st ed., pp. 47–63). Verlag Barbara Budrich. http://www.jstor.org/stable/j.ctvbj7k5p.8

Rose-Ackerman, S., & B. J. Palifka. (1999). *Corruption and Government: Causes, Consequences, and Reform*. Cambridge University Press. https://www.cambridge.org/core/books/corruption-and-government/94925B501D79FA0357060F5489DE2F1F

Slinko, I., E. Yakovlev, & E. Zhuravskaya. (2005). Laws for sale: Evidence from Russia. *American Law and Economics Review*, 7(1), 284–318. https://academic.oup.com/aler/article/7/1/284/118107?login=true

Stoyanov, Alexander, & Alexander Gerganov. (2019). State capture: From theory to piloting a measurement methodology. https://unwe-yearbook.org/en/journalissues/article/10158

Stoyanov, Alexander, Alexander Gerganov, & Todor Yalamov. (2019). State capture assessment diagnostics. Center for the Study of Democracy. https://csd.bg/publications/publication/state-capture-assessment-diagnostics/

Winters, Jeffrey A. (2011). *Oligarchy*. Cambridge University Press.

13 Promoting political equality in healthcare

Ximena Benavides

This chapter assesses opportunities for public participation in health systems and the pursuit of justice in U.S. healthcare. I began developing these thoughts during my doctoral studies at Yale Law School under the supervision and mentorship of Professor Susan Rose-Ackerman. Her scholarship on corruption, democracy, and executive power influenced my thinking on topics of health equity, within a framework of political economy and public policy. Following in the spirit of her work, this chapter interrogates the role of markets and the distribution of political power in the design and governance of accountable social institutions – while at the same time considering legal and policy reforms that can promote more equitable access to healthcare.

According to conventional wisdom, government-provided universal healthcare is the most effective means of promoting health equity. Yet, making healthcare available to everyone, irrespective of their economic status, is insufficient to achieve the democratization of health. The political economy of the U.S. health sector demands a closer examination of what constitutes the value of health and how legal institutions should be held accountable. Although access to medical services and medicine often is a natural place to ask why human rights, democratic values, and basic moral concerns are disconnected from the economics of health markets, there is more to the equation. Firms that control the pharmaceutical market can have an immense impact on the distribution of health services, determining what, when, and whom health innovations benefit. For example, in the name of spurring invention and innovation, legal entitlements, such as patents, enable corporations to control the path of pharmaceutical research. This leaves healthcare innovations vulnerable to patent gaming practices, the exercise of monopoly power, and the absence of competition – all of which affect drug prices and, as a consequence, the availability of consumer drugs. Similarly, the failure to develop new treatments that would not reach profitability and skyrocketing lobbying expenses suggest regulatory capture. Because concerns over economic efficiency and profit maximization shape the priorities of the health system, health laws and policies often fail to address people's primary healthcare needs. Even as healthcare technology continues to develop, it may very well be disconnected from the broader values of accessibility and human rights associated with democratic societies.

This chapter argues that there are serious discrepancies between the U.S. model of healthcare innovation and democracy. Political equality, not just the greater

DOI: 10.4324/9781003416234-15

availability of services, should be a condition necessary to secure the availability of healthcare. The first section of the chapter argues that the political economy of the U.S. health system is structured in accordance with neoclassical principles of economics, prioritizing the maximization of profits before the recognition of health as a fundamental human value. The second section shifts focus to the control of medical research, specifically, the ways that large pharmaceutical companies benefit from a legal and political system that preserves their market dominance. Citizens, including patients and caregivers, are sidelined and rendered politically unable to effectively channel medical research to prioritize people's needs or to hold legal institutions and health providers accountable. The third section examines policies that might help to address political inequality. The section focuses on the collaboration between parents and scientists to fight against a rare and fatal genetic condition known as Niemann-Pick disease type C, a cholesterol metabolism disorder affecting children's life expectancy (the "NPC collaboration"). This case study of cultivating citizens' political capacity suggests how citizens can become equal partners with researchers, becoming creators in addition to beneficiaries of scientific knowledge, engaged in acts that limit corporate power, and how they can collaborate with regulators to promote a more democratic health system.

The political economy of the U.S. market-based health system

Unlike other developed countries, the United States does not legally guarantee a right to health.[1] Guaranteed access to healthcare is not a matter of constitutional[2] or statutory law.[3] Formal recognition of the right to health could not alone guarantee a national commitment to its provision and assure the conditions necessary to promote its implementation and preservation. Nevertheless, the lack of such rights contributes to the belief that a right to health *for all* is out of reach in the U.S.

Following legal scholarship that recognizes that higher lawmaking occurs in more ways than enshrinement in the constitutional text,[4] health scholar Christina Ho contends that a right to health *does* undergird U.S. law.[5] Ho argues that there is already considerable groundwork established in ordinary statutes and case law that might serve as the legal basis for the right to health. Arguably, Medicare-for-All entrenches near-universal statutory health rights in law, at least for those 65 and older, as does the Patient Protection and Affordable Care Act (ACA) for the populations it applies to.[6] Other developments in U.S law suggest an expanded right to health. In a series of high-stakes cases, judges have framed their decisions as "valuing or honoring the sanctity of health and protecting it from unjustified compromise."[7] This "rights-building work," Ho argues, could be feasibly and meaningfully expanded through policies, making *health as a value* a priority.[8] Health reformers would then need to decide what that value is and how far they are willing to go to advance it.[9] Contemporary decisions of the United States Supreme Court[10] – including pre-pandemic decisions[11] – however, suggest there are sharp divisions over the right to health across political groups. Although court decisions ultimately deal with public health concerns,[12] and offer grounds for right-to-health thinking, making health a priority for the citizenry of the United States still seems not to be an institutional priority. Instead, constitutional decisions favor the wealthy and private sector dominant groups, with a general disregard for overall public health.[13]

U.S. law follows a similarly individualistic pattern when it regulates the health market. Although the U.S. healthcare model is governed by principles of choice and competition, paradoxically, it has fallen short when it comes to adequately serving the *needs of consumers* – especially in the domain of healthcare.[14] In denying access to affordable healthcare (e.g., prescription drugs), the model fails to uphold the value of health as a right.[15] It is for this reason that health law scholar Allison Hoffman, in examining laws and policies of the U.S. health insurance market, concludes that consumerist principles have produced "exactly the opposite result": a myth of choice and a market bureaucracy "captured by powerful, vested interests."[16] Already in the 1960s, American Nobel Prize economist and political theorist Kenneth J. Arrow, in his seminal piece on modern health economics, warned about the special characteristics of health markets. With information asymmetry significantly higher in medical care than other markets, people defer meaningful *choices* to others, not necessarily as expressions of freedom and trust, but of uncertainty.[17] Given marked information asymmetry and self-serving behaviors by medical suppliers and providers, the conditions necessary for a competitive market, such as the agency and free choice of users, are arguably lacking. Furthermore, healthcare may be a "credence good" that consumers have trouble evaluating even after they have obtained medical goods and services.[18]

Problems stemming from uncertainty run deeper than the difficulty that individuals have in making appropriate medical and lifestyle choices. Health is not solely determined by individuals' choices but by systemic features of society. For instance, certain populations are more likely to die from treatable conditions than others not as a result of their individual choices[19] or biological differences alone,[20] but rather "primarily [as] a product of systemic forces" that make health disparities endure.[21] Structural forms of *subordination*,[22] such as race and class divisions, are the result of policies, practices, norms, and culture; they hold down one social group while benefiting others. These have contributed to enduring differentials among population groups that affect their health and well-being.[23] Regulatory policies that view health disparities as resulting from "market failures" thus fail to confront the structural conditions that sustain these inequities.[24]

An individual's health is mediated by the person's broader political-economic context. Incorporating the value of health into social policy is difficult if political institutions and power structures conflict with policies that would facilitate more equitable health outcomes.[25] Since the Reagan administration, Democratic and Republican administrations alike have enacted social policies in an environment that "relies heavily on the industry to achieve social welfare goals."[26] Overall the healthcare industry has been extremely active in lobbying political campaigns at the federal and state levels,[27] and the pharmaceutical industry has the largest lobbying budget in the country.[28] Just in the last decade, the number of companies lobbying and their spending levels have significantly increased, growing more than 70% during the pandemic.[29] The biggest campaign contributions made by the pharmaceutical industry have coincided with periods when drug-pricing legislation was in contention. Lobbying activity was high before the passage of the ACA, during presidential elections where health was a crucial topic, during the COVID-19 pandemic, and surrounding the approval of novel mRNA technology vaccines for emergency use.[30] Individual companies and wealthy activists find multiple ways other than outright lobbying to influence the health system, preserve the status quo, gain an advantage, or fight proposals seen as damaging "its" market. Consider, for example, user fees that supplement the annual funding the Food and Drug Administration (FDA) receives from Congress, which are negotiated with the industry every five years in exchange for performance commitments, such as accelerated drug approvals.[31] Evidence of the industry's practices indicates that health disparities are not exclusively "market failures" but are mostly *policy choices* directed by a few actors unduly exercising their power. This state of affairs demands a stronger and more critical political-economic analysis of health institutions in law and policymaking.[32]

The value of health in access to medicine

Access to medicine is heavily influenced by vested interests. Market dominant actors and power structures influence the governance of health access. Law and policy fundamentally shape the market power of actors in the health economy. For example, research and production of new health technologies, from drugs and vaccines to devices and treatments, rely on a model of innovation embedded in a "patent culture" that, in the name of promoting investment in innovation, consolidates power in a few firms through "temporary" entitlements of exclusivity, making biopharmaceutical development highly dependent on the industry's need to make profits.[33] Under this model, the social benefit of innovation is determined by the marketplace; "getting a product to market is the goal."[34] In other words, a goal compatible with corporate interests. This is a departure from the "progress of science and the useful arts," the Constitution's language granting rights to authors and inventors.[35] Because of business influence over the health system, and medical research more specifically, today's critical challenges to biopharmaceutical innovation are not exclusively scientific (e.g., competent scientists and research facilities) or financial (e.g., available funding) but rather fundamentally related to the democratic governance of the knowledge economy.[36] As it continues to grow, the knowledge economy is increasingly disconnected from the basic values and broader concerns behind the constitutional goal of progress: distributive justice, institutional accountability, community, collaboration, *equality*.[37] The production of safe, effective, and quality health technologies and their equitable allocation to populations in need, rely on supply-driven regulations and market-driven mechanisms that remain in tension with public health concerns. Is there "progress" when science develops a lifesaving medical treatment that is widely inaccessible because of high prices and wealth barriers, beyond the reach of ordinary people, and leaving many massively undertreated? Consider hepatitis C, which afflicts some 2.4 million people in the United States. Remarkably effective drugs to treat the ailment were approved by the FDA during the last decade but remain prohibitively expensive for many people who need them most. Or, most recently at a global level, treatments against the coronavirus where drug innovation did not reach global populations timely and equitably, creating a vaccine apartheid across countries and regions.[38] Given rising health inequalities and looming public health crises, the pharmaceutical industry's claim that it needs property-like rights as an incentive to recuperate their economic investments requires critical examination.[39]

The pharmaceutical industry has not only become one of the most powerful actors in the global political economy, it has concentrated political power via regulatory capture and aggressive lobbying for protections and special treatment.[40] As noted earlier, the pharmaceutical industry is one of the most politically powerful in the United States.[41] The power of the sector extends globally. During the Covid-19 pandemic, for example, wealthy countries refused to waive multilateral agreements on intellectual property (TRIPS)[42] or exercise compulsory licenses authorized by law for reasons of public interest, or they subscribed to secret pre-marketization agreements regarding publicly funded vaccines. All of these actions, which were a response to lobbying by the drug industry, greatly disadvantaged developing countries.[43]

The U.S. government plays a fundamental role in driving the private sector's development of new therapeutics. The government does not engage in biopharmaceutical manufacturing itself, despite advantages of scale, distribution, and despite precedents for the government's legal right to use patented discoveries or to order production to address public health needs.[44] However, the government remains an important investor in early-stage research. Studies show that half to two-thirds of the most important or transformative drugs since 1965 were associated with public funding, especially in the discovery stages of basic science before scientific findings are translated into potential disease treatments.[45] Public contributions have increased over the years. All drugs approved by the FDA from 2010 to 2019 were developed with the help of funds allocated by the National Institutes of Health (NIH).[46] In the development of mRNA COVID-19 vaccines amidst a deadly pandemic, public investment was extraordinary compared to other publicly funded health technologies.[47] One study has estimated that the NIH, combined with other U.S. government grants, invested $31.9 billion to develop the mRNA technology and produce and purchase mRNA COVID-19 vaccines, early before the pandemic.[48] Pre-pandemic funding included at least $337 million in long-term capital to produce basic and translational technologies to create the mRNA vaccines and $1.8 billion for Moderna's clinical trials. During the pandemic, government buyers created the market for COVID-19 vaccines through advance purchasing agreements with a public investment of $29.2 billion for 2 billion vaccine doses.[49] Importantly, the U.S. government was a risk-taking technology investor and developer, essential in shaping all stages of technology development, production, and procurement of mRNA COVID-19 vaccines. Despite the public financing of basic research, "it is up to the private industry to get products to the public."[50] Traditional policy thinking still describes the government's funding role in private biomedical research restrictively as "fixing market failures,"[51] when what the government is actually doing is directing public resources to advance social interests, and in doing so, assigning them a public value. This narrow understanding of the government funding role limits the possibilities of conditioning funding agreements on health equity-access or to secure inclusion in innovation processes supported by public funding. For example, a recent 2019–2020 clinical-trials analysis found that close to 29% of federally funded clinical trials excluded participants with limited English proficiency.[52] Another study showed that over the past 25 years people from racial and ethnic minorities have accounted for only 4% of trial participants, including NIH-funded studies.[53]

Neglecting treatment

The profit motive can direct the development of medicines toward innovations, serving markets that are perceived to be high-value and away from the task of discovering cures for health challenges across the board. The proliferation of examples of scientific development being guided almost exclusively by profit versus the public value of the science is troubling. The uneven distribution of COVID-19 vaccines globally during the pandemic and the high costs of treatments for diseases considered top U.S. mortality causes, such as cancer or diabetes, are only some examples.[54] Preventive treatments and vaccines are often sidelined in favor of high-incidence chronic or lifelong medical treatments because the latter represent better prospects for sales.[55] Studies published over the last two decades show that drug makers' profit prioritization affects drug design and clinical testing.[56] Therapeutical treatments for diseases prominent in the Western market offer a higher financial value and, hence, are more attractive to develop and manufacture. Infectious diseases were marginal parts of research agendas between 1999 and 2018.[57] In the same vein, the Access to Medicine Foundation 2022 report reveals that only a fourth of the companies covered engage in bolstering R&D pipelines for emerging infectious diseases other than COVID-19.[58] The concern of underproduction is even bigger because decisions of biopharmaceutical innovation (e.g., when, which, and how many products to manufacture, for what populations, and at what price) are highly dependent on the production capacity and commercial motivations of a few biopharmaceutical firms. With U.S. pharmaceutical companies representing at least 40% of drug production globally, their approach to innovation exerts an extraordinary influence over global public health.[59]

Governments attempt to address the risk of underproduction of new products that are commercially unprofitable through a combination of tools such as prizes, patents, and R&D grants. However, unless conditions are imposed over these forms of funding, many of these tools can end up expanding health disparities in access to medicine. The inequitable access to mRNA COVID-19, despite significant public funding, is a prominent example. More recently, U.S. Senator Bernie Sanders proposed that the Pandemic Preparedness Act be amended to award cash prizes, in lieu of intellectual property protections, to companies when they invent drugs as a way to delink the costs of inventing drugs from their prices.[60] Despite these efforts, the concern remains that too few resources are being directed to vaccines or therapies aimed at infectious diseases.[61] A public pharma movement that encourages the government to get into the business of making medicines is gaining traction. This movement is urging U.S. states to respond to the national crisis on drug shortages and high prices, in contrast to supporting further public subsidies.[62] Ultimately, if inventions cannot leave the laboratory bench to reach the marketplace, lifesaving medicines face the risk of underproduction and timely access. Considering the dominant position of the United States in the pharmaceutical market, the risk of global health disparities increases as well.

Neglecting innovation

In addition to skewing the direction of investment and research, industry-government interactions *neglect the value of innovation*. As described earlier, the government regularly funds basic scientific research and drug discovery, which are performed principally by academic institutions or government laboratories. Findings are transmitted to the private sector for development, a strategy that contrasts with the original role of sponsors that the FDA envisioned for the industry in the 1960s.[63] Although the U.S. government's involvement in the development of science has been almost always significant,[64] it fails to direct public investment to the most socially valuable uses.[65] For example, when Pfizer and Moderna used their capital from sales of publicly funded mRNA COVID-19 vaccines to conduct massive shareholder buybacks, they signaled that their corporate goals were primarily to boost their share price rather than directly to reinvest in innovation. Between 2021 and 2022, Moderna announced or executed $7 billion in share buybacks and spent $4 billion on research and development.[66] Moderna is a newcomer to the pharmaceutical sector, that never produced a commercial drug before the pandemic,[67] but Pfizer's actions during the decade before the pandemic indicate a pattern of value extraction in the name of maximizing shareholder value.[68] Additionally, Moderna and Pfizer announced plans to charge more than $110 per vaccine dose in the United States in 2023 (though each dose cost an estimated $1 to $3 to manufacture). To many, it is morally troubling that big pharmaceutical companies are prioritizing profit amidst a deadly public health crisis. Even more troublingly, public funding for drug development lacks ties to health equity goals. In the context of inequitable access to mRNA COVID-19 vaccines globally,[69] a health equity goal could have required intellectual property rights (patents and trade secrets) and technology transfer to multiply efforts to produce vaccines, particularly in underserved regions.[70] Instead of public funding serving to maximize value for corporate shareholders, innovation ought to have been connected to health equity goals that can "translate public investments more fully in the service of public health."[71] Drugs reaching certain populations with unmet needs or making patients healthier and safer seem to have been afterthoughts, excluded from the priority setting of the innovation model.[72]

The pharmaceutical industry's power has also contributed to the high drug prices paid in the United States compared to other developed countries.[73] Intellectual property law does not provide a system to oversee prices, and antitrust laws do not police patents.[74] The Inflation Reduction Act (IRA), passed under the Biden

Administration, authorizes the federal health insurance program and the biggest client of drug companies, Medicare, for the first time, to negotiate the prices of some prescription drugs. It is too early to determine IRA's success in drug price reduction, but this law does subject the industry to scrutiny. Big drug companies such as Johnson & Johnson and Merck have already challenged IRA's drug-pricing program in federal courts, regarding it as a form of government price control and arguing that its provisions are unconstitutional – specifically, that they violate the First and Fifth Amendments.[75] The industry calls the IRA and programs for lowering prices that affect their revenues a discouragement to developing *innovative drugs*.[76] In contrast, pharmaceutical policy expert Ameet Sarpatwari contends that the IRA might incentivize the industry to focus on breakthrough therapies rather than drugs structurally very similar to old ones because clinically meaningful benefits are now required under the IRA in determining the price Medicare will pay for drugs.[77] The value of health will again be tested through the industry's litigation strategy to confront the IRA, which will probably reach the U.S. Supreme Court.

Political equality for health justice

The goal of health justice demands closer attention to power and politics.[78] A focus on power pushes us to interrogate the political process—powerful interest groups and business-government coalitions—that perpetuate health inequities.[79] Legislative and administrative processes can be exercises of technocratic expertise dominated by those *few* exercising political-economic power, both public (e.g., federal health agencies) and private (e.g., the heavy-lobbying drug industry) actors. Rules affecting society gain political legitimacy when they are set by those whom they affect rather than by a "ruling class."[80] Political legitimacy comes not just from the election of lawmakers and policymakers but also through participation in the processes of government that implement the law.[81] In contrast to compulsion and citizens' submission,[82] the essence of democracy is the opportunity to participate in the formation of the communal will.[83] To achieve health justice, those affected by health laws and policies – by their lack of enforcement, absence, or gaming – ought to play a role in their determination so the social benefit of healthcare innovation, for instance, represents their needs and interests.[84]

Susan Rose-Ackerman's scholarship identifies public participation and accountability as the foundations of modern democratic government.[85] To that end, a regulatory system encapsulates democracy in action as long as it invites and empowers members of society to work with a responsive administrative state to design and implement policies.[86] Policy choices ought not to be purely technical exercises; at the same time, policymakers should not displace technical expertise by turning policy decisions over to citizens. Rather, governments need technical experts' input without "leav[ing] final policy choices to technocrats with no special claims either to make value choices or represent the voting public."[87] Discussions about whether innovation has settled on the right solution, its impact on society, and whether there are unexplored alternatives or overlooked governance models become even more critical if one fears regulatory capture of technical experts by the pharmaceutical sector's lobbying practices.[88]

Those who wish to create a more just healthcare system need to change the structural political position of people and communities in political processes.[89] Citizens need the power to participate and the capacity to influence political environments. For Rose-Ackerman, there are two major obstacles to increasing public participation.[90] First, citizens often do not have the technical knowledge deemed necessary for constructive participation. They lack technical knowledge and medical expertise. The economic theory of credence goods goes further to recognize that patients may not be able to evaluate the impact of medical treatment even after they have experienced it.[91] Information asymmetry can overly narrow the range of deliberation by citizens and subordinate their input to that of experts.

Several illustrative community-led initiatives support my arguments for public participation in accountable political processes. A 2007 collaboration between parents – *citizen scientists* – and scientists and clinical researchers – *professional scientists* – is one U.S. example that shows how citizens can contribute to science access. Parents of children with a fatal genetic, cholesterol metabolism disorder, Niemann-Pick disease type C (NPC), organized a meeting at the NIH lab to capture the attention of scientific researchers and urge them to seek a treatment.[92] Children with the disorder experienced declining cognitive abilities and motor skills, most of them dying by the age of nineteen. By screening the drug libraries of skin cells of children with NPC, using a robotics system that rivaled those used by pharmaceutical companies, they generated a list of promising drugs and narrowed it to potential candidates for development. Parents set up a collaboration with researchers and doctors and endeavored to find an effective drug and accelerate the typical timeline for the development of new drugs. Of most significance, parents became "citizen scientists." They were not simply research subjects but creators of scientific knowledge.[93] They gathered and analyzed their own medical data. They tested a promising compound (cyclodextrin) in clinical trials. They co-authored scientific papers, sharing findings. Later, parents engaged directly with the FDA at each step of the drug approval process. These parents rebelled against traditional medical research, conducted in isolation by groups of researchers who wield more information and knowledge than patients or caregivers, with practically no rules that allow groups of patients and caregivers to drive science. Of course, the NPC collaboration was not free of moral concerns. For example, there were disagreements on whether their examination of the benefits of various drugs should consider what was in the best interests of their own children or what was in the best interests of a broader and future (unborn) community of patients. The absence of a clear way to resolve their differences led to the idea for a written agreement between all members of the collaboration.[94] Certainly, many research ethics rules were not written expecting parents to drive research. Overall, the parents-scientists NPC collaboration fundamentally tested the idea that, despite their different agendas and approaches toward the production of science, professional scientists can work with citizen scientists as *equal partners* to identify and develop potential treatments for diseases that were not attractive to pharmaceutical and health technology companies because they affect a small population.[95] They prioritized the common goal of finding a way to extend the lives of the affected children. This is a particularly important goal for certain lethal or rare diseases for which the market could be too small to justify expending the resources and investment required to identify and test novel drugs and get them approved.

A second factor that Rose-Ackerman identifies as further complicating public participation is that members of the executive often override agency expertise with regulation that maximize partisan political objectives.[96] Consider the drug-industry lobbying that accompanies the passage of crucial pieces of legislation. Equally complicating, yet less debated, is the unwarranted faith the system places in the expertise of health agencies, courts, and legal institutions, overlooking their political dimension. Legal scholar Aziza Ahmed has offered a progressive critique of the relationship between health law, evidence, and expertise, contrasting the anti-science policies of conservatives and the follow-the-evidence policies of progressives who defer to expert medical or scientific authority.[97] With a health justice frame, Ahmed challenges several assumptions of the follow-the-evidence approach: that expertise and evidence itself are apolitical and neutral, that evidence is settled, that evidence and expertise are generated distinct from law, and that basing health law on evidence rather than political considerations is preferable. These assumptions overlook the fact that legal institutions are part of a larger political ecosystem "that will legitimate particular ideas about whose health matters and why."[98] Ahmed claims that a follow-the-evidence approach does not necessarily "depoliticiz[e] decision making in health spaces and keep them in the realm of the technocratic."[99] Two controversial pandemic-era decisions, which reached contradictory progressive positions about evidence-based regulation, support her claim.[100] "Achieving health justice requires an active critique of expertise and evidence rather than a simple deference to it."[101] Moreover, the patron–client relationship between the industry and politicians, evidenced by aggressive health lobbying, reinforces the idea that expertise and evidence are politicized.

Providing citizens with the political capacity to foster public participation is not an easy task in the political economy of the U.S. health sector, which has historically been relatively insulated from democratic scrutiny.[102] Activist efforts, from HIV in the 1980s to cancer and disability more recently, have shaped participation policies (e.g., in clinical trials), and yet gains still fall short of full participation.[103] The attainment of *equitable access* to health (e.g., to safe, high-quality medicine) is a social justice value, and, as such, should not be sidelined to accommodate policies focused only on market efficiency. A renovated liberal perspective of social justice thinks critically about market rules and pays attention to the ways in which political roles and social practices can potentially generate social injustices. This contemporary perspective suggests that social justice is attainable in market-led environments through *power-balancing* tools, the redistribution of *political roles*, and structures that prevent the control of political processes by those with economic power.[104]

Health justice scholars frame power shifting in terms of *breaking and building* power.[105] Building power entails cultivating the political capacity of people who are disproportionately harmed by health inequities, including anyone whose health is imperiled under present conditions. Forms of empowerment include the revival of grassroots and social movements, community organizing, and the introduction of novel approaches to governance, policymaking, civil technology, and institutional design, as well as similar avenues for countervailing power against antimajoritarian political institutions,[106] rather than quick or opaque policy fixes.[107] NPC is a valuable example of power building with the NPC parents using the internet to find one another and get together with other like-minded patients or families in chat groups and organized communities on social media platforms,[108] building power for parents to become politically equal to scientists. Parents from six family-run foundations participated in the launch of the project. Over time, the number of families expanded and their roles diversified, from weighing in on the trials to helping fund the research and participating in meetings with the FDA or NIH, among many other contributions. "[W]hat connects many pioneers in citizen science is the ability to form social networks" through a combination of proxies for organizing a community.[109] Parents described cyclodextrin, whose development was at the center of the NPC collaboration, as "the community's drug."

Conversely breaking up concentrated power involves weakening and dismantling the existing political and economic configurations, including those embedded in social structures that help to perpetuate health inequities.[110] Efforts to break power may involve not only those who are most harmed but those in coalitions with "those who hold kinds of power that need to be broken."[111] Establishing limits to profiteering (e.g., cutting back on pharmaceutical tax benefits and exemptions) and encouraging state action to curb the power of actors (e.g., FDA regulatory capture) are strategies for breaking power.[112] These mechanisms to democratize the economy of health require the greater involvement of people in systems of government – "governing citizens" – and to avoid people becoming subject to unchecked private or state power[113] that "assert[s] its collective will over the economic order."[114] Again, the NCP collaboration is illustrative. Due to its strategic maneuvering with institutions (e.g., the NIH and the FDA), the NPC collaboration could also be seen as a case of breaking power. The NPC collaboration can be interpreted as contesting the morally troubling idea that the economy of science – the level of the investment and the size of the market – should determine which medical conditions deserve research attention and should be treated.[115] Professional scientists have declared a moral obligation to help citizen scientists in patient-led research.[116] Relations of power within community-led projects are important to monitor (e.g., whether members all belong to an affluent class) to ensure that social patterns of segregation and dominance are not replicated or expanded, and to avoid patient-led initiatives that only include powerful groups (e.g., patient-advocacy groups funded by the industry) involved in the administration of scientific research.

Conclusion

From ideation to production, the existing healthcare innovation model is programmed to achieve a narrow "social benefit" – one shaped by vested interests.

Such a model does not represent the values of a democratic society. Stark inequalities and intensifying public health crises require us to think harder about intellectual property rights and the governance of healthcare, refiguring the value of health and the meaning of progress. Because politics are not separate from the economy, and because we have the capacity to build the type of economy we want in a democracy, these goals are ultimately moral imperatives. Health governance ought to deliver *trust* to stakeholders and constituencies – those who fulfill the moral obligation of care that all stakeholders of a democracy owe one another – and hold them *accountable* to each other.

Political equality is foundational to the attainment of health equity and justice. Toward that end, community empowerment and public participation promise to democratize health decision-making processes and, as a result, the systems that result. Fostering political equality demands that law and policymakers provide a more careful assessment of legal institutions as democratic spaces. The NPC collaboration is only one example, of other many community-led initiatives, that suggests "the radical idea that science must belong to us all,"[117] and that "technical expertise does not equal social wisdom."[118] Integrating more diverse forms of community and expert input into the traditional innovation process brings benefits to technological development as much as to the public interest – at the least, it favors broad access to treatments. A power-shifting model in innovation governance processes offers an opportunity for end users to democratically participate and influence the governance of the health systems "that serve them;" for innovation to serve the public good; and for democratic governments to be less detracted from addressing health inequities and achieving health justice. In other words, an opportunity for users of health systems to act and be treated as *equals*.

Notes

1 Eleanor D. Kinney & Brian A. Clark, Provisions for Health and Health Care in the Constitutions of the Countries of the World, 37 *Cornell Int'l. L.J.* 285, 291 (2004) (concluding that 67.5% of the constitutions of UN member states – excluding the United States – have a right to health or healthcare provision); *see also* Alicia Ely Yamin and Tara Boghosian, Democracy and Health: Situating Health Rights Within a Republic of Reasons, 19 *Yale J. Health Pol'y L. & Ethics* 96 (2020) (arguing that the right to health and healthcare lacks a human rights perspective in the United States). The 'right to health' phrase refers both to a right to health and a right to healthcare. Following Norman Daniels' work on health policy and distributive justice, health refers to actions and conditions, beyond medical services and including health-related ones, that promote, restore, or maintain health and forbid its interference. A 'right to health' label, therefore, refers to securing the equitable distribution of those actions and conditions, regardless of the attainment of health outcomes. *See* Norman Daniels, *Just Health* 145 (2008).

2 U.S. Const. art. 1, § 8. *See* Kinney and Clark, *supra* note 1 at 290–91 (referring that the U.S. Constitution's provisions that authorize the enactment of general welfare laws do not refer to health as a duty or an entitlement).

3 Allison K. Hoffman, Health Care's Market Bureaucracy, 66 *UCLA L. Rev.* 1926 (2019).

4 Bruce Ackerman, *We the People: The Civil Rights Revolution* 26–27 (2014); William N. Eskridge and John Ferrejohn, Super-Statutes, 50 *Duke L.J.* 1215, 1216 (2001).

5 Christina S. Ho, *Normalizing an American Right to Health* (2023). (Ho's postulation is framed in terms of resistance against what failing to recognize the right to health represents to a national democratic identity.)
6 Ibid. at 2, 51–54, 57–61 (referring also to the work of Erin C. Fuse Brown, Developing a Durable Right to Health Care, 14 *Minn. J.L., Sci & Tech.* 439 (2013)).
7 Ibid. at 97–98 (referring, for example, to the litigation against tobacco companies in the 1990s and the U.S. Supreme Court decision about the FDA authority over cigarettes). *See* FDA v. Brown & Williamson Tobacco Corp., 529 U.S. 120 (2000).
8 Ibid. at 3, 23.
9 Marc J. Roberts et al., *Getting Health Reform Right. A Guide to Improving Performance and Equity* 55–58 (2008).
10 James G. Hodge et al., Supreme Court Impacts in Public Health Law: 2022–2023, *J. Law, Med. & Ethics* (forthcoming), https://papers.ssrn.com/sol3/papers.cfm?abstract_id=4507621 (last visited August 28, 2023).
11 Wendy E. Parmet, *Constitutional Contagion. Covid, the Courts, and Public Health* (2023) (documenting how the U.S. Supreme Court pre-pandemic cases helped to shatter social contracts, weaken democracy, and perpetuate the inequities that made the U.S. especially vulnerable during COVID-19).
12 Health Law Professors Conference, University of Maryland Carey School of Law. Plenary Session: Supreme Court Decisions and Their Implications for Our Health (Natalie Ram moderator, Greer Donley, Renée M. Landers, Michael Ulrich and Heather Walter-McCabe, discussants) (June 8, 2023) (suggesting "everything is about health"); *see also* Lindsay F. Wiley et al., Eliminating Racism In Health Care Before and After the Supreme Court's Affirmative Action Decision, *Health Affairs* (July 7, 2023), www.healthaffairs.org/content/forefront/eliminating-racism-health-care-before-and-after-supreme-court-s-affirmative-action (referring to the adverse implications of the Court's affirmative action decision for medical schools, programs that train clinicians and public health policymakers, and other realms where institutional leaders and policymakers rely on race-conscious policies to promote health equity).
13 *See* Parmet *supra* note 11.
14 *See* Deborah Stone, The False Promise of Consumer Choice, 51 *St. Louis U. L.J.* 474 (2007).
15 Ho, *supra* note 5, at 4.
16 Hoffman, *supra* note 3, at 1934 (arguing that neither of these promises has been – nor will ever be – realized).
17 Kenneth J. Arrow, Uncertainty and the Welfare Economics of Medical Care, 53 *Am. Econ. Rev.* 941, 948–54 (1963). ("As a . . . consequence of informational inequality . . ., the patient must delegate to the physician much of his freedom of choice." Ibid. at. 965.).
18 *See* Esben S. Andersen and Kristian Philipsen, The Evolution of Credence Goods in Customer Markets: Exchanging "Pigs in Pokes" (paper presented at the DRUID Winter Seminar, Middelfart, Jan. 8–10, 1998); *see generally* Phillip Nelson, Information & Consumer Behavior, 78 *J. Pol. Econ.* 311 (1970).
19 Emerged in the late 1970s, healthism blames bad health on bad moral character. For example, obese people are judged as lazy and ignorant. *See* Robert Crawford, Healthism and the Medicalization of Everyday Life, 10 *Int'l J. Health Servs.* 365, 365–78 (1980).
20 Eduardo Bonilla-Silva, The Essential Social Fact of Race, 64 *Am. Socio. Rev.* 899 (1999).
21 Jamila Michener, Health Justice Through the Lens of Power, 50 *J.L., Med. & Ethics* 656, 656–57 (2022). *See generally* Angela P. Harris and Aysha Pamukcu, The Civil Rights of Health: A New Approach to Challenging Structural Inequality, 67 *UCLA L. Rev.* 758, 766–67 (2020); Chloe Thurston, Racial Inequality, Market Inequality, and the American Political Economy, in *The American Political Economy: Politics, Markets,*

and Power 133 (Jacob Hacker et al. eds., 2022); Paula Braverman, What Are Health Disparities and Health Equity? We Need to Be Clear, 129 *Pub. Health Reps.* (Supp. 5) (2014), www.ncbi.nlm.nih.gov/pmc/articles/PMC3863701/ [https://perma.cc/X4LZ-EUBR]

22 Harris & Pamukcu, Ibid., at 792–805.

23 Michener, *supra* note 21, at 657.

24 Ximena Benavides, Inequitable by Design, 56 *U. Mich. J.L. Reform* (2023), (arguing that health inequities are avoidable policy choices).

25 Marc J. Roberts et al., *Getting Health Reform Right, A Guide to Improving Performance and Equity* 57 (2008).

26 Hoffman, *supra* note 3 at 1934; *see also* Frank Pasquale, The Hidden Costs of Health Care Cost-Cutting: Toward a Post-Neoliberal Health-Reform Agenda, 77 L. *Contemp. Probs*. 171, 176 (2014) (contending that health policies build an environment that overly seeks maximization of returns). *See generally* Paul Starr, *The Social Transformation of American Medicine. The Rise of a Sovereign Profession and the Making of a Vast Industry* (2017) (offering a sociological account of the political struggles over healthcare and the rise of a corporate system in the history of the U.S. healthcare system).

27 *See* Industries, *OpenSecrets*, www.opensecrets.org/federal-lobbying/industries?cycle=a [https://perma.cc/H5J8-72L6] (last visited July 13, 2023). (In 2021, the pharmaceutical industry spent an average of $353 billion on federal lobbying, followed by the electronics industry with $185 billion.).

28 Olivier J. Wouters, Lobbying Expenditures and Campaign Contributions by the Pharmaceutical and Health Product Industry in the United States 1999–2018, *JAMA Internal Med.* 180 (1) 2020.

29 Alyce McFadden, Pharma Loses Vaccine IP Battle Despite Record Q1 Lobbying, *Open Secrets*. May 5, 2021; Tara Suter, Lobbying Efforts by Companies Making COVID-19 Rapid Tests and Vaccine Fluctuate, *Open Secrets*. Nov. 8, 2021.

30 *Open Secrets*, *supra* note 27.

31 *See* www.fda.gov/industry/fda-user-fee-programs/fda-user-fees-explained (last accessed, July 21, 2023); Christina Jewett, F.D.A.'s Drug Industry Fees Fuel Concerns Over Influence, *New York Times,* September 15, 2022, www.nytimes.com/2022/09/15/health/fda-drug-industry-fees.html (citing Yale Medicine Professor, Reshma Ramachandran, who refers to the pressure the drug industry exerts over the agency).

32 Ximena Benavides, The Law and Political Economy of Healthcare in the United States, in *Markets, Constitutions, and Inequality* (Anna Chadwick et al. eds., 2022).

33 Benavides, *supra* note 24.

34 Shobita Parthasarathy, Can Innovation Serve the Public Good? *Boston Review*, July 6, 2023.

35 U.S. Constitution, Article I, §8, cl. 8. *See* Jessica Silbey, *Against Progress. Intellectual Property and Fundamental Values in the Internet Age* (2022)

36 *Kaushik Sunder Rajan, Value, Politics, and Knowledge in Global Medicine* (2017); Fatima Hassan, Vaccine Apartheid Is Racist and Wrong, *PLOS Global Public Health*

37 Silbey, *supra* note 35.

38 (May 23, 2022).

39 The 'grand incentive narrative' of intellectual property has been proved incomplete to false in several fields. *See* Simone A. Rose, The Supreme Court and Patents: Moving Toward a Postmodern Vision of Progress?, *Fordham Intellectual Property Media and Entertainment Law Journal* 23 (2013): 1197–219; Margaret Chon, Post-modern "Progress": Reconsidering the Copyright and Patent Power, *De Paul Law Review* 43 (1993): 97–146; Jessica Silbey, *The Eureka Myth: Creators, Innovators, and Everyday Intellectual Property* (2015). On health inequities *see* Health Justice: Engaging Critical Perspectives in Health Law and Policy Symposium, 50 *J.L., Med. & Ethics* 636

(Lindsay F. Wiley et al. eds., 2022). On looming public health crises, *see* Mun-Keat Looi, What Could The Next Pandemic Be? *BMJ* 2023; 381.

40 *See* Amy Kapczynski, The Law of Informational Capitalism. 129 (5) *Yale L.J.* 1276; Amy Kapczynski, The Political Economy of Market Power in Pharmaceuticals, *J Health Polit. Policy Law*. September 27, 2022. https://doi.org/10.1215/03616878-10234184

41 Nicholas Florko and Lev Facher, How Pharma, under Attack from All Sides, Keeps Winning in Washington. *STAT News*, July 16, 2019.

42 TRIPs is the World Trade Organization (WTO) Agreement on Trade-Related Aspects of Intellectual Property (IP) Rights, which introduced IP rules into the multilateral trading system applicable to WTO's members.

43 Horti et al., Who Killed the COVID vaccine waiver? The inside story of lobbying, threats and the desire to protect industry gutted a proposal that was meant to make vaccines widely available in poorer countries. *Politico. Investigation*. November 10, 2022.

44 *See* Christopher Morten and Charles Duan, Who's Afraid of Section 1498? A Case for Government Patent Use in Pandemics and Other National Crises, 23 *Yale J.L. & Tech.* 1 (2020); Dana Brown and Christopher Morten, Public pharma is the best solution to the ongoing problem of drug shortages. *STAT News*, Aug. 9, 2023 (offering examples of public manufacturing in the past and current state proposals for public drug manufacturing).

45 Iain Cockburn and Rebecca M. Henderson, Publicly funded science and the productivity of the pharmaceutical industry, *Innov. Policy Econ* 1:1-34., 2001; Ranjana Chakravarthy et al., Public- and Private-Sector Contributions to the Research and Development of the Most Transformational Drugs in the Past 25 Years: From Theory to Therapy, *Ther. Innov. Regul. Sci.* 50(6): 759–68. 2016.

46 Ekaterina G. Cleary, et al., Contribution of NIH funding to new drug approvals 2010–2016. 115(10) *PNAS* 2329–34. February 12, 2018; Showing updated data of funding of drugs approved until 2019, *see* Ekaterina G. Cleary, et al., Government as the First Investor in Biopharmaceutical Innovation: Evidence From New Drug Approvals 2010-2019, *Institute for New Economic Thinking* Working Paper Series No. 133. https://doi.org/10.36687/inetwp133 July 20, 2021.

47 Benavides, *supra* note 24.

48 Lalani, Hussain et al., US public investment in development of mRNA covid-19 vaccines: retrospective cohort study. *BMJ* 202 (indicating $5.9bn in indirectly related NIH grants).

49 Ibid.

50 Parthasarathy, *supra* note 34.

51 Victor Roy, *Financing Covid-19 mRNA vaccines*, *BMJ* 2023; 380: 413. March 2023. On fixing market failures, *see* Mariana Mazzucato, From market fixing to market-creating: a new framework for innovation policy. *Industry & Innovation* 2016; 23: 140–56.

52 Muthukumar et al., Evaluating the frequency of English language requirements in clinical trial eligibility criteria: A systematic analysis using clinicaltrials.gov. *PLOS Medicine* 18(9): e1003758 (2021)

53 Ma et al., Minority representation in clinical trials in the United States. *Mayo Clinic Proceedings* 96(1): 264–66 (2021)

54 *See* Benavides, *supra* note 24.

55 Elvira Thissen, Focus on pharma: Creating a market for disease prevention, *GreenBiz*, December 5, 2014, www.greenbiz.com/article/focus-pharma-creating-market-disease-prevention

56 UCL Institute for Innovation and Public Purpose (IIPP), *The People's Prescription. Re-imagining health innovation to deliver public value,* 2018: 17.

57 Federico E. Testoni et al., Whose shoulder is health research standing on? Determining key actors and contents of the prevailing biomedical research agenda, *PLoS ONE* 16(4): e0249661, April 7, 2021.
58 Access to Medicine Foundation (AMF). 2022. Access to Medicine Index 2022 https://accesstomedicinefoundation.org/medialibrary/2022-access-to-medicine-index-1668514482.pdf
59 Chris Kolmar, 26 Incredible U.S. Pharmaceutical Statistics [2023]: Facts, Data, Trends, and More. February 21, 2023. https://www.zippia.com/advice/us-pharmaceutical-statistics/ ("[U]p to 40.8% of the total global pharmaceutical market, by sales.").
60 John Wilkerson, Bernie Sanders wants to replace drug patents with prizes for breakthrough medicines. *STAT* July 20, 2023. www.statnews.com/2023/07/20/bernei-sanders-drug-patents-prize
61 William W. Fisher III, Regulating Innovation. A Response to Ian Ayres and Amy Kapczynski, Innovation Sticks: The Limited Case for Penalizing Failures to Innovate, 82 *Univ. Chic. Law Rev.* 251 (2016), 256–60.
62 Brown & Morten, *supra* note 44 (referring to the states of Michigan, Maine, and California).
63 Moses H. 3rd, et al., The anatomy of medical research: US and international comparisons. *JAMA* 313: 174–89. 2015. On the idea of sponsorship in science, *see generally* Daniel Carpenter, *Reputation and Power: Organizational Image and Pharmaceutical Regulation at the FDA* (Princeton University Press, 2014) (referring that the private sector was envisioned to sponsor a piece of legislation, rather than controlling all aspects of drug production as today).
64 *See* accompanying text to *supra* notes 46 to 49.
65 Roy, *supra* note 51.
66 Moderna. Moderna Earnings Call Presentations, 2021–2022. https://investors.modernatx.com/events-and-presentations/events/default.aspx.
67 *See* Peter Loftus and Gregory Zuckerman, Inside Moderna: The Covid Vaccine Front-Runner with No Track Record and an Unsparing CEO, *WALL ST.* J. (July 1, 2020), www.wsj.com/articles /inside-moderna-the-covid-vaccine-front-runner-with-no-track-record-and-an-unsparing-ceo11593615205 [https://perma.cc/3NR9-FCEH]; Julia Kollewe, From Pfizer to Moderna: Who's Making Billions from COVID-19 Vaccines?, *Guardian* (Mar. 6, 2021), www.theguardian.com/business/2021/mar/06/from-pfizer-to-moderna-whosmaking-billions-from-covid-vaccines [https://perma.cc/Z7SA-578G];
68 *See* Roy, *supra* note 51 (additionally referring that Pfizer spent $115bn in payouts to shareholders, $34bn more than it spent on R&D); Pfizer, Pfizer 2021 Annual Report – Financial Performance, www.pfizer.com /sites/default/files/investors/financial_reports/annual_reports/2021/performance/ [https://perma.cc /YKU2-PTKC] (Pfizer reported a record annual net income of near $22 billion in 2021).
69 Benavides, *supra* note 24 (referring the African region was dramatically sidelined in access to vaccines).
70 Roy, *supra* note 51. ("Imagine if, instead of Operation Warp Speed, the US government had pursued Operation Global Vaccination?")
71 Ibid.
72 Close to 75% of novel drugs were approved in 2021 through the FDA accelerated process. In the group of cancer drugs, only a third proved to be effective. *See* Andrea N. Monge, et al., Use of US Food and Drug Administration Expedited Drug Development and Review Programs by Orphan and Nonorphan Novel Drugs Approved From 2008 to 2021, *JAMA Network Open*, November 1, 2022.
73 Aaron S. Kesselheim et al., The High Cost of Prescription Drugs in the United States: Origins and Prospects for Reform. *JAMA* 2016 Aug. (concluding U.S. per capital prescription drug spending is the highest globally).

74 *See* Ellen F.M. 't Hoen, *The Global Politics of Pharmaceutical Monopoly Power* (2009) (describing how the high cost of medicine drew "attention [to] the relationship between patent[s]… and high drug prices"). *See also* Aaron S. Kesselheim et al., ibid. (referring monopoly rights like patents play an important role in high drug pricing).

75 Sheryl Gray Stolberg and Rebecca Robbins, Drugmakers Are 'Throwing the Kitchen Sink' to Halt Medicare Price Negotiations, *New York Times* July 23, 2023; Zachary Brennan, J&J and Astellas pile on two more bio-pharma industry lawsuits over CMS drug price negotiations. *Endpoints News*, July 18, 2023 (Astellas added violations to the Takings Clause and the Due Process Clause).

76 Stolberg and Robbins, ibid. (referring to an analysis by PhRMA, funded by Gilead Sciences, asserting that the industry would lose $455 billion over 7 years if companies negotiate with Medicare, and a study funded by Biotechnology Innovation Organization arguing IRA will represent in as many as 139 fewer drugs over the next 10 years).

77 Ibid. *See also,* Rachel Sachs, A Holistic View of Innovation Incentives and Pharmaceutical Policy Reform, *Health Affairs Scholar*, Vol. 1, Iss. 1, July 2023. https://academic.oup.com/healthaffairsscholar/article/1/1/qxad004/7203675

78 Michener, *supra* note 21, at 655. *See also*, Jamila Michener, Health Justice: Love, Freedom Dreaming, and Power Building, *Bill of Health Blog* (Sept. 9, 2021), https://blog.petrieflom.law.harvard.edu/2021/09/09/health-justice-love-freedom-power-building/. On health justice scholarship, *see generally* Health Justice: Engaging Critical Perspectives in Health Law and Policy Symposium, 50 *J.L., Med. & Ethics* 636 (Lindsay F. Wiley et al. eds., 2022); Angela P. Harris and Aysha Pamukcu, The Civil Rights of Health: A New Approach to Challenging Structural Inequality, 67 *UCLA L. Rev.* 758, 766–67 (2020); Chloe Thurston, Racial Inequality, Market Inequality, and the American Political Economy, *in The American Political Economy: Politics, Markets, and Power* 133 (Jacob Hacker et al. eds., 2022).

79 Michener, *supra* note 21, at 657.

80 Alexander Meiklejohn, *Free Speech and Its Relation to Self-Government* at 3, 6 (2004).

81 Nikolas Bowie defines democracy as the pursuit of political equality. *See* Nikolas Bowie, Antidemocracy, 135 *Harv. L. Rev.* 160, 167–69 (2021).

82 Meiklejohn, *supra* note 80, at 3, 5.

83 Robert C. Post, Meiklejohn's Mistake: Individual Autonomy and the Reform of Public Discourse, 64 *U. Colo. L. Rev.* 1109, 1115 (1993); *see also* Robert C. Post, Between Democracy and Community: The Legal Constitution of Social Form, 35 *NOMOS* 163, 170–71 (1993).

84 Meiklejohn, *supra* note 80, at 3, 5 (referring that democratic freedom requires citizens to have a voice in the decisions to which they are subject).

85 Susan Rose-Ackerman, *Democracy and Executive Power: Policymaking Accountability in the US, the UK, Germany, and France* 147–48 (2021).

86 *See, e.g.*, Alejandro Camacho et al., Memo to the Next President, *Ctr. for Progressive Reform* (2016) (challenging the idea that governments restrict people's liberty and suggesting how governments can become agents of liberty by promoting opportunity for all).

87 Rose-Ackerman, *supra* note 85, at 255.

88 *See* Parthasarathy, *supra* note 34 (considering ways in which the innovation process should incorporate ordinary citizens).

89 Michener, *supra* note 21, at 657.

90 Rose-Ackerman, *supra* note 85, at 147–50.

91 *See supra* note 18.

92 Amy Dockser Marcus, *We the Scientists: How a Daring Team of Parents and Doctors Forged a New Path for Medicine* (2023).

93 *See* Amy Dockser Marcus, Citizen Scientists Are Driving Medical Research. Now They Need a Constitution, *Time* (Apr. 14, 2023, 7:00 AM EDT), https://time.com/6268944/citizen-scientists-medical-research/.

94 Ibid.

95 "Researchers often pursued scientific questions that reflected their own interests rather than those of the patients they set out to help." Ibid. *See also*, Amy Dockser Marcus, The Cathedral of Science: On the Struggle to Find Clear and Satisfying Solutions, *Lit. Hub* (June 12, 2023).

96 Rose-Ackerman, *supra* note 85, at 147–50.

97 Aziza Ahmed, A Critique of Expertise for Health Law, 50 J.L., *Med. & Ethics* 682, 682–86 (2022).

98 Ibid. at 684–85.

99 Ibid. at 685.

100 In the first case, a district court judge undermined the Centers for Disease Control's judgment with an injunction in the context of a mask mandate arguing the mandate was not a sanitation measure under the Public Health Service Act. *See* Health Freedom Defense Fund, Inc. v. Biden, No. 21-1693, slip op. (M.D. Fla Apr. 18, 2022). In the second case, a district court judge entered an injunction against the FDA to lift an in-person drug dispensation requirement for abortion medication during the pandemic, as the court deemed the regulation as a substantial obstacle to abortion access and elevated the risk of COVID exposure. *See* Am. Coll. of Obstetricians & Gynecologists v. U.S. Food & Drug Admin., 472 F. Supp. 3d 183 (D. Md. 2020) (No. 8:20-cv-01320-TDC). While the first case was seen to be "disrupting public health policy," the second was celebrated as a "victory of evidence over politics," suggesting that the FDA "did not represent a technocratic body of experts" but was a political agency – and that the pressure on the agency by lower court judges was justified. *See* Ahmed, *supra* note 97, at 683–84.

101 Ahmed, *supra* note 97, at 685.

102 *See generally* Yamin and Boghosian, *supra* note 1.

103 Amy Dockser Marcus, Making Medical Science More Democratic, *Wall St. J.* (February 11–12, 2023).

104 Stephanie Haeffelle and Virgil Storr, Is Social Justice a Mirage? *The Independent Review* 24(1): 145–54, 2019.

105 Michener, *supra* note 21.

106 Ibid. at 659; *see also* Jacob M. Grumbach and Jamila Michener, American Federalism, Political Inequality, and Democratic Erosion, 699 *Annals Am. Acad. Pol. & Soc. Scis.* 143 (2022) (contesting that decentralization is beneficial for democratic politics and discussing how federalism at large unevenly constrains and enables democratic participation).

107 Corinne Blalock, Introduction: Law and the Critique of Capitalism, 121 S. *Atl. Q.* 223, 229 (2022), at 223, 229, 231; K. Sabeel Rahman, *supra* note 61.

108 Marcus, *supra* note 96.

109 Email from Amy Dockser Marcus to author (Sept. 11, 2023, 9:53am EST) (on file with author).

110 Michener, *supra* note 21.

111 Ibid. at 659.

112 Ibid. at 659–60.

113 Amna Akbar, Demands for a Democratic Political Economy, 134 *Harv. L. Rev. F.* 90, 113 (2020); *see* Erik Olin Wright, *Envisioning Real Utopias* 19 (2010) ("Radical democracy" requires "an expansive understanding of democracy," including "strong institutional mechanisms for blocking the translation of private economic power into political power").

114 Jedediah Britton-Purdy et al., Building a Law-and-Political-Economy Framework: Beyond the Twentieth-Century Synthesis, 129 *Yale L.J.* 1784, 1831 (2020).

115 Marcus, *supra* note 93.
116 Xaver Baur et al., Ethics, morality, and conflicting interests: how questionable professional integrity in some scientists supports global corporate influence in public health. *Int. J. of Occup. And Env. Health*, 21(2), 2015.
117 Marcus, *supra* note 92.
118 Parthasarathy, *supra* note 34.

Index

Page numbers in **bold** denote tables, those in italic denote figures.